Charles Gibbon

What Would You Do, Love?

A Novel

Charles Gibbon

What Would You Do, Love?
A Novel

ISBN/EAN: 9783337027414

Printed in Europe, USA, Canada, Australia, Japan

Cover: Foto ©Thomas Meinert / pixelio.de

More available books at **www.hansebooks.com**

WHAT WOULD YOU DO, LOVE?

A NOVEL.

BY THE AUTHOR OF

"WHAT WILL THE WORLD SAY?"

CHICAGO:
BELFORD, CLARKE & CO.
ST. LOUIS:
BELFORD & CLARKE PUBLISHING CO.
1881.

Printed and Bound by DONOHUE & HENNEBERRY, Chicago.

CONTENTS.

WHAT WOULD YOU DO, LOVE?

CHAPTER I.

THE OLD HOME.

NO one out in the world talked much of the beauty of Bar-sands, because few knew how beautiful it was, and only those who lived there loved it. Perhaps the fishermen might have wished that the iron-bound coast had been a trifle less picturesque, and by so much the less danger-ous, and that the mighty cliffs and long lines of sharp-ridged rocks running far out to sea and narrowing the passage to the cove to a mere thread, could have been exchanged for one of those quiet, smooth, land-locked bays where the sea is only a bigger kind of lake, and the fish take quietly to the nets, and keep in them when they get there. And perhaps the farmers cared less for the solemn grandeur of the wide and rugged up-lands, with their old-world memorials of granite quoit and crom-lech, "castle" and carn, holy chapel and haunted rounds of stone-struck "Merry Maidens," which gave the purple moors such a special character, than they did for the storms that swept over their fields, beating down grass and corn as if a troop of cavalry had passed through them, and ruining in an hour the labour of months. But the fishermen forgave the magnificent cruelty of the jagged and caverned coast for the sake of its wealth in cod and pilchard ; if the cliffs were barren of all save ling and heather, golden gorse and sweet shy sea-side flowers, they were just the right height for the "huers" watching for the "schools ;" and seine-fishing prospered if agriculture had but a hard time of it. And seine-fishing meant wealth and good living to the whole community when it wa

large "school," and poverty, distress, debt, and well-nigh starvation, when it fell short.

Then again, counting up the mercies, which perhaps is the
wisest kind of arithmetic when dealing with things human, the
children and women were healthy, and no doctor could have
picked up even half a living at Barsands, which saved the public pocket on that side ; and there were large tracts of common-
land swarming with rabbits, where the people had the right of
pasturage, turf-cutting, and free-warren, which somewhat compensated for the want of wood and productive gardens characteristic of this special stretch of coast land.

It was a breezy, healthy, untrammelled kind of place ; a place
which had no large landholders, no resident gentry, and which
did not seem to have any lord of the manor, resident or absent.
Or, if it had, then one who did not trouble himself about his
manorial privileges, but left everything as he found it, to nature and the community. There were innumerable rights of
way about, but very few made roads, and not one that could
be called good. A noticeable paucity of fences, and those
which existed generously dilapidated, with untrustworthy
gates and breached stiles, gave a haphazard communistic look
to the division of fields and farms which did not show great
territorial tenacity, but seemed as if everything belonged to
everybody alike ; and there was not a bolt shot nor a door
locked in the whole village by night or by day—whether the
house inmates were helpless through sleep, or absent at market,
or to "preachin'" at the Wesleyan chapel.

They were a poor set at Barsands doubtless ; unlettered ;
unmannered, if you will ; but they were innocent folk in their
way, hard-working, high-minded, and honest to a proverb.

This did not, however, make them amenable to law *quâ* law ;
and the man who would have taken it in hand to deprive the inhabitants of Barsands of what they considered their rights of cove
or cammon, or to coerce them into ways unaccustomed and uncongenial, would have had to fight for it, though he came with his
pockets stuffed full of the Queen's writs. They were a stiff-
necked, clannish set of people ; and, as their betters had left
them alone for so long now, the general feeling of the place was
decidedly in favour of being left alone to the end.

It was a small community, all told ; a mere fishing village

on the North Cornwall coast, where a handful of stalwart men fought with the sea for their daily living, and put money in the Penrose bank when their take of "fair maids" was more than ordinarily successful. The clergyman, who took pupils to eke out a scanty income, and who lived inland three miles over the hill, coming into Barsands only for an alternate Sunday service, and when he did come addressing empty benches—for the Wesleyans had got the majority of souls, as they have all through Cornwall ; Captain Kemball, an old naval officer, who lived with his niece Patricia at Holdfast Cottage, at the turn of the valley, and Miss Pritchard, who, with her two sisters, kept a young ladies' boarding school on the Penrose road, were the sole representatives of the wealth, rank and learning of the world. The rest of the community consisted of the fisher-folk, congregated for the most part in a little nest of huts and cabins between the cliff at the mouth of the cove where the fish-houses were ; the coast-guards in their shining black cottages, surrounded by dazzling white walls on the slope of Penthill and just below the signal station ; a handful of poorly living day-labourers, who did odd jobs about the boats or the beasts, the cove or the farms indifferently ; and the small traders in the village, who combined several callings in one, and, as in the post-office, mixed up letters and Queen's heads, bacon, tape, candles, pennyworths of medicine, sugar, and the like, with no more sense of classification than there was among the fish when the net was hauled in.

There was only one house that ventured to style itself an inn. This was the *Lame Duck*, kept by one Mrs. Jose, or, as she was generally called, Mother Jose, in whose hand lay virtually the whole of the inland trade of Barsands. Left a widow with five sons thirty years ago, she had made a good fight in her day, and she was now enjoying her reward, if not in ease of living, yet in worldly gear and local power. She was a potentate after a kind in the little village, and was reputed to be worth untold gold. She kept the *Lame Duck*, and she kept it well ; and she horsed, ran, and personally conducted the omnibus that went twice a week in summer to the market town. This was Penrose, fifteen miles off ; and the way lay over a wild, whisht country, with a road that was simply a dry watercourse in summer and a wet one in winter. It was not much

of a market when you got there ; but it was the best to be had,
and the Barsands people thought it could not be bettered.

The five sons who had been left as five dead weights on the
woman's hands in those sorrowful days of thirty years ago,
were now all parts of the clever mechanism of her life ; and
she took care that they should be paying parts. Not one of
them was his own master yet, not one married or in his own
home. Two worked on the farm and got journeyman's wages,
no more ; one helped in the house, brewed, kept the accounts
—and the peace when needed ; one drove the omnibus, and
looked after the horses on the off days ; and the last was a kind
of general agent for the house in Penrose, where he sold the
surplus produce of the farm and booked travellers and merchan-
dise by the Barsands coach—as they called the shaky old van,
omnibus-rigged. It was a powerful combination , and Mother
Jose, a mighty woman of sixty-three, standing five feet eight
"in her stocking feet," and as free with her fists as she was
close with her pocket, was more regarded in the place than
queen or clergy. All the people who were in debt (and they
were not a few) were in debt to her ; and the mixture of fear
and respect, gratitude, hatred and envy which was added to
the heavy interest she claimed "on account," was almost as
strong as a superstition.

In summer the little village was quite gay with such simple-
minded strangers as could endure the primitive arrangements
of the place, and find more pleasure in noble scenery than in a
good dinner. Sometimes a party of fashionable London tour-
ists would alight from Mother Jose's omnibus like a flight of
peacocks settling down besides the Dorkings. But they seldom
stayed long. Barsands supplies, with the meat running short
and no fish to be had because of the rough weather, vegetables
unattainable, and the "clomb" bread turning out as hard as a
stone and as bitter as the butter itself, was not very tempting
fare for fine folk accustomed to metropolitan profusion and
perfection. Bathing, too, in the open, with only sharp
rocks, black with close-set mussels and jewelled with sea-anemones, shining like rubies and emeralds in the sun, for a dressing room—unless they cared to run for at least a hundred
yards over the rough boulders, and take shelter in the caverns
tapestried with *Asplenium marinum*, or the fairy foliage of the

true maiden hair—going out into the water alone to do the best they could for themselves, when the long, green Atlantic waves came rolling in—was shocking to the gentlemen and ladies who could bear the full dress of the London season and the dangers of the streets. So the fashionable people came one day, and looked about them the next, and went away the third, hungry, tired and sleepy, not having been able to make life sweet or restful with such accommodation as the *Lame Duck* afforded. And Barsands, therefore, escaped the perils of popularity, and was left pretty much in its primitive condition.

To be sure, there was more stability of stay in the odd-looking artist men and women in hideous umbrella hats who might be seen trying to give the forms of those stern old granite cliffs, shaggy with pale grey moss and solemn with purple shadows, of which not the best could represent the true grandeur—trying to give the life and motion and purity of those heaving lines of liquid beryl which came on with such noble strength and splendour of curve and colour, to break against the rocks with a light and grace more exquisite still—and failing here too—all save one; but failing in a good cause and on a glorious mission. And sometimes a grave kind of elderly woman, may be with her young companion, might come down for several weeks at a stretch, spending her time chiefly in looking for wild flowers inland, and sea-anemones on the vein of slate that broke edgewise through the granite of the cove. The fishermen wondered what she wanted with her weeds and her "beasts," the creatures that used to crawl by dozens into their crab-pots, and were regarded as of no value to men or gods, being good for neither food nor bait: but when they had said, " Lord! the ridic'lous foolishness of they Londoners!" they had given reason sufficient and dismissed the subject as too trivial for more attention.

Barsands however did not place much store by these casuals, but got along in the best way it could with its regular inhabitants, who, at the most, were few.

The ladies' school kept by Miss Pritchard numbered some eight boarders, children of the well-to-do tradesmen in Penrose. The resident governesses were the younger Misses Pritchard, who had been expressly educated for that purpose, one having been six months in Paris and the other the same length of time in Germany, and both considered as good as natives of either country respectively. Added to the permanent eight, one day-scholar of an uncertain kind had also drunk of the Pritchardian spring. This was Patricia Kemball, the niece of that wooden-legged old captain at Holdfast Cottage of whom mention has been already made ; a scholar said by the three ladies among themselves to be eminently unsatisfactory, and doing credit to no one. Last year, however, Patricia being then seventeen, her education had been considered finished ; so that even the desultory kind of teaching which had gone by that name for twelve years had run itself dry, and no more schooling was held to be necessary for a girl who knew absolutely nothing of all that other girls are taught to prize as the best things women can learn.

This was the Captain's doing, not the ladies'. He did not like the " old maids," as he called them; sometimes "old cats," as a variation ; and they did not like him. They thought he should have married Miss Matilda fifteen years ago, and that he had behaved ill in consequence ; and he took it that they had made a dead set at him ; and as he wanted nothing with any of them, and least of all with Miss Matilda, he resented their attentions as indelicate, burglarious, and unfair. So there was war between the two houses ; and it told well for the Captain's generosity that he thought more of Patricia's well-being than his own distaste, and sent her to profit by his enemies' brains and to put money in their pockets in return.

It must be confessed, however, that his system was a trying one ; and it was well that Patricia was a good girl by nature, else his peculiar method of upbringing might have proved more meritorious in design than advantageous in result. To be sure he had taught her to speak the truth ; to be loyal to her word and faithful to her trust; to abhor suspicion ; to be obedient to her superiors, and to sacrifice herself when need was with cheerfulness and without regret. His moral motto had been " Thorough," if his intellectual system had been patch-work; and his pupil had learnt as he had taught. For the rest, he himself had instructed her in coast-line geography, in astronomy, and the art of navigation. She knew the name and purpose of every shroud and sail in the model of his old ship, the *Holdfast*, which he had rigged up on the lawn, the flags of all nations, and the meaning of ship-signals ; she could read off-hand the difference between the lines of a man-of-war and a merchantman ; and she cherished a grave contempt for iron-clads and steam. But she could neither tat nor crochet, for all that the Misses Pritchard had made both these arts salient accomplishments in their programme ; though, to do her justice, she could darn stockings, hem and stitch and sew, make a pudding, and bud roses, with the best. Also she could skate like a bird and climb trees like a squirrel ; and she liked galloping over the moors better than she liked any other pleasure in the world save boating in a breeze with the *Mermaid* in good humour.

The Misses Pritchard said she would be ruined if this kind of thing went on. When they saw her streaming over the country with her flapping straw hat half-way down her back, and her long brown hair flying like a mane behind her, they said the Captain was a very self-willed old man to let her go on so. It was downright shameful ; and he would live to repent it. And they said it so often that at last the Captain himself caught the echo, and became doubtful of the wisdom of his ways. Then he would send Pat, as he called her, for another quarter ; beginning regularly and with the strictest intentions, but invariably ending by keeping her at home four days out of the six, honestly convinced that he was doing the best for her in his power, and that his own private lessons, added to exercise and fresh air, were more to the purpose than all she could learn in the " kitten house," as he irreverently called the school.

Then again he began to doubt, when the Misses Pritchard had said something more than ordinarily tart, and he had heard of it, as he always did ; and tormented himself with conscientious scruples. But when he looked at her, and noted how she had thriven on her training, with such an exuberance of life, such a power and splendour of girlish health and beauty as he had never seen surpassed—not even in the South Seas where he had left a dusky, sleek-haired romance in old days that haunted him—he stifled his misgivings ; shut his eyes to all but the fact that she was perfect in constitution, in principles, and in temper ; lovely to look at and good to be with ; and that she had never given him a day's uneasiness during the twelve years of his guardianship. Still, he was conscious that at eighteen years of age she needed more in her home life than the society

of an old sea-captain, though he could tell her about the Chinese
war where he had lost his leg, and teach her the names of the
constellations and all the technicalities of the *Holdfast* model.

The question, however, was; What was it she needed? and
how could he get it for her, even if he found out? His means
were limited, and his knowledge of the world on a par with his
means; but he must do something all the same. So he took
the thought to heart, and racked his brains night and day to
discover what it was Patricia ought to have to perfect her education and condition—"the cats" being of no more good—and
when he had found it he would give it, let it cost what it would.

Meanwhile Patricia lived on, blithe as bird in bower, conscious of no loss in her life, feeling no pain, foreseeing no sorrow. Youth, health, a conscience as clear as the sky, and love
as warm as the sun, made up the glad catalogue of her days.
She knew no evil and she feared none. Her duty was plain
before her and her path had neither thorns nor dubious turns.
Truth, reverence, obedience; there was nothing hard nor difficult in these; bred as she had been, the contrary lines would
have been the difficulties. No falsehood had ever passed her
lips; no shadow of subterfuge, of sly pretence, of fair-seeming
which was seeming only, of disloyalty to her word, of insincerity to herself, or irreverent questioning or comment on
others, had ever sullied the stainless innocence of her soul.
Frank and free, loyal and loving, with the sea and the rocks,
the wild flowers and the wild birds as her playmates, Gordon
as her friend, her uncle to reverence, to obey, and God, who
was never her tyrant, to fear—only her Father Invisible to
worship—what more could she want? Had she been asked,
she would have said "Nothing." Her life was one of absolute contentment, of cloudless joy; and strong of heart and
energy, rich in vitality, in cheerfulness, in youth, she felt as if
nothing could ever touch or harm her; as if she could neither
die out of existence nor be crushed by circumstance; as if she
must always be as she was now—happy, free, and fearless, and
with a conscience void of offence towards God and man.

CHAPTER II.

IN THE SUNSHINE.

THE Captain was sitting in the porch of the cottage, which gave to the South and looked on the sea. The wind stirred the fringe of curly snow-white hair that hung about his ruddy weather-beaten face, and blew out the folds of the Union Jack flying from the flagstaff before his house. The white clouds scudded over the bright blue sky; the white waves leaped about the feet of the old grey cliffs and broke into backward streams of spray as they came tumbling in-shore; the birds sang as if they thought the spring had come again; a few brave bees hummed over the latest flowers; and the golden leaves of the autumn trees shook and rustled in the sunshine as the wind passed through the branches. Everywhere was movement, everywhere freshness and the sentiment of life and freedom. And this bright October day, this blithe and genial farewell of the golden autumn time, was in true harmony with the cheerful spirit of the old man sitting in the porch, and feeling—past seventy as he was—how good a thing it was to live.

If only he knew what was best for Patricia! When once this problem was solved he should not have a care left. It was his only anxiety; and she dear child—God bless her!—how unconscious she was that he was bearing this cross for her!

In a life so eventful as his, and with a temperament the reverse of indifferent—given indeed to exaggerate rather than reduce any question whatsoever took enormous proportions, and a difficulty of decision became a moral burden grievously oppressive with a sense of responsibilty though never making him downcast nor ill-tempered.

Sitting there in the porch, touched by the sun and stirred by the wind whiles sweeping the horizon with his glass, whiles fingering his round rasped chin as if counsel lurked among the stubbly beard-roots, suddenly the solution struck him. It came like an inspiration born of the sunshine, and the wind on this swift and hurrying October day. A lady companion! That was it. A lady companion who would teach her all those little feminine graces he could not supply ; nor, for the matter of that, could the Miss Pritchards, with all their pretensions and "parlyvouing ;" who would put the supreme touch on this jewel which nature had fashioned so nobly, and over which he had wrought so tenderly with such ability as had been given him. Yes, that was just it ; and his thought was the Eureka over again.

He heard Patricia's fresh young voice trilling out the "Minstrel Boy," as she was industriously fighting her way upstairs through a refractory bit of sewing. It was a rent in her gown, made yesterday when she climbed the apple tree and came down with a run, as a practical lesson on the folly of trusting to rotten branches.

"Hi there, my love !" he shouted.

"Yes, uncle," said Patricia thrusting her head out of the window, which was framed in by the crimson leaves of a Virginia creeper. It was like a picture by Jordaens, only better done.

"Come down, I want to speak to you," said Captain Kemball ; and Patricia throwing her work on the floor, came down the stairs, two at a time, and jumped across the hall like a school boy into the porch.

"Yes, uncle, she said in her clear voice, louder than most girls voices because the Captain was a trifle deaf. "What do you want ?"

"I want to speak to you, my dear," said Captain Kemball gravely.

She looked at him with a little surprise. The unusual solemnity of his voice struck her.

"All right, I am ready," she answered ; and sat herself down on the opposite bench, her hands folded on her lap, and her attitude "attention."

He raised his eyes to her fondly. There was nothing that pleased him more than this ready, heartsome acquiescence which was one of Patricia's characteristics. There was no skulking about her. Whatever she might have in hand she left it at a word or a sign from him ; always with that sunny smile on her

fresh fair face, always with that frank look in her dark grey
eyes, and that air of almost soldierly attention in her upright
supple figure, which gave the value of meaning to please to
all she did. She was alive, body and soul, heart and brain;
and even her silence was more active than many people's
words.

"Patricia," said Captain Kemball, " I have found it."

"Yes, uncle," she repeated for the third time. "What have
you found ?"

"What you want, my dear."

"Oh! But I did not know I wanted anything," she said,
with a pretty perplexity on her face.

"Yes you do, my dear," he answered positively.

"Very well." She smiled. "If you say so, I suppose I do ;
but I did not know it. What is it ?"

"A lady companion."

"A lady what ?" said Patricia with the air of one who has
heard and has not understood.

"A lady companion," repeated the Captain gallantly sticking to his guns. She was not going to be "nasty" surely—
and for the first time in her life ?

"What on earth can have put that notion into your head,
uncle ?" asked Patricia in amazement. "What do I want with
a lady companion ? She would be horribly in our way—yours
as well as mine."

"As for mine," he said resignedly, "I should not object to
anything that was for your good."

There was no affectation in this. He too thought this lady
companion would be horribly in his way ; but he would bear
this cross as cheerfully as he had borne that of his own perplexity before.

"But what do I want with a lady companion at all ?"
reiterated his niece. "I am very happy as I am ; as happy as
the day is long ; and I am sure we should not get on better with
a third person in the house. Why, uncle dear, what a funny
idea !"

"But you will like it, Pat ?" he said.

"I am sure I should not," said Patricia ; "and I cannot
think why you should say so. There would be nothing to like
in having a stranger always with one. Fancy never being able

to be alone to our two selves again! Oh, uncle, how horrid!"
And here she asked again: "Who can have put such an idea
into your head?"

"Providence," said the Captain gravely.

And Patricia did not laugh.

"Very well, uncle dear," she answered after a short pause.
"You know best, of course. If you really think it right that
we should have a lady companion here for my sake, we will
get one; but I hope you will be quite sure that it is the right
thing to do before you decide, because it will be difficult, look
at it how we will. You see the house is so small, and the
spare bedroom wants furnishing, and we ought to have a new
carpet in the sitting-room; Sarah and I have darned that old
thing till we can darn it no more. And we want some cups
and saucers, and lots of things in the kitchen, and a coal-
scoop; Sarah says she scatters the small coals through the
holes in the old one. And the dinner-set is all chipped and
half of it broken. There is no end to it all when we once begin! And a lady companion is an awfully expensive thing,
I have heard; and, of course, though we can go on very well
as we are, she must have everything ship-shape and nice when
she comes. But you know best," she repeated cheerfully,
leaning forward and laying her hand on his; "and whatever
you wish, you are very sure I shall say yes, are you not, dear?"

"God bless you! to be sure I am, my girl," answered the
Captain warmly. "And now that you tell me all this, I'll
look into my balance and think of it."

"Meanwhile, I must go and finish my mending, said
Patricia with a kind of conscientious solemnity.

Needlework was about the most sobering occupation she
knew; it kept her so still and took so much time.

"All right, dear. But I say, Pat, I do not like to know
that things are wanting in the house which we should be
obliged to have if the lady companion came. My girl ought
to be as well found as any lady companion that ever stepped.
Eh how have you let things go so far a drift? Have you
had a cat, childvean?"

Patricia laughed. "No; our cat has been time and wear,"
she answered. "That's enough, too, Sarah says."

"Well, well, we'll see to it," he said, adjusting his glass.

"Was that all you wanted with me, dear?"

"Yes, for the present," said Captain Kemball, his glass to his eye. "There's a fine Prussian, Pat!" he cried. "She'll give those poor mounseers some trouble if ever she comes across them. Bad sailors, those mounseers. Lord! what a fine ship!"

Patricia went over to him and looked through the glass too. "Yes, she's a beauty," she said as she handed him back his telescope.

Then she kissed the top of the dear bald head, as was her wont, and went back to her own room to darn her skirt. But she sang no more of the "Minstrel Boy." A chord beside these of his own harp was broken for to-day.

Presently her uncle called to her again. He had come out of the porch and was standing on the gravel-walk, whence he could see her as she sat by the window sewing.

"I have it, my girl," he said in a cheery voice. This was his second Eureka within the hour.

"Yes, uncle?" she answered looking up, her bright face slightly flushed.

"I will write to your Aunt Hamley and be guided by her advice."

For a few seconds Patricia did not speak. She was apparently too much occupied with a rebellious length of hair that would fall over her face to be able to give her full mind to Aunt Hamley; but she soon cleared her eyes and said, bravely enough if not quite in her usual key: "Do so, dear; you know best."

"I knew you would say that," cried Captain Kemball triumphantly. "Bless your dear innocent heart. I can read you like a book! Always the same steady discipline in the ship, and the old uncle's command submitted to without a murmur. If you knew how we old folks prize this ready obedience Pat!'

"Well, I should be very ungrateful else," said Patricia.

"And that would not be like you," he said.

"I hope not," she answered gravely.

"Now, I'll go and write to your Aunt Hamley," said the Captain. "She'll understand this matter, and I do not."

On which he turned and went into the house, and Patricia heard him knocking things about downstairs—opening half a dozen drawers for one, fighting over split pens and dried-up ink, and making as much noise and as many preparations before settling down to write a letter of a few lines to his sister as if he was going to board an enemy.

Now, Aunt Hamley was Patricia's one standing dread in life. She was her uncle's, consequently her dead father's, only sister; but since her marriage with Jabez Hamley, the rich brewer of Milltown, and possessor of Abbey Holme, which had relieved him from the necessity of her further support, she had kept up very little intercourse with her surviving brother, Both men had been objectionable persons, each in his own way, to her mind. The one was a long-haired artist who declined to go into the Church on conscientious (she called them unconscientious) grounds; the other was a sailor of democratic habits, with no manners to speak of, and promotion cut short by the loss of his limb. Had Reginald, Patricia's father, been even successful in his questionable career, and employed to paint the Queen and the Royal Family, instead of being a wretched dreamer who threw away his time over his ideas—ideas, indeed! as if a man could live by ideas !— or had Captain Robert not met with that accident and so had gone on to be an admiral and a K.C.B. like his father before him, she would not have minded so much ; but an unsuccessful painter and a shunted captain—they were vessels if not of wrath yet of very unrefined clay, and she declined handling them save at a distance.

When Reginald died, twelve years ago, she did certainly offer to take the penniless little girl to her own childless home and bring her up to ladylike habits and womanly refinements. She would have done her duty by her, had her offer been accepted, and she would have liked her the better the more entire her dependence ; but the Captain elected to take the child himself, and Aunt Hamley had never quite forgiven him. The plan had distressed as well as disappointed her. Men were doubtful creatures at the best, in her opinion. As husbands, she held theoretically by the doctrine of wifely submission and obedience, as women often do when the rod wherewith they rule is of iron sharply pointed ; but outside this theoretical premiership, beyond doing all the hard work of the world that women may live softly and fare richly, taking care of their ladies in a crowd, looking after the luggage and the tickets at a railway

station, and managing the business details of life, she did not
see of what good they were. When it came to an old sea-
captain, with a wooden leg and only his half-pay and pension,
taking charge of a little girl of six, and never a lady in the
establishment to see that her hair was properly brushed, or that
her boot-tags were neatly tucked in and her clothes nicely
made, she was more disgusted at the selfishness and home-help-
lessness of the sex than she had ever been before ; and this was
saying much.

This refusal to let her have Patricia had not only offended
her with her brother, but had given her a distaste for the girl
herself. Though she had never seen her since her cherubic
days of short frocks and scratched legs, she was sure that she
had " grown up undesirable by the logical necessity of her
training ; " and she did not care that Dora Drummond, Mr.
Hamley's young cousin whom she had adopted in default of
Patricia after her brother's refusal, should have such questionable companionship.

" She must be dreadful," she used to say when discussing her
unknown niece in family conclave ; and both Mr. Hamley and
Dora used to say, " Dreadful indeed ! " in concert.

Neither of these last-mentioned persons wanted to see Mrs.
Hamley become interested in her niece. To Mr. Hamley the
adoption of his own cousin had been a matter of intense pride
and satisfaction ; and such a cousin too !—fit to be a queen, he
used to think. And dear Dora, though not noticeably jealous,
naturally wished to keep her standing intact, and did not desire a rival. Hence, no word of praise—that was impossible,
for no one knew if she was praiseworthy or not—but no word
of indulgent hope was ever coupled with Patricia's name at
Abbey Holme, and the idea of her was associated with a certain
steadfast disfavour that bore its fruits in the time to come, and
made itself felt even now in the time at hand.

Patricia had thus some cause for the sudden dismay that
overcame her when her uncle said he would write to Aunt
Hamley for her advice and be guided by it. She knew by in-
tuition that all the advice they would have from Abbey Holme
would be hard and uncomfortable so far as she was concerned ;
and who knows ? perhaps her uncle would adopt it, whatever
it might be, even if it hurt himself to do so. He had his

crotchets at times, and was not always in the same humour;
and his conscience had a trick of self-torturing when he was not
quite well, which led him to acts of pain and penance, happily
of short duration if severe while they lasted.

Right or wrong, however, this idea of a lady companion had
taken possession of him ; and with it the necessity " of consult-
ing his sister Hamley in a matter so purely out of his line." So
acting on the theory of the providential inspiration of his
thought, he wrote now on the instant to Abbey Holme, at
Milltown, as has been said ; and in doing so felt he had washed
his hands of half his responsibility and all his difficulty.

CHAPTER III.

"WHAT WOULD YOU DO, LOVE?"

THIS was the first break in Patricia's life; a break as yet only potential, not actual. But it brought her up with a round turn, as she herself would have said, and made her reflect on her position, for the first time seriously. For the first time too, it opened the gate of the future, and gave her a glimpse of the possibilities lying within.

Her uncle's darling, to be sure, that she knew she was; the light of his days, the apple of his eye, He could no more get on without her than the trees and the flowers in the garden could live without the sun. She knew all this well enough; had always known it with more or less consciousness from the time when she was brought to the cottage in her little black frock, with her doll in her arms, and Uncle Robert, whose name was associated in her childish mind with perennial sugarplums and almost the only toys she ever had, had taken her on his knees and had kissed her and her doll too, and had told her with a husky voice that he would be her father now, and that she was to be a good girl and say her prayers, and never do anything behind backs she was afraid of all the world seeing.

From that time she had taken her place and had rooted. And she had been happy; who indeed happier? It had been just the life that had suited best with her physical temperament and her moral nature. She was nothing of a dreamer, nor yet of a casuist; she was contented with things as they were; things she could touch and understand without going to their roots or questioning eternal causes. She liked to know that she was doing right, but she did not care to analyse her own sensations, nor to understand exactly where her right might have broadened into wrong. Certainly she was not over well educated nor yet intellectually inclined. Hitherto she had not cared greatly for reading, save history, which was true and therefore

B

fascinating enough ; and her uncle had not made her read much beside the Bible and Shakespeare, which last he had Bowdlerised on his own account with a broad pen and very thick ink. But on the other hand she had learnt a good deal of natural history, and what she knew of life was by the village dramas acted before her eyes, not by theories thought out by others. As yet she had more conscience than consciousness, and a moral sense keener than her intellectual perceptions.

Her physical life, too, suited her as exactly as the rest. Two-thirds of it was passed in the open air, chiefly in strong exercise ; and her home occupations were for the most part active —outside her needle-work and her evening backgammon with her uncle. Her health was perfect, and her strength greater than the strength of most women, save such as work in the fields or the like. And she loved to use it. And as, happily for her, her uncle did not think it part of the eternal rule of right that women should be defrauded of their inheritance of health and development, she did use it, and to good purpose. Thus it was that she never knew what it was to be sick or sorry, depressed or doubtful, out of heart or out of temper, or at cross purposes with life at home or abroad.

But with all this fullness of joy in the present her future was not assured. Her uncle was not her father, and she had no claims hereafter, if many privileges now. If anything happened —she did not realise for the instant what could happen—so that she had to turn out into the world, what could she do whereby to gain her own bread ? Absolutely nothing, unless her physical strength might turn to some account; and how could it ? Women were wanted for fingers, not muscles ; clever heads, not powerful hands. If ever that day of need came, of all girls living she, so rich in life's best wealth now, would be the most to be despised then. It came to her with a shock, a blow. She almost started as she saw the truth of her position, and felt herself for the moment degraded by her ignorance, her uselessness, anywhere but where she was.

As she sat by the window, her work fallen from her hands, her eyes fixed on the sea that stretched from the familiar shore far away into the unknown, so like her own life—ah, so like all life !—she tried to reason it out fairly and to convince herself that the dear old man's instinct was right. She had been

happy and she had been well loved, as also she had loved. She
was strong and not afraid ; and she knew a few things that
were of use in their way, and had been of great use hitherto.
But she wanted more. She wanted the power of self-help if
she needed it ; she wanted more education and to be made
more like other women ; and she wanted to be taught how to
make money in the time to come when there would be no one
to give it to her. For must not that time come in the ordinary
course of things ? However far off—and until now, when she
was holding this innocent parliament with herself she had
never once foreseen either the time or the fact—was it not to be
expected that her dear uncle should die before her ? And if
he did, she would be left absolutely penniless. He had nothing
but his half-pay and pension ; and he had not saved, if he was
not in debt. He had told her so, many a time ; and how could
she wish him to save when distress was about, and the poor
men and destitute women and children had to be fed and
clothed in the hard winters of bad fishing years ? Perhaps that
was what he was thinking of now—the real meaning of this
new idea of his about his sister's advice and the lady companion.
He was thinking of what would be best for her in the future
when he should not be with her—dear, good, unselfish uncle !
And she had shrunk from the proposition—what a wicked thing
to do ! Ah, she would be so good to-night ! She would show
him that she was sorry she had been so cowardly, and that she
was ready to do all, accept all, he proposed. How grieved she
would be when she was alone in the world to remember her
misdeeds ! When she was alone—when the supreme decree
had gone forth !

Like a picture actually before her she suddenly realised the
loss of her second father, and saw him lying there dead, and
gone for ever from her. It was so vivid, she felt as if she could
have touched him. With a kind of startled cry she put up
her hands to her face, and broke into sobs with a strange and
bitter pain.

If her uncle had seen her at this moment he would have
thought she was crying because of the lady companion, which
would have made him more determined than before ; and he
would have thought her temper had " turned nasty," though that
was not her way ; and he would have been wounded and annoyed.

No one however did see her, and she soon dried her eyes again ; tears not being luxuries to her as they are to some— being indeed amongst the rarest events of her life.

" Crying never did any one any good yet," she said to herself ; " and I had better make my dear uncle happy while he lives than sit here and sob over his death, which would make him unhappy, and will not be till I am an old woman. And I will not vex him any more about this lady companion who is to come. I don't like the idea, and I don't want her for pleasure ; but it is my duty to be obedient, and I dare say she will teach me a lot of things I ought to know. Oh, I dare say it will be all right !—only I hope she will not be like Miss Pritchard who always looks as if she had been eating green gooseberries. Perhaps she will be a darling. Why not ? There are more good people in the world than bad, and why should she not be one of them ? But if Aunt Hamley chooses her ? Well ! if Aunt Hamley chooses her she will perhaps be nice all the same, and at any rate I will try to love her and to make her happy."

On which she shook off her hair from her face, threw back her shoulders, straightened her slender figure which had drooped together as she had pondered, looked out frank and brave to sea and sky ; and then, as if to meet her brighter mood, she heard a firm, swift, manly step come down the lane and stop at the little wicket-gate of the garden. Immediately after she was leaning out of the window framed in by the crimson foliage, with the sunlight pouring on her like a golden glory, laughing to a fair-haired young man in a sailor's cap and jacket who stood on the lawn below,

" Why, Gordon ! I thought you had run away without bidding us good-bye !" she said.

And Gordon Frere, laughing too, answered with just the faintest dash of Irish accent in his voice : " Ah now, Patricia, could you think so meanly of me as that !"

" Well, it was not like you, certainly," said Patricia ; " but people do odd things sometimes, you know "

" I don't think I should ever do anything quite so odd as that," he said.

On which she laughed again, and said, " No !"

Presently the Captain, who had finished his letter to his sister Hamley, came out into the porch again.

"Hullo, Gordon! where have you been all this time?" he said.

"That's just what I have been asking," said Patricia.

Not that she had in words, but her thoughts had meant the same thing.

"To London, sir," said Gordon, with a look up at the face framed in the scarlet leaves.

"Ay!—and what may you have been doing there, boy?"

"It was only an uninteresting bit of family business on my coming of age," said Gordon. "Lawyers and deeds, and no end of fees to pay and musty old courts to visit."

"Lawyers—sharks!" said Captain Kemball with a shudder.

He was not an enlightened old gentleman, though he was a good one; and he cherished his superstitions.

"Well, perhaps," answered the young man hesitatingly. "And yet it saves a world of trouble to have a fellow at one's elbow who knows everything where you know nothing, and who sees so jolly far ahead! It is like telling fortunes by the cards; and when that old family lawyer of ours, that Mr. Fletcher, whom I believe I once mentioned to you—but you know him for yourself, don't you, sir?"

"To be sure I do. The Fletchers come from Milltown where I was born and bred," said the Captain, "and that Fletcher you speak of has been our family lawyer for three generations —at least, not that man, but the house."

"I thought three generations a long time for one life," laughed Patricia.

She had come downstairs while they were talking, and was standing now by the door. She had bathed her eyes and put up her hair afresh, and had even gone to the coquettish length of a bright bit of ribbon about her throat and a bow of the same colour—dark sailor-blue—among the glossy brown of her luxuriant hair; and as she stood there she made a picture more beautiful, Gordon thought, than ever poet imagined or painter drew.

"We must mind our tackle now the pilot's aboard—eh, Gordon?" said the Captain, looking at her proudly.

And Gordon said "Yes," with full meaning.

"I am glad you know the Fletchers," then said the Captain. "One likes one's friends to be in good hands. There is a

Catherine Fletcher too," he added, looking with an odd kind
of expression at Patricia. "She was a beauty in her young
days. All Milltown was mad after her. "She and her brother
Henry live still at Milltown, I believe. He was a doctor, but
he left the profession when the old man died ; and a fine fellow
he used to be, I remember."

"So is Mr. Fletcher in London," said Gordon ; "and so
sharp and clever ! When he used to come in with his mathe-
matical way of putting things that I thought were all different,
as I said, it was like fortune-telling somehow. I know he used
to make me feel the most of a fool I have ever felt."

"Eh ? Then he must have known his alphabet," said the
Captain waggishly ; and Gordon laughed and blushed.

He was a fine young fellow, brave and strong, but not beyond blushing like a girl on occasions.

"True all the same," he continued. "What I thought was
as plain as that two and two make four, he showed me had
this bearing and that meaning I had never seen, and that my
two and two made five or six or nothing at all ! I used to feel
in a foreign land in that old office of his, where I knew neither
the language nor the country and had to walk as if blindfold,
under guidance."

"Long may it remain a foreign country to you and us all ! "
said the Captain fervently.

"I think there must be a born antipathy between sailors and
lawyers," put in Patricia.

"Land-sharks and sea-sharks," said her uncle quite gravely ;
"and, of the two, the land-sharks are the worst."

"But this special shark of Gordon's, this Mr. Fletcher, he
seems to be harmless enough ? " she said.

"Fletcher ?—yes, he's about the best you'll find," her uncle
answered. "If he was not one of the devil's advocates I should
say he was about as good a man as ever walked on the face of
the earth. He has a strain of honesty, that man, which has
stood in his way more than once ; he'll never make his fortune
out of the ruin of other people's."

"He'll do better—he'll deal justly by other people's," said
Gordon ; and then the conversation dropped.

But it left on Patricia a cheery impression. She was glad
that Gordon had an honest man for his legal adviser when he

had business on hand, a man he could trust as the caretaker of his fortunes while he was away at sea doing his duty to his country, which would not be half grateful enough, she used to think, if he came to grief in her service like her uncle, or mourn him as he deserved to be mourned if he went down altogether in the fight.

She and Gordon were great friends. When she spoke of him, and was conscious that she had to account for the familiar terms on which they were together, as happened sometimes, if rarely, she invariably said, " We have been brought up together, like brother and sister." And this was true. He had been educated at Mr. Ramsey's, the clergyman who lived at St. John s and served Barsands as well ; while his mother and sisters did battle with small means and large pretensions in Germany. And as the journey was expensive and the Frere finances limited, he had seldom gone over to them ; a big, healthy, English boy, destined for the sea and as wild as a colt, not being the kind of thing specially desired by a nervous woman in a small foreign apartment, with a couple of showy-looking daughters to dress and marry. By which it had come about that the captain had taken possession of him in his holidays, and Patricia had learned to regard him as a brother, or something very like one.

When he first went away to the *Britannia* training ship she felt as if she had lost part of her very self. She was but a little lassie at the time, but she always remembered how she had cried when he turned the corner, and she saw him for the last time out on the Penrose Road, waving his cap ; and how for days and days after there seemed to be no sun left in the sky. Now she was glad he had chosen the profession. Naturally, to her mind it was the finest a man could choose. Had not her dear uncle, and her grandfather before him, been its shining lights ? For though when he had got fairly afloat it took him away so much, yet when he did come home —St. John's Vicarage and Holdfast Cottage were always " home " to the poor boy who had never known any other—it sent him back with such an atmosphere of youthful heroism about him, such a sense of dangers braved and difficulties overcome and a noble life's work nobly begun, that she could not grudge the separation which had borne such glorious fruits already, and which was to bear others even more glorious in the days to come. She would not, if she could, have kept Gordon "moidering" away his youth at Barsands. Pleasant as it was to have him as her companion when she tore about the country on her shaggy, ill-groomed pony, or beat up against the wind in the *Mermaid*, she knew that a life of idleness, though ever so delightful, was not the right thing for a man. And it gave her a little joy to feel that for his good she could conquer her own desires, and even rejoice at the cause if she grieved over the fact of their separation. But let him be gone as long as he would, she was ever entirely loyal to him in his absence, never forgot him in her prayers, never took any one else to be her brother in his stead, but always kept him first in his generation in her heart, as beseemed a steadfast and affectionate sister.

She loved him as young things of the right kind do love each other, without fear or introspection. She scarcely could remember the time when Gordon Frere was not part of her life, and when she did not love him as much as she loved her uncle, if differently. It was not a thing to think about at all. It was a fact; just as much as sisterhood or daughterhood is a fact. Gordon was Gordon to her; and when she had said that she had said all.

And yet this time she had been conscious of the slightest possible little change in their relations. It was not coolness — by no means coolness; but just a dash of shyness and reserve, as if there was something of which they were a little afraid to speak, and as if they both felt they must be more careful somehow than they used to be. But it was so slight a change that Patricia was resolute not to accept it; and as Gordon, on his side, seemed to struggle against the shadowy influence in the best way he could, the old joyous harmony that had been for so many years unbroken between them still went on, and this visit of the bright young sailor to his friends at home was as happy as all the others had been.

"Any news when you join?" asked Captain Kemball.

Gordon looked at Patricia; Patricia looked at him.

"In three days," he said, and turned his face to the sea.

"Oh, Gordon! that is a month too soon!" cried Patricia in frank sorrow. "I thought you said you were to stay till the third week in November?"

"So I did; but the Lords have ordered us away the third week in October, you see," he answered.

"What a pity ! We do miss you so when you go. It seems to get worse every time !" said Patricia.

The young man's eyes glistened. "Well, I am glad you are so sorry, Patricia !" he said frankly.

"You are ? What a horrid speech—and how Irish !" she laughed.

"Isn't it better than to go and think not a living soul on shore regrets you ?" asked Gordon looking at her earnestly.

"Yes, Pat," said the Captain taking up the strain ; "you don't know what it is to keep watch on a dark night, and be thinking of the dear ones at home, and knowing that they are thinking of you, and feeling their blessed hearts so pitiful to hear the wind blow."

"It's hard lines for the poor fellows who have no one to care a button for them," put in Gordon ; "and I, for one, don't envy them. So you'll please keep on being sorry, Patricia, do you hear ?"

"Well, Gordon, I suppose we shall," said Patricia, with her hand on her uncle's shoulder. "We miss you horribly when you go away, don't we, uncle ? Life isn't the same thing without you, and you will take away the last of the summer this time. However "—and she sighed. The sigh meant resigna-tion and "what must be, must be."

"Don't make a Molly of him, Pat," said the old Captain, going into the house.

"It's good news you tell me ; I wouldn't have it altered; I like you to miss me when I go," continued Gordon gravely.

Without knowing why, Patricia suddenly felt herself grow pale, and an odd kind of tremor passed over her.

"I hear Sarah with the tea-things ; come and have some tea," she said abruptly.

"All right. And you will sing me ' Dermot asthore' after ?" asked Gordon in a rather lower voice than usual ; for he too, generally spoke as if a northwester was blowing in his teeth.

"Yes, if you wish it," was the reply.

"I do wish it, very much, Patricia. I want to hear 'Der-mot' and 'What would you do, Love ?' and when I am toss-ing about at sea I shall remember them and you—and this evening."

"Why this evening specially?" asked Patricia.

But though she tried to speak in her usual frank way, something—it was almost like wool—seemed to have got into her throat that changed the quality of her voice, even to her own ears. Neither could she look at Gordon as she was accustomed to look at him. She felt bashful, and as if her eyes refused to go his way. Altogether it was uncomfortable, and she felt inclined to run away and hide herself where he could not find her. Nor was he quite the same to her. A trouble, dim, formless, but real, seemed to have fallen between them; and yet it was not the trouble of unkindness.

"Why? I will not tell you now, Patricia; but some day I will," said Gordon, looking at the gold band of his cap as if it was something he had never seen before, and sinking his voice, which trembled.

"Mysteries? oh, I hate mysteries!" she cried, making a sudden effort to conquer her strange sensations, and laughing in a way scarcely natural to her, as with an odd feeling of escape she ran into the dining-room—where she mismanaged the tea, or, as the Captain called it, "spoilt the brew."

As she did not know very well what she was about she scalded herself, which effectually awakened her from the confusion of her state; and she did not get entangled again that evening, not even when she had finished "What would you do, Love?" and Gordon had asked her, with his honest blue eyes raised fully into hers, "Is that what you'd do, Patricia, to any poor fellow who loved you and had bad chances?" and she had answered heartily, "Yes, I would, Gordon."

"You'd not believe an ill word, and not be frightened by a cold fortune?" he asked.

"I? No! not all the world could turn me from one I loved!" she said warmly.

"I believe you, Patricia!" said Gordon; and his face beamed with something more tender than a smile, deeper than mere pleasure. "You are the truest-hearted girl that ever stepped. Man or woman would be safe with you!"

"Gordon, how can you talk such nonsense!" said Patricia.

But her cheeks flushed with pleasure, and she felt very happy that he thought her so true-hearted.

CHAPTER IV.

THE "MERMAID."

NATURALLY the chief amusement at Barsands was boating, for those who owned anything that would float, between a tub and a cockleshell; though for the matter of that, there was only the Captain to keep a pleasure-boat at all—the rest being fishing and seine-boats only, of larger or smaller dimensions. And, naturally again, Captain Kemball, and Gordon Frere when he was on shore, were never happier than when they were cruising about the rocks and islands which made this special reach of coast so dangerous.

Patricia was generally with them, in accordance with the Captain's idea that the right kind of feminine education was to make women as brave as men, heroically indifferent to danger and clever in getting out of it; courage and presence of mind being the qualities he most admired after truth and loyalty. And Patricia was really a very good seawoman. She could handle the tiller ropes as well as if she had been a pilot on her own account, and she knew every shoal, and rock, and current as accurately as if she had been the hydrographer of the station Her uncle used to call her "the mermaid" sometimes; and when he hit on the idea, he re-christened his boat, which, unti then had been the *Young Holdfast*, the *Mermaid*, too, in honou of her. He was fond of innocent little jokes, decent man and one of them was to declare gravely to such strangers as he might have seen gaping at her pranks in the water—f she could swim like a fish—that he had seen many mermaid in his time; shoals of them about the Pacific Isles; and tea this creature there was half a one, web-footed inside her shoes and with the neatest little dorsal fin, just like a lady's tail between her shoulders. And he always maintained that some of them—benighted Londoners for the most part—looked as if they believed him. So that, instead of being in the way on board the *Mermaid*, if a gale came on and they had to dodge the wind to slip by the Gridiron, she was of as much use, save in absolute strength of muscle, as the best A.B. on the Admiralty books.

The next day the three went out for a long cruise. It was a bright breezy day, just such as yesterday had been, only perhaps more brilliant and more vigorous ; with a full wind that sent the little boat merrily along, and just enough sea on to make her "dance like a lady," said Gordon, as she slipped from wave to wave and laid over to the breeze till her sail dipped into the water. The " white horses" were out, but they only gave greater animation to the scene ; and they were not so much horses as ponies, said the Captain, bonny little beasts, sent out by Neptune to view the world and report below ; but to see them breaking and leaping beneath the wind, and to see how the *Mermaid* danced and courtesied as they met her, would have made a landsman shudder. As it was, it was a sea and sky which to sailors and sea-birds were perfection.

There was no wool in Patricia's throat to-day, no mist before her eyes. The strong north-east wind seemed to have cleared both her and Gordon from that formless trouble of the night before, and the happy companionship they had always known, affectionate and unconscious, had come back as if it had never received a check.

Long after, both Gordon and Patricia remembered this morning as one of the golden memories of their youth. It was the last sail the pleasant triad had together ; the last time the Captain did the ordering and Gordon the hard work—which, however, was not very hard—while she, with the ropes in her hand, steered close or clear, luffed, fell off a point, or put the helm hard a-port as she noted the signs of sea and land ; the last time she watched the sail flap heavily against the mast as they shifted the boom and she set the tiller sharp, then felt the seaman's glow of satisfaction as she saw the canvas slowly fill, in sign that the little boat had not missed stays, and that they were off on another tack, cheating the wind and zigzagging defiantly right in its very teeth ; the last time she served out their simple dinners on the cuddy roof—she eating hers standing while the Captain took the tiller ropes for a spell, and looked at his boat and his niece with about equal admiration. How well the one sailed, how grandly the other grew ! How

the new white canvas of the *Mermaid* filled and bellied with
that perfect line, in its way as beautiful as the curve of a swan's
neck or the slant of a bird's wing! And how prettily the wind
caught the girl's dress and eddied it into billowy wreaths like
a purple cloud, while it tore her bright brown hair from its
slender fastenings, and blew it in shining tangles across her
face!

Beautiful Patricia always was. Her enemies, if she had had
any, must have confessed this; but to-day she surpassed herself.
Even her uncle, who had nothing of that sickly sentimentality
which moons and maunders over a woman's beauty as if it was
a thing to reverence like a virtue, and who cared more for
what she was than for how she looked—even he, as we have
said, was filled with a strangely vivid sense of the nymph-like
splendour of her loveliness as she stood there so young and
fresh, so full of happy life, and so unconscious of her charm!
Gordon Frere made a surreptitious sketch in his pocket-book,
of which she, intent on an enormous sandwich, was in nowise
aware. She nearly caught him though, as she suddenly looked
back to the little world on board from her alternate contempla-
tion of the horizon and her hunch of bread. But he smuggled
away the book in time, and all she saw were two blue eyes
looking at her roguishly and a handsome face lighted up by a
smile. Then she smiled too, in her responsive way, and the
sketch never got discovered nor completed. Gordon scarcely
needed it to remind him of the girl or the boat, or his own
thoughts and feelings of this day.

There was something that seemed to move them all to remain
out as long as possible on this cruise. It was one of those days
which make an ineffaceable impression on the memory, and
which seem different altogether from others. There are times
when the fields and the sea and the sky seem nothing more
than a mere face—something to look at, to admire if one will,
but not to understand, and not to remember with special delight; and there are days which seem to show us something
beyond and behind, and to put us in harmony with the inner
heart of nature. And these we never forget, nor the aspect of
the world as we looked at it then. To Patricia it was as if the
universe had been swept and garnished afresh, and life had just
begun, and all things been made beautiful and new since the

sun broke over the hills this morning. There were no ghosts of dead loves, no sorrows, no sighings about earth and sky to-day. It might have been the first day of creation, for its sense of buoyant freshness to her—the first hour of time when was no Past with its tears and funeral faces, only the glad Present and the hope of the Future ; and she might have been Eve ere yet the Serpent had whispered to her, and before the flaming sword had been drawn.

In Gordon's mind ran a strange confusion of texts about the sons of men and the daughters of God that came down to them, and it did not trouble him that he read the words wrong-handed ; while the Captain's heart went back with his memory some forty years and more, when the world used to be newly swept and garnished for him too, and the sons of men fell in with the daughters of God on the roads by which he travelled.

So they sailed and laughed and talked and had long spells of silence ; sometimes of a silence that meant dreaming, sometimes only watching ; while the little *Mermaid* ran before the wind with a clean sweep and a light pair of heels, and shook and swayed and tossed impatiently, as they put her about and forced her out of her natural course, and art and science conquered nature and the elements in the old way. And now it was getting dusk when they finally put her head straight for Barsands, and steered for home.

As the evening drew in the weather changed. The bright flecked sky became thick and grey, the sun went down behind a heavy bank of purple clouds, the wind rose, and the rain began to fall. A storm was coming up with the tide, and the tide was running swift and high. This dangerous caost-line, full of sharp sunken rocks and strong currents as it was, needed both clever seamanship and clear weather to render it practicable ; and it was a constantly recurring triumph in a small way when the Captain and his niece brought the *Mermaid* safe into harbour again, and defeated for another time Mother Jose's standing prophecy, that the pair of them would be drowned one of these fine days ; and then where would they be ?

This time there seemed a desperate chance that the prophecy might be nearer fulfilment than was desirable. But the party on board did not take much heed. They put the boat about, and she answered gallantly to the helm. So far well; but the freshening gale obliged them presently to close-reef their sail, and then they began to look somewhat anxiously to their stays and bolts. Even such a slight press of canvas as the *Mermaid* carried was soon more than she could bear in the weather that had come on; and now their only course was to make all snug, to steer well and carefully, edg away before the wind, and to do the best they could with a difficult job.

Moment by moment things looked worse. The evening settled down darker and wilder at every quarter of an hour that passed. The wind, which had backed sharp from north-east to south-west, had risen to a gale setting dead in-shore, and the tide and the currents swept along with tumultuous violence. Already the Gridiron, that dreaded reef of rocks, was one line of boiling surf from end to end; and the tide was not yet more than half high; and the cliffs were dim with the spray that was cast up about them. But while they steered well, and the boat obeyed the helm, they were in no real peril; though, sometimes buried in the trough, sometimes flung up to the crest of the giant waves, the little *Mermaid* looked as if her last hour had come, and as if she could not possibly live in such a sea.

On they went, each face gradually getting graver, each heart more anxious, but the bonny boat holding her own bravely, when suddenly a tremendous wave, breaking athwart, tore away her rudder and left her masterless in the storm. As the sea struck her she gave a lurch and heeled over on her side; but she righted herself in time, and rose gallantly to the wave, trembling in every inch of her as she went forward with a leap like a race-horse touched by the whip and the spur. Gordon did what he could to utilise the sweep as a rudder; but the sea was too strong; and after trying all the expedients open to them they were forced to let things be, and to take counsel of hope and courage only. On she went, driven with a force they could neither check nor resist. Under bare poles as she was, the storm swept her before it like a leaf in a mill-race. They were powerless to prevent or to guide. Hitherto, man and science had been the masters, now the elements were supreme and man was the slave, and too probably, the victim.

The boat drifted fast, and the precious moments flew with it. If only they could weather Penthill Point, where many a good ship's bones lay bleaching at the bottom, the wind would

serve them well; they would leave the Gridiron clear to the
left and be blown straight into Barsands harbour. Would they
weather it ? Yes, if the wind changed but half a point, so as
to set them straight for the harbour; no, if it blew dead in-
shore, as it blew now; and no, too, if it changed more than that
half-point, for then they would fall on the Gridiron. But it
did not change. It carried them on to their destruction straight
as an arrow flies. Every wave that rose bore them nearer,
every moment of time that rushed into eternity drove them
closer to the cliff, and diminished their chances of escape by so
much. It was an ugly look-out ; and they knew their danger.

Not a word was spoken. The two men, with the girl between them, sat in the stern, holding on by the gunwale and
lightly lashed as well; a quiet, resolute, silent triad ; each as
brave as the other, and each thinking for the others, "If only
they could be saved, I should be content to die !" Sea birds
wheeled and screamed above their heads, and dipped their
slanting wings in the foam that flew over the masthead, as the
crests of the waves were cut as if by a knife and scattered into
plumes and streamers of spray. The wind howled through the
darkening sky, and whistled shrilly among the straining shrouds;
and the huge billows came thundering after the *Mermaid* as she
flew wildly before them, and overtaking her, deluged her with
water that swept her deck from end to end, and tried the temper of the wood and hemp and iron of which her life had been
made. Faster and faster she drove before the gale, caught by
the wind and the tide and hurried dead upon the Point. They
seemed to be drawn as if by a magnet in this mad race of theirs
with death; as if they were being hunted by the wind and
waves behind them. And then suddenly the huge black cliff
stood up sharp and square before them, and the spray cast off
from the face fell back on them in a blinding shower.

" Hold on !" shouted the Captain.

And at the word came a shock that threw them all forward,
and a tearing, ripping noise, that told its own tale.

" Keep steady, girl ! There's a God in heaven !" he said,
passing his arm around Patricia's waist as the boat reeled back,
quivering at the blow.

Divining more than hearing what he said, for the wind and
the waves drowned all other sounds but their own, Patricia put

her arm about him too; but she did not speak. Then she turned to Gordon, and smiled with a kind of sad but brave cheerfulness as she held out her other hand to him.

He took it and pressed it between both his own; but he could not answer back her smile. His handsome ruddy face was set and blanched, his brows were contracted, his teeth clenched tight. Brave as he was—a man who emphatically had never known physical fear—he was sick with terror now. Not for himself; he would have died resolutely enough for his own part; but it seemed to take the manhood out of him somehow, to think of her perishing before his eyes, and he unable to save her by his strength or by his own sacrifice. There was no help for it. The strongest swimmer that ever lived could not have breasted the breakers foaming over the rocks at Penthill Point; the cliff had not a foothold where the waves might fling them and leave them clinging till they were seen and taken off; and a life-boat, even if there had been one at Barsands, could not have put out.

The time, however, for any kind of suspense was shortening with each pulse of the tide. Whatever sin each soul there was conscious of, let it be confessed now in whispered prayer, humbly but in trust. The Great Secret stood very near to each, and in a few moments all would be over and all learnt.

Again and again the *Mermaid* was lifted by the waves and flung like a toy against the cliff. It was pathetic to see the way in which she bent to her fate, unresisting, trembling, tossed by each incoming wave against the cruel granite, and beaten by wind and water savagely. Her seams were opening; her outer planks were torn away and ground to splinters as she struck. The work had been good to have held out so long. In the midst of his solemn thoughts the Captain caught himself measuring the quality of his boat as tenderly as he had reckoned up Patricia's virtues; but even the best work that ever man laid could not have saved them now. It was the question only of a few moments. She could not possibly hold out for more than five at the longest against the strain that was put upon her.

Five minutes—and then of those three brave loving hearts, the old and young, not one would be left to mourn the other! So far this would be merciful. The old life full of honour and

c

the young full of hope—they seem welded so closely one with
another, that the one without the other would be a blank.
But ah! how much poorer the world would be for their loss !

Involuntarily they pressed closer together; not a tear, not a
murmur, among them ; only a closer grasp of hands, a stronger
strain of arms, and a sweet and calm farewell looked lovingly
from each to each. The one who, up to now, had seemed to
suffer most was the Captain, because he was in his own mind
the one to blame. He ought to have been more careful for her
—so young, so good—and that brave fellow there ! It was a
mournful ending for two lives so full of promise : and he had
tasted more than the bitterness of death for his own part in his
self-reproach and sorrow for them. So it had been up to now ;
but now, in the very presence of death, at the very footstool of
the Supreme, a strange calm had fallen on him as on the others.
It was a farewell, but it was also love ; it was peace, confidence,
resignation ; but again, and above all, it was love !

Again the *Mermaid* struck, again reeled back; and then, just
as the last flutter of hope was stilled and they had all looked
firmly in the face of death, loving and not afraid, a bright light
shot through the air, and the whizz of a rocket passing over
their heads brought a rope athwart the deck. The coastguard
on the look-out had seen them, and the imminence of their
peril had been their salvation. Close under the cliff as they were
the pitch was easy, and if there was time all would be saved.

Gordon sprang for the rope, and Patricia shrank back, pushing forward her uncle ; but the old man took her in one arm
like a child and thrust her to the front. To debate the point
was to lose all, and to yield to his unselfishness was her own
best unselfishness. So she stood quite calmly, and helped Gordon to lash the rope about her ; and in a few seconds she was
safely corded and the signal to haul away given. They watched
her in the dim twilight as she was drawn up by the men on
the cliff ; she, guiding herself by one hand away from the sharp
jags and points of the rock while holding on to the rope by the
other, keeping her eyes turned downward to the sea where the
men she loved were still floating side by side with death, seeming to make her own safety the assurance of theirs by the very
closeness of union among them ; as if one could not live or die
alone.

Then, over wind and surf they heard the men's glad cheer as the girl was safely landed ; and immediately after another rocket came for the Captain's help. Him too Gordon secured and watched drawn up as Patricia had been before him , and now only the poor lad was left, sole captain, crew, and pilot of the wreck. But now he was comparatively indifferent. If the *Mermaid* broke up before he could be saved—and he knew that though she still kept the form and semblance of a boat she was no better than if she had been made of paper. and might break up at the next blow—if she went down and he with her, at least the girl he loved was safe ; and the dear old Captain —he was saved too, to still care for her and protect her.

Looking always upward, he saw clearly, dark as it was, the face of Patricia bending down from the heights, as if encouraging him by her love. He saw the long, dank, dripping hair falling like a veil as she bent ; he saw her eyes looking frankly, yearning and loving too ; her lips parted with the same tender smile, the same kind of dumb speech that he had seen before to-day, and that seemed to say so much in its silence. Doubtless it was all fancy, and what he saw was a mere dream ; but at the time it was real, and he took heart as he looked—heart for her sake.

Then came another muffled cheer from the cliff, and again, for the third time, the rope fell ; and Gordon Frere caught it and was saved. But just as his foot left the deck at the first haul from above, the *Mermaid's* mast fell by the board, and in a second the boat had disappeared as if by magic, and only a mass of splintered wood eddying in the boiling surf told where she had been. It was like taking a life by violence, and they all felt when she went to pieces as if a playmate and a friend had died.

The peril was past ; but could Gordon ever forget the cry of joy with which Patricia wound both her arms about one of his, as she clung to him for a moment with girlish abandonment ? —could he ever forget the look in the dear eyes that met his, a look so full of the very ecstasy of joy that they seemed to shine like stars in the darkness ? And what was there in her voice when she said : "Dearest Gordon—oh ! my brave, dear boy !" that went to his heart as if she had said much more than the words ?

It was not five minutes since he had sat by her in the boat, hand-in-hand, looking at death together, yet it seemed now as if it was a lifetime since. But that he was a man, and the two coastguards were standing there, and the Captain was on the other side of him wringing his hand, Patricia would have learnt more of his heart, and her own, than she had yet fully fathomed. All he could do, even for his own sake, to give back her caress, was to press her clasped hands against him warmly, and say in a voice that would tremble in spite of himself, "Brave and dear, yourself, Patricia! You helped to save us all."

"The one *Mermaid* has gone, the other is left," said Captain Kemball, looking at his niece. Taking off his cap, he stood bareheaded in the storm : "I thank thee, O Lord, for her life!" he said reverently. And Gordon, taking off his cap too, said "Amen."

Suddenly he blanched and staggered.

"Dear Uncle! Gordon, what is it!" cried Patricia, as she caught him in her strong young arms just in time to prevent his falling.

The old man had fainted : a thing he had never done in his life before.

The coastguardsmen and Gordon took him up among them, carried him into the little shelter-hut by the signal ; where they rubbed him and gave him brandy, and by care and tender treatment, if rough method, succeeded in bringing him round. But it was a long while first ; and at one time it seemed almost hopeless. However, he came to himself at last, and sat up and looked about him as usual. They wanted him to have a car or cart, anything on wheels, sent up for him as far as it could travel. Gordon would have run down for it ; but the Captain, who had a will of his own insisted on walking home. He was never better in his life, he said ; and he rubbed up his curling white hair, slapped his rotund chest, and chafed his chilly hands with vigour. He did not know how he came to be such a fool, fainting like a sick girl! It was only because of that gipsy, he supposed, pointing to Patricia. When he thought it was all over with them he was sorry for her, and blamed himself for it. He ought to have kept a smarter look-out, and not have stayed so long. So he imagined the faintness was just the reaction when he found his little girl safe. He was up to the mark now ; no fear ! and he declined all further coddling. Coddling was not the thing, he went on, when he carried her Majesty's commission, eh, Gordon ? and he'd show them yet that he was man enough for any two of them !

So, with a kind of innocent rollick that yet was not like himself, and with a certain dazed look about him he bade the men good night ; emptying his purse among them sailor fashion ; and set off down the steep cliff path gaily enough.

It was a weary tramp. The night was pitch dark by now; the storm was raging furiously ; they were all drenched through and through—to their bones, said the Captain ; and the cliff path was difficult for the mutilated pedestrian at the best of times. To-night it was doubly so, being slippery as well as rugged, and difficult to find in the blackness overhead. They got down in sufficient safety on the whole; though the Captain had one or two bad falls by the way which shook him terribly ; and, weakened as he was already by excitement, fatigue, and that strange fainting fit up above, he was fearfully strained by the time they reached home.

"Ah, my dear, I am getting an old man!" he said to Patricia with a half-humorous melancholy, as he flung himself exhausted on the sofa. "I must leave off these pranks for the future. For the future, indeed! I have lost my boat, and needs must, I'm thinking."

"Oh, we will save up our money and get another *Mermaid !*" said Patricia cheerfully. "We should be lost without our boat ! We must have another just like her—the poor old *Mermaid !*"

"We'll have to content ourselves with you, my dear, as the sole representative of the tribe," said the old man. "Hey, Gordon ? "

"We might do worse," said Gordon with a sudden flush, as he looked at the girl tenderly—as a man looks when he loves.

The old man caught both the flush and the look.

"Give me your arm, boy," he then said with a strange softness of manner. "I feel a little the worse for wear to-night ; do you help me upstairs. You won't be jealous, Pat ? "

"Of Gordon ? No indeed, whatever he were to do for you, dear !" she answered frankly. "Jealous of Gordon !" she laughed.

"That's right, my girl. Of all the fiends that ruin happiness,

and dignity too, jealousy is one of the worst. Never give it
harbourage in your heart, lass. Keep out jealousy and keep
in truth; and remember that a friend is a friend, and that your
word once passed, you must go to the stake before you break
it! Now give me a kiss, and good night."

Patricia laid her hand in his. "Dear Uncle!" she said
fondly, bending her face to his.

He took her hand; then laid it side by side with Gordon's
as if measuring both together.

"It's a pleasant *patte* enough! he said to the young man,
smiling. "Not a fine lady's useless little fist, but a good, serviceable, womanly hand that can handle a rope and dandle a
baby, both as they should be done. I'm thinking it will be a
treasure some day to some one."

"Uncle!" she remonstrated, with a burning face; while Gordon gave her hand one strong silent pressure, answering, and
not looking at her:

"It will so, sir. And I hope he will get it who will prize it
most."

"Good night, lassie," said the Captain with a smile half
pleased, half pathetic. "It's all right. When I'm gone you'll
have him to take care of you. Sleep well and don't dream;
or if you do, dream of those who love you."

"Good night, my dear—my dearest dear!" she exclaimed,
and threw her arms round his neck and kissed him fervently;
he pressing her to his heart with a kind of passionate solemnity
of which Patricia had never seen the like in him before.
"Good night, Gordon," she then said, her eyes downcast, her
cheeks dyed crimson, and tears, she did not know why, beginning to start.

"There, boy, give her a kiss; you have earned it to-night,"
said the Captain, standing as it were between them, holding a
hand of each. "Kiss your friend, Pat, who has been so near
to death with you and who helped to save you."

Trembling as much as herself, Gordon drew her gently towards him. The tears had come fully into her eyes by now, and
were falling slowly and heavily down her cheeks—tears that
were alternated with a smile and a blush, and a wish that her
dear uncle had not said what he had; and yet, what harm was
there in kissing her old friend?

Feeling that to obey his wish frankly was better modesty than to object, she lifted up her face all wet as it was, and Gordon, with almost as much bashfulness as her own, trembling, proud, happy, and yet shy, stooped his head and kissed her full on the lips, with a reverent tenderness if also a frank affection not lost on the Captain.

"Thank you for all you have done," said Patricia simply; and lighting her candle went off to bed with a trouble at her heart she had never felt before.

She heard her uncle, helped by Gordon, stumble heavily upstairs. He walked as a drunken man might, and somehow the failing footsteps struck a chill to her heart that seemed like the beginning of disaster. Then she heard the young man's voice and his in lower earnest talk; and then a "Good night" said cheerily, as Gordon closed the door and strode downstairs. And after this she heard no more.

Thronging thoughts perplexed and possessed her, so that she could not sleep, weary as she was. It seemed to her as if all things had suddenly gone astray, and life was different altogether to-night from what it had been this morning. In the morning how bright everything had been; in the evening how dark and full of dread! The *Mermaid* lost; her uncle unlike himself; Gordon going away for at least two, and may be five, years—and he too not the same old friend and chum that he had been all these past years—but this was not a change that gave her the same pain the others gave her; in the distance Aunt Hamley and the lady companion who would introduce a new order of things, and perhaps an order they would not like. —these thoughts kept her awake far into the night. Her head would keep on talking to her, as was her phrase; but at last she dropped asleep with the heavy slumber of the young, and did not awake till quite late into the morning.

CHAPTER V.

MORS JANUA.

SHOCKED to find how late it was when she awoke Patricia hurried over her dressing, afraid of having kept her uncle waiting for breakfast; which was one of the domestic offences he found it hard to forgive. The temper of the commander still clung to him, and with the kindest heart in the world he had one of the tightest hands when he exercised any discipline at all. He was always captain in his own ship, he used to say, and always intended to be ; and if his laws were few they were positive.

Patricia however was needlessly alarmed. When she got downstairs, full an hour after her usual time, she found that her uncle had not yet risen. She was glad of this as it enabled her to help Sarah with the breakfast ; and with a womanly instinct of the right sort she took pains to make it a breakfast of special niceness, in reference to her uncle's fatigue and seizure of the night before. But though it took rather a long time to get ready, still the Captain, usually so punctual and so early, was not astir.

She went up to his room and knocked at the door. There was no answer. She knocked again ; still no answer. Again and again ; each time louder than before as the imperiousness of fear made itself felt. And then, holding her breath for she knew not what unspoken dread, she opened the door and went in.

On the bed lay the old man still in the wet clothes of the evening before. He had evidently flung himself there, weary and exhausted, when Gordon left him ; and so had fallen asleep. Asleep ? Was that white face sleeping ? When she took his hand, and it hung so coldly strange and still in hers—when she kissed his face and found that so cold too, so rigid underneath the skin, the glassy eyes not quite closed, the mouth opened, the jaw dropped—was that sleep ? Was it not rather the thing she had seen only a day ago ? It was Death ; and she knew it.

Soon the servant came hurrying up to her loud call; and then the doctor from St. John's, who happened to be passing through the village at the moment, was brought in; and in less than ten minutes the house downstairs was thronged with eager questioners crowding up to hear the news, which had spread as if the birds of the air had carried it, confirmed at the fountain head. It was like a social earthquake in the village; and even brave men felt scared when they saw the cottage flag floating half-mast high—the coastguardsman who came in had done that; it would have been shameful and indelicate else, as bad as a piano playing, or the first Sunday at church in bright colours—and heard that the fine old captain who was like a father in the place, had been found dead in his bed—God save his soul alive!—and that a life which looked as if it had had many years yet to run was cut short just when it was most wanted. For the fate of the poor fatherless and motherless girl, whom they had seen grow up among them like one of their own, touched them all with pity; and many a man's eyes were moist that day, and many a woman felt her mother's heart ache with pain, for the bright and friendly "maid" who had always been the first to lend a helping hand when a neighbour was down; but who now wanted a stronger hand to help her than any to be found in Barsands.

Whether she was pitied or deserted Patricia neither knew nor for the moment cared. She would not leave the room where her dead uncle lay, and she would not let go his hand. She did not speak nor cry nor stir, but stood quite still with a dazed kind of air, looking at him. Only once, when the doctor handled him as she thought roughly, she put her arms over him in the manner of protection, saying, "Don't do that—you will hurt him."

She could not realize the fact that this body, this person of the one she had loved so tenderly and lived with so long was no more now than the stones in the fields or the wood in the forest. She was intellectually conscious that he was dead, but she had still the feeling that he felt and saw and understood though he was not able to speak to her, and that she must take care of him against those who did not love him as she loved him. But indeed she had not much conscious thought of any. kind. She had only a general sense of darkness and a dull

kind of pain, mixed up with a mocking and incongruous activity of eyesight that seemed half sacrilegious, as when she found
herself counting the worn buttons of his waistcoat and the
stripes on his grey flannel shirt.

The doctor spoke to her, and tried to reason with her; but
though she heard his voice clearly enough, she did not understand what he said. She wondered why he talked to her, and
she wished he would leave off; but outwardly she was patient,
and at one time he thought he was doing her good. Knowing
his profession, he did not like that tearless, half-bewildered and
half-stony look she had. If she had shrieked and sobbed, and
been even petulant and unreasonable, he would have understood it better; but this silent tenacity had an ugly look of
pressure, and he wanted to rouse her out of it.

Presently, in the midst of his talk, Gordon Frere, pale and
breathless, came rustling through the garden and up into the
room where Patricia was standing, still keeping guard over the
dead.

The news had met him as he came in from St. John's, and
half a dozen people had stopped him in the village to repeat it.

"Patricia!" he said, touching her lightly on the shoulder.

His voice seemed to break the spell. She turned hastily and
held out her hand.

"Oh, Gordon, how glad I am you have come! you are all
I have left," she said. Look there, Gordon! Gordon! he is
dead?"

Then she turned away her head, and covering her face with
her hands broke down into passionate sobs and tears,

And the doctor, looking at her critically, gave a little sigh of
relief and said to himself, "Now she'll do."

"My darling! what can I do for you?" said Gordon, taking
her into his arms with a strange mixture of tenderness, protection, and shyness. "Patricia, don't give way like this, dear;
you break my heart to see you!"

"He was so fond of you, Gordon!" said poor Patricia, looking up into his face. "How he loved you!"

"And how I loved him?" answered the young man, brushing his hand over his eyes. "We are one in our sorrow, dear!
He was almost as much to me as he was to you!"

"Ah, yes, you knew him, and he loved you," she repeated.

" And I love you too," he said in a deep voice.

" Yes, I know you do," she answered simply, " You are the only person in the world who does now—all I have left."

" And I will be always yours—always part of your very self, if you will have me, darling ? We will never desert each other—never—never ! "

" Never ! " she said, tears breaking her voice ; the poor young people transacting their love affairs so innocently before the doctor and in the presence of the dead ? " But oh ! do not let us think of ourselves ; let us think of him," she added with sudden remorse, turning towards the bed, where, flinging herself on her knees, she took the cold hand again in hers and kissed it fervently as if asking pardon for her momentary disloyalty.

And Gordon was not ashamed to feel his own eyes dim and his eyelashes wet for sympathy and sorrow too. But he soon lifted her up again, and made her sit down while he stood by her, holding one of her hands in both of his ; her other laid lightly on the dear dead. No more was said between them. Quite quiet and silent they remained there, she gazing at the white face with its falling wreath of snowy hair before her, thinking only of him ; he looking at the white face too, but thinking most of her and her desolate future. And in this silent companionship of sorrow they felt drawn closer together somehow than if they had spoken for hours. They were unconscious of time, or who came and went about them. They were together in the presence of the man they had both loved, and whose spirit seemed with them still.

So they would have stayed probably till night ; but the women who had been sent for—those mysterious death-bed women—came to fulfil the last offices, and the doctor gave Gordon a sign to take Patricia away. He thought there would be a difficulty and he had prepared his exhortations : but there was none of that feminine exaggeration of character in her which makes sorrowing women so often unmanageable. Besides, she felt that Gordon was her master now ; that it was her duty to obey him as she had formerly obeyed her uncle. When he said she was to go, she looked at him piteously, mutely beseeching him for leave to stay ; but when he repeated his words, drawing her as if to lift her from the chair, she got up at once, and though she wept afresh she went with the simple obedience of a child.

Gordon kept with the poor desolate young thing the whole day through. But the long hours came to an end at last, and he too must leave her. It was his last leave-taking. He must be off early in the morning for Portsmouth, and neither pity nor sorrow, nor yet love, could make the time longer. They had talked but little through the day, but they had kept very near together. They seemed afraid of losing sight of each other ; as if something would happen to separate them for ever if they drifted apart for a moment. There had been no pretence of reading, or of doing anything whatever with a purpose. They had either sat in the little sitting-room, side by side on the black horse-hair sofa, or they had wandered out into the garden, scarcely noticing how gloomy the day was—and how bright yesterday !—but looking at each familiar tree and flower as people do who look for the last time. And they had stood by the model of the old *Holdfast*, and had touched it with a lingering fondness as if it had been a creature that could feel. But as they walked round it, both Gordon who had sense, and Patricia who was not fantastic, turned pale and looked at each other with a sense of awe upon them, when they saw that, by some means not evident, the storm last night had broken off the figure-head of the resolute-looking being that had symbolised the name, and that the legend underneath, painted by his own hand, " Robert Kemball, R.N., Commander," had been torn away with the device. They made no remark to each other when they saw this. They only looked up, and both were very pale. It foreshadowed nothing, explained nothing ; but it gave them a feeling of superstitious dread that made the present burden heavier.

The hours passed, as all hours do, and the last moment had come. Many a time during the day Miss Pritchard and old mother Jose had come down, wanting to be of use ; and now the former, thinking that Patricia would be none the worse for at least the appearance of womanly countenance, was knitting a brown woollen antimacassar by the dim light of one kitchen candle, lamenting in her heart the selfishness of the young in Patricia's absorption in her grief for the one and her love for the other, and thinking it was a good thing, as matters had turned, that her sister Matilda had never married that old man. And yet, if she had, she would have had her pension, and Patricia would have gone to her own relations. Yet Miss Pritchard was by no means a bad-hearted woman. She was only human; and she lived in a small place, with a very narrow field in which to work out her life.

"Well! time's up; I must go, Patricia." said Gordon.

He was pale and desperately agitated. Up to this moment he had been the calmer, and more self-controlled of the two; now their positions were reversed, and it was he who had to be comforted.

"What o'clock is it?" asked Patricia, waking up as if from a dream.

"Ten," said Miss Pritchard demurely.

"Yes, it's time for you to go," she answered. "Uncle likes the house shut up at ten."

"You'll write to me?" he said, standing and holding her hands in his. "You know you will probably have to move from here; you cannot stay here alone; so I shall not know where you are unless you tell me."

"You need not be afraid of her being left, Mr. Frere. I will look after her till she gets a better protectress," said Miss Pritchard in her precise voice.

She meant it kindly, but her words came in with a horrible jar on the young lovers. They had forgotten she was there, forgotten all but each other: and now her voice broke in between them like a sign of the world and the future, and the conventionalities too, which were about to divide them.

"Yes, of course I will write," said Patricia, "And I shall want to hear from you too, Gordon. I shall have only your letters to make me happy. Happy! I shall never be happy again!" she cried. And she believed what she said.

The ancient schoolmistress shook her head softly; and though the tears were in her eyes, tears of honest human sympathy falling over her unlovely work, she knew by experience that time is not eternity and that the "never" of the young is of very short duration.

"Come upstairs with me," then said Gordon. "I would like to say my last good-bye to him."

"God bless you, dear!" cried Patricia, flinging back her

head with a gesture peculiar to herself, and which meant an out-
pour of love and thanks greater than she could put into words.

Her lips quivering and his set firm, hand in hand they went
up the stairs and into the shabby little room that was now a
sacred temple to them.

"Make a prayer with me, Patricia," Gordon said.   "It will
be good to remember."

"Yes," she answered ; and she looked at the dead man—so
she would have looked had he been alive—for his approval.

Kneeling down by the side of the bed they said the Lord's
Prayer together, like two children at their good-night ; nothing
more ; but both felt it their sacrament. Then they stood up
still holding by each other.

"And you will not forget me ?" said Gordon in a husky voice.

"Forget you ! How can I forget you ?" she answered.

"Nor love any one else, nor let any one else love you ?"

"What do you mean, dear ? How should I love, or whom ?"

"You feel then you are engaged to me, Patricia ? that you
have promised to be my wife through good report and evil report, through poverty and all loss ?"

"Was that what you meant last night ?" said Patricia
simply, "I did not understand you quite. If it is I am glad.
Yes, I will be your wife, Gordon, and I will not love any one
else, nor let any one love me."

"God bless you ! Oh, how can I thank you enough for these
dear words ! *He* would have been glad, darling. He said so
to me last night, and I was to have come to-day to get your
promise. He wanted to know that you loved me, from your
own mouth, before I went away. You do not mind having to
say now at such a sad time, do you, dear ? You do not think I
am selfish in putting it to you now—and here ? I could scarcely
go away and leave it in doubt."

"It would have been cruel if you had," she answered.

"You like to feel bound to me, pledged to be my wife, to
care for no one else, only me, all through your life ?"

She looked him full in the eyes : "Like it, dear ! it is the
only comfort I have," she said.

At another time she would have been shy and bashful, she
would have laughed and cried and blushed ; but the whole
thing was too solemn now for any of the pretty follies or trepi-

dations of love. It was an oath they were pledging, not a man wooing and a woman being won.

"And you will always feel that I am yours? as much as if we were married already?" continued Gordon. "If there is any thing in which I or my affairs—my money, Patricia—can be of use to you, do not hesitate to go to Mr. Fletcher, and tell him who you are, and that I sent you. It breaks my heart to think how utterly alone and unfriended I am leaving you. If it were not for the dishonour I would stay and look after you."

"I shall have your love and his," said Patricia, struggling against her tears and conquering them; "and I will not let any-thing make me cowardly or complaining. I will bear my fate cheerfully, whatever it may be, for his sake and yours. I will be worthy of you both, Gordon."

"I trust you, Patricia darling, beloved! I trust you for all strength and honour as I trust the sun for shining," said Gor-don fervently. "Never let us lose trust in each other—I in you, and you in me. Darling, promise me that."

"Never, Gordon! I could not live if I did not trust you. Will you always believe in me?" she said, with a yearning kind of look.

"Will I always believe in the sun? Could I doubt you, Patricia? If you came to me in rags, loaded with the world's scorn, I would believe you before the world! Now, good-bye, and God bless you, my heart's dear love!"

"Good-bye, Gordon; and God bless you too!" said Patricia.

"You will give me one kiss again to-night? You may, now you are my promised wife. I would not ask you if you ought not."

"I have given you my love and my word, and that may well follow," she said, and put her arms round him frankly.

He held her pressed close to his heart with one arm, passing his other hand lovingly over her hair, holding back her face while he looked long and tenderly into it.

"My beloved!" he said, and kissed her.

With a great sob he loosened her arms and his own, and she heard him dash down the stairs, and through the gate and so on to the stony village road. She heard no more; and Miss Prit-chard running up at the sound of her fall, found her lying pale and senseless on the floor. Her strong spirit had given way, and the brave heart yielded to its pain at last.

CHAPTER VI.

NOVÆ VITÆ.

NEXT day's post brought a letter from **Aunt Hamley** to her brother. It was not a very long letter, but it said a good deal in its space. It was written in a fine pointed hand, with long, sweeping tails and graceful curves that ran far into the next line, giving the page a tangled and cobwebbed look, more ladylike than legible.

It set forth in the beginning, as if it had been a legal declaration, the writer's womanly satisfaction that he, Robert Kemball, had at last seen the fatal mistake he had made, before it was too late, if indeed it was not already too late to remedy it. No one but himself, it said, with one of what the Captain used to call Rosanna's characteristic digs, would have thought of bringing up a young lady without some older lady to guide and instruct her. Whatever harm came of it however, her brother Robert must never forget that she, Rosanna Hamley, had lifted up her voice against it from the first—though vainly. As it was, she was glad to see him awakening to a sense of his true position ; and she decidedly recommended him to look out for a lady companion forthwith—or rather, she proposed to do so for him herself. There were one or two highly-trained persons at Milltown of whose circumstances she knew something ; poor, and for whom a small salary with a comfortable home would suffice ; women perfectly well-bred and fitted for the work of reducing an undisciplined young person to the ladylike demeanour demanded by society. She assumed that Patricia was undisciplined ; poor girl, how indeed could she be anything else ! Then she went on to say, that if her brother and his niece—she said " your niece," not " my " nor " our "—would like to come over to Abbey Holme for a week or so she would be better able to give advice ; and she would be glad to welcome them there. She could not deny, nor would she, that there had been differences between her brother Robert and herself, and this would be a good way of healing them, besides being of use to both himself and his niece. She could say no more. If he would accept her offer, he was to write at once and say when they were coming; if he rejected it, she did not see how she could help farther in the matter, as, on second thoughts, it would be undesirable to engage a lady so entirely in the dark as she would be were she not made better acquainted with his niece before she looked out. The letter ended with a postscript: "Dear Dora Drummond," it said, "Mr. Hamley's cousin, and the child of my adoption—failing Patricia, whom you refused to me—is the best proof I can give of *my* fitness for advising on the subject of young ladies' education; also of what *my* training would have done for your niece. I think, when you see Dora, you will acknowledge that the grace, good breeding, and perfect self-command I have laboured so hard to inculcate have been thoroughly well learnt. Her association will do Patricia good; and her principles are, I am happy to say, too firmly fixed for me to be afraid of undesirable associations on her own account."

This was the elaborately-worded letter that came in answer to the Captain's brief and bluff request for a few words of advice: "Should he get a lady companion for Patricia? She was eighteen now, and he wished her to have the best of everything. What did his sister Rosanna think?"

Patricia read this letter as if it had reference to another life. Her vague disquiet at the idea of the lady companion seemed so childish now in the face of the terrible reality that had come; and so far off! It seemed as if it was months ago, and at the other side of a wide river, since her uncle had called her into the porch to listen to the project over which he had been brooding, and which startled her so much. It was only three days since, but a lifetime lay between. Three days ago she was a happy child; now she was a sorrowful woman. It was like waking up from a dream; or rather, it was like a dream itself —as if that happy past was the reality still, and this dreadful present a mere vision, a nightmare, from which she would awake in the morning, to hear her uncle knocking up the house as usual—his kind old face, framed in its silver hair, beaming with affection, and freshened with the morning air, looking up to the window from the lawn as he called out, "Hi, there lazy-

D

bones! Past six o'clock, and you still abed! Tumble up, tumble up, or I'll be at you !"

But, ah! it was all too real! He was dead; Gordon was away; there was no return, no escape to the beloved past; she had to realise the present, and to live through it.

Fortunately for her she had no one at this moment on whom she could fall back. She was the sole mistress of all that was left, and she must exert herself. Men may die, but men must live ; and those who are left must be provided for on the day when the beloved lie dead all the same as on other days. The morning breaks and the evening wanes, and there is the uprising and the downsitting, as if no light had gone out, and no one's life was the poorer for its loss. But a short time can be spared from active work for the filling in of a grave, let who will lie there. To the young this is impious and horrible ; but it must be. Patricia would rather have sat in sackcloth and ashes by the side of the dear dead than have worn her ordinary gown—that very skirt which she had mended in the sunshine on the other side of the gulf, and so many years ago ! But sackcloth and ashes and giving oneself up to mute mourning on the floor do not square with the ordinary run of things in daily life, and she had to bestir herself ; to enter into consultations with Miss Pritchard and Mother Jose, the one about her mourning, the other about the undertaker at Penrose, to whom word must be sent—to morrow being Mother Jose's " day in." And when she had read Aunt Hamley's letter, she had to write to Abbey Holme to tell them of the loss that had befallen her. The chances are that without this letter as a reminder she would have forgotten her aunt's existence for the first part, and would then have shrunk from bringing herself before her notice for the second.

The answer came by telegram—Mother Jose brought it in to save the expense of the messenger ; and before Patricia had read it herself, all Barsands knew of it and half the village had spelt it over. It was short but important :

" Mr. Hamley sets off to-day for Barsands. He will bring you back with him."

Mors janua vitæ. Not only for the beloved dead but also for her. Through the gate of his grave she walked straight from the old to the new, from the known to the unknown, from joy-

ous security to doubt and dread. Life at Aunt Hamley's! She
shivered, and thought how cold the night was and how soon
the winter had come this year! But she was not going to mope
and give way for a fancy, she thought. She was not of the kind
to create spectres for want of a braver resolve to meet cheerfully what was before her. At the worst, Aunt Hamley was
her father's sister and her dear dead uncle's : and with too such
men for her brothers she could not be all bad. And then the
natural buoyancy of youth came in to help her. She had
known only love and liberty hitherto ; and may be love and
liberty would brighten out on her from the foreboded gloom of
Abbey Holme. And, if not, what was the good of her promise
to bear all things cheerfully, if her strength could not stand a
trial? It was easy to be brave in the air ; better to prove by
deeds and be proved by trial!

With this she dismissed herself and her future from her
mind. And if she had thought of either, it had been rather in
reference to being and doing as her beloved uncle would have
wished, not because she cared much at this moment what would
or would not become of her.

The next day, just as the evening was beginning to draw in,
a post-chaise dashed through the village. It was the smartest
chaise to be had in Penrose, with a couple of postilions in rather
shabby jackets ; but it was a sight not often seen in Barsands,
and it brought the people out as if the Queen or Wombwell's
wild beasts had been passing through. After stopping at the
Lame Duck to inquire where Holdfast Cottage might be found,
and being told by a dozen people at once, the full-fleshed dark
haired man who had put his head out of the window to ask
said, "Drive on!" authoritatively, and drew it back again,
smiling to himself while the carriage dashed on to the cottage,
followed by all the children of the place yelling their Io pæans
in west-country language and with seaside lungs.

Patricia was upstairs in a back room, and neither heard nor
saw the arrival ; but the servant came rushing in to summon
her, breathless and jubilant.

"Your aunt's master!" she said. "And as fine a looking
gentleman as ever you see!" she added excitedly ; quite glad
that her young mistress had such a showy piece of humanity for
her future protector.

"Mr. Hamley here!" cried Patricia, involuntarily catching her breath. She felt the room go round and the floor slide from her feet, as she afterwards told Miss Pritchard; who put her dynamics right for her. But she could not afford to lose time in noting odd sensations; so, standing up and clearing her eyes, pressing back something at her heart as if with a strong hand, without waiting to arrange herself, to put up her hair or to put on a ribbon—not having the ordinary woman's instinct that way, though she had done it all for Gordon—she ran down stairs to the little parlour, for it could not be called a drawing-room, tumbled, unkempt, disordered as she was.

Mr. Hamley was waiting for her; and, while waiting, he had been examining with a critical eye the extraordinary collection of rubbish and real curiosities intermixed, disposed by way of ornamentation about the chimneypiece and on the side table. Magnificent bits of coral were flanked by paltry sixpenny figures of lambs and dogs with broom-stick tails; an exquis-itely-carved vase in jade-stone had for its pedestal a common seashore pebble worn flat enough for a stand; the oleographs distributed by certain weekly papers were pinned unframed against the walls, but Patricia had hung them round with wreaths of yellowing oak-leaves and fronds and tufts of sea-weed, green and scarlet and duller purple; which was an arrangement that betokened taste if it also spoke of poverty. Mr. Hamley, however, did not respect taste if allied with poverty. What he liked was a good, heavy, handsome, gilded frame about a fine strong-coloured oil-painting; not your hand-ful of withered leaves and slimy seaweeds festooned with pins round a twopenny-halfpenny print given away by a weekly.

"Not worth a pound the lot!" he was saying to himself as Patricia opened the door and came in.

She saw a tall, largely-framed man with dark curled hair; a clean-shaven face save for a pair of thick whiskers that met in a frill under his chin; small, deeply-set eyes, bright, black, and keen; a large obtrusive kind of nose; and heavy, clumsy, cracked-looking lips that squared out when he spoke, and showed a close row of sharp rodent-shaped teeth and all his upper gums when he smiled. He was a fine-built man, with an unmistakable look of good living and prosperity about him. In the smooth lines of his sleek figure, tending to stoutness, but as yet only sleek ; in his showy attitudes and parabolic gestures ; in the measured accents of his level artificial voice ; in the glitter of the massive gold chain across his ample front, the sparkle of the huge diamonds on his large hands; from the cleanly-drawn parting of his shining hair down to the tips of his shining boots, and in the superb fineness and glossiness of all his clothes, could be read the self-complacency of the man and the success of his life. He was Mr. Hamley of Abbey Holme ; and he liked people to know it. He was not ashamed to add, the man who had begun life as an errand-boy on six-pence a day ; the son of a brewer's drayman, born in a hovel and bred in a stable ; but who by industry, good conduct, tact, and natural ability, had risen to be the rich brewer of Milltown and the husband of Admiral Sir Robert Kemball's daughter. He was a self-made man, and he gloried in his maker, and asked the world to glorify him too.

He had early decided on his tactics, which were to stick to the place where he had known hunger and had made a colossal fortune, and to force society there to recognise and admit him. The closed paradises of his past were the only ones the gates of which he especially cared to open ; and he would rather be re-ceived on an equality by the poorest Milltown gentleman whose horse he had once been glad to hold for a few pence, than be courted by people whom he had not known, and who had not known him in his bare-footed days. Milltown was his world ; and that world he had set himself to conquer. And he had succeeded.

He put his face into the proper expression of sympathy as Patricia entered ; but in spite of himself a look of surprise took the precedence, and his forced sympathy dropped away like a mask. He had not expected to see anything so beautiful ; and he showed that he had not. Not that hers was the kind of beauty he liked best; certainly not. He liked very fair women; gliding, caressing, insinuating women ; women who were timid and who screamed easily ; women he could protect and domi-nate, and who confessed his masculine superiority even when they put on pretty airs of social queenhood—he giving up to them this social queenhood in consideration of holding all the other sceptres in a sheaf together ; women who were fond of warmth and good living, luxurious seats, fine clothes and sparkling jewelery; women he could buy with gifts and subdue through their senses, as he could make cats purr by pleasant treatment. He hated all enthusiasm in women, save maybe for trivial amusements; all decision of opinion; all power of reasoning or show of learning; and the doctrine of their rights (which however he did not understand) was anathema maranatha. He easily forgave a little graceful deception, especially if in his own favour. Indeed, he used to say that truth was indelicate in women—not that he ever called them anything but ladies—and that nature meant them to fib as she meant canaries to sing. Neither was he severe on their want of honour in love affairs or money matters, providing they did not jilt nor cheat him. He called them little "rascals," when they were found out; but if they were pretty he laughed as at a good joke. He had an idea too that they should take very short steps—pretty pit-a-pat useless kind of steps—in fact, a Chinese woman's walk modified; and that they should carry their heads bent downwards, looking up from under their eyebrows shyly. And he liked trim, well-buckled figures where the art of the stay-maker and the milliner was apparent; and the only kind of appearance that fascinated him was that called stylish.

Patricia fulfilled none of these personal requirements. She bore her head straight and her shoulders square, and looked out from her large, well-opened eyes held quite level. She walked with a swift, free step, and took what he mentally noted as strides. She was not especially neat; rather the reverse; and her manners were singularly fearless, and with an air of independence and unconsciousness that set her at odds with her aunt's husband at first sight. Her hair was in loose masses that showed the shine and varied auburn tints and broad rich wave upon it, such as artists would have loved; but as it was not smooth and silky like Dora's blonde and elaborate chignon, nor crimped and curled like Mrs. Hamley's faded tresses, to Mr. Hamley's eyes it looked undressed. As to her figure, to be sure she was as upright as a dart, yet as supple as a willow wand; all her lines were long and slender, and she was exquisitely proportioned; but she evidently wore no stays, her dress was of poor material and badly made, she was neither trim nor well-buckled, and, in fact, she was not finished off anywhere. That was the word—she was not finished off; still in the rough ; good material but having no value, no more than an uncut diamond or a block of brute marble—or a pocketful of hops thought Mr. Hamley, before it had seen the malt.

All this would come ; Mrs. Hamley would know how to do it, and Dora's example would complete the process. Meanwhile he had to condole, not criticise ; to forget that the pretty girl before him had neither stays nor style, that her hair was undressed and her whole person unfinished, in his efforts to make himself agreeable, and to impress on her untutored mind that her aunt's husband was by no means a common sort of man, and that she might hold herself fortunate in falling into such good hands.

" My dear !" he exclaimed, with that kind of enunciation which makes all the leading words end in h, "I cannot express how truly grieved Mrs. Hamley and myself are at your bereavement. Such a sudden termination !—with no time for prepara tion !"

" He was prepared," said Patricia hastily.

Mr. Hamley knew very little of religion, experimentally or intellectually. Nevertheless he had a few catch-words, and the probable lost condition of a soul suddenly called away was one of his strongholds.

He smiled with a kind of bland sorrow. "I devoutly hope so," he said, his voice showing that his hope had not taken on itself a very lively assurance.

" He was good. No more is wanted than that !" said Patricia, looking him straight between the eyes.

He hated to be looked at straight between the eyes, especially by women. He thought, too, she was defiant when she looked at him so fearlessly and spoke up so warmly. She was not : she was only in earnest.

" The Bible tells us more, I think," he said a little tartly.

This first introductory interview had not begun on velvet.

" Oh, do not speak as if you doubted !" she said in real pain. "There never was a better man than Uncle Robert ! I ought to know—who so well ?" she added, her voice breaking.

" Ah ! well ! we will converse no more about that aspect of the case," said Mr. Hamley with his soothing manner, taking her hand in his ; and his was large and fleshy and moist. " But you must resign yourself, my dear young lady, and remember that no amount of tears, not if you cried those fine eyes of yours out of your head, will bring a dead man back to life again. We must be reasonable even in our mourning. Don't you agree to this?"

"Yes," said Patricia, controlling herself without much effort. Something seemed to pass over her that made it almost sacrilege to show more of her heart to this man. "And yet," she added with perhaps a natural movement of opposition, "it seems strange to talk of reason at such a time."

"Reason always is strange to ladies," said Mr. Hamley. "Ladies feel; they do not reason."

The girl looked at him in frank amazement. Truly his words were plain English enough; but the meaning of them? For all the essential purposes of language he was speaking to her in a foreign tongue; and her face betrayed her perplexity. He caught her look and it pleased him. It seemed to confess that he could teach her something, and Mr. Hamley liked to hold forth.

"But you will be reasonable, my dear," he continued in that strange mixture of fine words and familiar, not to say vulgar, colloquialisms which made up his style. "I make bold to assure myself of this. What you have to do now is to reflect on your position and to make the best of it. I hope you will not find it such a bad job in the end as it seems in the commencement. That is, I hope you will find Abbey Holme not so very unpleasant, all thing considered, and that you will be able to make your life there to your liking." He said this with a smile and a little bow, as if he had been talking of a cup of tea.

"Thank you very much," answered Patricia, looking into his face. "I hope rather I shall be what you and my aunt will like."

"No doubt, my dear, after a training in our harness. When Mrs. Hamley has put her touch on you, and dear Dora has shown you what a real lady should be, I make no kind of doubt we shall be satisfied with you. Your aunt must take you in hand, and I bet that before long you will be turned out the real article too."

"Yes," said Patricia vaguely.

"We must get the angles down," said Mr. Hamley, rubbing his hands.

" Yes," she answered in the same vague way, wondering what the man meant.

" Mrs Hamley is a disciplinarian, my dear ; a tight hand, as you'll find ; a good soul though, and a real lady ; but," plucking at her loose sleeve and ill-cut bodice, " she'll not stand this kind of thing long ! Mrs. Hamley likes what the captain would have called ship-shape, brailed up; don't you understand ? Never mind now ; you will come right in time, and meanwhile we must do our business. And the first bit of business to attend to, if you'll excuse me, is the fortification of the inner man. Can your servant cook me a chop ? I am a plain man myself, and a well-cooked, juicy chop, with a nicely-done potato, steamed not boiled, satisfies all my wants."

" I am afraid we have not such a thing as a chop in the house," said Patricia in distress : " we have only a bit of cold mutton."

Mr. Hamley's face darkened.

" What part ? saddle ?" he asked.

" No ; I have never seen a saddle of mutton in my life," she answered innocently. " It is a bit of the breast, and I am afraid not very nice. We have not a great choice here."

" But you knew that I was coming ?" he said.

He was gravely displeased. A man of Mr. Hamley's stamp thinks much of fatted calves, both for honour and toothsomeness ; and a cold breast of mutton, with no special preparation for his arrival, was a sin greater than half a dozen falsehoods would have been.

" I daresay I can get something at Mrs. Jose's " then said Patricia, her face brightening at the thought ; but Mr. Hamley stopped her as she was about to rush out of the room tumultuously.

Don't give yourself quite so much trouble, my dear," he said with a certain ill-concealed irony. " I will go to the inn, and you can enjoy your own mutton in peace. I daresay you would rather be alone at such a time ;" with a half sigh : " and, after all, I came to help, not to make more work. Not a word ! I shall go to that house we pulled up at ; I presume they can toss me up some little thing that will suffice ; and then I will return to you and take off my coat to it."

On which he took his hat and conveyed himself out of the

room. No other word would give an adequate idea of the showy
dignity and ostentation with which he walked across the shabby
little parlour, which indeed he seemed to fill, and stooped his
head in the doorway, though there was no necessity for him to
do so—he could have passed through well enough. And when
he had gone Patricia sat down and took a long breath, feeling
as if a weight had been taken off her breast, as when we fight
off that shadowy hand at night which is throttling us in our
sleep.

This then was her aunt's husband, the uncle who was to be
her friend and guide and guardian in place of the dear dead
whom she had reverenced so simply and loved so truly ! It was
an instinct and not an act of reason that led her feet upstairs,
when she heard the garden gate shut as Mr. Hamley swaggered
out. She went to her uncle dead, as she would have gone to him
living, for counsel and if need be reproof. And when Mr.
Hamley came again he found her with red eyes truly, but more
cheerful somehow than she was before. And he said in his
letter to his wife that evening: "I am happy to state that my
coming has been of marked advantage to your niece, and that
she has already picked up wonderful."

Once installed master of the situation nothing could exceed
Mr. Hamley's energy and kindness. He took everything on
himself in a natural matter-of-fact way as if he had been born to
the work. His business faculty came in as almost another
sense, and reminded Patricia so often of what Gordon had said
about the fortune-telling of lawyers. But valuable though he
was, he extinguished her in the neatest manner possible. She
had not a word to say on any matter; and if she ventured an
opinion, he told her that was his business, not hers, that two
could not be masters, and that she was to give herself no kind
of trouble, but leave all that to him—he was there for that
purpose. For what else were they, great hairy men, born, but
to take care of the ladies? He wished her to sit down and
amuse herself; and he would do all the work if she would only
be quiet and enjoy herself.

What could she answer? She could not but feel grateful;
he meant it kindly; but still she wished that she might have
been employed too in these last arrangements of the old life—
these last gatherings of the dead roses. Lavish in his profes-

sions of consideration, irresistible in his high-handed assumptions, he swept her aside out of the path altogether, and Patricia suddenly found herself plunged from a life full to the brim of activity and love into a void where were only echoes and reflections.

In one thing, however, she was resolute; she would go to the funeral. Mr. Hamley thought it indelicate in a lady even to wish to go; but she was firm; and in the first real conflict of wills between them his had to go down before hers. He owed her a grudge for it, and never quite forgave her. For the matter of her following however, all the village went, coastguards, fisherfolks, the Misses Pritchard and all; so that her absence would have been remarked not to her advantage. This concourse, poor as it was, gratified Mr. Hamley. It pleased him to see that *his* brother-in-law had been popular; and it also pleased him to have such a good opportunity for showing himself off. He was conscious of his height and breadth and glossy black clothes, and general air of substance and prosperity : and as no homage came amiss to him, it made him feel quite his own man again when he saw the women whisper together as they looked at him, and the men cast those appraising glances as he passed which measured him and weighed him, and found him satisfactory. He was the make-believe hero of the day; and though the real hero was the one they loved, he could afford the rivalship on the principle of the dead lion and the live dog.

The Captain had left no will. Such men as he never do leave a will, except perhaps one they themselves write out on a sheet of note-paper, without witnesses to the signature; also partly because such men seldom have anything to leave. Of a surety the poor Captain had left neither will nor effects; so that all Aunt Hamley's husband had to do was to arrange the details of the funeral, pay the undertaker's bill presented at the conclusion, see what small debts were owing in the village, and sell off the furniture to meet them.

This was the hardest part to Patricia. In vain she besought him not to have a sale, but to let her give the things away.

"Give them away!" he said. "My dear young lady, you must be dreaming! Why give?"

"I know the people, and they are all so poor," pleaded Patricia.

"If they are too poor to buy, then they will not spend their money," Mr. Hamley said ; "and the other way on. Don't you trouble yourself about them. They can take care of themselves ; and you may be sure every one of them has an old stocking somewhere up the chimney with a hoard in it that would astonish you. Bless you ! I know the class as well as I know my alphabet ; always crying Peter Grievous, and putting money in the bank, the rogues ! You leave them alone, and turn your own pennies when you can."

" But it seems so disgraceful to sell to them," she said.

She had been brought up practically like a good democrat ; and she was a good democrat by nature as well as training ; which did not hinder a fine flash of the true old spirit that was once known as "Noblesse oblige." So disgraceful, for the comparatively rich to make money by the poor !—so far the better thing to give royally to those who needed, instead of chaffering for the miserable pence they could not afford to spend.

When she said all this, Mr. Hamley put his hands into his pockets and laughed aloud. He could not stop himself, he said ; such an extraordinary idea !—quite a backwood's kind of notion. To give away your property when you could make it into money !—to care two straws whether people were richer or poorer than yourself so long as you make your market of them ! The dear young lady was fit to be carried about in a show ! Lord ! it was lucky for her that he had come to save her from herself ! And as for making presents to any of them, the coastguards or the old women or any man-Jack alive, not he, not a farthing ! They had made a pretty penny out of the old Captain when he was alive, no fear ! and now he, Mr. Hamley, as the orphan's guardian—with a flourish—would save her little inheritance in every way he could, and do the best for her he was able under the circumstances.

So, in spite of all she could say, the sale was arranged and took place ; and everything was sold, save one or two intrinsically valuable "curios" which Mr. Hamley selected as "agreeable memorials for your aunt of her poor brother."

All told, it was not a weighty matter. When the last account was settled, and just as the fly was preparing to take them away, Mr. Hamley handed Patricia the net balance— nineteen pounds odd—as her sole independent fortune.

"Keep it, my dear," he said, when Patricia, full of youthful honour, also full of youthful distaste to its source, wanted him to take that sum as part payment of her prospective expenses. "Make it go as far as you can, but keep it. Remember it is all of your own that you possess. When it is spent you will have to come to *me* to replenish your purse. I wish to impress this on your mind. I am well off—I may indeed say very well off—but I do not encourage extravagance. I know what it is to earn sixpence a day and live on it; but I climbed up, you see, and got pretty well ahead by my own exertions; and I always advise other people to do the same."

"Indeed, Mr. Hamley, I am willing and ready to do anything —that I can," said Patricia, with a sudden hesitancy that explained everything.

"No doubt"—he stuck his thumbs into his waistcoat armholes. "But that is just where the hitch is—what can you do?" She turned pale. "Nothing!" she said looking down.

"Of course not! I knew that; only you need not have confessed it. Such an education as yours, scrambling and rambling about the country like a tinker's daughter, getting wrecked here and tossed like a bale of cotton there, and knowing no better than to have a cold breast of mutton for a gentleman's dinner after a long journey—how could you have learnt anything? Why you have not learnt even your own trade of lady! But never mind. I confess I should not like to see dear Dora obliged to work for her living—ladies ought to be worked for," —he put this in gallantly, standing there on his six feet one and ponderous breadth of shoulders; "and your aunt may have the same feeling for you. If she has, Abbey Holme is large enough for you, and," jingling the money in his pocket, "the Hamley funds can bear your additional burden, I daresay. Now here comes the fly. Are all your things ready? Say good-bye, my dear, to the old and make your courtesy to the new. No! no tears if you please. I can't abide a crying lady—it makes one damp!" To himself he said, almost aloud —"Lord! that the fool should cry to exchange this horrid hole for Abbey Holme."

CHAPTER VII.

THE HOME-COMING.

THE journey from Barsands to Milltown was a cross-country one; consequently full of delays, and tedious. There had not been much either in the scenery or the circumstances to amuse Mr. Hamley or interest Patricia. When he had pulled up both the windows, tucked himself and his charge well round in heavy railway rugs, bought the day's papers for himself and a trashy novel for her, he had done all that politeness and the circumstances of the case demanded of him; and Patricia had borne the feeling of oppression and suffocation consequent on his care as the sacrifice of self due to him for gratitude. But not even gratitude could make her read the book he gave her. Her education had been lamentably neglected with regard to modern fiction; and, save Sir Walter Scott and one or two of Dickens's earlier works, she had never read a novel in her life, and had no desire to begin. They seemed such wretched make-believes to her—much as an opera seems to a young person of ordinary common-sense perception and a keen idea of fitness, who sees and hears for the first time the hero die in an aria and the heroine go mad in a recitative. All she did, therefore, was to look out of the window; watching while she could; feeling, as every station with its well-known name was passed and left behind, that she was lengthening her chain of sorrow, cutting off so much from her life; and when she could no longer watch, dreaming. Meanwhile Mr. Hamley slept, and when he slept he snored.

It was a drear, dull day; one of those late autumn days which seem to have suddenly leapt into winter since yesterday. Here and there a tree, bright with gold and brown, had kept its foliage in a loose and feathery way still about its branches; but for the most part only a few deep red or russet-purple leaves fluttered in the chilly air, like the last good-byes of a friend.

Clumps of square-headed rag-wort, a few late hawkweeds, and some shabby tufts of milfoil were the sole representatives of the gracious flowers of spring and summer. The day was raw and damp. Not a bird twittered in the hedges; and the leaden sky looked as if it would never shine again. All this dreary dullness, all this melancholy of earth and sky, seemed quite natural to Patricia. She would have been surprised if the sun had shone, and the birds had sung, and the earth had been gay and sweet with flowers. It was not a conscious thought, but it was there all the same—the thought that nature was in mourning as well as herself; and that her uncle's death was known to more than the world at Barsands.

It was evening when they reached the station which served Milltown for its point of contact with the outer world. In old days when railroads were considered vulgar by some and immoral by others, Milltown had resolutely refused to be polluted by iron and steam. The clergyman had preached on the dangers to be dreaded by the influx of navvies; speaking of them —poor honest fellows!—as if they had been brigands or burglars; the ladies were afraid that their horses would be frightened by the engine, and foresaw the most frightful catastrophes; and the gentlemen objected to the "strange blood" which the line would introduce among them. Social influence —always strong in such a place as Milltown—had therefore managed to secure intact the exclusiveness which had been one of the characteristics of this little aristocratic south-coast queen of the sea. A station nine miles off was quite near enough for the conservative respectabilities which ruled in Milltown; and, though some now rather regretted this exclusiveness—they were the people who did not keep carriages—most stood by their colours, and thought they and their fathers had decided well in the past. These were the people with carriages and horses, who were able to leave home as often as they liked, and get abroad all the variety that home denied them. To them it was shocking to contemplate the invasion of their cared-for, well-trimmed, garden-like valley by hordes of excursionists from the neighbouring towns; and the idea of retired tradesmen, aping gentility, being enabled to rent houses, or maybe buy land and build amongst their own sacred seats, was one not to be borne for an instant. Whether by opening up mar-

kets and thus causing a brisker trade a railway would do
the farmers and smaller shop-keepers good, was not an item in
their calculations. It would bring strange residents, London
visitors and cheap-trip excursionists; and the Milltown gentry
wanted none of them.

When the train deposited Patricia and her companion they
found the Hamley carriages and the Hamley servants waiting
for them. Their arrival caused that excitement which the
coming of the rich men of the neighbourhood always causes in
such places; and the station-master and the two porters bustled
about and ran hither and thither to serve the owner of Abbey
Holme with alacrity and zeal. Flies round the honey-pot they
buzzed with expectant emphasis; and to do him justice the
great man paid for their buzzing liberally. Though by no means
generous by nature, pride disposed Mr. Hamley to public acts of
ostentatious liberality; and he understood that a character
must be paid for as well as other things more material. He
was thus quoted by some as the freest-hearted gentleman
of the district; while others with whom he had graver business transactions, spoke of him between their teeth as—well !
one who would skin a flint and make broth of the remainder.
Besides, small as the triumph was, he was pleased that Patricia should see the estimation in which he was held when at
home. He was aware that he had failed to impress her very
profoundly so far as he had gone yet, and he thought that
these evidences of his local dignity would do her good.

All she noticed however was, that the men seemed sickeningly
servile; and she wished they had not bowed so low or said
"sir" so often. He, not knowing this, was wonderfully affable
to-day, with the affability of a superior person condescending to
his brethren of low estate; and the honey ran over at all sides,
to the satisfaction of the limp-backed flies that gathered it.

Handed ostentatiously to the carriage, Patricia stepped in
with the wrong foot first; by which she entangled herself in
her dress and had to untwist herself before she sat down. The
result was not unlike the action of a dog turning round on the
hearth-rug while making his imaginary bed.

" We must have you instructed how to step into a carriage,
my dear," said Mr. Hamley blandly, when they had fairly rolled
away.

"Yes!" she answered. "Is there a right and a wrong way?"

"Is there a right and a wrong way?" He gave a scornful kind of snort. "Ask Dora," he added, in the tone of one who propounds something that is indisputable.

"I suppose Dora understands all these little things perfectly?" Patricia said, by way of courteous question.

"Little! Not so very little, let me tell you," Mr. Hamley answered hastily. She was touching his gods and profaning his sacred shrines. He had not been Mrs. Hamley's husband for fifteen years not to have learnt the full value of the minor graces. "These are things which all ladies should understand; and of which, if you'll excuse me for saying so, you are as ignorant as a cat. You will have to be learnt them without delay; and you will never progress if you commence by regarding them as little."

"I call them little only in comparison with the really great things. I daresay they are quite good and right in themselves, only not so important as some others," said Patricia, with the steady look which Mr. Hamley disliked so much, visible under the carriage-lamp shining full upon them. "Uncle always used to say that if we got the main things right, the rest would come when they were wanted."

"I do not exactly see how the main things as you call them —and I do not know what you mean either—will assist you to step into a carriage with the right foot foremost. And more than this, I cannot allow you to argue with me," said Mr. Hamley in a firm, heavy voice. "There is nothing more offensive to my mind than an argufying lady. You will remember this in future, I am sure."

"But is expressing an opinion arguing?" asked Patricia.

"There you are! at it again! My dear young lady you are positively dreadful! I say dreadful, and I mean it. What will Mrs. Hamley say to you? or dear Dora, the gentlest of her sex? Dora never argues, never objects. When Dora hears these pert remarks of yours she will be shocked; I know she will. A very little shocks both Dora and Mrs. Hamley."

"I will try not to shock them," said Patricia, patient but astounded. Truly life was having its new readings printed heavily for her benefit.

"You must not ; which is more than trying. And for one thing you must really be less radical than you are now. You are out-and-out the most independent radical for a lady I have ever seen. Positively astònishing ! And wherever you could have picked it all up, and your uncle the son of a K.C.B. and the brother of such a woman as Mrs. Hamley, I don't know.

"But I am not a radical at all, Mr. Hamley," said Patricia, opening her eyes and speaking very earnestly. "I understand nothing about politics, and am neither radical nor tory—scarcely indeed know the difference between them !"

"And I say you are," repeated Mr. Hamley, who had used the word in a provincial and not a political sense ; " so let us have no more discussion. Your duty is to be humble-minded and obedient; to order yourself lowly and reverently to all your pastors and masters and those who are put in authority over you," he added, with a happy reminiscence of the catechism as the sling and stone he thought would have most effect on this odd young person.

Patricia was silent. She wondered why, when her dear uncle's lessons had always awakened such a full response in her conscience, such a fervent desire and resolve to live up to all he said, and had seemed to lift her over every little moral difficulty in which she might have been at the time, Mr. Hamley's only pained and irritated her. What he said was of course the right thing so far as words went, but a certain something in her heart seemed to rebel rather than to acquiesce.

"You do not agree with me ?" then said Mr. Hamley with an unpleasant smile. He had been watching her face with its large eyes fixed on the darkening line of hedge and bank, and her lips closed tighter than her lips were wont to close. "You do not perceive the truth of what I say about humble-mindedness and obedience ?"

" Yes I do," said Patricia, still looking out of the window.

" But you are annoyed that I have said it ? "

For a minute she was silent. Then she turned to him frankly; "No, I am not," she said, and put both her hands into his.

"Very right," said Mr. Hamley with an indescribable assumption of superiority. He felt he had conquered and had driven in the thin edge of the wedge. " But you need not put your hands into a gentleman's when you speak. Ladies do not do such things in good society," he added, with a patronising smile ; not unkindly, rather the contrary ; the smile of a man who accepts his obligations and fulfils them at any cost, even that of being cold and disagreeable in checking a youthful enthusiasm towards himself, which however pleasant was perhaps dangerous.

No more was said after this ; and the carriage rattled on in silence till at last it turned out of the main road into one narrower and even smoother, flanked on each side by high banks topped with hedges, which, dark as it was, Patricia saw were closely trimmed and sheared.

And here Mr. Hamley said graciously, " We are close on home now. Your home too, my dear, as well as mine, if you are wise and will learn how to conduct yourself like a lady should. And I hope you will find it so, till," laughing, " you meet Mr. Right, and then I reckon it will be, 'Up Killick !' and away in no time !"

While he was saying this, Patricia understanding only his words and not the sense of them, they were driving through the lodge-gates with the woman who opened them curtesying to the very ground ; then through the chestnut avenue of the park, and so to the gates of the garden-lodge, with another woman to open them also curtesying to the ground ; up the shrubbery-drive, and finally to the broad sweep before the hall door.

The instant they drove up the doors were flung open with a clang, and two dogs, and what seemed to Patricia a crowd of men in scarlet and buff, appeared in the brilliantly-lighted hall. The small dog barked shrilly, and the servants all came forward under the marshalship of a solemn-looking man in black whom Patricia took to be a gentleman, and probably Mr. Hamley's uncle, or a visitor : he was only the butler ; and then Mr. Hamley got out of the carriage—he would have called it descended from the carriage—and the servant offered his arm to Patricia. The poor girl got out rather more awkwardly than she had got in, knocking her hat against the roof, stumbling over her dress, and taking the man's proffered elbow underhanded, as if it had been a rope.

Mr. Hamley turned and as a relief to his feelings kicked

the big dog that was standing quite still, leisurely surveying
the new-comer. If she had blushed and looked ashamed he
would not have minded so much; but that "confounded coolness of hers," as he called her innocent unconsciousness, annoyed him perhaps more than her awkwardness. However,
there was no help for it. He only hoped the men had not
noticed her; but he made sure they had; and for them to
know that Mrs. Hamley's niece had not been a carriage-lady
all her life was a bitter mortification to the former shoeless
little street-boy holding horses for coppers, and the present
master of Abbey Holme.

Concealing his annoyance in the best way he could, the
butler leading the way, Mr. Hamley took Patricia's hand upon
his arm and walked solemnly with her across the hall and
through half a dozen ante-rooms to the small drawing-room
where they always sat, and where he would present her to her
aunt.

The small drawing-room at Abbey Holme was about thirty
feet in length, and of proportionate width; and to Patricia,
accustomed to a sitting-room just a third that size, it looked
interminable. It was heavily furnished, but feebly lighted, a
couple of silver reading-lamps, casting two little islands of
light on two little velvet tables drawn close to the hearth,
being the whole of the illumination. By one table sat Mrs.
Hamley, by the other Dora Drummond.

A tall, thin, fashionably-dressed woman, noticeably upright,
and with a small waist tightly belted; wearing her own hair
not dyed, but restored—as she was careful to tell her friends
—her scanty puffs and braids, helped out by art, profusely
ornamented with white lace and shining black flowers, her
rustling black silk gown also glistening with beads and bugles,
and multitudinous jet ornaments clinking lightly as she moved
her head or hands; a tall thin woman, with a look partly of
ill-health and partly of ill-temper on her pinched and sallow
face; with cold light grey eyes and closely-drawn pale and
narrow lips—a woman fully twenty years the senior of her
sleek and prosperous husband—rose slowly from her seat as the
pair came up to where she sat.

" How do you do, Mr. Hamley?" she said in a thin voice
to her husband, shaking hands with him coldly. The Hamley

marriage was not one of the caressing sort. "I am glad to see you safe. And is this my niece, Patricia Kemball ? How do you do, Patricia ? How tall you are ! You are like poor Reginald, and like my poor mamma too, I see."

"How do you do, Aunt Hamley ? I am very much obliged to you for your kindness in taking me here," said Patricia, in her loud clear voice ; a little subdued, perhaps, because she was partly shy and partly moved, but louder and clearer and fuller than the normal register heard at Abbey Holme. It sounded like a silver trumpet, full, rich, sonorous, after Mrs. Hamley's tinkling wires ; but it was louder than Mrs. Hamley liked, and sounded the note of discordance at the outset. She and Dora Drummond looked at each other, and each understood what the other thought.

"How do you do, Patricia ?" said Dora Drummond in the sweetest flute-like notes. She had a dainty little lisp, especially becoming—a catch rather than a lisp—and she spoke slowly and softly.

Patricia turned and looked at her. She saw a young woman of about four and twenty, of middle height, by so means thin, but of singular grace of line and movement ; she saw a fair face with a small head round which coiled and twisted innumerable braids of golden hair as smooth and glossy as spun glass; blue eyes with light lashes—eyes that did not look straight and steady like her own, but that had the most bewitching little trick of shy observation, fleeting, half ashamed to be caught observing, such glances as Mr. Hamley liked, and which he had once confessed to Simpson the lawyer, when he was making his will, "fetched him, as nothing of the kind had ever done in his life before," but which others had been heard to say they wished were franker and not so sly ; a small, moist, rosy mouth ; a small, round, dimpled chin ; a waist that you could span—only eighteen inches ; and dimpled tiny hands, pink and unpractical. This dainty little person was dressed in a pretty costume of peach-blossom set about with black lace and ribbon to mark her share in the family mourning—a costume all frills and lace and coquettish arrangements of bows and ends, as beseemed her youth and beauty, and making her graceful figure look more graceful still by contrast with the billowy puffings which concealed some lines to betray others to greater advan-

tage. Altogether she was one of the loveliest creatures Patricia
had ever seen ; and yet the girl's first movement towards this
fairy was one of repulsion. Her second, when Dora looked at
her so kindly, spoke to her so softly, and pressed her hands
with such tender warmth, was one of gratitude; and with
gratitude and admiration together the rest was not difficult.

Especially graceful and . well-mannered, as was also Aunt
Hamley in her own severe way, both women struck the home-
bred girl as of a different type and mould from ordinary
humanity. Not even Miss Pritchard-had ever invented lessons
of deportment that came near to the lovely grace of Dora
Drummond, the ladylike self-possession of Aunt Hamley.

"Now I know, why dear uncle wanted me to have a lady
companion," she thought, and looked at Dora with a beaming
face that seemed to that young person "infinitely funny."

She was accustomed to be admired, but not by girls ; and the
naïveté of Patricia's admiration amused her. But she accepted
it with a sweet and friendly smile, mentally determining to turn
it to good account, if she should ever want a help as blind as
Patricia's would be.

"She will not be my rival, and I will make her my slave,"
Dora thought, as she looked up with the sweetest friendliness
into the clear eyes gazing down so honestly into hers ; and,
pressing the large hand that held her taper fingers quite en-
closed, suggested that Patricia must be cold, and apologized for
standing between her and the fire. Which she was not doing ;
but it sounded hospitable to say so.

On which Mrs. Hamley rang the bell for her maid, and
Patricia, under her guidance, was led through hall and passage
and corridor, till the way seemed as if it would never end, before she was finally ushered into the room assigned her ; where
the first thing she did was to draw back the curtains from the
window, open the window-shutters, then the window, point
with a look of dismay to the huge fire blazing in the grate, and
say piteously, "Oh, please take that away ; I never have a fire
in my bedroom !" and altogether show the savage simplicity of
her up-bringing to her aunt's prim and genteel maid as clearly
as if she had given her a sketch of her whole life, and proved
mathematically that Uncle Robert had been "no gentleman,"
and that she herself was not a whit more of a lady.

And while she was upstairs scandalising Bignold by her unladylike simplicity of personal habits in the first place, and by
her unfashionably cut garments in the second, the three Asses-
sors down-stairs were passing judgment on her from first impressions.

"She has a nice face," said Mrs. Hamley ; "but she is dreadfully uncouth."

"Quite in the rough, Lady, as I told you," said Mr. Hamley,
shifting his feet noisily. ·

"She will look better when she is better dressed," suggested
Dora amiably. "She is untidy now, and looks tired and
tumbled. To-morrow perhaps she will be better."

"There you are out, Dora," said Mr. Hamley ; "she'll be no
better to your liking to-morrow than she is to-day. I tell you
what it is, Lady," turning to his wife, "you've got your hands
full with that young woman, and your work's cut out for you
and no mistake !" .

"I shall be able to make her all I could wish. She is my
own niece," said Mrs. Hamley coldly ; and Mr. Hamley was too
well drilled not to be able to note signs with accuracy.

"No doubt no doubt !" he said, spreading out his large hands
to the fire. "At all events "—with his grand manner ; the
manner he put on when he wanted to impress women with the
consciousness of his bigness and manliness and strength and
magnanimity—"at all events this is her home, poor young
lady, and we must do the best we can for her. What we've
done for Dora we'll do for her ; and I'll never grudge the outlay. Whether she'll turn out as good a job as Dora is another
matter ;" here he smiled on his fair cousin ; "but we'll try,
Lady, we'll try. Faint heart never won fair lady, and we can't
top the hills if we sit down at the foot."

"You speak as if she was a savage," said Mrs. Hamley
tartly.

"You might have made a worse guess, Lady !" replied the
brewer composedly.

CHAPTER VIII.

FENCED IN.

ILLTOWN was eminently a residential place. Visitors were discouraged, and the enterprising or impecunious householders who ventured to exhibit " Apartments " in their windows were not well regarded by the gentry, who seemed to regard such an announcement as a personal impertinence, as well as a liberty, for which the householders deserved reproof. To let lodgings to strangers was held to be a base sacrifice of Milltown respectability to filthy lucre ; and gentlefolks with a good balance at their bankers are generally strict in their estimate of the mill wherein their poorer brethren grind their corn.

Being thus residential nothing was done to attract the outlying public. There was no parade, no evening band, no pier for the display of pretty boots and neat ankles on windy days, no Rooms, and next to no baths. The inhabitants thought it indelicate to bathe ; so there were only two machines : one for the ladies, painted blue and white, and one for the gentlemen, painted green and black ; and even these the proprietor said he was working at a sacrifice and on the ground of public spirit.

Though a seaside place, the sea was only a passive adjunct not an active part of Milltown existence, A land-locked placid bay, shallow and barren, it was artistically valuable on account of its colour, and the changing lights lying on its cliffs ; but nearly worthless for fishing and very little used for boating. Only one house in the place had a yacht in the basin within the breakwater. This was the *Water Lily*, a pretty little toy belonging to the Lowes ; young Sydney Lowe, with his father the Colonel, generally contriving to have all they wished to have, though by no means wealthy people ; indeed, being the most out at elbows of all the Milltown gentry. But the more nearly insolvent a certain kind of man is the more he contrives to spend on his pleasures. Colonel Lowe, of Cragfoot, was this kind of man, and his son Sydney was like him. Being thickly inhabited by the gentry every rood of land had its exclusive owner and its artificial as well as natural value. The very cliffs were fenced off against trespassers; perpetual attempts were made to stop old-established rights of way, which sometimes succeeded, if at others they failed when some man of more public spirit than his neighbours was personally inconvenienced; and the open paths across the fields, which were inalienable, were grudgingly marked off by lines of thorns, with fierce warnings of prosecution should the narrow strip be departed from; while all the gates were padlocked and the stiles made unnecessarily high and difficult. It was a jealous, "this is mine, and you have no right here," kind of system that was not good for the higher feeling of the people.

The country was noted for its garden-like neatness. Every hedge and bank for miles round was trimmed and combed like a croquet lawn. No wild flowers were allowed on the Milltown public waysides; no trailing growths, rich and luxuriant, to enchant an artist and distress the highway board and private gardeners, twined and hung about the well-clipped hedges of thorn and privet. If you wanted to study botany you must go some five miles or so inland, where a certain stretch of unreclaimed land gave the growths that flourish in peat and neglect, as well as affording squatting ground to a few half-starved miserable sinners whom the Milltown people regarded with a mixture of fear and contempt, as if they were of another order of beings altogether from themselves. The Milltown people paid no reverence to nature in the rough, and at the best held her as only brute material, without value till man had come with his tools to pare her luxuriance and bring her into subjection.

If the face of the country was fenced and trimmed and curled, till not a vestige of wild beauty or natural grace was left in it, the society of Milltown was in harmony therewith. It would have been hard to find a more rigidly respectable or more conventionalised set of people anywhere, than were those who ordered their lives in this pretty hypæthral prison by the "safe," if untrue, gospel of repression and condemnation. They were all retired admirals and colonels and landed gentry, who lived there; all emphatically gentlemen, with the Earl of Dovedale at

the Quest as their patron social saint, when he came down.
And up to quite late years not even a millionaire, who had
made his millions in trade, would have been admitted among
them.   It was a place where the dominant social sentiment was
caste.   The gentlefolks were one thing and the commonalty
was another ; the one represented the sheep and the elect, and
the other the goats and the discarded. The gentry classed
these last all together in a lump ; and the idea that they in their
turn could be split into minor subdivisions, wherein the baker
and the boatman, the farmer and his hind, held different degrees, seemed to them as ridiculous as the wars of pigmies or
the caste distinctions of savages. But the commonalty followed
their leaders, and the example of class exclusiveness set in the
higher circles was faithfully copied through the lower.

Milltown was respectable ; as a rule intensely so.   No one
got into debt publicly, or did wrong openly ; and whatever
sins might be committed were all out of sight and covered down.
The majority, too, went the right way in politics. No confessed
Republican had ever troubled the clear stream of Milltown Con-
servatism.   The worst of the pestilent fellows who canvassed
for the wrong side, voted blue instead of yellow at the elections,
and stood up against the rector at board meetings and vestries,
were nothing worse than mild Whigs who would have been
shocked to have heard themselves classed with Odger and
Bradlaugh, or as sympathising with even the " real gentlemen "
who had associated their names with advanced opinions.   But
even mild Whiggism was abhorrent to Milltown respectability,
and voted disreputable and low.   A confessed Republican or
Freethinker would have been considered capable of picking
pockets or cutting throats, had he held up his head and testi-
fied in the market-place ; and " not regular in his attendance at
church," or " not sound," was the worst condemnation that
could be given in a society where " chapel people " was used as
a term of reproach, and where a gentleman would as soon have
put on an apron and sold figs as have gone inside the Wesleyan
or the Baptist place of worship.

The parish church where Mr. Borrodaile, the rector, preached
his weekly orthodox sermon on what may be called dogmas of
a second intention, not wholly moral nor yet wholly theological,
was a fine old building of the Early English style. The services

were conducted in what they called "a proper and decent manner." There was no ecclesiastical vagueness at Milltown; no tampering with the unclean thing in any way. Extreme opinions were tabooed to which side soever they leaned, and enthusiasm was regarded as both vulgar and silly. Ritualism, Evangelicism, or Rationalism, an attempt to attain superior spiritual nobleness, or to carry out into action the Christian precepts in their simplicity, or to make the services of the church more gorgeous—all these things would have been equally despised had they been presented. Milltown prided itself on being English—English to the backbone; and as England was to its mind the Delos of the religious as well as of the social and political world, and as the Thirty-nine Articles were nourishment enough for the most hungry soul, any line of thought which would have led it a hair's breadth away from ecclesiastical Christianity as decided by Act of Parliament would have been considered a heresy and a treason.

The inhabitants did their duty and the rector did his. They went to church; heard what he had to say with more or less attention and more or less personal profit; then went home to what amount of earthly comfort their rents or wages provided, and dismissed the subject of religion till the next Sunday, when they took it up again with their best clothes and a superior dinner. He prepared his sermon, wherein he either exhorted the poor to contentment and honest industry, or lectured his congregation on the sins and temptations to which those of low estate are specially prone (he dropped the subject of the sins of those in high places); or else he said a few words about elementary dogmas, which the more vigorous Wesleyan Minister serving the little chapel by the water-side called milk for babes; then he too went home to his well spread table, where he drank his fine old crusted port and eat his Dartmoor mutton with a good appetite and a tranquil soul, in nowise troubled with disturbing applications or vitalising convictions. For the rest, he was fairly active in his degree: he presided over the schools, where he allowed no reading-book but the Bible; was the head of the Board of Guardians and not guilty of the sin of charity in excess; sat as a magistrate every Wednesday, like any other gentleman, and mingled the precepts of the pulpit and the judgment of the bench with admirable dialectical skill; gave hospitable dinners and accepted invitations to the like; when a few uneasy spirits demanded and organised a workman's reading-room or Mechanics' Institute, as it was called, he took care to lead the movement he first tried to suppress, and to have his hand on the rules so as to render the institution "harmless;" and on the whole got through life in a calm easy kind of way, earning his twelve hundred a-year without much trouble; and if but an indifferent shepherd for the lost lambs, making a tolerably inoffensive one to those content to go quietly in the beaten track, undisturbed by doubt, not troubled with over zeal, and unstained by public sin.

Furthermore, there was the usual sprinkling of widows with marriageable daughters; of old bachelors who could and yet would not; and of spinsters from whom hope, like chance, had long since fled. Of these last were the two kinds familiar to all who understand provincial life in England: the one strict and severe, who ignored all individual rights as well as the rights of human nature in favour of the conventional law, to whom most things were shocking, and the worst interpretations came easy; and the other who could read French, had been to London, had a slight tendency to plain speaking, tolerated cigars and did not encourage scandal, and was considered lax by mothers and strong-minded by men. Furthermore still, and different from the rest of the Milltown world, were Dr. Fletcher and his sister Catherine; of whom more when their turn comes.

None of the questions agitating the world outside this little Sleepy Hollow of Philistinism found a sympathetic echo here. Woman's rights were considered immoral, unrighteous and indelicate; strikes, and the theory of the rights of labour, were criminal and treasonable; the education of the poor was the knell of England's prosperity; and the democratic spirit abroad boded the downfall of the empire and the ruin of society. But where all else was evil, one place at least remained pure. Milltown held itself clear of the prevailing sins, and constituted itself the Zoar of English social order and political righteousness.

The shopkeepers were the fitting pendants to the gentry. They were of noticeably bland and respectful manners; did not trouble themselves with public questions, which they left to those who understood them ; charged high, and preferred yearly bills to ready money. But they did not, as the fishermen and the farmers, think to please the rector by asking for weather prayers according to their own immediate wants, nor speak of rain and drought as the consequences of topographical iniquities. To sum up in a word ; all through, the gentlefolks were the masters of the situation, and the "common people" of all degrees were made to understand that they existed primarily for the comfort of those gentlefolks, and only secondarily for their own.

It was a bold thing for Mr. Hamley to decide on forcing his way into such a caste society as this of Milltown. But Mr. Hamley's ideal masculine virtue was will, and he lived up to his pattern. He put small faith in chance and less in Providence, and believed in no towers of strength of which a man does not make the bricks by his own exertions. He laughed at the idea of luck, and preached frequent after-dinner sermons on the text that "conduct is fate." Unconsciously paraphrasing the axiom which tells each French soldier he carries a marshal's *bâton* in his knapsack, if he has but the wit to find it, he vigorously maintained, in positive accents if his grammar was shaky, that success is within the reach of all men, independent even of the first start, and that it is merely a question of energy and will whether a man wears broadcloth or fustian, and lives in a palace or dies in a hovel.

"Look at me," he used to say, tapping his spread fingers on his ample chest while his thumbs were hooked into his waistcoat armholes. "What made me ? Energy and will. What has ruined scores of other men ? Want of energy and will. Set your teeth, sit square, and go at it as if the devil was behind you. That is what I have done, gentlemen, and where am I ? At Abbey Holme, from office-boy at Ledbury's on sixpence a day and find yourself. And those who have not sat square and gone at it, but smouched and slouched and wanted this help and that lift—I'd lift them, the lazy dogs !—are just where they were when they commenced."

These sermons, practically self-laudations, were apt to run into space in rather a formidable way ; and his hearers often wished he was back at Ledbury's, that they might have the privilege of telling him to "shut-up" or of "cuffing his head"

if he went on. But a prosperous man never fails to find practical patience where he has won acceptance; and the men who
stifled the most yawns were sure to cry " Hear, hear ! " the
oftenest, and to shake hands with him with most ostentatious
friendliness when he had finished. After all, Milltown was only
the world in little, and its clean-handed Pharisaism was never
so clean as to damage its own interests.

Mr. Hamley, setting himself to conquer this caste-beridden
society, had succeeded. Step by step he had climbed the ladder dexterously and boldly—now from an office-boy to a clerk,
now from a clerk to a junior partner, then to be that senior
partner himself, and finally to be sole possesser of the brewery
which had made the fortunes of all its sole possessors time out
of mind. And when he was firmly established there he made
an offer of marriage to Miss Kemball, the very poor and very
genteel daughter of Admiral Sir Robert Kemball, K.C.B.,
whose relations with the upper classes would put the finishing
touch to his success. And Miss Kemball, being then past fifty
and wholly dependent on her brothers, who were very nearly
as poor as herself, while Jabez Hamley was a showy young
man worth a great many thousands, swallowed her disgust for
his low birth, for his inherent vulgarity, for his rodent teeth,
his bushy black whiskers and his indefinite syntax, and married
him ; with misgivings ; but with a determination never to let
the world see that she repented her decision. He, on his part,
determined the same. Thus the marriage had kept together
with a wonderful show of harmony, and had accomplished all
on either side for which both had sold themselves. Thus again,
the result sanctifying the event, it had become respectable in
the eyes of the Milltownians ; and as Mrs. Hamley was certainly a lady, and Mr. Hamley a man of irreproachable character—though he had sprung from nothing—a man, too, of the
right political colour, and rich, why, society relaxed its exclusive rule in his favour ; which however was not to be taken as
a precedent. Gradually house after house opened to him ; and
the wealthy brewer sat as an equal at the table of the men who
had given him pence in bygone days and had sent him into the
yard to get a hunch of bread from the cook.

The only house to which he had not yet been invited was
the Quest ; but from information received he had reason to be-

lieve that he would not be passed over this season, and that
his humble suit and service of many years would at last meet
with its reward.   For Mr. Hamley had always been a far-seeing kind of man.   He had early taken the measure of the
heaven into which he desired to be admitted, and had ordered
himself and his ways accordingly.   Having set out in life determined to conquer society, he had been scrupulously careful
never to offend it.   No one could recall an offensive word from
him against his social superiors or the institutions of his country.   He had always been a good Conservative and a staunch
upholder of the aristocracy.   He professed a romantic attach
ment for the Queen and Royal·Family, and whenever he could
bring in " the throne and altar " with effect, he did.   To have
done otherwise would have been suicidal, a fouling of his own
future nest which, one day, who knows ? might also harbour
eagles.

But no one had yet seen Mr. Hamley in power, or with the
neck of one of those gentlemen who had flung him coppers in
times past, ignored him in his earlier efforts, and only recognised
him now when he had bought them by his possessorship of
Abbey Holme, under his heel.   When that day came, the man
whose neck was under his heel might be pitied.

He was also strong on the subject of sex ; holding the doctrine of the rougher rights of men, and the gentler privileges
of ladies ; and, while denying anything like elemental equality,
conceding, as has been said, all kinds of social superiority.
His favourite simile, which was evidently not original, was that
men were as the oak, born to brave the battle and the breeze ;
woman, the clinging ivy.   This doctrine applied only to ladies ;
to women in the rough, women of the people, servants, pea-
sants, and the like, he was simply what only one word can express—brutal.

An old servant who had lived with him in his bachelor days,
once heard him bring out this favourite flourish of his about
the oak and the ivy.

" Ah, oak and ivy 's all very well when you've got friends at
your back to look after you," she said, setting her lips tight,
" but what I say is, it's the toad and the harrow when you
haven't ; and it ain't pleasant for the toad.

Mrs. Hamley approved her husband's doctrines, if sometimes

his manner of setting them forth made her feel that to be even mistress of Abbey Holme had its drawbacks. For her own part she advocated domestic discipline, as well as upheld theoretical feminine submission. Her central creed was the plasticity of human nature when taken young and firmly handled; and absolute obedience to social ordinances stood in her mind next in importance to obedience to the Ten Commandments. She had no tolerance for the wild humours, the erratic notions, the wayward fancies of youth. She liked all things to be in order; and minds and hearts with the rest. There was one settled and unalterable way of right, to her thinking, and every divergence therefrom was distinctly wrong. The doctrine of venial faults revolted her; and she refused to admit the plea of extenuating circumstances, whatever the provocation. She was one of those women who can look neither before nor after, and for whom their own country, day, style of living, and manner of thought, their own views, ways, habits, friends, and associations are all focussed exactly right, and are impossible to be bettered. She had an odd irrational kind of opposition to people and things that were different from herself; as if she had been born absolute in taste and judgment, and what she did not like was therefore deserving of condemnation. Thus, she could nor tolerate foreigners nor dissenters nor free-thinkers in any sense; and she disliked even friends and backers who went a hair's breadth beyond herself. If they did, steeped in opposition as she was, she used to turn round and demolish her former theory, leaving them dismayed and discomfited. She wanted only the exact echo of her opinions, the most nicely graduated reproduction; and those who gave more gave too much. She had a good intellect of its kind; but she was too positive in her assertions, and too inaccurate in her facts, to be a pleasant conversationalist. She was unable to reason to a point, and always got angry over an argument. Her religious views were sharply defined and entirely unelastic, and she was equally hostile to doubt as to enthusiasm. No inconvenient spiritualism for her; still less the anguish of struggling souls seeking for a better way and a truer light. The world has all it wants, she used to say; and modern English society is the final outcome of the Best.

She was by temperament grave, by temper fretful; seldom

laughed, often chided ; she could do generous things on a large scale, but she was mean in small matters, and though not unkind, must be supreme. For though she talked of feminine submission as much as Mr. Hamley talked of masculine authority, and inculcated it on others, somehow she seemed to exempt herself from the rank of womanly slaves, and was always the mistress, absolute and autocratic.

This was quite well understood at Abbey Holme ; and Mr. Hamley, though he might stick his thumbs into his armholes and play tunes on his chest, never in her presence commanded man nor maid, uttered a decided opinion of his own, nor differed from hers, nor indeed held his own flag aloft in any way. She was always referred to humbly as "Lady," and he followed in her wake deferentially.

In some things indeed she honestly possessed him. She had had a better education than he, and made no difficulties on the score of conjugal delicacy in showing him where he tripped and how he had exposed his ignorance. And when a woman has sufficient strength of mind to do this very often, and always quietly, she is sure to end by subjugating her husband, whatever his number of inches ; and, perhaps, the bigger the man the more thorough his subjugation. Then she was invariably self-possessed, and always in the attitude of a superior being. She allowed no enthusiasm, no loud laughter, no noise, no fun, no rudeness in her presence. Life with her must be well-oiled in all its hinges, and regulated by the strictest rules of common-sense. She went regularly to church twice on Sundays ; not because she felt the need or the comfort of going to church, but because it was the right thing to do as an example to the common people, and what was owing to the rector as a gentleman whose function it was to read the service and preach for five-and-twenty minutes after. And she had morning and evening prayers at home ; the latter punctually at ten ; because it was respectable and might do the servants good, and certainly enabled her to see that they were all safe under the roof and sober. But when she said in those prayers, which she herself read, that she was a worm and a miserable sinner, she said the words with no more inward conviction than if she had confessed she was an elephant or a giraffe. They were words with her, no more ; and she did not feel a wish to make them more.

F

Between these two, Dora Drummond, Mr. Hamley's young cousin, had had but a compressed kind of existence during the ten-years of her adoption. Masculine supremacy on the one hand, and feminine discipline on the other, had taken all the courage out of a nature never brave nor strong, and more prone to yield than to withstand. Her sole object was to avoid contention and secure peace; and as she found submission easier than fighting for freedom, she slipped under the yoke with perfect grace and obedience, and gave no more trouble to the authorities at Abbey Holme than Patricia had given at Barsands. But the difference of method by which these two girls had been taught obedience was not inconsiderable. Neither were the results.

This then was the kind of place into which Patricia came from the freedom, the happiness, the practical democracy of Barsands. Not a line of the old ruling remained to her. Even the sea, her old friend and playmate, was not the sea of her love. Tamed down to a mere mill-pond, it seemed to have lost all the life and meaning it had when it came lashing round the cliffs and foaming over the Gridiron out on that wild Cornish coast. And even such as it was she could not see it. Her windows at Abbey Holme looked only on a steep bank of trimmed and patterned flower-beds surmounted by the wall which hid the offices. Now, in the late autumn time, when there were no flowers to fill them, the beds were ribboned with coloured stones; which Patricia admired about as much as she admired earrings, rouge, or face-powder.

If the place was inharmonious, the life at Abbey Holme was even more so. Into that sternly-fashioned method of existence, so still and so subdued, her breezy vigour came with a kind of tempestuous force that frightened Dora, horrified Aunt Hamley, and disgusted Aunt Hamley's husband. Voice, step, manner, gesture, everything carried with it the impression of a whirlwind to these quiet, well-regulated people; and Mrs. Hamley often said, with her lips drawn close, that she looked after her when she left the room, expecting to see her leave sticks and straws behind her. She was so noisy! so unsubdued! lamented the poor old lady who would have been glad to have loved her dead brother's child if she could have brought her down to the proper point of discipline. She seemed as if she should have been a boy, not a girl, she was so distressingly strong and healthy, so large altogether! And how obtuse! It was impossible to make her understand anything unless it was put into the plainest language; and as for a hint, you might as well expect a blind man to see you beckon to him as Patricia to receive a hint. How different from dear Dora's marvellous delicacy of perception, and that tact which was almost like another sense!

Mrs. Hamley had some reason for this last lamentation, for Patricia was indeed impervious to all the lessons conveyed by the way of dignified carriage and silent reproof. When Aunt Hamley answered her loud and frankly-worded questions in a voice so low and level that the girl's quick senses could hardly catch the words—answered her vaguely, without looking at her, never if possible giving her the information she asked, saying, "I do not know," when the thing was part of her very existence, and speaking with a deep sigh and an oppressive politeness—Patricia used to think that perhaps poor Aunt had a headache; poor Aunt often seemed to have headaches; and she used to look at her so compassionately that Mrs. Hamley sometimes rebuked her for her pertinacity, and told her sharply that it was ill-bred to stare.

When the girl wished to surround her with those little attentions which some girls like to show their elders, and which certain women hate to receive unmasked—when she carried sacred pillows as if they had been kittens by the middle under her arm—sacred pillows from sacred sofas, which dear Dora would not have deranged for worlds—and wanted to stuff them into Aunt's easy chair where they did not fit, and only threw her too far forward and made her uncomfortable; when she plunged about for footstools, and denuded corners of their rightful ornaments, and made a commotion for kindness, when all that Mrs. Hamley asked was peace and quietness; the poor, starched, self-centred lady thought she should have gone distracted. She could not bear it; nor did she attempt to conceal that her niece's zeal without discretion made her headache worse than ever.

She used to call dear Dora to undo in her quiet, gliding, soothing way what Patricia had done with such enthusiastic goodwill and tumultuous philanthropy. And then Patricia

used to feel snubbed in spite of her determination to see only
the best side of everything, and to be satisfied with her fate
whatever it was. She used to wonder vaguely what it all
meant, and how it was she so evidently failed to please when
she tried so hard. After which she would redouble her efforts
by the very fact of her failure ; continuing in the vicious circle
that never knew a break for better things.* If her aunt had
only spoken to her straightly and kindly, the whole thing
would have been put right. But she wanted her to divine
what she would not explain ; and then was annoyed at her
denseness of perception.

Perhaps the person most to be pitied at this time was Dora.
She knew exactly where the hitch was, but she had not sufficient generosity or truth either to warn Patricia or to defend
her. She was of the order of false prophets who prophesy
smooth things, and cry peace when there is no peace. She was
of those who are all things to all men, and always adopted the
colours of her company. She played echo in private to Mrs.
Hamley's complainings and agreed with her that Patricia was a
dreadful infliction, and the most badly brought-up young person
of her degree to be found within the four seas. But she was
careful not to go a line beyond her pattern ; else, if she had,
Mrs. Hamley would have been down on her for injustice, and
would have taken Patricia's part with vigour if acridity.

To Patricia, when alone, she was sweet and flattering as if to
atone for the burden of snubbing she had to bear ; but in public, before the Hamleys, she was quite well-bred but not even
familiar, still less affectionate ; which sometimes amazed Patricia, and seemed to make her whole life a thaumatrope where
things jumped about and changed places, she could not tell how
or why. For the matter of that however, she had fallen in
love, girl-like, with Mr. Hamley's pretty, graceful, well-mannered young cousin ; and love with Patricia meant the patience
as well as the steadfastness of loyalty.

Meanwhile, Mr. Hamley looked on and chuckled. It was a
triumph to him, and he enjoyed it. That the blood-cousin of
Ledbury's office-boy should be such an undoubted success, and
the grand-daughter of Admiral Sir Robert Kemball, K.C.B.,
such an undeniable failure, tickled him between the ribs of his
vanity deliciously. He took no open part in the small femi-

nine warfare going on in the drawing-room, further than by
almost ignoring Patricia altogether ; for which he received
more than one sharp rebuke from Mrs. Hamley in private, and
a cold demand whether he did not think her niece deserved a
little more courtesy at his hands ? But he knew too well the
shaky character of the ground he had to traverse daily to act
on the spirit of this rebuke. If he had befriended Patricia in
the smallest degree, he would have been called to order on the
charge of affording comfort and support to a rebel ; and, of the
two, he thought the attitude of non intervention the safer.

CHAPTER IX.

DORA DEMONSTRATES.

PATRICIA had been about a month at Abbey Holme, and things had not mended. She still filled the domestic atmosphere with sticks and straws, and still made poor Aunt's headaches greatly worse by her endeavours to make them better; fighting bravely the while against the material and moral inharmoniousness of her life, and refusing to confess to herself how unutterably lonely and misplaced she was. She had never greater need than now of all her courage and all her cheerfulness. Overheated rooms; no personal liberty; no fresh air; no exercise—for she did not call driving in a close carriage, with only one window open a couple of inches, either fresh air or exercise; the staple occupation of the day needlework enlivened by novel-reading aloud—and the stories such trash! thought unimaginative Patricia, who had not matriculated in the college of light literature, and who cared for nothing that was not true;—cards in the evening—bézique, or three-handed whist—and she did not know a king from an ace, and could not learn the simplest rules; food a world too rich and too frequent for a girl brought up as she had been on the plainest fare, and who, naturally unsensual, had been taught asceticism over and above—a girl whose appetite for bread and-butter, at its highest point, was never satisfied at a table which gave everything but simplicity, cold water, and reasonable " rounds": all these things together were as much as her strong health could bear without breaking up under the change. Add to material circumstances so uncongenial, a life of moral repression, of lovelessness, and the sentiment of being always in disgrace, and it is easy to understand that if Patricia was not an acquisition, for her own part, to the new world which had received her, this new world was not of the kind to give her happiness or to bring out the best that was in her.

One day, after she had been making more than her usual

amount of whirlwind in the drawing room, and had been snubbed with even more than Aunt Hamley's usual amount of cold acerbity, she went up-stairs to her own room to overcome a certain miserable sensation of loneliness and mistake which threatened to overcome her.

When she had gone Mrs. Hamley laid her work and her hands into her lap with a gesture of angry despair. Dora looked at her, and laid her work down too with a look of sympathetic annoyance.

"Dora," said Mrs. Hamley severely, "I had hoped that you would have helped me in this affliction, this trial, as I may call it. For though she is my own niece, and I should wish to love her and do my duty by her, she is an affliction all the same, wretched child! I have been disappointed in you, Dora. You have shown less than your usual tact, and not the amiability I might have expected from you."

"I am sorry that I have failed in any way, dear," said Dora sweetly. "What can I do to help you? I will do anything I can, as you know."

She spoke with her slight lisp and put on her prettiest air of feminine subjection; and Mrs. Hamley felt a little relief in remonstrating severely with so unresisting a creature. It soothed her, on the principle of passing it on.

"Why do you ask me what you are to do?" she answered irritably. "Does not your own common-sense tell you? have you no conscience to dictate your duty? You ought to talk to her, Dora, and tell her not to be so noisy and officious, not to speak till she is spoken to, and not to take so much on herself. It will come easier from you than from me, and perhaps you will have more influence than I should have."

"I will tell her, of course, if you like, dear," said Dora, desperately troubled in spite of her suave manner. She did not want to wound Patricia any more than to offend Mrs. Hamley. For if it was difficult for her to refuse a request, or to stand up for her own rights, it was still more difficult to voluntarily offend. Face-to-face aggression was not in Dora Drummond's way, and she would have rather Mrs. Hamley had deprived her of every kind of enjoyment for a week than have bidden her do this thing.

"Yes, it will come better from you," said Mrs. Hamley.

"You horrid old coward!" thought dear Dora, with a timid,

plaintive little smile that meant the sweetest, most complying submission.

"You are girls together, and can make her understand her position here and her duties better than I," continued the lady. "Take her out for a walk to-day. You can talk better when you are walking than driving. You have not been out for a walk, too, for a long while, and it will do you good: you are looking quite pale for want of exercise, Dora; you sit far too much in the house—and then you can talk to her. But don't go beyond the town, and don't let her think that I have told you to speak to her. I want it to come as if naturally from yourself; as indeed it would have done if you had had as much common-sense as I always gave you credit for."

"Very well, dear, I will go and I will do my best," said Dora with graceful obedience; very quiet in action but a little flushed, her eyes eager beneath their long, light, silky lashes as she put away her embroidery, deliberately, noiselessly, neatly, as she did all things.

She kissed Mrs. Hamley on her forehead, and saw that her ready obedience had dispersed the little cloud and reinstated her in her old place of prime favourite; then went to her own room, where she first wrote a short note very rapidly, and when this was finished ran lightly along the thickly-carpeted corridor to Patricia's room. She found her also writing—to Gordon Frere; not saying that she was unhappy, but unconsciously showing that she was so by the very pains she took to conceal it.

"Busy, dear?" said Dora, putting in her gracious head as if timidly asking permission through the half-opened door.

"Oh, no, not if you want me!" cried Patricia, attentive, upright, alive at all points as usual. "Come in—do come in!"

"Thanks. I came to ask you if you would go for a walk with me," said Dora, gliding forward and carefully shutting the door after her.

"Yes, indeed, that I will," Patricia answered with unnecessary alacrity. "I am longing for a walk! It seems a year since I had a breath of fresh air."

"Good gracious! what do you call this?" said Dora, shivering as she pointed to the open window. "Sitting with the window open, and no fire even, just before Christmas! I wonder it does not kill you!"

"No, it is the only thing that keeps me alive, I think. But I need not torture *you*, dear," said Patricia, shutting down the window as she spoke ; and as she shut it with good will she did it somewhat noisily. "If you only knew, Dora, how I long sometimes for the great strong wind of Barsands!" she went on to say. "I feel as if I should like to sit on the top of an iceberg in a gale of wind after I have been down in the drawing-room for a few hours. How you and Aunt Hamley can bear the stifling heat and want of fresh air of your lives is more surprising to me than my open windows can be to you."

"Then you are not happy here ?" said Dora, going nearer to her and laying her hand on her shoulder.

"Don't think me ungrateful—indeed, I am not that !" answered Patricia hastily ; "but I do miss the boating and fresh air and freedom of the old life ! This seems to me like being in a hot-house prison in comparison." She drew a long breath, and looked out on the beds of coloured stone that rose up close against her window, surmounted by the grey stone wall which shut out all view of the country beyond ; her eyes full of infinite yearning, and the brave, cheerful face saddened.

"We have been used to such a different life from yours," said Dora soothingly. "It must be strange to you."

"Yes, it is," said Patricia simply, and sighing.

"I should like to make you happy," continued Mr. Hamley's cousin, her lips quivering slightly. She was skating round the central subject, and amiable coward as she was, she did not like it.

"If I could be always alone with you I should be happy," said Patricia. "I daresay it is my own fault that I do not get on so well with my aunt and Mr. Hamley as I ought. They don't seem to understand what I mean sometimes, and perhaps I do not understand them ; but with you it is different—when we are alone," she added by an after-thought; "then I am quite happy !"

Dora kissed her with her butterfly kind of kiss. "You dear little thing, you know I like you, don't you ?" she said to the tall girl who stood a couple of inches or more above her, and whose strong hand was like a man's compared with her own useless little compress of rose-leaves.

"I hope so," answered Patricia, looking at her fondly.

"Hope !" remonstrated Dora.

"Sometimes I think you do, and sometimes I think you do not," said Patricia candidly. "At all events"—frankly, warmly—"I love you Dora, and would do anything in the world I could for you; and that you know."

Dora gave a graceful little deprecatory shrug. "But there is nothing in me to like," she said sweetly, glancing at herself in the glass and putting up her hand to smooth back her glossy hair.

"Oh!" cried Patricia, who took everything literally. "How can you say so, Dora! Why, you must know what a darling you are!"

Dora cast up her blue eyes shyly. This love-making between girls seemed to her odd beyond measure; but she was glad of it, as it made her task so much the easier.

"Do you really think so? That is because you are so nice and good yourself," she said.

"No; it is because you are so nice and good," flung back Patricia as antistrophe.

"You dear thing!" breathed Dora. "If you think so, really and truly, and do not merely flatter me, you must let me be your guide and mentor here." She was looking at Patricia steadily enough for her, but lisping more than usual. "You see, dear, I am worlds older than you, and I can tell you some things, perhaps, you do not know."

"Every kind of thing," said Patricia.

"No, not quite that, but some things. For instance, Mr. and Mrs. Hamley are the dearest people in the world, and I am immensely fond of them—as indeed I ought to be, for they have done everything for me—but they are just a little particular and peculiar. I can quite see where you will rub against their angles, you dear thing, and get into trouble, if you do not take care. I know them so well, the dears! and you do not, you see."

"But I only want to please them," said Patricia, opening her eyes. "I try all day long to please my aunt. It is my duty, you know," she added gravely.

"Yes, I know that, dear," Dora said, looking down. "But," raising her eyes suddenly as if a thought had just struck her, "wanting is not enough—we have to learn how; and you must learn how."

" Tell me where I fail ; I will learn anything from you," said Patricia in her loud, clear, open voice.

" That is very nice of you ; so let me give you your first lesson," lisped Dora. " Do not speak so loud ; Mr. and Mrs. Hamley do not like it. They have a horror of all noise. Don't you notice how softly every one speaks here, and how silently every one moves about, and how quiet the whole house is ? "

" Yes, and I thought I spoke softly too. I am sure I do ever so much more than I used at Barsands ; for dearest uncle was a little deaf, and I had to raise my voice there. But here I thought I spoke as soft as possible !"

Dora gave a little smile. It was a faint, evanescent little smile, but it was eloquent.

" Do you really mean to say, Dora, that I speak too loud ?"

" Rather," said Dora in the tones that conveyed the sense of " very much."

" I feel stronger and bigger than you and Aunt Hamley, certainly," Patricia went on in a reflective kind of way. " Am I too strong and big for you ?"

" A little," repeated Dora.

" I did not feel so at Barsands, but somehow I feel different altogether here," said Patricia sorrowfully.

At that moment she felt as if she was all wrong everywhere. Hitherto so unconscious, never thinking of herself, scarcely knowing whether she was tall or short, dark or fair, she suddenly awakened to the perception of a vulgar, ungainly, unlovable personality of which she had been wholly ignorant. It was not so much wounded vanity that she felt, as sorrow that she was so disagreeable to others ; and—how horrible she must be to Dora ! Tears stood in her eyes, but even Dora could see that they were something deeper and purer than tears of mere petty girlish vexation.

" But now that I have told you, dear, you will try to improve, will you not ?" Dora asked coaxingly, sorry to see her humiliation but glad of her sensitiveness.

" Yes, I will try. I am sorry I am so big and loud," said Patricia humbly.

" Yes, it is a pity," said Dora in a matter-of-fact way. " And now that we are on the subject, let me give you a word of advice about Mrs. Hamley. Dear thing, she is just—what shall I say ?—the least bit in the world fidgety ; and you must not fidget her if you want to please her."

"But do I ?" asked Patricia, in the same surprised way as that in which she had asked if her voice was loud.

"Dreadfully," said Dora.

"Dora ? how ?"

"By fussing about her; bringing her cushions and footstools, and wanting her to have tea, and all that kind of thing."

"But if she has a headache ? It seems so unkind to leave her to herself and do nothing !" urged Patricia.

"I think you will find that the wisest plan though," said Dora dryly. "I know her better than you do, and my advice to you is not to notice her headaches, and never to ask her if you shall bring anything or do anything for her till she tells you. You never see me fuss about her as you do."

"No, but then I am her niece," said Patricia naïvely.

Dora shot a glance at her from under her lashes that was not quite so dovelike as her usual glances.

"And I have lived with her all these years," she said quietly, "and am like her own child. Which do you think has the most right to take things on herself, you or I ? And if I do not hang about her, and worry her with requests to do this for her, or jump up to fetch that without asking her if I may, and without her telling me that I am to do so, need you, do you think ?"

"No ; I see you are right," said Patricia.

"You do not mind my saying all this to you, dear ? it is only for your own good," then said Dora with a little sigh. Her *corvée* was accomplished, and she was glad it had been so easy —glad, too, that Patricia had been so obtuse in some directions if so amiably impressible in others.

"Mind ? I am very much obliged to you !" cried the poor girl. "I only wish I was like you, Dora, and then I should be all right. No, I do not," she added with sudden reflection. "I am better as I am for my own life ; for if I had been like you when the *Mermaid* went to pieces we should have all been drowned. You would never have held on ; and you would have fainted when you were hauled up; and then there would not have been time to have saved dear uncle and Gordon. Oh, Dora ! it was awful to look down and see that tremendous surf,

and the poor little *Mermaid* just like a live thing beaten to
death, and dear uncle and Gordon on board her, looking as if
they must go to the bottom at every wave. I shall never forget
that moment; and I dream of it so often. Ah, that was real!"

And all these petty crosses and distresses and tempers and
unfitnesses, they were not real, her heart said. They were fac-
titious, rootless; and as she looked back the truth of the past
overshadowed the small and wearying falsehood of the present;
and she forgot the ugly self just revealed to her, and the loud
voice and the officious activities of her misplaced sense of
duty; and even the importance of Aunt Hamley's headaches
was diminished in her vivid recollection of the living love of
Barsands, and the desperate peril of that awful hour.

"Well, don't think of it any more just now," said Dora
briskly. She was disinclined by temperament to things sad
or horrible. "The best of the day is going and we must
have our walk."

"Very well," said Patricia, shaking back her hair, and
brushing her hand over her eyes as if to free them from some
picture that would remain in them. "I shall be ready in a
minute."

"And I not for ten," lisped Dora, laughing. "But then I
take pains with myself, and am more particular than you how
I put on my things."

This was meant as another lesson; for the girl's want of
personal trimness annoyed Aunt Hamley almost as much as
her overplus of attention. But hints were lost on Patricia, and
her toilet was performed to-day in the old rapid way of yesterday and as it would be to-morrow Dora thought disdainfully,
unless she was fairly forced to pay more regard to herself.
What an uncouth, clumsy, horrid way of bringing up a girl!
she thought again, scanning here an end adrift and there a tie
askew. Captain Kemball could not have been a nice man, and
Dora questioned if he had been a good one; for was not personal attractiveness the main part of the religion of life in her
estimation as also in Aunt Hamley's? and was not a woman's
indifference to appearance worse than even her indifference to
virtue?

The walk was a pleasant one, albeit neither eventful nor
exciting. It was simply a walk through the garden and the

park and down the lane fenced in by two high, trim, closely-sheared banks, and so on to the main road, which had a side walk like a gentleman's garden-path, gas-lamps, telegraph wires, and more shear-work visible. But it gave Patricia a sense of relative freedom to be outside Abbey Holme gates without a footman behind her, as had been insisted on the only time when she had been beyond the grounds alone and on foot since her arrival.

Her aunt wanted to break her of this love of rambling among other undesirable propensities. She did not choose to do it by denial, so she adopted the plan of nullifying the pleasure. And it had answered. A footman at her heels was even worse than home-keeping, and Patricia had never repeated her request for a long walk by herself ; consequently the little expedition to-day was a glimpse of better things that inspirited her. And Dora, having fulfilled her disagreeable task, and said her say successfully, was sweeter than ever, as if to make up for reproofs in which Patricia saw only the truest friendliness. So they walked and talked and laughed—at least Patricia laughed and Dora smiled—till they came to the High Street of Milltown, whither they were bound.

Patricia was neither observant nor suspicious. Had she been either to even a moderate extent, she would have seen Dora's fair face flush gradually a deeper and deeper, if prettier, rose-pink as they approached Milltown ; she would have seen her blue eyes look furtively from side to side, as if expecting to see some one beside the day-labourers and petty shop-keepers, who lounged up the roadway, or stood in their shirt-sleeves by their doors ; she would have seen her slide her hand into her pocket, where her fingers played nervously with the little note she had written in such haste before leaving home, ready to drop it into the post as they returned, unless —— And seeing all this, she would probably have connected therewith the handsome young man who came suddenly out on them from the Bank as they were passing that establishment, and greeted Dora with a strange look of eagerness and familiarity.

"How do you do, Mr. Lowe ?" said Dora, her face dimpled into the most enchanting smile as she put her hand in his. When their hands unclasped, Mr. Sydney Lowe's held the note. "Miss Kemball," she added, indicating Patricia.

The young man gave the new arrival a sharp, bold stare—that comprehensive, analytical kind of survey which women resent as an impertinence—and which is one, and is meant to be one. Then, as if he had seen nothing in her worthy his attention, he turned again to Dora with the same eager and familiar look as before, and began talking to her rapidly in French. As they were going up the street, he walked with them ; and because the side-walk was too narrow for the three abreast, Patricia went on alone before and the two kept behind, still talking. And even when they had executed Mrs. Hamley's weighty commissions of matching a skein of wool at one shop, buying a yard of ribbon at another, ordering a tin of preserved lobster at the grocer's, and getting an order for thirteen and fourpence from the post-office, even then this young, handsome man with the bold black eyes, thin nose and loose lips, kept close to Dora's side, always with the same unmistakable expression of imperiousness and familiarity on his face, and always talking to her in French.

After having walked with them till they came within sight of the Abbey Holme gates, he finally took his leave. But his last words were many and apparently difficult to say. He and Dora stood together in the road, face to face, so long in the bitter December twilight that even Patricia was chilled ; and when they parted Dora's eyes were moist with tears and the young man's dark with anger and impatience. But they finally said good-bye for the last time and the two girls walked in silence up the lane.

Then said Dora in her softest and most caressing voice, glancing sideways at Patricia, not looking at her openly : "Patricia dear, if Mrs. Hamley asks if we met any one, you need not say Mr. Lowe walked with us. Of course I shall say that we saw him if she asks me ; but you need not tell her more.

Patricia turned her large grey eyes full on the fair face with its sweet look trying so hard to appear unconscious beside her, and succeeding marvellously well.

"Why not ? she asked in a tone of surprise. "What harm was there in it ?"

"No harm at all," Dora answered. "But Mrs. Hamley, though the dearest darling in the world, is a little particular, and perhaps she might not like it."

"Then we ought not to have done it," said Patricia gravely.
"I should like to know how I could have helped it when he
would come!" cried Dora pettishly.

And Patricia had an uneasy sense of something wrong, she
could not say exactly what. There was surely nothing to be
ashamed of in two girls meeting a young man and his turning
back and walking with them! Gordon had done so to her a
hundred times and more; and she had never felt she ought not
to tell her uncle, or that he would have disliked it when he
was told. But she thought to herself that if she had not
wished Gordon to turn back and walk with her she would have
made him understand so clearly. She would not have talked
to him so much, and then complained that he *would* come. But
Dora was so amiable, she could not give pain, she thought
again, half angry with herself that she had felt even this passing
sense of wrong.

Patricia, however, was not put to the test. Her aunt asked her
no questions; and when she had gone upstairs, and Mrs. Hamley
reproached Dora fretfully for being so late, Dora answered
with the tenderest little air of patience and contrition united:

"Yes, I know we are very late, dear; but Patricia wanted so
much to see the town I could not refuse to show her everything I could think of."

"That girl is always wanting something she should not!"
said Mrs. Hamley irritably.

"It is better when people are accustomed to things a little
before they are quite grown up," Dora put in sensibly.

"Oh, I hate your blasées girls who know everything," said
Mrs. Hamley; and Dora answered "Yes, so do I," with un-
ruffled serenity.

So Mrs. Hamley never knew anything about Sydney Lowe
and his eager and familiar looks, his long and rapid conversation in French, those difficult farewells, and Dora's troubled
eyes. There was evidently a secret connected with this young
man, and a secret that gave Dora some concern. For she cried
that night when she went to bed—just a little; she had too
much respect for her eyes to cry much; and once flinging her
pretty head impatiently on the pillow, said half aloud: "How
I wish I had never seen him! and oh! how I wish I had refused and never done it!"

CHAPTER X.

OVER THE WINE AND WALNUTS.

IN almost every country place there is at least one young man who has, sometimes vaguely, sometimes manifestly why, what the world calls a bad character. Perhaps no definite charge can be brought against him, but none the less ill-repute has crept like a mildew over his name. Respectable people are cool to him; careful mothers keep their daughters out of his way; prudent fathers warn their sons against too close intimacy with him; and he is the acknowledged black sheep of the community, tolerated only because of his family and the name he bears.

Mr. Sidney Lowe was of this kind to Milltown. No one knew exactly what he had done that was more disgraceful than the ordinary silly scrapes of youth; and it may be presumed that he had neither robbed a church nor committed a murder. He was the son of Colonel Lowe, of Cragfoot, who had married Lady Anne Graham's daughter, an heiress and a personage; and the Lowes had always been among the first people in this little heaven of exclusiveness. Nevertheless, no one about Milltown cared to be much with him, and those who knew him best liked him least.

Yet he was handsome and clever—too clever by half, they said in the town, where he had been known, man and boy, these five and twenty years, and never any good known of him in the time! And as for his handsomeness, there were those who professed not to see so very much in him when all's said and done, and without any reference to the old proverb which makes handsome is that handsome does. But there were others who said that he was well to look at if bad to do with—a fine young man, if a scamp. It was the young men who, for the most part, held his good looks cheap, and the women who rated them high.

He was one of the light-weight men, about five feet nine in

G

height, supple, active, well proportioned ; with good points,
such as small hands and feet, broad shoulders, narrow hips,
and a waist that would have matched a French officer's.　He
had a general air of smartness and dressiness about him, wore
light gloves, perfect boots, and clothes of noticeable newness ;
and he always buttoned his coats tightly about him when they
were coats with waists and skirts, as they generally were, by
which he showed off his points and magnified himself in the
eyes of the Milltown womanhood.　But with all this he looked
like a gentleman and not like a snob.　In features he was
sharply cut and darkly coloured.　He had a profusion of black
hair that shone like silk and curled in multitudinous little rings
over his head ; a broad, low forehead, olive-tinted ; long, arched
brows of the pencilled kind above black eyes that never looked
straight at men, though, to make amends, they had the habit
of staring women out of countenance.　His mouth was rather
wide, thin in the lips, and curved in the lines ; his chin was
sharply pointed ; his face smooth-shaven, excepting for his well-
waxed moustaches ; and there was a great width between his
ears.

All this was very much like other people, and bore nothing
on the surface to account for the odd kind of disesteem which
hung about his name.　Grant that he was idle, as indeed every
one must allow, yet he had no need to work.　When his father
died he would have Cragfoot and his mother's fortune, and
come in for everything.　Why should he toil through the best
years of his life, heaping pound on pound, and wearing away
his youth like a nobody instead of enjoying it like a gentleman ?
As he was the only one to ask this question, he was the only
one to answer it ; and the answer came, as might be expected,
in Mr. Sydney Lowe's using his youth according to his pleasure—sowing many bushels of those disastrous oats which make
no bread for a man's future.　His father had but little influence
over him, and what he had went the wrong way.　A tyrant
over his wife, he was a slave to his son ; and though he sometimes affected to adopt a bullying tone, when his liver was out
of order or he had lost an unusually large sum on the turf,
Sydney for the most part came off master in any collision that
might take place between them.

Colonel Lowe was a proud man with a high temper and a

weak will; selfish in his nature if spendthrift in his habits, and unable to rise above his desires. Though it would manifestly have been the proper thing for Sydney to have gone to school, if only to complete the gentleman's part of his education, his father had kept him close to his side ever since he left the nursery, because the boy's liveliness amused him and he wanted a companion. He had only a taciturn and ailing wife to whom to speak when Sydney was away, and he had long out-lived his pleasure in that association. So he educated his son at home, and prevented his making a career for himself, that he might fill the place of filial jester at Cragfoot, that he might boat and hunt and shoot, and play billiards with him when desired; that is, be his plaything indoors and his playfellow abroad.

As time went on ugly rumours, as has been said, began to gather round the young man's name. Young, idle, fond of pleasure, and loosely held, were they to be wondered at, with all the weight of Milltown respectability to keep him straight! Kind friends gave the Colonel hints as to what was said and done; but the Colonel turned a deaf ear to them all. Young men would be young men, he said, and he would rather his son was a natural, high-spirited young fellow who did kick over the traces at times, provided he kicked as a gentleman should, than be one of those mealy-mouthed Joseph Surfaces who are as bad as their brothers, but are not found out because they are more cunning and hypocritical. Whatever then he knew of Sydney's husbandry in the matter of those wild oats with which he was credited he kept to himself; and the lad had never been corrected of bad habits nor educated to nobler things from the time when, as a little fellow, he killed his pet rabbit because it would not learn to beg like a dog, and then tried to hide what he had done by stealing one of Tommy Garth's in its stead.

Of one thing only was Colonel Lowe determined; Sydney should make a good marriage. No one knew so well as himself the necessity for this; for no one knew so well as himself how much of his wife's fortune had gone into the pockets of the bookmakers at Doncaster and Newmarket, and what a mere shell Cragfoot was; and in his own mind he had fixed on old Lady Manley's daughter, Julia Manley, the heiress of Waterfield, with five thousand a year in her own right, and the grand niece of a duke. To be sure, poor Julia was no beauty. She was a tall, angular, sandy-coloured young woman, with weak eyes and freckles, very good, considered clever, and decidedly silly; but five thousand a year to a young man mainly occupied in sowing wild oats on his own account, and whose father has been a godsend to the bookmakers, will gild even weak eyes and freckles; and as Colonel Lowe used to say, it really does not signify whom you marry! After a couple of years one woman is just like another woman; but the five thousand a year remains.

On the evening of the day when Sydney had met the young ladies of Abbey Holme, and had talked so much French to dear Dora, Colonel Lowe and his son sat by the fire after dinner, sipping their claret with the velvet on and cracking their wal- nuts as usual.

" Who was that tall young person with the Hamley girl to- day ?" asked the Colonel suddenly.

Sydney's dark eyes went down.

" That niece of Mrs. Hamley's," he answered.

" That niece of Mrs. Hamley's ? —what niece ? "

" I don't know exactly. A brother's child, I believe," said Sydney, with indifference.

" Which brother? There were two, Robert and Reginald," the Colonel said.

" I am sure I don't know. The old fellows were before my time. You must know more about them than I possibly can !" answered Sydney, concentrating all his energies on peeling his nut without a break.

The truth was, both father and son knew perfectly well who Patricia was. It was simply their mode of fencing.

" That Hamley girl has some good points," said the Colonel, with a kind of contemptuous admission, as if he had been speak- ing of a dog or a cow ; for he too, notoriously gallant to ladies, was by no means respectful to women. Sydney still looked down intent on his task, and this time made no answer. " She wants style, of course," his father went on to say. " It is a good pro- verb, if a coarse one, that you cannot make a silk purse out of a sow's ear ; and the Hamley grain is not silk. Blood will out, my boy, whether it is blue or brown ; and that Hamley girl, if a pretty thing of her kind, is of a low kind all the same."

"She is only distantly connected with Mr. Hamley," said Sydney.

He, too, hated the ear which was not silk; but he ignored it in Dora.

"Lucky for her. I confess I should not feel very desirous of being connected with a man who once held my horse for twopence, though he is now the owner of Abbey Holme—worse luck for Milltown! Still you know, Syd, she is a parvenue, make the best of it you will. I own, not so bad for a parvenue, and might be made something of if well handled. I doubt, though, if she could ever be really refined—rubbed up beyond the outside."

"She is well bred enough," said Sydney, seeing that his father waited as if for an answer.

"Is she? I know so little of her! She is long in getting a husband for a pretty girl. She ought to be looking about her now, I should say—five and twenty if a day!"

"No; only just of age," said Sydney hastily.

The Colonel raised his eyebrows. "You are deep in a lady's confidence, Syd, if you know her age!" he said, with a satirical laugh.

"I happened to know this by chance," answered Sydney with a sulky look.

"And I remember when she came to Milltown ten years ago; and she was fifteen then, I'll swear. Will you swear to your figures, Syd? Are you sure you have not been hoodwinked by a year or two?"

The young man laughed uneasily. "Well, really I have not made Miss Drummond's exact age a profound study," he said half insolently. "Nor do I offer one, two, three, or four and twenty as a profession of faith. I said what I thought; but, faith! I may be wrong; and it is of no great consequence either way."

The Colonel looked at him, a smile not wholly of pleasure on his face. "Good," he said; "I don't want you to get too intimate with the Abbey Holme people at any time. They are all very well to be on civil terms with. That old shoeblack understands wine, and his wife gives decent dinners; besides, she is a gentlewoman if a fallen one. But we don't want them as friends, you know, Syd—you and I—we are a flight too high for that."

"It is difficult to keep on very formal terms with people one meets so constantly in such a small society as this," said Sydney, throwing a fly.

His father rose to it, but in the wrong way.

"People one meets so constantly?" he repeated with a surprised intonation. "My dear boy, you must be dreaming. Where, in the name of fortune, do we meet the Hamleys so constantly? Why, they are just beginning to be noticed in the place, and are yet only barely tolerated. You cannot call half-a-dozen dinners in the year meeting constantly! And the old shoeblack has not got beyond that—and that's too far!"

"No, certainly; half-a-dozen dinners in the year do not make a great intimacy, as you say," returned Sydney, finishing his wine and lounging up from the table as one profoundly uninterested, not to say wearied of the subject. "Shall you be long, dad?" he asked. "I am off to smoke."

"Go, if you like; I'll follow," the Colonel answered; and Sydney went, yawning ostentatiously.

When he had closed the door, his father said to himself, as he poured out another glass of claret; "I don't like his manner. I'd lay my life there is something in the wind there. How he looked when I spoke of her! But he fenced cleverly, the young dog—too cleverly. I wish he had been franker, and so had given me a better opening. I'd swear I heard him call her *chérie* when they passed by the *Black Lion*, and did not see me in the passage ; and his manner said as much as her face. Hamley's cousin for my son? No, not if she brought a million in her skirt! Hard up as I am I'll live and die as I was born ; and my son shall not fall below me with my consent!"

He sat as if pondering for a few minutes ; then he added, still holding solitary counsel : "I will have them here, and then I can judge for myself. After all, if he likes the girl and the old ruffian gives her a good dowry? But it will not be equal to Julia Manley's. Only, if Syd has set his mind on her, and I have no good excuse, I know him well enough ; he'll marry her in the teeth of everything, and then there will be the devil to pay!"

On which he drank yet another glass of claret ; then crossed the hall and went into the drawing-room.

Mrs. Lowe was lying on the sofa, comfortably packed up and half asleep.

" My dear ! " said her husband in a high key.

" Yes, Colonel ! " she answered with a start.

" I do believe you were asleep again, Matilda ! " he said tartly.

" Asleep ! What nonsense ! when you know I never sleep ! " was her reply made peevishly.

It was an old battle-ground between them, and the weapons were never suffered to grow rusty by disuse.

" I think we will have a dinner party, Matilda," said the Colonel, stirring the fire.

" A dinner-party ? " she echoed.

" Did I not speak plainly, my dear ? I said a dinner-party ; and I meant a dinner-party," returned the Colonel ; the accompaniment of falling coals lending a curiously warlike clang to his words.

" Yes, Colonel, certainly. Who are they to be ?" said Mrs. Lowe, with that air of frightened submission which always irritated her husband. It is only fair to her to say that an air of anything else would have irritated him just as much.

" Let me see. Suppose we say the Rector and Mrs. Borrodaile, Fletcher and his sister, the Collinsons, Dr. Wickham, and the Hamleys. There's a new girl there ; Mrs. Hamley's niece —Reginald's daughter I imagine she must be—the Captain never married. We'll have her out, and see what she is like."

Mrs. Lowe repeated the names. " That makes eleven," she said.

" Yes ; fourteen with ourselves. Seven of a sort," said Colonel Lowe. " Nobody likely to take anybody else by the throat, and two pretty girls as the enliveners among you old women. So perhaps you will write the notes at once, my dear ; and John can take them round. This day fortnight— January 3rd—unless you are too sleepy."

" How fond you are of saying disagreeable things ? " said poor Mrs. Lowe in her ill-used tone, as she slowly unpacked herself from her comfortable nest of shawls and pillows and went shivering and tumbled to her davenport.

But she dared not remonstrate. Colonel Lowe was not the man to sleep on a project ; and when he began to stir the whole house must be up and doing. It was always taking time by the forelock with him and striking while the iron was hot ; and his thoughts and plans were full grown Minervas, matured at their birth and never needing nursing. So the notes were written and the servant sent out with them on the instant; for all that it was a damp, dark, unpleasant night in December, and to-morrow would have done just as well. But to men like Colonel Lowe servants are only animated machines who have to do as they are commanded, and who are not allowed the effeminacy of taking cold in bad weather or feeling fatigue after hard work. If he had brought nothing else with him out of the army he had brought the habit of command ; and there was not a living creature about Cragfoot who did not recognise the master's hand when he raised it—save Sydney ; and even with him there were conditions and barriers he could not pass ; if few, yet immovable. And one of these was—he must marry money or he must accept disinheritance.

DILEMMAS.   105

CHAPTER XI.

DILEMMAS.

THE invitation to Cragfoot came to Abbey Holme just as Dora and Mr. Hamley were settling to their evening bézique. Mrs. Hamley was not playing to-night. She was deep in a quarterly article on the latest book of scandalous chronicles, where all the highly-spiced bits were extracted fenced about by an editorial padding of reprehension ; by which means was accomplished that feat, so dear to English respectability, of enjoying impropriety under the pretext of condemnation.

"An invitation to Cragfoot !" said Mrs. Hamley, with a perceptible sneer. "How strangely even people who should be well-bred forget themselves ! As if Patricia or myself could possibly go out in our first mourning ! For you are specially asked too, Patricia, though they have not called on you yet. Odd manners for Lady Graham's daughter, to say the least of it !"

"I do not want people to call on me, and I do not want to go out to dinner," said Patricia hastily.

"Don't be silly," returned Mrs. Hamley sharply. "And don't be affected. Of course you will have to go out like any other person when your first mourning is over. I hate these pretences of being unlike other people ; and you are far too fond, Patricia, of posing yourself as something special and peculiar, and, I suppose, something better than any one else."

"I did not mean it as a pretence or affectation," said Patricia.

"Yes, you did ; and do not contradict," snapped her aunt. "And I would make you go now, only it would be absurd in your deep crape. And she ought to have remembered this, silly little woman ! That eternal catarrh of hers seems to have really softened her brain."

Fortunately for Dora the name of Sydney Lowe's mother was not mentioned.

"What is all the row about, Lady?" asked Mr. Hamley in his rolling, unctuous voice, with his terminal h's and odd mixture of pomposity and vulgarity.

She looked at him with cold annoyance; when she was displeased, no one was right and Mr. Hamley more often wrong than another. Then after a pause she told him—an invitation on the third to Cragfoot, for all of them; adding "Of course we cannot accept,"

"No?" he said, dealing his cards leisurely, but dealing three instead of two. "Cannot Dora and I go as your representatives?—unworthy ones, I admit—but just to carry the flag for Abbey Holme, and show the neighbours we are alive?"

"If you like to make a marked division in the house, yes," said Mrs. Hamley coldly.

"Not to annoy you, Lady," said Mr. Hamley, throwing away his bézique knave.

"No, not for worlds," echoed Dora, who had been warned by a touch from her partner's foot that she was to "follow his lead," and "back him up."

"I really do not care a snuff about it. It was only for the credit of the house," said Mr. Hamley. 'Royal marriage; Dora, forty."

"And I am sure I do not, dear," said Dora, looking at Mrs. Hamley sweetly. "It is awfully cold too, turning out at night to drive a full mile!" shrugging her shoulders with a shiver.

"To drive a full mile!" echoed Mrs. Hamley crossly; none of these well-bred people had learnt the little politeness of not repeating foregone phrases. "And what of that? When we were girls we thought nothing of walking to Cragfoot in Lady Graham's time. I don't know what the girls of the present day are coming to with their indolence and inability to exert themselves. And you are as bad, Dora, as any of them."

Patricia looked and listened with her big eyes wide open, and her astonishment at this new view of her aunt's visible on her face. Remembering the frequent lectures which her own unladylike vigour had drawn down on her head, how her strength and hardihood had been counted to her as sins, she wondered where the right line was drawn and what was the exact amount of energy allowed before it became vulgarity, and where ladylike delicacy ended and reprehensible self-indulgence began.

"But Dora is too delicate to walk out at night!" she said in eager apology. "She would catch cold with the night air. Why! she does not go out enough in the daytime even!"

"My dear niece," said Mrs. Hamley in her most freezing tones, and with her most elaborate politeness, "oblige me by not interfering in matters which do not concern you. Miss Drummond and I can settle the business between us without your assistance. Now, Dora, if you will give me a moment's attention—that is, if you can abstract yourself from your ridiculous game—perhaps you will have the kindness to say whether you wish to go to this dinner or not?"

Again Mr. Hamley touched her foot.

"I wish to do just as you and Mr. Hamley like, dear," said Dora cheerfully.

"That is no answer; yes or no, if you please."

"If Mr. Hamley likes to go"—she hesitated with an appealing look. Mr. Hamley still making signs under the table, kept his eyes on his cards, taking no part in the discussion.

"Mr. Hamley can answer for himself," said his wife, compressing her lips. "We will come to Mr. Hamley by-and by. I have only to deal with you at this present moment. Do you wish to go to Cragfoot to dine on this day fortnight, or do you not? Quick, if you please; the messenger is waiting."

"If you were going, dear, I should like it," stammered Dora.

"But I am not going," said Mrs. Hamley; and paused for a decision.

"I think I would like it, then," said Dora with her eyes down, knowing too well that the authorities whom she made it the business of her life to conciliate equally were in opposition, and that she must offend one which way soever she took. In general, like a wise girl who knows where the staying power as well as the real influence lies, she sided with the wife; but the temptation in this case was more than she could resist; and an evening spent at Sydney's home, with the opportunity of making herself charming to his father and mother, was worth a few days of Mrs. Hamley's ice-bound manner, in her rapid estimate of values. Besides, there was Mr. Hamley's heavy foot under the table, and she knew what that meant too.

" You shall have your wish," said Mrs. Hamley stiffly. " I
have no desire to impose my sad mourning on you or Mr. Hamley.   The sympathy which is not given freely from the heart is
of no value in my eyes ; and I am glad you have decided as you
have done with such unmistakable candour.   Truth is always
valuable, even if unflattering."

Dora reddened, but said nothing.   Mr. Hamley went on
quietly with his game, but took care to score in silence, not
calling out his declarations.   They knew their world and what
was their best wisdom.

But Patricia, who was only honest and who knew nothing
but what she saw, cried out in real pain : " Oh, aunt, you
misjudge her ! Dora does care for you ; does sympathise with
you ! She said herself to me that she felt like the daughter of
you both !"

Mr. Hamley's eyes gleamed viciously at this, now at Dora,
now at Patricia.   Dora looked inexplicably confused.   Mrs.
Hamley took no notice.   She merely half shut her eyes, which
made them look something like a cat's, and after much unnecessary trial of pens and paper wrote a long and elaborately-
worded note of explanation and regret for her own part and for
that of her niece, for the necessity they were under, owing to
their recent bereavement, of declining, but ending with the pleasure which Mr. Hamley and Miss Drummond had in accepting
Colonel and Mrs. Lowe's polite invitation for Thursday, the 3rd
of January.   This she folded, directed, sealed—Mrs. Hamley
did not patronise stamped and gummed envelopes ; and on the
instant Patricia, who had been watching her, rang the bell un-
bidden.

" My dear," said Mrs. Hamley, still with her eyes half shut,
showing just a line of cold glitter between the lids, " may 1 ask
you never to do that again ?   I allow no one to ring the bell
in my presence uninvited."

"I beg your pardon, aunt ; but I thought it would save time,"
said Patricia.   " It was getting so late for the poor messenger,
whoever he is."

And you are this messenger's care-taker ? I thank you for
your lesson in humanity, though I was not aware I needed it.
I have generally had the character of extreme consideration
for others ; but it seems we older people know nothing, and

you young ones have exclusive possession of the wisdom and virtue of the world."

Patricia rose and went over to her. She put her young, supple arms about the angular and well-girt body of her aunt, and laid her fresh face against the withered cheek efflorescent with its Bloom of Ninon.

"Dear aunt," she said tenderly, "have patience with me! I want only to please you, and do what is right; but I know that I blunder more often than I succeed. I have been brought up so differently from your ways that I cannot help offending you. But indeed I do not want to vex you. You believe that, do you not, my dear?"

Her grey eyes were full of honest pleading and tender wishes as they looked with pathetic yearning into the hard face that turned itself away from her caress.

"Yes, yes," said Mrs. Hamley irritably. She hated anything like a scene; and to have her moods noticed, save by tacit submission to the course they indicated, was an offence she found it hard to forgive. "I daresay you will improve in time, child; but I must confess you are very trying now; and my poor brother lamentably failed in his duty to you. There, that will do! Don't you see you are crushing my *fichu?* And, good gracious, Patricia, what a mess you have made of my cap!"

On which she pushed her away angrily; and Patricia felt herself in deeper disgrace than before.

When they went to bed that night, Dora stole quietly into Patricia's room. She found her sitting half undressed, by the uncurtained window, looking at the starry sky—so much of it, at least, as she could see between the top of the wall and the roof of her window. She was not crying, as another girl might, but just wearying her heart out to know what it all meant. She felt in a maze to which she had not the clue, and where every path was wrong, every trial abortive. She could understand nothing; neither why she had offended her aunt because she had spoken the truth, defended Dora, and thought for the poor messenger—all of which were simple duties; nor did she know why there should have been such a bitter under current about such a simple thing as a dinner-party; nor why Dora— dear Dora, whom she so much loved—was so reluctant to say what she wished. And then why she had been told to hold her

tongue about the young man they had met to-day ?   And who
was he ?   As only " Cragfoot " had been mentioned downstairs
when this mysterious dinner was discussed, and as Patricia
had not .the smallest idea who lived there, the name had told
her nothing.   Had she heard of Colonel or Mrs. Lowe, the
chances are she would have made some kind of exclamation which
would have caused a considerable. draft on Dora's inventive
faculties and have necessitated a profuse coinage of her current change—white lies.   As it was, it was all a mystery ;
and Patricia's whole nature abhorred mysteries.

This initiation of hers into a certain phase of life, unhappily
only too common, was as painful as physical suffering; and the
confusion it was beginning to create in her mind was working
infinite sorrow, and might in time—who knows?—work as
infinite mischief.   For the most honest nature in the world,
the most pure and crystalline, if humble, loving, and loyal, may
be warped to doubt by the very virtues that are its charm.   Patricia knew what she had been taught in the early days of her
life, and her lessons and their teacher were dear ; but how could
she maintain her honesty, her candour, her sincerity, in a
household where these qualities were not only unpopular but
condemned as sins?—a household, too, so far superior to herself
in training and wisdom.   Was she really the only one right and
all the rest wrong?   Or was there another virtue beside those
which she had been taught, and which must at times be supreme—the virtue of seeing wrong-doing without remonstance,
consenting with sinners, and sliding down the incline with her
superiors? Humility or truth ? Obedience or sincerity ?   She
knew what she would have said at Barsands, and what her
uncle would have taught her there ; but things which were
clear then were confused now, and she seemed to know less as
she learnt more.

Sitting there, with her rich brown hair falling over her bare
shoulders, and her eyes fixed on the stars with a childish yearning for her uncle's spirit entangled somewhere among them to
come down to her this night and tell her what she ought to do,
she heard her door softly opened, and Dora, in a dainty wrap-
per of blue and white and lace and ribbon, supplemented with
an ermine cape—for she knew the temperature of Patricia's
fireless room—came gliding in.   Her hair too was about her

neck, very picturesque and pretty. But what a small amount it took to build up that magnificent structure of braided coils! thought Patricia. Her own great heavy masses which were three times as thick and long as Dora's could not be made to do half the work.

Coming up to her in her graceful, gliding way, Dora said softly:

"Dear thing, I want to help you."

Patricia's arms were round her in a moment, and the light of her love brightened her eyes to their old radiance.

"You are my good angel," she said enthusiastically. "I do not think I could go on living here without you, Dora!"

"But you really must let me teach you how to live here peaceably and happily, with me or without me," said Dora; and then began her lisping lecture on the propriety of absolute silence and submission to all Mrs. Hamley's words and ways. There was no good in opposing her, she said. Mrs. Hamley, dear thing, was mistress, and would always be mistress to the end of her life; and not one of them, from Mr. Hamley downward, dare contradict her or hold their own against her.

"Remember," she gave as her last exordium, "never defend yourself or any one else, however unjust she may be. It is only a mood, and will pass if you do not notice it; for she is really a kind-hearted woman at bottom, though such a difficult temper to deal with. Never take anything on yourself without her express permission, if it is only the pulling down of a blind, or the suggesting more coals on the fire. You may very likely be scolded for not pulling down the blind if the sun comes into the room, and for not putting more coals on the fire if it goes out or gets too low, but if you are you must just take it quietly, and pretend that you were to blame. If you do things of your own accord, you are sure to catch it; and it only fidgets her to see any one move without her permission. So, why do it? If she says black is white, good gracious, say it is white too! What does it signify? If you say no, it is black, you make her angry and have a row; and where is the good of that? In fact, you must just efface yourself, dear; and whatever you think say nothing, but make your mind apparently the shadow of hers."

" Dora!" cried Patricia with unfeigned horror. "Such a life as that! I would not lead it if I had to die! I will do all I can to study and please my aunt—it is my duty—but I will not listen to her injustice when she is unjust without protesting : and I will never say what is not true for her pleasure."

"Then you will never get on at Abbey Holme," said Dora.

"No I hope I never shall, if this is the only way in which I can," answered Patricia stoutly. The doctrine of sham and untruth, brought nakedly before her, broke through the cobweb meshes of her doubts and set her soul clear and free. "I would rather that my aunt disliked me even more than she does, than that I should despise myself."

"Why can't you leave yourself alone !" asked Dora, unconsciously touching one of the deepest problems of spiritual life. "Do what you ought to do—what it is only wise to do—and never mind whether it makes you despise yourself or not. We have to live for others, not for ourselves."

"And we have to live to God and Truth before all," said Patricia, looking up.

The fair face heroically suppressed a smile. Patricia was so funny! She might be a Methodist parson talking like that ; and to another girl too ! No *kudos* even to be got by it !

" Well, you must do as you think best, of course ; say all you think and make Mrs. Hamley very angry, and yourself most horribly uncomfortable ; but I hope you will not quarrel with me dear, because I am a cowardly little thing and care only to keep peace," Dora said coaxingly.

"I Dora ! In the first place, I never quarrel with any one. I don't think I ever had a quarrel in my life, not even with Miss Pritchard, whom I did not like; and least of all could I with you ! Dear, clever, gentle, good Dora! I think you are an angel ! Why, I offended my aunt to night because I could not bear to hear her so unjust to you—you, of all people ! "

"Which you need not have done," said Dora a little coolly. " I am used to that kind of thing from her and do not mind it. Hard words break no bones," she said lightly ; "and your little brush made it only all the worse for me."

" What an unlucky girl I am !" sighed Patricia.

"No, you are not a bit unlucky, but you are very self-willed," said Dora, with an admirable appearance of not knowing that she was saying anything that would offend the most susceptible.

"No! no! don't call me that, Dora! I am only trying to live as I have been taught," cried Patricia, really pained.

" You may call it what you like; I call it self-will. When you are advised again and again, as I have advised you, how to conduct yourself here for everybody's peace, and you will make yourself and every one else miserable by going your own way, what is that but self-will, I should like to know? At all events, if you determine to follow out your high and mighty line of conscience and righteousness," with a little grimace, " you must expect to suffer. Martyrdom may not be pleasant, but it is what you go in for; so you must accept it patiently, remember that!"

"I try to be patient in every way," said Patricia, looking at her with an agitated face.

" Yes, it is all very well for you to say that you try to be this, and try to be that, but it is we who suffer," said Dora, shrugging her shoulders. "You make us all—Mr. Hamley, poor dear Mrs. Hamley, and poor dear me too—as wretched as yourself, simply because you will not have a little common-sense and less egotism. But now I shall say no more. I have said all I want to say, and all you are to remember; but please, dear," passing the tips of her fingers playfully down the girl's upturned face as she stood beside her preparing to go, while Patricia still sat by the window listening to her, " *do* remember it. And now, good night." She stooped her pretty little fresh face and kissed her affectionately. " You old goosie!" she said, as Patricia gave her a great hug and called her a darling; and laughing, glided to the door. "Oh!" she then said quite indifferently, just as her hand was on the lock, turning back and speaking, in the tone of a person who has been struck by a sudden thought; "if a note comes for you to-morrow morning, dear, will you give it unopened to me?"

" A note for me to be given to you?" said Patricia, in her well-known tone of frank amazement.

Dora's fair face flushed with annoyance.

"She is positively maddening!" she said to herself. "Please, dear," aloud, quite tranquilly.

" But why should it come to me, and not to you direct," asked Patricia, looking at her with her bewildered look.

H

Dora glided back to her old place by the uncurtained window.

"Now don't ask me any questions, there's a dear," she said caressingly. "It is just my little secret, and of no consequence to any one but myself. You will get me into dreadful trouble if you do not help me ; that is all I can tell you ; and you will do no one any harm if you do. But you will help me, will you not, darling?" She laid her small hand on the girl's shoulder, and looked down into the noble, troubled face pleadingly.

"I do not mind, of course, giving you a note that does not belong to me though it may be addressed to me," said Patricia, distressed, disturbed, uncertain. "But if Mr. Hamley or my aunt sees it, and asks who is my correspondent, what am I to say? You see I have no letters ; and there is no one to write to me excepting Gordon ; and I cannot hear from him yet for two months or more. So they will be sure to ask ; and then what can I say?"

"Say? Anything! That it is from Miss Biggs, the dressmaker."

"I cannot do that," Patricia answered gravely. "I have never told a falsehood in my life, and even for you, Dora, much as I love you and much as I would do for you, I cannot begin now!"

"And how do you expect to get through the world, if you will not help a friend with a harmless little white lie like this?" said Dora, indignantly. "And you, who make so much fuss about your loving people so much, and your loyalty to them! It is perfect nonsense, Patricia, setting yourself up as so much better than any one else, and pretending that you are too good to do the things we all have to do!"

"Don't be angry, Dora," said Patricia humbly. "There are very few things that I feel sure of now—fewer, a great deal, than I did three months ago !—but this I do know, that it is mean and cowardly to tell falsehoods for any purpose whatever. Even if I ought to hold my tongue, as you say I should, and let people think I agree with them when I do not, I am sure I ought not to say what is not true."

"Then you will betray me ?—for the note will come!" said Dora, very pale.

"No, I will not betray you, Dora. I could not do that at

any cost. But neither will I tell a falsehood to screen you, if there is anything you do not want known."

"Well, leave it to me, you tiresome girl!" said Dora after a moment's pause, and speaking more ill-temperedly than Patricia had imagined she could speak. "I shall know better than to trust to your friendship for me another time; but as I did trust you this time you must not tell of me, and I will do the best I can. You have promised you will not betray me?" earnestly.

"I will not," the girl answered, as if she had been taking an oath.

"Then I will trust to my own brains for the rest," laughed Dora; her good-humour returned with the scheme that had occurred to her, and, nodding to Patricia gaily, she slid out of the room and nearly ran against Bignold as she was leaving Mrs. Hamley for the night. If she had, that virtuous female would have told of her next day, and Aunt Hamley would have administered a lecture on collusion which would have had more words in it than meaning.

This night it was, when, safely locked in her own room, Dora indemnified herself for the suppressions and vexations of the day by crying a little when she got to bed, and saying half aloud, shaken with fear and repentance, "How I wish I had refused and never done it! It was too bad of him to make me, when he knew what was at stake!"

CHAPTER XII.

HER FATHER'S FRIEND.

WO for me; one to you, Lady; none for you, Dora; and one for you, Patricia ;" said Mr. Hamley, dealing out the letters like cards the next morning at break fast.

Patricia crimsoned with undisguised embarrassment as she received a letter written in a strange hand—a man's hand— with the local postscript on the cover. She said nothing, but quietly laid it beside her plate and began to eat her breakfast.

Her aunt looked at her sharply. It seemed strange to her, first, that Patricia should have a letter at all ; next, that she should be so indifferent about reading it as not to open it, as any one else would have done ; or if not indifferent, then so much the reverse as not to be able to look at it before other people. Who could be her correspondent ? There was something here defying and mysterious ; and Mrs. Hamley never forgave either independence or mystery. People of arbitrary wills, and with a disposition to herd souls like sheep, seldom do.

This is one of the reasons why she liked dear Dora so much. She used to say, when speaking of that young person as she often did, and giving a reason for the faith that was in her, that dear Dora had not had a secret from her since she came under her roof ; and had never been ashamed to give her the most minute and circumstantial account of every event in her innocent life. It was as good as being on the spot herself, Mrs. Hamley said, when Dora had been away for a day or two and came home with her budget. When she went to London last October, for instance, and stayed there for a week with the Borrodailes—Mrs. Hamley not being able to accompany her, owing to what she called a chilblain and her doctor gout—her sprightly reminiscences were really amusement enough for weeks. She had kept a diary, dear child, on purpose to please them ; and the care she had taken to put down everything she had seen and every place she had visited was beyond praise both for its cleverness and frankness. There was not an hour of her time that she could not account for; and how delightful it was to have to do with a person so thoroughly candid and trustworthy ! *She* had no secrets indeed !—except, Mrs. Hamley might have added, when she herself wished to conceal anything from her husband ; and then how clever and discreet and full of nice helpful tact the girl was ! And so said Mr. Hamley on his own side when he had it in hand to hoodwink the Lady, and dear Dora was his confederate. But as they never came to the comparison of notes they never found that the tact each thought consecrated to him or her only was common to both, and so went on accepting as special and private a quality which was serviceable for more purposes than their own.

If, however, this strange noisy girl was going to add to her natural misdemeanours the acquired sin of making mysteries and having secrets, Mrs. Hamley felt that her cup would then indeed be too full; and that this would be just the one drop of overflowing bitterness which she could not and would not accept.

" Are you not going to read your letter, Patricia ?" she asked tartly.

" No, not yet, aunt," replied Patricia, not looking up.

" Who is your correspondent, pray ? "

" I do not know, aunt."

" You do not know ? A young lady, my niece, receive letter and not know from whom, and not open it to see ? What an extraordinary thing !—not quite according to my ideas of the natural action of well-bred girls," said Mrs. Hamley, very slowly, very deliberately.

" I dare say it's from the dressmaker," said Dora, coming to the rescue in her sweet peace-making way. " Give it to me Patricia, if you are afraid to open it dear."

Patricia, not looking up from her plate, flung the letter across the table with a shy and awkward jerk, while Dora gazed at her with a reassuring smile and candid eyes. The one looked guilty and ashamed, the other showed a fine, snow-white, well-ventilated conscience which had no dark corners to hide.

" Yes, it is," she said, as she opened the note down in her

lap and showed a printed circular—as the contents. " 'Miss Biggs has the honour to announce to her kind patrons, the Nobility and Gentry of Milltown,' &c. &c. I thought I knew the Biggs style of doing business," laughed the girl, with a pretty triumph at the difficulty being so happily ended. " Did I not tell you, Patricia, that you would be sure to have a notice, all to yourself, as soon as our local Madame Elise found you out ?" she added.

" What an incomprehensible girl you are, Patricia ! and what mountains you contrive to make out of molehills !" said Mrs. Hamley with displeasure ; Mr. Hamley adding, as the masculine view of the subject ; " My dear young lady, never throw away your powder and shot on trifles. When you have anything that you wish to conceal from Mrs. Hamley and myself, conceal it—if you can ; but for goodness gracious sake don't begin a game of ' I spy I ' with nothing to run for ! "

" I was not playing any game and I had nothing to conceal," said Patricia, a little nettled, and looking straight up at Mr. Hamley.

She had borne her aunt's rebuke in silence, but when her aunt's husband took her in hand she found humility and the acceptance of undeserved blame difficult.

" Whew !" said that gentleman with a prolonged whistle ; "but we can show fight then when we get our blood up, can we ?"

" Oh, Mr. Hamley !" broke in Dora, her fair face dimpled into the loveliest little labyrinth of smiles, " I wish you would tell us that delicious story of yours—that fight between the Irish carmen ! "

Mr. Hamley laughed noisily. This fight between two Dublin carmen, which took place on the Quay when he once went over on business to what he always called Paddy-land—men of Mr. Hamley's stamp are sure to be ethnologically insolent— was his favourite battle-horse ; and to be asked to repeat it was always pleasant to him, and never fatiguing. So, stretching out his legs, he began with more than usual gesture and emphasis ; and the incident of the letter passed without further comment. But it shook the Hamley trust in Patricia's honesty, and inclined them to doubt her gravely, and to debate whether her apparent straightforwardness was not rather the artfulest kind of sham.

"Now then, Miss Prue, what was there to make such a fuss about?" laughed Dora when she and Patricia were alone in the drawing-room. "You ridiculous old simpleton!" very prettily, quite in the manner of a caress.

"I don't know," said Patricia. "I don't understand what it all meant, nor why I might not have opened the letter at table before everybody without a word being said. It was only to please you, Dora, and because you told me not, that I did not."

"You dear old thing, said Dora, "it was just a little joke! I wanted to see if you could be depended on, that was all—if you were really as loyal to your word as I believed you to be."

"I think you might have been sure of that," replied Patricia with a certain reproachful sorrow in her face. "I would trust you, Dora, without testing you."

"Well, don't look as if you were going to cry! Mrs. Hamley will be asking what is the matter, and then there will be more complications;" said Dora, shrugging her shoulders.

And Patricia was as much startled as if a cold wind had suddenly blown over her, by the cool, half-annoyed and half-indifferent tone in which the girl spoke. It did strike her as being just a little bit ungrateful after she had been going through such a disagreeable experience for her sake.

"Dr. Fletcher," said the servant opening the door.

People call early in country places, and though it was not yet quite noon there was nothing in the hour to cause a remark, so far as Milltown habits went; but Dora shrugged her shoulders again; this time petulantly. Dr. Fletcher was evidently not one of her favourites.

A tall, lean, angular man with iron-grey hair and leathery lanthorn jaws came with a kind of lazy awkwardness into the room. His eyes were large and bright, but meditative rather than observant; his face was grave, even sorrowful, like the face of a man who has thought much on the miseries and perplexities of life; but his smile was sweet, more sweet than joyous, and a wonderful grace of patience and kindness rested on him. He looked older than his age and he was evidently in delicate health; which was perhaps another reason why his face had that unmistakable look of a man to whom life is tragically real, not a mere summer day's holiday, and who has taken

it to heart to live manfully according to that reality and to
leave the summer pastimes to the children.

He was a man of private means, but by no means wealthy.
When old Mr. Fletcher died he left just enough for his son and
daughter to live on, without the need of sordid economy on the
one side or the possibility of self-indulgent extravagance on the
other. And on his death Dr. Fletcher retired from the profession which had always been irksome to him in its practical
and business aspect, and came back to the old home at Milltown where he could study without interruption. He was one
of the quiet men who think and are still, not one of the active
sort who go out into the world to fight and cry aloud. His
life was mainly an endeavour to disentangle some of the many
problems which perplex society, and to create for himself some
kind of intelligible hypothesis in the midst of so much that is
dark and undetermined. And to do this, he went for his light
to science.

Of course he was considered fatally unsound in Milltown.
The most independent thinker that respectable community had
ever had, he was naturally styled Atheist by people who
thought religion consisted in denying the right of private judgment or individual interpretation. Men said, with a kind of
shudder, that he believed neither in God nor Devil—but to
disbelieve in the latter was the worse crime of the two ; he was
known to deny eternity of punishment—which was an awful
questioning of God's mercy ; and his scientific pursuits were
subjects of some scorn, much reprehension, and the profoundest disbelief in their truth or value. And those who knew
least about them despised them most, and flouted him with the
challenge to explain how or why a tree grew, and to recompose
into life the elements he pretended to weigh and measure and
tabulate in death.

His want of ambition, too, was disapproved of and held to be
a shameful wrapping up of talents ; and every one agreed that
with his abilities he ought to do something—indeed ought to
have done something long ago. They considered he had done
nothing yet, because fame had not beaten her tomtom before
him. The quiet rendering of a noble life seemed to be worse
than nothing to the children of an age which reverences chiefly
blare and tinsel. For his own part, when he was told that he

ought to do something and make a fortune, he answered that he thought that those who had enough should be contented; and he held it ignoble in the well-endowed to still further crowd the glutted labour-market, lessening the wages of the workers by necessity by just so much as they earned for their superfluities. This might be bad political economy he used to add with a smile. Some of his friends said it was ; but it was human justice all the same ; and, for the rest, political economy must go. He deprecated the race for wealth, the greed of gain, characteristic of the present day. He deprecated the tumult and excitement and clamour of our social life, the luxury and the sensuality of our homes ; and what he deprecated in others that he refused for himself. But Milltown did not endorse his doctrines. Indifferent to fear, to pleasure, to ambition, merely a calm, wise, just thinker, who appraised things at their real value, and was content to accept certain theorems as unprovable—the well-fed lives and uninquiring minds of that little paradise of conservative respectability had no sympathy with such an iconoclast and blasphemer of its gods ! The old proverb was verified ; the prophet had no honour among his townsfolk, and the most charitable interpretation of a life that dared to be real and a mind that dared to be ignorant was, that Henry Fletcher was mad. And many added, his sister Catherine with him.

Dr. Fletcher seldom called anywhere, but perhaps less frequently at Abbey Holme than even other places. Dora Drummond's pretty manners pleased him, certainly, for he had a benign kind of pleasure in contemplating children and young people and all other things fresh and beautiful ; but he did not feel at one with Mr. Hamley. Not because he was a self-made man—his sympathies would have naturally gone that way—but because he was a vulgar and ostentatious man, one whom he mistrusted and took to be a mask, of which the reality was very different from the appearance. Also, he could never overcome a certain repugnance for Mrs. Hamley. That a woman of her pretensions to ultra-refinement of character, whose birth and breeding were her strong points, and who spared no sister in her sorrow, no brother in his weakness, could have sold herself to a man of Mr. Hamley's stamp for money and a settlement, was so far out of his ideas of womanly dignity and purity, not to speak of that other virtue of his for which the world said he was mad—the virtue of sincerity of life—that in spite of his long acquaintance with her and her family, he could never feel for her cordially, nor look on her as other than self-degraded. And yet he pitied her. He thought the need which had forced her into such a marriage must have been indeed a crushing one! And in pitying her he tried to forget his repugnance, and perhaps went up to call as if in silent atonement for the personal distaste of which he had been conscious for both her and her husband.

Dr. Fletcher had been from home of late and had only just returned; by which it came about that although Patricia had been at Abbey Holme for some time now, he had neither seen nor even heard of her. He looked at her curiously as he came in, but in Mrs. Hamley's absence Dora did not dare to take on herself the responsibility of an introduction. If Mrs. Hamley's life was made up of small things, was not dear Dora's success due to her clever comprehension thereof? But though not introduced, Dr. Fletcher took a liking to the new girl. There was that kind of fearlessness which is born of innocence and unsuspiciousness in Patricia's eyes and bearing that interested him, even through her silence. She looked a new specimen for Milltown; and he liked new specimens. Then she was beautiful; and beauty, even to leathery skin and iron-grey hair, is interesting. And the mental trouble of her late state had given her a yet greater charm than of old. If something of her former exuberant radiance had gone out of her, more of depth had taken its place; and the abounding vitality which had given her happiness such infinite enrichment gave now her sadder phase as much pathos.

Then the two girls made a pretty picture and harmonised by the very force of contrast. The one was dressed in a simple gown of some soft black material, hanging in straight, deep folds, the severity of which was relieved round the throat and wrists by a line of transparent white; the other was in the daintiest and most coquettish grey that had nothing of mourning but its newness. The one was richly coloured yet in a low key, her dark brown hair, brightened with gold, framing her creamy skin heavily, gorgeously, her figure generously designed, but as yet showing only the long unfulfilled forms of youth;

and the other was fair, dainty, all pink and white, and blue and
gold, and every tint clear if slightly crude, every line rounded,
every form fully moulded. They made indeed a pretty picture ;
and Dr. Fletcher looked at them with his quiet eyes approvingly. In character, too, that superficial kind of character
which lies on the outside, how different they were! Patricia,
a woman nobly planned by nature, left pretty much to nature
to complete ; and Dora, the careful creation of art and education, pretty, graceful, well-bred, good-natured, but not real :—
Patricia looking as if she was capable of being a heroine in
more directions than one, from a Joan of Arc to a Saint
Theresa and onwards to a hospital nurse or a poor man's loyal
helpmate ; and Dora fit only for the soft things of life, a drawing-room lady from head to heel, to whom it would be martyrdom to be without a maid for four-and-twenty hours, and
whose sole endeavour in life was to avoid unpleasantness, get
her own private gathering of pleasures, and outwit the Nemesis
belonging.

All this Dr Fletcher took in in a fragmentary, hazy sort of
way, and then, after a few words to Dora, he turned to the
silent girl who was doing nothing less feminine than working
square stitches on coarse canvas as badly as a child would
have worked them, and said, apropos of nothing : "You are a
stranger here ?"

· It was rather a self-evident proposition, but it served for an
opening as well as anything else.

"Yes," answered Patricia, looking up with her big bright
eyes ; "I came here about six weeks ago."

"Do you make a long stay ?"

"For ever, I believe," said Patricia a little mournfully and
looked at Dora.

Dora was looking down, occupied with a difficult stitch in
her modern point. Dora's stitches were often difficult when
she wished neither to see nor to show.

"Ah ?—who are you then ?" asked Dr. Fletcher, as if he
was asking the most matter-of-fact question and not commit-
ting any offence against good manners.

Miss Kemball is Mrs. Hamley's niece," said Dora, glancing
uneasily at the door.

"Ah !" he said again ; then after a moment's reflection, he

asked, in his slow meditative way. Are you Robert's daughter?"

"No, that was my dear uncle. He was like my father and I loved him like one, but my real father's name was Reginald. I don't recollect him though," said Patricia tenderly.

"No, I suppose not. You must have been a very little child when he died. I remember him quite well, poor Reginald!" said Dr. Fletcher.

"You remember my father?" she cried eagerly, bending forward to look into his face."

"Quite well. We were lads together here at home, then at the same school, and afterwards together at college. He was the youngest of the family, you know, and Robert was the oldest. Robert must have been eighteen or twenty years older than Reginald. We always called him the Captain, even in the days when he was only a lieutenant. Has not your aunt introduced you to your old family friends? Milltown is your native place."

"I remember now all about you ; and you have a relation, a lawyer in London!" cried Patricia in a breathless kind of way ; as the scene, when Gordon was telling her uncle in the porch about his journey, and the good fellow, the lawyer, he had met in town, came like a photograph before her mind. The sunshine ; the blue, bright freshened sea ; the white sails of the passing ships ; the crimson leaves of the Virginia creeper round her window from the midst of which she leaned, looking at the fair-faced youth standing in the sunlight talking to the kind and generous guardian of her past life—all so full of colour, of careless joy, of fearlessness and freedom ! Dr. Fletcher became at once something nearer and more special than anyone else. He had a secret link with that happy past which no one else had, and of which no one else knew.

"I am glad to know you," she said with a passionate ring in her voice.

All in a flush and a tremor she rose from her seat and went over to him, offering both her hands. Was he not her dear dead uncle's friend ? And had not his relative, whoever he might be, been good to Gordon ?

Dr. Fletcher took her hands as she offered them. He was not a demonstrative man, and he had a wholesome horror of ordinary young ecstasies ; but Patricia's excitement seemed of a different kind, and if it embarrassed him it did not revolt him. Not that he knew what to do with her hands when he had them, and he wished she had not held them out to him; but he pressed them in a nice comfortable way and looked into her face kindly; and that was reception enough for Patricia.

He was holding her thus, she standing before him bending down her face looking into his, and he just saying, " You must come and see my sister Catherine, child," when the door opened and Mrs. Hamley entered. She had that habit of coming into a room when she was least wanted.

" I see there is no need of an introduction between you and my niece, Dr. Fletcher," said the lady of Abbey Holme in a cold voice.

Before she had married Mr. Hamley, by-the-by, he had been Henry and she Rosanna; as is the way with people in the country who have been brought up in the same place.

" Miss Kemball and I have fraternized over the past," said Dr. Fletcher. " She did not know that I had been her father's chum, and the Captain's too in a minor degree."

" And, in return, she seems inclined to accept you as her uncle, *faute de mieux*," Mrs. Hamley made answer with a sarcastic smile.

Oh, aun., you do not know what it is to meet some one who knows something about one in a strange place l " said Patricia impulsively.

" No doubt, **my dear**," **Mrs.** Hamley answered drily. " Of course I know nothing of you or your family."

" But I heard uncle speak of Dr. Fletcher only the day before "—— she hesitated—" the wreck," she added, after a pause.

" My poor brother must have been singularly reticent if Dr. Fletcher is the only one of his numerous Milltown friends of whom he spoke to you. He knew every one there was to know, and naturally every one knew him," said Aunt Hamley with the same dry tone and unpleasant smile.

" Still, it is something to hear those one loves spoken of with love," cried Patricia fervently.

" The inference is neither flattering nor just," returned Aunt Hamley with a formal movement of her head. " Now we will

drop the discussion, if you please. It is one in which Dr.
Fletcher can scarcely feel an interest, and of which I hope he
will not accept the interpretation you have endeavoured to
insinuate."

She waved back the answer that rose to the girl's lips with
the manner which, when she put it on, no one had yet been
found able to withstand. It was her slave-chain with which she
compelled her husband ; the grand air which had always carried
Milltown, and which, more than anything else, had maintained
that queer shadowy thing called position both when, as a penniless lady she had been as it were a lioness with her claws cut,
and now, when the wife of a moneyed nobody she was a lioness
with her claws well grown, though she was yoked to a very
low-bred and clay-carrying cart-horse. In the former case she
had never, as she said, forgotten herself nor suffered any one
else to forget her : in the latter, she insisted that Milltown
should accept the axiom which tells how the greater includes
the less. Given the lioness and the cart-horse in the same yoke,
and the regality of the one shall overshadow and merge into itself the clay-carrying of the other. So far she was both wise
and brave, and her grand air merited the reward it gained.

Her grand air, however, was not very formidable to Dr.
Fletcher. He knew his old friend, Rosanna Kemball, pretty
well after half a century's intimate acquaintance ; and, for his
own part, doubted her zoology. So, undisturbed and undis-
mayed, he talked as much to Patricia as he did to Mrs. Hamley
herself, and made her tell him all about her past life and her
uncle, Barsands and the *Mermaid*, till the girl was quite rapt
away at last, and for a few moments was oblivious of everything
but her memories.

" Dear old Barsands ! " she said, throwing back her head ;
and one thick twist of hair came loose and fell down her back.
" Oh, life was good then ! " she cried.

Her face lighted up as she spoke with a sudden effulgence of
passion and beauty that gave it a totally different character
from the ordinary expression it wore. Even her aunt was
startled, and Dr. Fletcher looked at her with half a smile and
half a sigh.

" You must come and see my sister Catherine," he said again ;
and touched her arm.

She started, and looked at him as if he had awakened her; passed her hand over her forehead, and drew a deep breath; was conscious of the straying length of hair, of her aunt's cold eyes, of the heavy, gorgeous drawing-room, of all her loss and all her change. The brightness, the rapture, the effulgence passed; she was only one of the inmates of Abbey Holme; and Mrs. Hamley disapproved of dreamers.

"I shall be very glad," she said in her frank way, after a pause. "When shall I come?"

Mrs. Hamley's thin lips crisped and Dora's pursed in sympathy.

"Are you quite sure, Dr. Fletcher, that your sister will care to be troubled with so young a companion?" she said coldly.

"You know Catharine!" he answered. "Your niece—what is your name, child?—Patricia?—Patricia," he continued, turning back to Mrs. Hamley, "is just the kind of thing she will like. You know of old we have no nonsense at the Hollies. When can you come, do you say?" to Patricia. "When she comes home. That will be in about a week's time; and then I expect you two will make great friends."

"It will not be my fault if we do not," said Patricia simply. And Dr. Fletcher stroked his beard, and said "No," gravely.

When he had gone the trouble began. Aunt Hamley was put out, and life was difficult when the mistress of Abbey Holme was cross. She first scolded Patricia for her "abominable forwardness;" and Patricia unwisely defended herself, and assured her, with quite superfluous energy, that she never dreamt of being forward, and was only glad to see Dr. Fletcher because he spoke so kindly of dear uncle and poor papa. And then Mrs. Hamley turned against Dora, and told her very coldly and with a great parade of politeness, that she had no business to introduce any one in her absence. How did she know what her wishes were with respect to Patricia's becoming acquainted with the Fletchers? They were old acquaintances, certainly; but they were very odd people, and Patricia was quite eccentric enough as things were, she scarcely needed being made more so by outside influence. A great deal, too, was said of Dr. Fletcher's peculiar opinions; and though she had never sounded him herself, having no patience with him, she knew

that he held crotchets in theology—of itself a most undesirable
thing.

The doubts of striving souls struggling for light amid the
darkness had no kind of sympathy from Aunt Hamley! And
when she came to this part of her subject she went off into a
long disquisition on the folly and impiety of thinking for oneself on religion, or indeed on any matter whatsoever settled for
one by authority.

" As if any one could understand a thing we were never meant
to understand!" she said contemptuously. "Such presump-
tion! Just like Henry Fletcher, though!"

On which she blamed Dora again; and drawing a vivid picture of Patricia's subsequent infidelity and lost condition, made
her a present of it as her work and the result of this morning's
introduction. But drawing it as she did, with her broadest
colours and most comprehensive manner, she pleased herself so
much that she forgot she was angry. It was a clever, artistic
sketch, and the composition of it soothed her.

And when she had ended, dear Dora raised her eyes and said
very meekly, "I know all you say is quite true, dear, but what
could I do? He said he knew Patricia was a Kemball because
she was so like you, and he asked to be introduced."

" In that case you could scarcely have refused," said Mrs.
Hamley, who, with her eyes full of that brilliant face she had
just seen, felt the flattery pleasant.

" Dr. Fletcher seems to have taken quite a fancy to Patricia;
perhaps it is a *réchauffé* of the *very* friendly feeling he seems to
have had for you," laughed Dora significantly.

" Nonsense, child!" said Mrs. Hamley.

But she smiled. She was old enough to be Dr. Fletcher's
mother—what of that? Was she not Mr. Hamley's wife, and
was not Mr. Hamley born in the same year as Henry Fletcher?
Old enough for maternity or not, the multiplicity of her lovers
was one of Mrs. Hamley's weak points. No man had ever
spoken to her with any appearance of interest in the conversation but he had been marked in her diary as "another victim."
According to her the main fact of her own unwritten history
was that every marriageable gentleman in Milltown had some
time or other in his life yearned to make her his own; and
though she could not always add that he had expressly said so,

she was never at a loss to account for his silence—the signs by
which the poor fellow had betrayed his broken-hearted condition having told her more than his enforced reticence had been
able to conceal. In truth she has been a handsome girl in her
day, tall and showy, insatiably vain and as insatiably ambitious.
In truth too, one honest young fellow whom she had led on and
then denied had really blown out his brains for love of her;
and the sacrifice had so far touched her own that she had ever
since then considered herself irresistible and fatal.

"No! no nonsense at all, dear," returned Dora. "Why! how
can you say so?" with remonstrance. "Why else has Dr.
Fletcher never married? All Milltown knows that!"

"Dora, you stupid child, I will not have you talk such rubbish!" said Aunt Hamley laughing; then turning to Patricia
she said kindly: "I dare say, dear, it did a little upset you to
see an old family friend. That was perhaps natural, as you
have been nowhere yet in the neighbourhood. But you must
indeed learn to suppress your feelings, child, and be more like
other people, else I don't know where we shall be!"—good-
naturedly. "So now take what I have said in good part, and
remember *I* am your best friend—the truest you have in the
world, in every sense. Though I know my duty to you too well
to spoil you."

Patricia went over to her and kissed her; and dear Dora,
who knew that she hated to be kissed and loved to be praised,
said in her most caressing way:

"Friend! You are the friend of everyone, you darling! What
should we all do without you, I wonder?"

"Badly," said Mrs. Hamley, and sighed.

For the moment she was, to her own mind, a kind of Mary-
mother-martyr, bearing on her hands the sorrows and incapa-
cities of the whole neighbourhood.

"Dora! I did not hear Dr. Fletcher ask to be introduced to
me; on the contrary he asked straight out who I was; and I did
not hear him say I was like Aunt Hamley," said Patricia in a
tone of surprise when Aunt Hamley had left them alone
again.

She had advanced so far in worldly knowledge as to keep
these interrogations for her *tête-à-têtes* with Dora; of itself something.

I

" Nor did I," answered Dora coolly.

" Oh, Dora ! "

"Oh, Dora ! and what then, you dear little prude ? Now Patricia be reasonable !" said Dora, changing from banter to earnestness. " Have some common-sense, child, or you will make your life here simply intolerable ! What possible harm was there in saying what I did to Mrs. Hamley ? She would have gone on scolding till now, making herself and everyone else ill and miserable, unless I had turned her thoughts by my master-stroke. To say that the stupid old man thought you like her, pleased her ; of course she understood the compliment ; and 1 dare say you are like what she was, for she must have been very beautiful in her time "—that scored one for Patricia in her own mind ; but Patricia was too stupid to see the compliment implied—" and to say that he asked to be introduced to you took the load off my head. He wanted it if he did not ask for it, so what harm did I do ? "

" What is not the truth is always harm," said Patricia.

" Bah, my dear ! you will have to unlearn that nonsense before you have done with Abbey Holme, that is all I can tell you ! We have to get through the world in the best way we can ; and if a white lie that hurts no one helps us to keep peace and avoid pain, it is lawful," said Dora with a dash of scorn.

" No, Dora, it is not !" replied Patricia, earnestly.

" Don't be silly," she answered. " If you had been brought up between Mr. and Mrs. Hamley as I have been, you would have learnt the same lessons that I have. I would tell any story in the world, perjure myself anyhow, to prevent scolding and quarrelling. And so you would have done ; and so you will do before you are many months older ! "

" Never, Dora ! Rather than condescend to a life of false-hood I would leave, no matter what I did !" cried Patricia. " 1 would beg my bread first."

" And I like mine baked for me with plenty of butter," laughed Dora. Then suddenly changing her voice she said, rather loudly, " I like home-made bread, don't you ? " She had heard Mrs. Hamley's footstep in the hall, and knew that they would linger just a moment by the door before she opened it ; and they had home-made bread at Abbey Holme.

Nothing further happened till the day of the Cragfoot din-

ner, beyond the troubles between Patricia and her aunt which
would break out in spite of Dora's care. For, as if to make up
for her loose morality by personal kindness, she had constituted
herself Patricia's guardian angel at all points. She had
patience with her inept fingers and tried in vain to teach her
tatting ; she worked a point-lace butterfly for her hair, with the
Venetian stitches put in in black ; she made her head ache by
dressing her hair in a responsible-looking chignon ; laboured
over bezique, in which the former steerswoman of the *Mermaid*
was simply hopeless ; defended her against herself : and somehow brought out her most glaring misdemeanours against the
Hamley laws as shining virtues of intention, or at the worst,
the venial mistakes of ignorance ; she wound herself more and
more round the girl's heart—that heart which only asked leave
to love !—till Patricia fairly worshipped her, and would have
gladly died to save her an hour's pain ; she became more and
more the peace-maker of the house, faultless in tact, in temper,
in kindness, in quickness, faulty only in sincerity and truth.
On the whole, the last fortnight had been a happy one. Dora
had been delightful ; equal to every emergency ; at the head of
every occasion. Patricia, guided by her, was beginning to understand the virtue of leaving things alone, and especially the
necessity of leaving her aunt alone when she had a headache.
Mrs. Hamley, being less irritated had been less irritable than
usual ; and Mr. Hamley too, had helped to keep her in good
case by his blandest and most flattering attentions.

For his own part he had been radiant : sleeker, more
shining, more abundantly prosperous than ever. He had
once or twice even spoken genially to Patricia, and he had not
spoken so much, before folk, to Dora. It was all that dinner-
party in prospect at Cragfoot ! Life had narrowed itself very
much in that monotonous house when an ordinary dinner-party
half a mile off, was an event to be chronicled by changed tempers and higher spirits. It might be so to Dora well enough.
She was young ; Sydney Lowe was handsome, and a note had
passed between them. , But why should Mr. Hamley be so
pleasantly moved ? His chains must be heavy if, to have four
hours away from the Lady and alone with dear Dora, was a
chance for so much inner rejoicing. However, so it was ; and
to the good of Colonel Lowe's account must be carried the

fortnight's spell of comparative brightness that had ruled the
household of Abbey Holme.   His account did not always show
so much to the good ; nor good indeed of any kind in the home
that owned him for its master, and where poor, frightened,
nervous and catarrhal Mrs. Lowe called him husband.

CHAPTER XIII.

CANIS IN PRÆSEPI.

MRS. LOWE had not ceased for a full fortnight daily to express her astonishment at her husband's sudden proposal, first to have a dinner-party at all when they did not owe one and when money was so difficult to get out of the Colonel, and then to ask the Hamleys whom he so much disliked. Why should he have asked them of all people in the world when, from the first, he had opposed the rich brewer's reception as an equal among them, had been the last to ask him, and had never called Mrs. Hamley anything since her marriage but " old hag," " mercenary jade," and the like ? He himself had married Lady Anna Graham's daughter for money ; but let that pass. Few of us carry pocket-mirrors in our conscience ; and Colonel Lowe was not one of the few. What he might have done counted for so much ; but what Mrs. Hamley had done was a different matter.

Sidney was even more astonished than his mother at this proposed dinner-party. Crafty, therefore suspicious, and clear-sighted as a rule, this time he was off the track. Hope, so natural to the young, his belief in his power over his father, and the passion of his love, all helped to confuse him. For he did love Dora in his own way ; and if his own way was but a poor kind of thing, still it was the best he knew. He scarcely knew how to take this proposed dinner-party. Was it a trap or a chance ? inimical or providential ? Did his father suspect something, and so resolve to see on what terms the young people stood together, for their future discomfiture ?—or had he by a generous impulse wished to give them a chance, and himself the opportunity of measuring Dora Drummond's fitness to become the future Mrs. Lowe of Cragfoot ?

Sydney passed a good deal of his time debating these alternatives ; and as if by mutual consent the Hamley name had not once been mentioned between him and his father since that

little tentative brush of theirs over the wine and walnuts.   His
mother, however, many times bemoaned her hard fate to him
in having to receive Mr. Hamley at all, and specially at an unnecessary dinner ; and he had condoled with her sympathetically, and confessed it was an infliction, but it would be all over
this day month and be forgotten as if it had never been, and
she was not to bother herself, everything would go right ; with
other of the consolatory speeches he sometimes employed in
those rare moments when he played at being an affectionate son
to his maternal parent.   But, as she remembered afterwards,
he had ever said something kind of the Abbey Holme family.
Even while he agreed with her that Mr Hamley was a wretch
for whom hanging would be too good, he had managed to
make his abuse vague and his encomiums precise.   She had not
noticed it at the time, being so much taken up with her dishes
and her chills, the entrées she could not get, and her eternal
cold that would not go ; but she remembered it in the days
when the past was read by the light of the future.

When the .day arrived, and they were settling the order of
precedence and the necessary arrangements of pairing off, &c.,
Colonel Lowe, smiling pleasantly to his son, said, " And you
shall have the pretty heiress, Syd ?   For I suppose she will be
the old ruffian's heiress ? "

    " I should think no doubt of that," answered Sydney, briskly.

    " And I dare say he will cut up well when the devil claims
his own ?" continued the Colonel who used more bad language
than any other man in Milltown.   If he was minded to do his
son a kindness too, he was also minded that some of the worth
of it should be taken out in annoyance.

    " It looks like it.   I do not suppose there is anything flashy
about *his* means," Sydney answered innocently.

    " 'It looks like it !' you don't know what he is worth ? You
mean to say, Syd my boy, that you do not know more of your
Abbey Holme friends than ' suppose,' and ' looks like ? ' " cried
the Colonel with aggravating astonishment.

    " I ? no! Why should I inquire into Mr. Hamley's affairs ? "
said Sydney, shifting uneasily under his father's eyes.

    " Well ! that is being disinterested and confiding, and all
the other Arcadian virtues in a heap ! " cried the Colonel with
a long breath something between a whistle and an ejaculation.

Sidney flushed and tossed back his hair, but he did not take
up the glove.

"This new girl may come in for her share," put in Mrs.
Lowe following the main text, but in happy ignorance of all
that was to be read between the lines. "She is a Kemball ;
and the Kemball's are a good family."

"That shows how capable you are of giving an opinion on
such matters ? " sneered the Colonel. "How can you talk such
nonsense, Matilda? The old shoeblack holds the money, and you
may be very sure he will not slice his estate to make his wife's
niece equal with his own. He will go in for founding a family,
and making little Miss Twoshoes his heiress, with the proviso
to keep the illustrious name of Hamley for all future generations. Those fellows of mud and money always do go in for
founding a family, poor misguided wretches !"

Still Sydney did not answer. That discretion which is the
better part of valour was in the ascendant to-day, and Sydney
would have borne much rather than have given his father an
excuse for a quarrel. The Colonel knew this, and pricked him
with his verbal assegais accordingly.

"It is lucky for her that little Twoshoes is tolerably
looking," he went on to say. "She is not bad style, all thi.
considered." Sydney shot a glance at the handsome, contemptuous face, that meant a remembrancer, but failed ; and the
Colonel went on in the same offensive tone. "If she had been
a healthy young woman, with the good tough brown hide and
milkmaid's paws of her degree, she would have lowered her
chances by as many points as she would have gained in wholesomeness. Being scrofulous, she has therefore the superficial
refinement of the scrofulous—a high price to pay."

"Scrofulous ! how can you say such a thing ! " flamed Sydney, caught on a tender point. "Her health is perfect and
her blood is as pure as my own."

Colonel Lowe's eyes twinkled, and he smiled beneath his
moustache. "Hit ! " he said to himself ; then aloud, "Bah !
those pink and white, blue-eyed golden-headed things are
always scrofulous, and Miss Drummond cannot escape the inevitable. She is paying the penalty of a half-starved ancestry,
and the vitiated air of centuries of hovels, while you, dear boy,
have always been a gentleman when you were your great-grand-

father, and his great-grandfather to boot. The flesh-and-blood
theory is all very well for hustings claptrap, but don't talk to
me of your natural equality and one man being as good as
another, or any of your cursed Radical rubbish ; a gentleman's
a gentleman, and a snob's a snob, and God Almighty himself
can't make them different ! "

" Do not lose your temper with me, dad. I am not a
Radical, nor am I going in for the flesh-and-blood theory," said
Sydney ; while Mrs. Lowe remonstrated humbly in a horrified
whisper, " Colonel ! before the boy, too ! "

" No, I don't say you are. Egad you'd be no son of mine if
you did ! " said the Colonel. " But it vexes me to hear you
couple yourself any how with such a beggar's brood as that
Abbey Holme man's ! A ruffian I have switched in the streets,
as many times as there are days in the year, and now he is
dining like an equal at my own table, and I hear my son say
' we,' as if speaking of one of his own blood ! It galls me Syd,
though he does happen to have a pot of money, and could buy
us Lowes from garret to basement ; and though she is a pretty
girl, she is not one for you to look at. A Lowe should have
more pride ! "

" Bother pride when a pretty girl is concerned ! " said Sydney
with a forced laugh. " A Lowe has always had tolerably keen
eyes for that !—and I never heard of one among us who asked
whether the petticoat was of silk or stuff that covered a clean
pair of ankles ! "

" My boy ! " said Mrs. Lowe, tears starting into her poor
pale eyes.

She would have been in her right place as a placid old maid
given to small economies and smaller charities ; or as a by no
means broken-hearted widow with a quiet girl who would have
taken all the house-keeping trouble off her hands, and given
her no anxiety about her morals or manners ; but as the wife
of one gentlemanlike roué and the mother of another, her lot
was exceptionally hard. Small wonder at her persistent vili-
fication of the marriage state, and the morbid horror she always expressed at the responsibility of giving life ?

" Beg pardon, mater, if I have offended you," said Sydney,
following up his cue of filial amiability. " I ought to have remembered that you were there. Be a better boy for the

future ; and now I'll go and puff out my iniquities in a weed."

On which he beat a retreat, and drew himself rather hastily out of fire.

" You are a clever dog, but you don't blind me, Master Syd, nor get over me either, if I can find a way out of this cursed hole on any other side !" said his father under his breath, by way of parting shot. " Now, Matilda," viciously, " I advise you to go and put yourself under the hands of that old fumbler of yours. She takes an hour to make you the most of a scarecrow of any woman in Milltown, and you have not much more before you."

" You do say the most disagreeable things, Colonel !" cried poor Mrs. Lowe, hurrying aimlessly about the room.

Her husband's sarcasms acted on her nervous system like wind on a heap of chaff, and her thoughts, never remarkable for clearness nor precision, became utterly chaotic when he took it into his head to gibe and taunt ; which was the reason why he did so.

Having thus set his son's blood on fire and turned his wife's brains upside down, Colonel Lowe went off on his own side to the library, where he took a sheet of paper and read over an elaborate calculation between a long row of figures on the one side, and a very small item, taken from his banker's book, on the other. It was evidently an unpleasant process, for he frowned over it heavily, bit his cleanly-trimmed, filbert-shaped nails as if to gain inspiration, and several times he swore. This was an accomplishment in which the gallant Colonel, whose pride was in his inherited gentlehood, was notoriously proficient.

" Money I must have ; but that cursed mud !" he said, evidently with no kind of misgiving that the mud itself might have other views of direction ; evidently with but the one difficulty, that of stooping his proud head with a good grace and picking up the riches lying at his feet.

This was not exactly the estimate in which Mr. Hamley held his fair young cousin, nor the future for which he had secretly destined her ; not exactly the estimate in which she held herself as she stood before the pier-glass in her room, radiant in the white silk and pearl ornaments with which she hoped to charm Sydney Lowe's father and mother, and win their hearts to favour.

Evidently the task these young people had set before themselves was of supreme difficulty. On the one hand stood the
pride of the gentleman, on the other, the pride of money ; and
neither seemed likely to give way. Colonel Lowe thought no
girl too good for Syd ; Mr. Hamley thought no man good
enough for Dora. Colonel Lowe had decided that his son
should redeem the tottering fortunes of his house ; Mr. Ham-
bly had determined that his cousin should marry no one whose
alliance was not of so splendid a kind as to compensate him
for her loss. Each held the other infinitely beneath him ; and
when birth said " mud," money answered " beggary."

If there had been only the Colonel to soften, things might
have had a better outlook. Needs must when the day of need
comes ; but what was the influence that could move Mr. Hamley ? Dora knew of none. Wherefore it was, that believing
the Lowe finances to be as flourishing as they looked, and im-
agining that the Colonel's consent was the only thing to make
the affair a brilliant success, caring nothing for Mr. Hamley
though much for what she got out of Abbey Holme, she had
done—what she had done. Had she known that Cragfoot was
mortgaged from kitchen to garret ; that Sydney had not sixpence because his father had not a shilling ; and that her dower
was part of the speculation, even with her lover—well, matters
would have been different, that is all !

There was nothing very noticeable about the dinner-party.
It was much like any other where the host does not hold his
guests as first-class, and therefore permits himself to be condescending to some and unduly familiar to others. For even
gentlemen allow themselves these pranks sometimes. Not the
best kind, granted ; but the gentlemen whose consecration has
come from circumstance only, not by nature ; men, may be the
sons of a long line of well-endowed, who have places, and that
shadowy substance called a stake ; men who have been at
public schools with Oxford or Sandhurst to follow ; who know
how to come into a room with grace and to meet a social difficulty with tact ; who speak with a pure pronunciation and
accurate grammar ; read French and the classics, Balzac, Hor-
ace, and the like with ease ; who ride well to hounds ; shoot
right and left flying ; play billiards, and fence, and do all that
gentlemen should do ; but men whose inordinate pride of race,

pride of caste, and pride of person, have stifled the real humanity in them, and who, in idealising selfishness have degraded nobleness. These are the men who, because they are Gentlemen of England, think themselves patented kings of all other races and all lower conditions. Kings? If tyranny to the weak, insolence to the inferior, contempt for all differences, if this constitutes kingship, then was Colonel Lowe of Cragfoot a royal man—of a kind. Consequently a dinner party which consisted of a rich parvenu and his plebeian, if pretty, relation; the rector, respectable and a gentleman, but possessing only a scantling of brains according to the estimate of a clever reprobate whose predilections were for "life;" the medical man who, as a "professional," was of small account; two common place mediocrities like the Collinsons; and two queer, enthusiastic Radicals, free thinkers, woman's rights people, and who knows what absurdities besides, like Dr. Fletcher and his sister, was not a dinner-party for which he put on his best breeding nor brought out his best wine.

Nobody however cared much about the Colonel, nor his nicer shades of manner. Country friends have that kind of indifference for each other which is born of perfect familiarity; and if a man is known to have a "nasty way with him" on occasions, when those occasions arise and his peculiarity is made evident, nothing more is said than that he "showed himself off," or "his fit was on him," or "he was nastier than usual last evening." Of the two from Abbey Holme, Dora was happy because she looked pretty and knew that she shone out like a star in the midst of the faded elders, not excepting even Miss Fletcher, noble of look and of true queenliness of bearing as she was—but then she was past forty, and did not know how to dress; and Mr. Hamley was happy because Dora was there and Mrs. Hamley was not. The Borrodailes were glad to spend an evening out of their own house. They were of the jovial order of parsonhood in a mitigated way, and thought life was given as much for enjoyment as for work; and Dr. Fletcher and his sister took their part patiently in what they considered a personal sacrifice to the claims of a long acquaintance, and which had promised more pleasure than it had fulfilled in the disappointed expectation of meeting Reginald Kemball's daughter.

Only the Colonel's own family understood the run of the undercurrent of which the company at large saw nothing but the surface. They knew that his humour was insolent in its very jocularity, and that the more familiar his manner the more contemptuous his feeling. And the knowledge was enough to make Mrs. Lowe's naturally cold and nervous manners more than usually uncomfortable, giving her the appearance of being personally offended with all her guests save Mr. Borrodaile, to whom she addressed herself almost exclusively because he was long-winded and perorated, and liked to talk better than to listen. As for Sydney, knowing that every word and look was watched, he became so much on his guard towards Dora that he piqued her for a moment into evident displeasure. And this betrayed a greater amount of intimacy than even the dimples and the blush which broke out suddenly over her face when the young man took her hand under the table, and squeezed it with more fervour than Mr. Hamley would have quite liked, had he known.

All of which the Colonel saw and noted, and made his future game thereon.

After the ladies had retired and the gentlemen had drawn close, Colonel Lowe, who had been taking his wine freely, turning to Mr. Hamley who had been taking his freely too, said with a laugh that might have meant anything, from honest admiration to the profoundest insolence :

" That girl of yours grows prettier every day, Hamley."

Mr. Hamley's eyes glistened. He threw back one lappel of his coat, and smiled the proprietor's smile of proud humility which deprecates while it accepts.

" She's well enough ; she'd pass in a crowd," he said, waving his large hand with its big diamond flashing in the light ; " but she's better than pretty, Colonel—she's good."

" Good !" echoed Colonel Lowe ; " who cares about women being good ? All we want is. that they should be pretty and love us when we ask them. No woman is good who is worth her salt—such salt as it is ! "

" I must beg to differ with you," said Mr. Hamley sententiously. " I think ladies should be very good to enable them to encounter their little temptations and bear their little crosses ; ladies, when they are weak, do a great deal of harm."

"There I meet you," said Colonel Lowe with a laugh: "women, when they are weak and brainless, are I grant you the deuce and all; but your niece is not *that*, I take it."

"She is not my niece; Miss Drummond is only my cousin," said Mr. Hamley. "I cannot think why you should all say she is my niece! From the commencement it has always been your niece here and your niece there, confound it! in spite of all I could say to the contrary."

"So?—your cousin is she? Mrs. Hamley is trustful," said the Colonel dryly.

"Miss Drummond is as valuable to Mrs. Hamley as to myself; she is Mrs. Hamley's right hand and mine too," said Mr. Hamley in a distinct voice. "Mrs. Hamley enjoys but poor health, as perhaps you know, and Miss Drummond is quite the angel of the house, if I may say so without offence to Mr. Borrodaile."

"Ah! that is very nice," said Colonel Lowe. "Quite the right sort of thing for an adopted daughter."

Mr. Hamley frowned; but he drank a glass of wine, and therefore made no answer.

"Still," continued the Colonel in a meditative kind of way, "the more valuable she is to you now, the more you will miss her when she leaves you."

"I was not aware that Miss Drummond entertained the intention of leaving us," said Mr. Hamley stiffly.

"No? Why, you cannot expect to keep a pretty creature like that always by her mother's side, can you?" laughed Colonel Lowe. "You will be losing her some day when Prince Prettyman make his appearance."

Mr. Hamley's face flushed; Sydney's turned pale.

"I don't know anything about Prince Prettyman," he said; "but what I do know is, that I have never yet laid eyes on the man I would choose to give her to. Fact is, I care nothing about her marrying. She has no call to marry while Abbey Holme has a roof to its rooms and a fire in its kitchen. Who would be as good to her as we are? who would treat her as so much the lady? She is happier now than she would be elsewhere, and there's time enough before her." He spoke warmly, wiping his upper lip more than once; and the Colonel looked at him curiously, as if trying to read the man's inner thought.

"Yes, that is all very well as a matter of sentiment, I dare say," he said; "but you surely don't intend to prevent her marrying if a suitable occasion offers!—a gentleman of good blood, say "——

"Good blood!—good fiddlesticks!" interrupted Mr. Hamley coarsely. "Good blood makes as bad a job of life as bad blood does, and sometimes a precious sight worse. I would refuse the highest lord in the land if I did not think him good enough for her."

"I should have thought a lord, not quite the highest in the land, might have been considered Miss Drummond's equal," said Colonel Lowe smoothly.

"Look here, Colonel, I'm a self-made man, I am," said Mr. Hamley, moving his chair sideways to the table and thrusting out his legs; "and I'm used to price things by value and not by name. Lord or no lord, I know Miss Drummond's figure, and I tell you he'll have to weigh pretty heavy who'd come up to it and get my yes."

"But if you did like the man and the match?" pressed the Colonel. "You would then, I suppose, make the running smooth for the young people?—you would not send her to her husband empty-handed?"

Mr. Hamley took it all in at a glance. He sat upright in his chair planted his feet firmly, flung back both lappels this time, and looked at Colonel Lowe steadily with another steady look at Sydney; handsome faces both of them, each in its own way, but both bad—the one reckless and the other shifty. Then he said in a slow, ponderous voice as if he was giving judgment on the bench: "I desire it should be distinctly understood—distinctly understood—that I would not give Miss Drummond a brass farthing if she married. What I shall do for her if she remains single, and continues to act as she has done towards Mrs. Hamley and myself, is another matter. But the man who wants to be her husband will have to wait for my death if he wants to step into my shoes; and then I don't say they'll fit. Not during my life will he touch my money, married or single."

"That's explicit," said Colonel Lowe with a sneer.

"Yes, that's explicit if you choose to call it so," echoed Mr. Hamley. "I'll have no fortune-hunters nibbling around me, Colonel; you may take your oath of that."

He said this in such a loud voice that it broke into the conversation which Dr. Wickham was holding with Henry Fletcher respecting one James Garth, a yeoman in difficulties whose land Mr. Hamley was wanting.

"Who talks of fortune-hunters?" said Dr. Fletcher lazily. "Are there any in Milltown?"

"Perhaps you are one yourself, and can answer your own question," said Colonel Lowe. "Who knows? you may be Hamley's standing bête noire, Fletcher. We all know you admire Miss Drummond."

"She is very pretty, and one likes the young creatures one has seen grow up," said Dr. Fletcher.

"Now Fletcher, for heaven's sake don't *you* interfere! I hate to hear the ladies of one's own neighbourhood discussed in public as if they were so many servant-girls," cried Sydney fiercely. "It is such vilely bad form, I cannot understand how any gentleman can allow it!"

"I agree with you. It is bad taste, and not my way generally," answered Dr. Fletcher in the manner of an apology.

"I am much indebted to Mr. Sydney Lowe for his consideration," sneered Mr. Hamley. "But some affairs are best discussed in public when the time is ripe, that there may be no doubt remaining in the neighbourhood. And that Miss Drummond will have no fortune if she marries during Mrs. Hamley's life-time, with Mrs. Hamley needing of her daily, cannot be known too far and wide."

"Let us trust that the fowls of the air, not to say the beasts of the field, will carry the secret to all whom it may concern. Fletcher, Wickham, both of you—do you hear?—you are not to make love to Miss Drummond. She is *la fée défendue* of Abbey Holme, and Mr. Hamley's motto is ' canis in præsepi.' "

Colonel Lowe said this in a loud voice, with perfect breeding as to accent, inflection, gesture ; but his smile and his eyes were not pleasant to look at, and Dr. Wickham, bending his head, said in a half-whisper to Henry Fletcher, "Mephistopheles, by Jove!"

Sydney was white with rage. He looked first at his father and then at Mr. Hamley, and seemed only with the strongest effort to prevent an outburst. No higher motive of restraint than "at his own table" prevented him. Still, we may be thankful for any curbs at mad moments; and that Sydney Lowe was prevented from striking his father and flying at the throat of his guest by a mere consideration of conventional politeness was so much to the good of general morality. When we cannot have gold we must be content with brass; and paste answers the same purpose as diamonds, except for analysis.

"I don't know what you mean with your foreign tongues," said the rich brewer tossing off his wine and smacking his lips after it. "I never had much schooling in my days; and all I know about mottoes is that, when I married Mrs. Hamley and set up my carriage and a livery, I took for mine 'Victrix fortunæ sapientia,' which they tell me means 'Wisdom conquers fortune.' And so I say, and so "—with a roll of aggressive self-satisfaction in his voice and manner—"I have always found it."

"It is a motto that holds good for two," said Sydney insolently.

"No doubt, no doubt," returned Mr. Hamley, sticking his thumb into his arm-hole as was his favourite gesture, and playing noisily with his fingers on his chest, while with his elbow on the table and leaning back in his chair he helped himself again to wine. "But when you can catch a weasel asleep, Mr. Sydney, you have done the trick—hey? When Greeks meet then comes the tug of war. Doesn't somebody say that? I believe it's in a book."

"Very true," said Colonel Lowe gravely; "but we are not Greeks at Milltown," with a sly look to his son. "Gentlemen "—looking round the table—"you seem to be taking no wine. No! shall we then join the ladies?"

"And apologise to Miss Drummond for having committed the unpardonable offence of making her the subject of our discussions," said Sydney with a dark look.

"Right," echoed Dr. Fletcher.

"Save your breath to cool your porridge, gentlemen," said Mr. Hamley with undisguised insolence. "Miss Drummond has need of no man's protection where I am!"

"You should have fulfilled your functions better just now," sneered Sydney; and Mr. Hamley, not to be outdone, turned his head just as he was leaving the room, and said, "Pass that on to the Colonel," as he swaggered through the hall.

In the drawing-room, because he was a little flushed with wine and a great deal excited by wrath, Sydney paid Dora the most marked attention, and seemed disposed to set everything at defiance—his father, Mr. Hamley, the opinion of the world, and possibilities. It was by no means his best policy; but he was too angry to be politic. Besides, he had by nature a large share of that kind of feminine unreasonableness which cares more for the indulgence of its momentary spite than the furtherance of its views by self-control; and if he could strike to-day he did not look forward to being struck in return to-morrow. And because Colonel Lowe, too, was given up for the time to one of his haunting demons, and because he wanted to annoy Mr. Hamley and to punish him for his insolence in daring to hold his own against a gentleman's desire, he paid Dora as much attention in his way as did his son; and both together bewildered and somewhat disturbed that young lady, though they enchanted her too. Or rather, they would have enchanted her had she been left in peace. But Mr. Hamley had no intention of leaving her in peace. He drew a chair close to hers, and no stratagems nor inducements could tempt him to leave it. He mounted guard over her by his looks; a black and savage guard; and though he took no active hostile part against the compliments and pretty speeches which Sydney and his father showered like fireworks over her, yet he let them see plainly enough that they were not to his liking, and made her understand that what she accepted now she would have to pay for afterwards.

He spoke to her himself frequently, interrupting the two men rudely, with a fierce and familiar manner of ownership that nearly maddened Sydney—a manner, too, strangely at variance with the artificial and lumbering formalities of his usual company habits.

Dora, who had not the mot d'énigme, was at a loss to understand its true meaning. She did her best to steer clear with her usual clever temporizing; but she failed. For every smile and blush and pretty acceptance of gallant words from father or son Mr. Hamley spoke to her savagely; for every deprecating look to him and sweet-voiced endeavour to join him into the talk, Colonel Lowe laughed disagreeably, or Sydney pressed her foot beneath the chair with a savage pressure which it was

J

wonderful Mr. Hamley did not see. Still, all this turmoil
excited her vanity, and pleased it. To see herself the battle-
ground, as it were, of these three men, was charming to her;
and she felt quite like a little Queen of Beauty sitting on the
dais and watching the tilters in the field below. She had never
come out so prominently before; and the other ladies of the
party looked on, and either wondered what it betokened, or resented the fuss being made with her, according to their own
pretensions and private moods. As for poor Mrs. Lowe the
whole thing was a mystery from beginning to end; and she
had but one intelligible thought connected with it, that the
Colonel was more than ordinarily disagreeable, and that she
wished he would not lead Syd into mischief.

CHAPTER XIV.

PAYING THE BILL.

AT last the evening which seemed interminable to more than one, for the dinner had not been a success, came to an end, and the guests melted away as they do, whether they melt by degrees or with a rush. "Sic transit" was Dora's plaintive sentiment as she wrapped herself in her ermines and managed to make herself look even prettier than ever, though she put her unspoken lament into more homely language. Now, too, that the excitement was over, she was beginning to fear the consequences. It was the bad quarter of an hour when the bill was to be presented. To be sure, Mr. Hamley had always been good and kind to her, but that was because she had always been meek and obedient to him. She was a wise little girl in her generation, and knew that more than half the love given to us is because we please, not because we are worthy. And she was perfectly aware of the fact that her tenure at Abbey Holme, even now at this day, depended solely on the amount of use and pleasure of which she could be to her employers. For were they not her employers? she used to ask herself with cynical disdain of the sham she made it her life's business to practise. There were times when even she, Dora Drummond, took the truth in her hand and confessed it.

She knew now the task lying before her; and thrusting back into her heart all her gratified pride, and all the sweeter hope which this strange evening had aroused in her, bent to her yoke with easy grace habitual to her, and prepared to quench the fire and still the storm.

For her initial apology she looked up into her cousin's face and smiled tenderly as innocent of all offence, so soon as they were shut up in the carriage alone. He met her flattering little look with a close mouth and hard eyes. He was grim and angry.

"I hope you enjoyed your evening?" he said abruptly, after they had been silent for some time.

"Yes, I did," she answered pleasantly. "Did you?"

"Not at all." He spoke with savage decision. "I never enjoyed myself less."

"I am so sorry, dear!" said Dora sympathetically. She seldom called Mr. Hamley dear, and only when they were alone. She had her reasons for keeping on distant personal terms with him, and it was a sign that she had to put out all her strength when her address became affectionate.

"Humph! you did not look like being sorry for anything, I think," said Mr. Hamley, frowning.

"I did not see you were uncomfortable, else I should have been very unhappy," she answered.

"No! you saw nothing but that puppy young Lowe, and his beast of a father," thundered Mr. Hamley. "Because they made a fuss with you I suppose you got your head turned. But don't mistake them or me, Dora. I told them down stairs, as plain as a pikestaff, that I would not give you a brass farthing if you married—not a brass farthing! And so I flung their dirty fortune-hunting manœuvres down their throats, and I wish it had choked them. And I drunk their wine when I said it. If _I_ have taken you up and made a lady of you, that says nothing for nobody else; and by the Lord, if they count on that, they will find they have reckoned without their host."

"I don't suppose they have counted on anything connected with poor little me at all," said Dora quietly, sliding her hand into his. "You are vexing yourself for nothing, dear. No one wants to marry me with fortune or without, such a silly little thing as I am."

"And if they did, Dora, what then? Would you go?" he asked, his manner still savage if a shade less brutal.

She laughed lightly. "Not unless you wanted to get rid of me," she answered, looking up at him prettily.

"Will you promise to wait till then?" said Mr. Hamley, seizing her arm with a rude gripe. "Promise me that, Dora, and I'll defy them all, and the devil at their head!"

"Yes," Dora answered, raising her eyes with that shy yet candid look which she knew always scored honours in her favour.

" Then you will never go," said Mr. Hamley in a softer tone.

" I am very happy as I am," lisped dear Dora, choking back her tears and pressing his hand caressingly with her little rosebud-like fingers, while saying to herself: " Oh, how I loathe you—how I-wish you were struck dead to-night !" when he, taking up his grand manner—lordly, patronizing, condescending, yet not unkindly—as if afraid to commit himself to further sentiment, answered majestically, "You ought to be. I have done my best to treat you as the lady, and if you weren't happy with all I've done for you, you'd be more ungrateful than I'd like to think ! "

" And I am not ungrateful," returned Dora.

" I don't believe you are ; and we'll prove it some day to those two hounds yonder," said Mr. Hamley, as they drove up to the door, where he assisted her to dismount, as his phraseology went, and, offering his arm, walked with her in state to the drawing-room.

"How late you are !" was Mrs. Hamley's greeting, made sourly.

" How pretty you look, Dora !—like Catskins in the fairy tale !" was Patricia's.

She and her aunt were in the dimly-lighted drawing-room, both silent and both weary. If the evening had been long to the guests at Cragfoot, it had been longer to the ill-assorted inmates of Abbey Holme. Patricia had done her best to make things go smoothly, by which, of course, it came about that she had made them all go roughly. She had loyally set out by trying to please her aunt ; which was the sure way to displease her ; especially when she was inclined to find her path in life more than usually crooked, as it was to night, because Dora and Mr. Hamley had left her to herself and her niece ; and Mrs. Hamley had felt bound to improve the occasion, and give unpleasant if useful lessons on humility and obedience, which had pained the poor girl, who could not see where they applied to her, nor therefore why they were bestowed. So that at last, after several abortive efforts on Patricia's part to find the clue that could guide her out of the maze of mistakes in which she was wandering, there had settled down between them a dull, sad silence which Mrs. Hamley resented as an additional offence, yet would not break on her own side nor allow Patricia to break on hers.

The fact was, the mistress of Abbey Holme wanted to be amused in her own way and as dear Dora would have amused her. The woman who would not suffer that the best of the men and women she knew should hold doubts where she had certainties, or walk to the right when she chose the left, was not likely to submit to the independent action of a girl like Patricia; even though that independent action was for her benefit. Why did she ask her if she would play backgammon, and not wait until she herself had proposed it? It was not her place to propose backgammon or anything else. What she ought to have done was, to hold herself in readiness to play if she was invited, and then, when duly bidden, to bring the board from the what-not where it stood, set it square on the little velvet table, arrange the lamp to the proper focus, and do all this quietly, without strewing sticks and straws about the room. And if she was snubbed for clumsiness or noise, as it was almost impossible she should not have been, she ought not to have taken any notice save by silence and increased docility. "She was such an unmanageable young person," Aunt Hamley had been thinking all the evening with cumulative bitterness.

No wonder, then, that she said sourly when her husband and Dora came in: "How late you are!" her tone and manner telling the sense of injury under which she was labouring.

"Why, yes, we are late," said Dora, looking at the clock on the chimney-piece, which had stopped, and speaking with her deprecating, soothing smile.

"You must have been singularly well amused," sneered Mrs. Hamley.

"Quite the other way, Lady, we have been particularly badly entertained," said Mr. Hamley.

"You would have done better to have taken my advice and have stopped at home," she replied with a grim laugh. It comforted her to think that they had been bored as well as herself. "We have had the most stupid evening, Patricia and I—have we not, Patricia?"

"Rather," said Patricia frankly. "We have not got on very well together."

"There, I told you so," cried Mrs. Hamley with a look that would have made Dora quake had it been given to her. "You are candour itself, my dear!"

"Oh! it is always better to tell the truth," said unsuspecting Patricia.

Dora gave her one glance, and Mrs. Hamley another. Mr. Hamley rubbed his hands softly and smiled.

"I cannot say I am sorry for you," continued Mrs. Hamley, turning to Dora. "You see all you have got for your greediness for pleasure, you two, is to have spent a stupid evening yourselves and to have given me a worse."

"But you know you always prophesy rightly, dear," said Dora, sitting down by the fire and close to Mrs. Hamley, with the look of one who has something to say.

She was longing to go up-stairs to be alone that she might think over it all, and try to understand her position; but she knew what was expected of her, as well as she knew the terms of her holding; and has it not been said that she was wise in her generation?

"That's right, Dora; I am moped to death. Now tell me all about it," said Mrs. Hamley a little briskly.

"She'll not have much to tell," growled Mr. Hamley between his teeth.

"Well, I'll do what I can," Dora answered with her pleasant facile sweetness; and then began an account of the dinner, and Mrs. Lowe's cold, and Mrs. Borrodaile's hideous crimson gown, and Miss Fletcher's familiar manners to the lady's maid, and Dr. Fletcher's absence of mind and how he had taken salt for sugar and mustard with his mutton, and Dr. Wickham's round eyes, and Mr. Collinson's dyed moustache, and what this one said and that one did; till the grim visages waxed smooth and jocund, and more than once the two wrathful authorities fairly laughed.

In the midst of it all Patricia took her candle and bade them abruptly good night. She was pale and looked distressed. She could not bear to listen to Dora's ridicule. To have just accepted hospitality, and then to come home and laugh at those who had given it—to wear one face at Cragfoot and another at Abbey Holme—Patricia's honest soul rebelled at the hypocrisy there, the ingratitude here. And so, unwilling to blame and equally unwilling to be false to her own sense of right, she took the (as it seemed to her) cowardly part of flight rather than of protest; and, escaping to the solitude of her own

room, gave her aunt an opportunity of being Shahrazád in her
turn, and of telling them of all that " odd girl's" misdemeanours ; whereat the three condemned and condoled in concert.

Safe in the solitude of her own room, Patricia wearied herself
again, as so often before, with her one standing difficulty.   Between the two opposing duties of testifying according to the
truth that was in her, or silence in the presence of her superiors
whom her testifying only annoyed and did not reform, which
was she to follow ?   Ah ! others beside Patricia Kemball have
ere now stood at the cross roads, and not known which way
to take when virtues were divergent and duties incompatible !
If we could all have our infallible direction ever plain before us
we would all do what is right ; for it is by ignorance, not wil-
fulness, that we mostly fail ; and even when we have gone into
the deepest waters, and are at our worst, we have drifted into
the breakers by mischance rather than made intentional ship-
wreck.

But this was a step as yet beyond Patricia.   To her, life was
still in the stage of the absolutes, and a thing was right or
wrong—clearly, crudely—without softening shade or modifying
circumstance.   She knew nothing of those delicate little dove-
tails by which vice can be fitted into the mosaic-work of virtues,
and proved by reasoners and economists to be the very thing
that was wanted ; nothing of the pigeon's neck quality of circumstance through which lies are made more beautiful than
truth, and to bow the knee to Baal a holier deed than to confess for Israel.

So she sat and wearied herself, while Dora, with her white
satin boots shining on the crimson fire-stool, and her white silk
dress shining on the crimson firelight, played with her pearls,
and racked her brains and invention as she lounged in the prie-
dieu down-stairs ; amusing Mr. and Mrs. Hamley with her
playful sarcasms and dramatic cleverness, until she brought
them both from gloom to cheerfulness, not to say radiance.
By which she prevented an attack of ill-temper that would
have been felt in the remotest recesses of the house and by the
humblest member of the household for many days, and thus
contributed just so much to the general stock of morality and
happiness.

After this she went up-stairs, and only Alice Garth, her

maid, saw how she collapsed as soon as the door was shut between her and the house to which she acted.

" I tell you I did right ? " was her defence and answer when Patricia expostulated with her the next day.   " I did no one any harm, and I stopped a week's misery to everybody ; and what is that but good work, I should like to know ? "

" Not good work if you hurt your own soul," said Patricia.

" Soul !—hurt my own soul ?—what nonsense," Dora cried scornfully.   " My opinion is, Patricia, that nothing is so selfish, nothing so cruel, as that thing you choose to call sincerity.   I am sure if I was always thinking of my dirty little soul as you are of yours, I should go mad—certainly I should never expect to do a decently civil, not to talk of politic, thing again. Don't talk to me of truth and honesty !—I am sick of the very words. Talk rather of selfishness and cowardice and obstinancy ; confess these when you refuse to help in setting things straight or keeping them smooth, and then I will believe you."

" I do not think I am selfish for trying to be true to my own sense of right, or cowardly for refusing to tell falsehoods," said Patricia.

But Dora said, " You are, Patricia," so decidedly and so crossly that the girl gave up the point : shaking her head in deprecation, but keeping silence, not caring to justify herself afresh in Dora's present belligerent mood.

To uphold the right and to be condemned therefore, while those who do no wrong are rewarded, was a sorrow and perplexity not peculiar to Patricia's experience. Has life ever given aught else but condemnation to those who maintain a standard of truth and inner nobleness higher than the popular measure in use about them ? Aristides has not been the only man ostracised simply because he was just ; nor Socrates the only sage who has had to be effaced because he taught a virtue greater than his time. Patricia in her small way was simply repeating the experience of such as these ; and there are many living Patricias at this moment learning the same hard lesson by heart, and bearing the same heavy burden on their hands.

CHAPTER XV.

DEMETER.

THERE is a time in the history of most of us, while young, when the mind takes a sudden awakening and we enter into a new order of thought. We cannot always say how or why this has come about ; but sometimes we do know the precise moment when our eyes first opened to the higher truths, and can state how it was that the current of our inner life was changed. We can single out the one from whom we received the ineffaceable impress, and give the pattern of the altar from which we took the living fire that kindled our own. Up to that moment we had been waiting or wandering ; after then we knew where our Mecca stood, and set our faces toward it.

Such a moment was coming for Patricia. While her uncle lived she had had no need of extra direction. She had led, as has been said more than once before, that healthy and un-reflecting kind of existence wherein youth grows strongest and loveliest, but wherein is no conscious mental development because no spiritual struggle. She had never known the doubt of conflicting duties, nor suffered the anguish of moral uncertainty; the law under which she had lived had been simple and absolute, and no subtle Advocatus Diaboli, skilled in compound ethics, had held a brief at Barsands.

But now at Abbey Holme everything was changed, and her moral standards were fluctuating with the rest. The old and the new had come into collision, and her soul was yearning for an authority outside itself which should settle her difficulties and help her to fashion her life anew ; an authority that should show her how to order herself in accord with her present conditions, and yet live nobly after the teaching of her uncle.

If her mind was out of tune, her outward existence was no more harmonious with her real self. Her personal freedom denied threw her time on her hands ; and, though she was too

strong-minded to **allow** herself **to** mope, and too healthy **to fall**
ill even at the unwonted seclusion, the unnatural inaction of
her life, both spirits and health were **sorely tried. The time**
thus flung on her hands hung there so **heavily! She could not**
filter it, hour by hour, in the essentially mindless and frivolous
work which filled up Dora's and **Mrs. Hamley's days so plea-**
santly if less than profitably. Indeed her fingers, rough and
hard even yet with the ropes and **tar of the** *Mermaid,* could not
conquer those mysterious ins and outs of shuttles and needles
which occupied them as gravely **as if the results were of real**
importance. **And she** neither **admired nor coveted those**
results when attained. Neither was she an artist by education,
whatever she might be by nature. She had no available knowledge of music; **and the** utmost she could do in the way of
what Mr. Hamley **called** performing on the piano, was to
scramble over a simple accompaniment while she sang her
ballad songs in her sweet and fresh young voice, as untrained
as a Swiss peasant's. Her drawings were a mere school-girl's
carefully measured copies of prints and the like, of no technical
worth whatsoever, and even favouritism, which was not accorded
to her, could not have found them beautiful. And thus it came
to pass that Mrs. Hamley had some show of reason in her frequent rebukes administered for idleness—to Patricia, who had
so lately been the very embodiment of activity. And when she
complained that this uncomfortable niece of hers was always
either doing what she ought not, or. doing nothing at all, she
was justified by the outsides of things if scarcely by inner
realities.

However, as Patricia had sense enough to see that she was
very far below the right mark, taking Dora as her standard,
she wished to raise herself up to that mark ; and, as she had
brains, she desired to use them. She wanted to learn something ; she was very vague as to what; now that she had time.
She wanted to make herself as charming and cultured as Dora
—that pretty piece of stamped pewter polished to look like
sterling silver ; that Hamley model of feminine perfection, held
up to her at all times and in all ways as the one to copy and to
endeavour to approach as near as might be. So she began to
read with the floundering desultoriness of the eager and the
untaught ; and Mrs. Hamley found more fault than before.

To be sure, Mosheim's "Ecclesiastical History," for example, which was one of the tough pieces of literature the girl undertook of her own motion, was not exactly the best beginning she could have made. It was creditable, but, as Aunt Hamley said, she might have started with something less ponderous and more serviceable for general conversation; something that would help her to bear her part in society rather more effectively than at present—Tennyson, now, or Longfellow, or even Froude or Macaulay, or anything whatsoever that other people knew or were likely to talk of; but Mosheim's "Ecclesiastical History"—who ever heard of a girl in her teens attacking such a monstrous bit of literature as that! "It was scarcely feminine," said Mrs. Hamley severely; and she was not quite sure that it was altogether proper.

Poor, uneasy, cross-cornered soul! it was not given to her to applaud any one's independent action; least of all Patricia's; and if one stanza chanced to be cut off her Ballad of Burdens another was immediately added, so that the tale of them never lessened.

Had Patricia gone to her for help and advice in her new pursuits, everything would have been smooth. She would have accepted her confession of ignorance and request for instruction as so much tribute to her own superior attainments; for Mrs. Hamley prided herself on her knowledge and her mind; she would have been very careful with her, very pedantic, very hard to please, very thorough; but she would have been gratified. She would have put her to the elements like a little child—probably have given her a page of spelling and a sum in simple addition; but she would have liked the child's docility—for Patricia was docile though also independent; her love of managing would have been gratified; and she would have seen some of the best points of the girl's character, while some of the worst of her own would have been appeased. A real affection might have sprung up between them over Murray and Hume; and "Auntie, what is the meaning of this?"—"Auntie, please explain this to me," would have been a continually recurring homage paid to her superiority which would have soothed and flattered her

But she had checked Patricia too often to make it possible for such a proposition to come from her. Lacking the power

of insight into petty humours, taking all things seriously, and
too honest for tact or management, the girl had accepted her
aunt's moods as permanent dispositions, and had taken to
heart the need of effacing herself, as Dora had said. Not in
Dora's way of self-effacement, only to make herself the better
mirror, the exacter shadow, but by absolute withdrawal from
sight and sound; so that day by day saw her more in her own
room up-stairs, and more silent when with the family. And
both these habits annoyed Mrs. Hamley "beyond expression."
As she said bitterly to Dora half-a-dozen times a day, that girl
would kill her before she had done with her !

To which Dora always answered dutifully: "Dear ! I am
so sorry for you ! She *is* trying ! "

Thus Patricia began her task of self-education unguided;
and, as may be imagined, she did not make much headway,
but stumbled about among the " hard books " of the library—
chiefly dry old history—very much as the men stumbled about
the tombs at the foot of the Delectable Mountains.

One day she was in the grounds by herself. It was about a
week after the Lowe's dinner party, and Dora was at home.
She had caught a little cold on that famous night, and Mr.
Hamley had insisted on her keeping the house. He did not
wish to see her in the enjoyment of bad health all her life, he
had said ; and the sooner she commenced to take care of herself the sooner she would be recovered.

So dear Dora had nothing for it but to smile sweetly and say
she would do as he liked, all the while knowing that nothing
was the matter with her, that Sydney was expecting to hear
from her, and that a letter from him was in her pocket waiting
a safe Mercury. Presently, while Patricia was standing on a
little eminence in the avenue, facing the strong north-west
wind with a kind of rapturous delight, as if it was an old friend
with whom was connected the glad life of the dear past, Dr.
and Miss Fletcher passed through the lodge-gates, she coming
expressly to see the new girl of whom her brother had reported
so pleasantly.

In person they made a decided contrast, and yet they were
alike, with that kind of family likeness which depends more
on harmony of expression than on similarity of feature or
colour. He was tall, angular, serious, lean ; with grizzled

hair and leathery-brown cheeks ; a man who looked as if he
might have been a monk in one set of circumstances, or an
Arab chief in another.   She was tall, too, but stout, smiling,
rather short-breathed, and of a generous kind of beauty that
had almost an Italian expression in it.   For though she was
past forty, she was handsome even now, and was of the kind
to be handsome to the end.   People wondered how it was that
Catherine Fletcher had never married ; but mothers wondered
more how it was that not having married she should understand children and young people as she did, and have such an
accurate sense of their needs.   They said she was like a mother
herself, and asked each other, with amazement, how had she
come by it ?   For there is no error more popular than the belief that motherhood of itself gives natural insight, save that
other—that the maternal instinct is universal.

   Miss Fletcher was one of those women who are consecrated
by nature to marriage and maternity ; and yet her spinsterhood
was a greater gain to the world than her marriage would have
been.   Had she been a wife she would have made one man
happy, and she would have been the wise and loving mother
of probably many children.   But she would have concentrated
within the four walls of home the energy and intelligence which
now found their larger service in humanity.   As it was she
was the helper of all who needed ; a kind of modern Demeter,
with her hands full of gifts and her lap full of babies, offering
the grace of her womanhood and the power of her love to the
poor and the weak, the lonely and the loveless ; a democrat
because noble, and pitiful because strong.   Her whole being
was penetrated through and through with sympathy.   Not
sympathy of that vague and graceful kind which speaks tenderly of suffering, even sheds tears when it hears of woes and
wants, then passes on to its own individual happiness undisturbed ; but sympathy which includes active help at the cost
of personal sacrifice, sympathy which means patience with
folly, patience with ignorance, with prejudice, with selfishness, with impatience even—the hardest effort of all !—sympathy which cares for the real good of the person concerned,
and not for self-expression ; and so gets less credit than if it
contented itself with talking sweetly of Christian charity,
weeping for hypothetical woes, growing indignant at the in-

justice of society and sorrowful at the misfortunes of men ; and in the end saving itself all further trouble by a clever delegation of work and a small money subscription.

"Good morning, Miss Kemball ; my sister has come to see you," said Dr. Fletcher, shaking hands with Patricia ; and "Good morning, I am glad to see you," added Miss Fletcher with her kindly smile and warm grasp.

Patricia's face brightened. The fresh wind had given her back her strong free look, and the young have instincts of strange accuracy. The same expression came into her eyes as used to be there in old days, when her uncle spoke to her. Something in the voice, the hand-press, the face of her new acquaintance struck a chord that vibrated to her heart ; and a light seemed to have suddenly burst forth that turned the grey day into gold.

Her ready responsiveness made the elder woman smile. She liked this bright, tall, handsome girl with her frank eyes and unconventional address. She was human and not spoilt, she thought. Her brother had prepared her for a "candid, untutored kind of young person, very transparent and unaffected, but apparently as wild as a hawk ;" but she had not expected to see anything so beautiful in person or so innocently affectionate in manner. She had moreover her own reasons lying in the far past for a natural readiness to like the daughter of Reginald Kemball ; and as they walked up the avenue together, she improvised an invitation for the two girls for that day, wishing to see more of Patricia than she could see in a visit, and thinking that, as her life at Abbey Holme could not possibly be congenial to her, perhaps she might be of use and help to make it pleasanter.

"Perhaps she might be of use."

This was the law by which Catherine Fletcher lived. This queenly kind of woman, this Demeter of modern life, held herself as just the servant of her race, no more, and found in that servanthood her happiness and her honour.

"Yes, I shall be very glad indeed," said Patricia, " if," with a certain hesitancy, "Aunt will let me go. I do not think Dora can come ; she has a cold, poor girl ; so," very sorrowfully, far more sorrowfully than the occasion seemed to warrant, " perhaps Aunt will not let me go alone."

Miss Fletcher looked at her kindly. She felt all the tyranny and want of liberty included in this probable prohibition to a girl of Patricia's independent look and bearing. And Miss Fletcher disliked tyranny. That was why she had never liked Mrs. Hamley. Much older than herself, she had always remembered her as a tyrant; and she knew that age and prosperity had not widened her borders.

"I hope she will let you go with me," she said.

"I hope so too," Patricia answered gravely. "I should like to go with you."

"We will manage it then; don't be afraid," said Miss Fletcher.

And Patricia found trust in this pleasant-visaged, soft-voiced woman come marvellously easy. She felt as if she had known her a long time ago, and was only taking up an old love not beginning a new one. She kept wondering to herself "of whom she reminded her;" but she could give no answer, simply because she reminded her of no one, she only wakened up again a former cherished feeling.

"You are very kind Catherine, I am sure," said Mrs. Hamley stiffly, when Miss Fletcher proffered her request to take the two girls back to the Hollies, "I am afraid I must say no; thank you. Miss Drummond is not well enough to leave the house—Dora my dear, had you not better move over here to the other side of the fireplace?—you are just in a line with the door where you are. There is nothing so bad as a draught."

And Dora, who was already stifling under the shawls and flannels in which Mrs. Hamley had wrapped her, and who had only the most insignificant little head cold imaginable, pulled her Shetland shawl daintily over her chest, and carried herself and her workbox into the draughtless corner; making herself supremely uncomfortable with the gentle grace and submissive tact that characterised her.

"I am very sorry for poor Dora, but your niece? she has no cold, cannot she come?" said Miss Fletcher.

Mrs. Hamley turned to Patricia. Luckily for herself she was looking down. Had she raised her eyes and appealed with them, as she might easily have done, her aunt would naturally, not with intentional ill-nature, but by the mere cross-cornered law of her being, have found some good reason why not; but

as she kept her tell-tale looks to herself, partly for the relief of
getting rid of her, and partly because she thought she ought to
find pleasure in the society of two elderly people of grave pursuits, albeit tainted with strange heresies—though probably
she would be bored to death, when she would appreciate home
the more—Mrs. Hamley said yes ; and Patricia's sudden flush
was so vivid that it set Miss Fletcher wondering why.

She was either very dull at Abbey Holme as she had imagined,
and so hailed any diversion with exaggerated pleasure, or sadly
too excitable, she thought. In either case Catherine Fletcher
was glad she had asked her—if the former to make her happy
for an hour or two, if the latter to give her counsel. For being
both maternal and direct, she had more love than respect for
young people, and treated them all with a certain affectionate
familiarity with which they were seldom offended, even when
it included unwelcome counsel and may be rebuke.

"Shall you pass Martin's ?" asked Dora, with her lisp rather
strongly marked. Martin was the draper whom all right-
minded Milltownians patronized.

"Certainly if we can do anything for you. It will not take
us five minutes out of our way," Miss Fletcher answered.

"I am so much obliged to you. I do want some ribbon very
much !" said Dora. "I will not trouble you, dear Miss Fletcher ;
Patricia will do it for me ; won't you, dear ?"

"Of course, with real pleasure ; if I can serve you, anything,
darling !" was Patricia's hearty answer, all the louder and
heartier because she was glad to go with the Fletchers.

"What a dreadful fuss she makes about everything ; and
how she emphasizes the most trifling action !" thought Mrs.
Hamley. "As if there was any necessity for making a profession of faith about a yard of ribbon—answering Dora as if she
was her lover !"

"Will you come up-stairs with me, and I will give you the
pattern !" asked Dora.

"My dear, throw the shawl over your head, and cover your
mouth. I don't like your running about the passages," said
Mrs. Hamley. And Dora, with a shy glance of gratitude,
smiled as she said, "The house is very warm, dear," and
obeyed.

The girls left the room ; and when they were well out of

K

hearing Dora, flinging the shawl off her head, said with a quick little sob—

"How absurd it is of them to keep me mewed up in the house like this ! There is nothing the matter with me ; and I wish I was going with you ! I am sick to death of this dull drawing-room, and that detestable lace-work and eternal bézique !"

To Mr. and Mrs. Hamley themselves she said that evening when they were playing—he scoring a sequence, Mrs. Hamley holding double bézique, and she herself left to the excitement of three queens she could neither marry nor join to a fourth— "How much I enjoy our dear little evenings ! They are so quiet and pleasant ; and I am so fond of bézique !"

Then said Patricia, " Why don't you say you are not ill, Dora, if you are not ? I would not be kept in the house like this if I were you. You have only got to tell the truth, and say you are all right."

"You know nothing about it, Patricia," Dora answered irritably. " When Mr. and Mrs. Hamley say you are ill, you are ill ; and nothing but a doctor from London would convince them that you are well. And perhaps he would not. As if I did not know them !"

" Then Dora if you choose to give way to them like this, you should not complain. There is no good in rowing one way and looking another," said Patricia gravely.

"Don't talk nonsense !" returned Dora crossly. I know how I ought to act, and I don't want your advice."

"I did not mean to vex you, dear," said Patricia lovingly. I only do not like to see you annoyed ; and oh, Dora ! I cannot bear to see you so dreadfully afraid of Aunt and Mr. Hamley !"

" Better be afraid than bullied," said Dora, a little sulkily. "One must be one or the other here. I take the former, and you prefer the latter ; and I don't envy you any more than you envy me. So we need not talk any more about it."

After Dora had found a bit of ribbon for which she desired a match—and, considering that she wanted it so much, it was odd what a long time it took to turn up—she put her hand into her pocket, and, looking at herself in the glass to see if the powder showed too much about her eyebrows, said quite carelessly ; " Martin's is close to the post-office ; will you post this letter for me, dear ?"

" Has the post-bag gone? asked Patricia suspecting nothing, but astonished ; for the bag never went till six o'clock and it was only three now.

" I suppose not; but I don't wish it to go in the bag," Dora answered, still brushing off the superfluous powder.

" No ? Why not ? " was her quick word ; and then she stopped and looked at Dora distressed.

" Because I do not want any one to see it," Dora answered. " Now Patricia," turning round from the glass, " do not ask questions. You are my friend, and I trust you. Put that letter in the post for me. Do not look at the envelope, and do not let any one see it. See how I rely on you ! " she added with a good imitation of pathos, as she held the girl's hand, into which she had slipped the letter, and looked up with her pretty blue eyes, tenderly, beseechingly.

" I would do anything in the world for you, Dora—you know I would," said poor Patricia with the old conflict in her heart. " But oh, my dear, my dear, how I hate all this manœuvring and secrecy ! Oh, Dora, how I wish you had not a secret in the world ! "

" Some day I will tell you what I have, and then you will pity me," said Dora plaintively. " Now I cannot ; yet you must help me—blindly."

" It breaks my heart," began Patricia.

" It need not do that," interrupted Dora with the faintest little sarcasm in her voice; " that would be a pity ; for the posting of a letter for a friend without telling any one about it is scarcely worth the fracture of such a heart as yours. Now don't be a goose, darling," she said, changing her manner to a caressing banter that was infinitely becoming, and which was one of her weapons of conquest over Patricia. " There is nothing so dreadful in posting a letter, and it is only the tremendous "—she was going to say tyranny, but, having recovered from her momentary attack of discontented candour, she stopped herself and substituted " care—which Mr. and Mrs. Hamley, dear people, think it right to take of me that obliges me to do things secretly."

" But I would not be obliged, Dora," said Patricia returning to her old charge. " I would either obey them loyally or defy them openly. I would not condescend, if I were you, to all this underhand work. I would have more courage, more self-respect!"

"All very well, Miss Patricia, but we shall see you with your little plots and plans before we have done with you."

"Never, Dora! never while I live!"

Dora smiled. "And your letter from Miss Biggs?"

"Ah! that is cruel, Dora!" She turned away.

"Well, it does sound ungrateful, does it not? But all I meant to show, dear, was that if I had secrets for one reason you could be brought to have them for another. Say that it was to please me and not to get any good for yourself, still it was a secret all the same; was it not?"

"Yes; and I must have no more," said Patricia.

"Oh! that is not at all the right view to take," laughed Dora. "You have to put this letter in the post for me."

No, Dora." She laid it on the table with the directed side underneath.

"Yes, Patricia, if I ask you," said Dora in the most caressing, the most enchanting way.

She shook her head.

"Now look here, Patricia," said Dora, speaking in a quiet argumentative way, not usual to her. "I just want to show you a little of yourself to yourself. When I first asked you to do this for me, you hesitated; when I pressed you, you consented; when I hurt your pride, you refused. I like consistency, I must say!"

"It was not because you hurt my pride, Dora."

Dora shrugged her shoulders. "Prove it then!"

"No; it is because I hate having to do with secrets. They degrade one's very soul."

"Yes, that is just what I say; your own soul, always your own miserable little soul, and your poor friend's soul and body both may go to destruction for what you care! You say you love me, and I have tried my very best to make your life here happy, and to stand between you and Mrs. Hamley; and yet you are not brave or unselfish enough to do such a little thing for me as post a letter without proclaiming it on the housetop!" She turned away petulantly and began to cry.

The strong heart went down before her tears.

"Don't cry, Dora," said Patricia taking her in her arms.

"Don't cry, darling, I will do what you asked me—I will do anything you ask me!"

"Post that letter for me?" sobbed Dora with her back turned.

"Yes dear; post that letter for you."

"And not let the Fletchers see it?"

"No; I will put it in myself."

"You are a darling," said Dora, drying her eyes with despatch. "I thought you could not be such a cruel, cold-hearted thing as to make me so unhappy."

"I cannot make you unhappy, Dora," said Patricia fervently; "I love you too much."

Dora stood up on tiptoe and kissed her; but the kiss did not altogether sooth the poor girl. The glory seemed to have gone out of her day somehow, and the cold grey, characteristic of Abbey Holme, to have come back again. Had she been asked she would have rather given up the Fletchers altogether than have undertaken this surreptitious posting; which after all was only a symbol. But things had to go on now as they had begun, and she must carry her sorrowful heart and changed grace to as good a conclusion as might be. So the girls went back into the drawing-room, and Mrs. Hamley scolded them for the long time they had been up-stairs.

When the trio prepared to set out, the lady of Abbey Holme wished them all a stiff farewell, arranging to send for Patricia at half-past nine precisely; and Mrs. Hamley's fractions meant fixed quantities, not floating margins of elastic dimensions.

"I shall expect you home at a quarter to ten," she said with a severe glance at the clock, as if administering the oath of witness. "You must be ready when the carriage calls for you, Patricia, and do not keep the horses waiting this cold weather. It is quite cruel to take them out in such nights!" as if personally injured.

"Shall I walk home, Aunt?" suggested Patricia, ever ready with her remedy.

"Don't be silly," was the rejoinder.

"And do not forget my commission, please," said Dora with her coaxing smile.

"No dear," said Patricia with embarrassment.

And Miss Fletcher, who had the faculty of observation, caught
the difference in her tone as well as in her face, and remembered it.

When they got to the town, Patricia first matched Dora's
ribbon with a maddening exactness as to width and shade—
though the little lady wanted no ribbon at all, save as an excuse
—and then saying, "I must go to the post-office, please," put
her hand into her pocket and looked disturbed.

"Have you a letter to post ?   Give it to Henry ; he will do
it for you," said Miss Fletcher.

"Yes, give it to me," said Dr. Fletcher.

"Thank you. I must post it myself," answered Patricia, her
disturbance deepening.

"I am safe, I assure you.   I will not drop it," he laughed
holding out his hand.

"Thank you very much, but I promised to do it myself," she
answered eagerly ; and then she crimsoned with the sudden
consciousness that in her very honesty she had committed an
indiscretion, and for the sake of more effectual hiding had betrayed more than she ought.

All of which Miss Fletcher noted with those quiet brown
eyes of hers which had the trick of seeing everything without
seeming to notice anything ; casting up one of those sums in
moral arithmetic by which she deduced meanings from actions
—the product generally coming right. She drew the conclusion now that Patricia was being used somehow by Dora ; and
in the course of the walk she spoke with earnestness of the
moral deterioration sure to result from manœuvring and secrecy,
and the obligation laid on us not to mix ourselves up in matters
where we can do no good and might get harm.

"But if we can do good ?" asked Patricia earnestly.

"Then the question would resolve itself into one of 'comparative values,'" said Miss Fletcher. "But it would be only
some most important good for others that could reconcile me
to any line of action which was not essentially candid and
straightforward."

Patricia sighed. Then she looked into her new friend's face,
her own kindling :

"It does me good to hear you speak," she said, sliding her
hand under her arm. "It is like dear uncle speaking through

your voice. May I come to you when I am in doubt what is the right thing to do ?"

"Surely, dear child !" said Catherine warmly. "I can understand that, with all sincerity of liking and respect for your aunt, you do not find it possible always to ask her advice on all subjects."

"No, I do not," she answered. "She is so different from dearest uncle, and I feel so out of place somehow among them. I cannot tell at times what I ought to do, and I have no one to advise me."

"Make me your mother confessor, and perhaps I can help you," said Catherine, pressing her hand kindly against her warm, comfortable side, and Patricia thought to herself, " If I had known my own mother I should have felt for her as I feel for Miss Fletcher."

"I want you to look on this as a kind of outside home, and on us as your unregistered relations," said Catherine. "We have known your family so long that you do not come to us as a stranger, and both Henry and myself are prepared to take you to our hearts. Do you hear ? You are to come to us in your troubles, and give us your confidence and love. We will help you with our advice, child ; and love always does good— both to those who give and those who receive."

She said this just as they reached the Hollies' gate. It was a good omen for the disturbed young soul needing enlightenment and the living warmth of friendly direction as it did.

CHAPTER XVI.

BY PRINCIPLE.

THE Fletchers were people with principles and ideas of which they did not only talk, but by which they lived. It was not enough for them to eat, drink, and be decorously merry; to pay their tithes and taxes as gentlefolks should; to keep to the broad way of elemental morality; to do little acts of charity out of their accumulated balance, by which they sacrificed nothing they desired to possess, but, under the idea that they had, counting off all their possible purchases as so many offerings cast into the treasury of the Lord; but they were people who have taken to themselves the great law of duty, and who had set out to live up to their ideal.

They went to first principles and did not give much weight to expediency. They did not believe that because things are they must therefore be upheld, and they were not afraid of the right even if iconoclastic and subversive. To be sure they knew that it is always troublesome, and at times personally damaging, to maintain the right of God in the face of the wrong of society; but they thought life meant ever trouble in some shape or other, especially in the difficulties which beset endeavour, and they deferred their lotus-eating to another sphere.

The great facts cherished by them were, the honour due to humanity irrespective of social condition, and the duty of the strong to help the weak. Hence their own lives were organised on a plan of almost patriarchal simplicity of manners and habits, and they dedicated more than the prescribed tenth to their poorer brethren. They were laughed at of course, and sometimes more than laughed at; Milltown was not the kind of place where they were likely to find sympathisers; but they took their own way as tranquilly and steadfastly as if society had crowned them with roses not thorns, and right for right's sake was a law good enough for them by which to live.

Yet they were very different each from the other, for all

their sympathy and harmony of views and circumstance. Woman-like, she had the more arbitrary singleness of logic in her feelings, and carried out her views to the ultimate where he discerned an opposing law. She had more passion in her love for those she admired; but then she brought the same warmth of nature into her dislikes. He, a man without much weakness of soul or flesh, was therefore possessed of a certain philosophical pity for frailty of all kinds which never grew to anger save when the question of wrong-doing was one of oppression; and then he was implacable. But as a rule he took things more quietly than she did; striving to get to the roots of a man's action, searching for the physiological causes, the influencing circumstances, where others, and she too at times, condemned only the fact. This made him eminently just. Not the justice which means legality, retributive punishment, and the like; but the ability to see all round a question, and to decide on it according to its root-work and surroundings. Thus no one could count on him as a partisan irrespective of justice; by which it came about that he had the knack of offending all sides in turn because he would not be unfair to any. The popular verdict on this brother and sister was, that he was the more mischievous of the two, and she the more foolish.

They were both hard students and knew many things outside the ordinary grooves of education. The one luxury they allowed themselves in their simply-appointed home was the luxury of books and scientific appliances. They had a first-class microscope and a first-class telescope, which last they had fitted up in a rude but efficient observatory that excited more ridicule than admiration by its cunning contrivances of little cost. The subject too, met with as little sympathy as the method by which it was followed. People said with a sneer they supposed the learned doctor was devising a new system of astronomy which was to upset the Newtonian; and because he busied himself with certain biological experiments, which included boiled flasks, infused hay, and a cloud of moving creatures as the result, they asked him if the old axiom *ex nihilo nihil fit* was all a mistake, and was dead matter God?

All these studies were taken to be a kind of flying in the face of Providence; and when, tempted by the desire to let a little

light in upon those brains which seemed to him to cherish
their darkness too fondly, he suffered himself to mention any
facts bearing on the great scientific questions of the day, the
after-summary was invariably set in the one unchanging key—
the doctor was an infidel, and his conversation was absolutely
impious. Add to this, essentially " radical " political doctrines,
of which the Milltown translation was that he and his sister
were " known to be socialists, red republicans of the deepest
dye, wanting an equal division of property, and desirous of
pulling down king, lords, and commons to the one muddy
level of unwashed ruffianism," and it may be imagined that for
people who valued truth they had sometimes rather a hard
time of it.

Strange to say, with all this they were not entirely approved
of by the class they upheld, and not personally unpopular with
the class they offended. The peasantry and little people in
country places like to feel the gentry far above them. They
do not care to be caught up into the empyrean of an equal
humanity, but enjoy the poetry of their self-abasement in the
belief that their superiors are indeed their betters. They
think that those who treat them with respect lower themselves
to their own level, and would rather their gods came about them,
awful and effulgent, carrying their lightning in their hands
and their crowns above their brows, than as simple men and
women benign and unarmed. They liked the good things
which came to them from the Demeter of the Hollies; and the
women, when in personal trouble of sickness, sorrow or dire
necessity, turned instinctivly to her as possessed of all knowledge and all healing power ; but in daily matters they would
rather not have been made to sit in her presence ; they were
bothered by her advice as to the management of their children ;
her recipes for cooking puzzled them ; and the way in which
she opened windows and doors in cases of fever and the like
seemed to them barbarous and downright heathenish, as well
as murderous.

So too, her insisting on cleanliness and fresh air in her
tenants more than compensated for the low rent at which Miss
Fletcher's cottages were let ; and their undeniable superiority
in wholesomeness was paid for, they thought, by the greater extent of surface there was to keep clean, and the fidfads, called

improvements, which were not wanted and seldom properly managed.

All of which she and her brother knew well enough. But when twitted with the old simile of the pearls and the swine by those who held to class degradation as the righteous ordering of society, and who thought that class ignorance is and should be irremovable in the lower for the greater convenience of the higher, they used to answer quietly : "The less such things as we have grown to consider the first necessities of decent living are appreciated by our poorer brothers, the more pressing our duty of educating them up to that point of appreciation."

But the doctrine did not take.

The Fletchers got the lash on all sides. If a man was too poor to send his children to school and they paid for him, as they were sure to do, his neighbours, just able with hard pinching to pay for theirs, railed at the cunning which knew how to get the length of grand folks' feet for the one part, and at the simpleness which let that length be got at for the other ; while the Milltown gentry, who to a man disliked the scheme of educating the poor, denounced " those Fletcher fools " as playing the very mischief with class usefulness and parental responsibility. If, they said, a man brings children into the world for whom he cannot provide, he must suffer for it through them ; and to assist him by assisting his little ones was to go against the laws of God himself.

When winter came, and with it supplies of food and clothes and firing from the Hollies as surely as the frost and snow, those whose alpha of political economy was that the weaker must go to the wall in the press, and suffer that the strong may be made glad, and whose omega was the sin of charity, declared that the place was becoming revolutionary by his wickedness and pauperized by her folly, and that soon every gentleman would have to make himself a beggar that the beggars might be gentlemen. When they bought up small tenements and lowered the rents, such men as Colonel Lowe, whose tumble-down hovels stood at a rack-rent, said they ought to be prosecuted for interfering with market values ; and when they lent money to small landowners, to prevent the necessity of selling their little farms and fields, Mr. Hamley, who had the land-hunger on him, had been heard to say with an oath that

this tampering with the natural flow of capital and land ought
to be made as actionable as the lowered rents, and that some
day " Yon hound Fletcher would find himself in the wrong
box, and the Lord make it hot for him !"

No Milltown lady would take a servant from the Hollies.
To be sure there were not many opportunities, for the place
was good and sometimes the maids were wise. But sometimes
they were not, and preferred change for the sake of change to
the loving home they had found under Miss Fletcher. And
then their chances in Milltown were but slender. The ladies
said they were spoilt by over-indulgence, and were good for
nothing after they had passed through Miss Fletcher's hands.
Even the labourers who worked for them at odd times had difficulty in finding jobs on the off-days ; employers disliking the
contrast between the wages given at the Hollies and those pre-
cribed by the labour-market, and resenting the surplusage as a
wrong done to themselves who did not choose to give so much.
This too was counted to the Fletchers for unrighteousness ; and
because they were the friends of the poor they were held to be
the enemies of the rich, and condemned as undermining the
rights of capital in proportion as they recognised the rights of
labour.

But haunted by that odd resolve of theirs to do the absolute
right as between man and man, seeing everywhere Humanity
and nowhere social arrangements, they cared for none of the
hard names wherewith they were assailed. When society was
unjust, they stepped in with their reconciling measures, and
they found their reward in the worth of the things they did,
not in the euphony of the verdict with which the world received them. They lived neither for praise nor for thanks, but
for humanity and the right ; but they had to bear their cross
in return, this being just the line to which society is ever most
fiercely inimical.

These then, were Patricia Kemball's new friends, and the as
yet unknown sphere of thought and feeling into which she was
to be introduced.

When the door was opened and they went in, the girl was
struck by the house as different from anything she had ever
seen before. Her old home at Barsands had been bare and
rugged, scrupulously clean, but as plain as the old *Holdfast* it-

self. Abbey Holme was rich with gold and crimson, elaborate ornamentation, large tracts of mirror, huge vases of modern French porcelain, papier-mâché chairs and tables, and a great deal of bright steel, cut glass, and showy pictures. It was filled with size and glitter rather than beauty—a house of first-class upholstery, resplendent in its way, but that way one wherein both art and harmony were made subservient to expense ; and it was singularly unhomelike, and though monotonous destitute of all which gives the sensation of comfort or rest. The Hollies was simple, but strangely quaint and beautiful; for beauty was part of the Fletchers' religion of life : only it was beauty that did not with them necessarily include costliness. The materials were everywhere inexpensive, but the colours were pure and harmonious. The ornaments were few but of good design and workmanship ; books made up much of the wall furniture ; and though it was winter, flowers and growing plants were in pots and hanging baskets about the windows. There was evidently a central idea in the arrangements of the various rooms and passages. Incongruous things were not massed together without regard to epoch, style, intention, as is the rule with most houses ; but each thing seemed to fall naturally in the place where it was put, and if aught had been removed the rest would have been imperfect. And yet, with all this artistic exactness of arrangement, the house had the free possibilities of home-liness and comfort. The tables were for use not show ; and with rooms not half the size of those at Abbey Holme there was more than double the space available.

The effect of the whole was old-fashioned and un-English. This last was due partly to the wooden structural chimney-pieces, built up with shelves and pigeon-holes for bits of old china, where the looking-glass belonging was set deep in the shadow, lightening what else would have been a dark space, but not obtrusive as a universal reflector ; partly to the tiled, square fire-places, and the bold Italian dogs; to the waxed oaken floors, and squares of carpet and loose rugs in place of the conventional Brussels ; to a large amount of dark simply-carved wood in one room, and of plain deal, squared, and painted by Miss Fletcher's own hand, in another ; to lines of quaint blue pottery ; and a general background of flat grey, variously tinted and patterned, against which the bits of rich colour and gold

came out with gorgeous yet subdued strength. It was a house
of so much evident plan and design that a guiding principle of
life seemed the fitting ethical outcome.   •

The manners too, at the Hollies were as different from the
ordinary manners of society as all the rest. When the maid
opened the door—no man was kept save for the garden work
and to do the rougher jobs of the house—Miss Fletcher smiled
to her a friendly greeting, and the girl looked back one as
friendly. She was a pretty young person and nicely dressed,
without the " flag," and lady-like because happy and refined ;
and she gave the impression of having supplemented her servanthood with a fine kind of human affectionateness, and of
having added self-respect to her code of duty. But she was a
girl whom no one in Milltown save Catherine Fletcher would
have taken into service at all ; a mother and no wife, and
drifting fast into ruin when the bountiful Demeter caught her
up in her strong hands and cherished her back to happiness
and virtue.

" My dear," said Miss Fletcher kindly, " when you lay the
table will you set a place for Miss Kemball ? "

The girl looked at the young visitor pleasantly. Her manner meant a welcome.

" Yes ma'am," she said, and helped her off with her goloshes,
as her daughter might ; not servilely, but with friendliness.

" Thank you, my dear," said Miss Fletcher ; and the girl,
gathering up the things, smiled again and said—

" I hope you have taken no cold this blustering day. Shall
I bring you a cup of tea ?—and the young lady ? "

" Well, do so, Mary Anne ; it will be refreshing," was the
answer.

" If you will take your things off now it will be ready for
you when you come down," said Mary Anne ; " and there is a
good fire for you in the drawing-room."

" Thanks," said Miss Fletcher, " we will."

Particia stared. In her old life she had been kind enough to
the servants at the cottage, but she had always been the mistress in her own way. She had, perhaps, imbibed a certain
sense of discipline from the captain, and she had thought it her
duty to keep them up to the mark, and to see that they did not
waste, nor gad about, nor slight their work, nor fail in daily

godliness of service. For even Patricia had her share, if comparatively a small one, of the hardness characteristic of virtuous youth. At Abbey Holme the servants were spoken to as if they were intelligent dogs who could understand what was said to them, but of whose sensibilities or self-respect no one need take account; or, if as men, then men eternally in disgrace, with the master and mistress resentful and displeased. Mr. Hamley's manners, always dictatorial, were at times brutal; Mrs. Hamley's were glacial, as if she had been quite recently annoyed; and no one asked, but all commanded service, for which they never returned thanks. But Catherine Fletcher smiled at her maid and spoke kindly, and said "My dear" as to a young girl of her own rank; giving her order in the form of a request; seemingly too secure of her dignity to be afraid of lowering it by the practical confession of human equality. She saw Patricia's look of astonishment, and as they went into her dressing-room, she said laughing, "You were surprised at my calling Mary Anne, 'my dear?'"

"Yes," said Patricia, frankly. "I have never heard a mistress call her servant 'dear' before, and it sounded odd. But I like it," she added.

"Do you? It is one of my ways, as the people here say; and I always see when it startles."

"But do not the servants take advantage of it, and become impertinent?" asked Patricia.

"Sometimes; not often. And if they do, what then?"

Patricia looked straight into Miss Fletcher's face.

"You turn them away, of course," she said.

"No, I do not; I keep them, and try to teach them better," answered the lady; and this time Patricia turned her eyes to the fire and looked perplexed. Keep a servant who had been impertinent! It was a strange doctrine, and it puzzled her.

"Why should I not keep them and try to teach them better?" Miss Fletcher continued. "Think of the difference between us. I am a middle-aged woman, old enough to be their mother, with a better education than they have had; with more experience, more thought; and consequently I ought to have more wisdom and self-control, which is part of wisdom. Do you not think it would be a shame in me if I had not

patience with these young creatures, so much more ignorant
and undisciplined than myself?"

"Yes, put that way, you are right," said Patricia; "but"
———— she hesitated.

"But, you would say, they are servants born to obey and
take what they can get from their superiors; and that this
kind of personal consideration is against the laws of society. I
grant it. But, on my side, I say that the way in which mis-
tresses, good women in their own spheres, allow themselves to
treat their servants is one of the authorized sins of society; so
you see, my dear, between an authorized sin and my own conscience I choose the latter. And I think I am right."

"But what should we do if servants were made equal to
ourselves?" said Patricia; "we should have to do our own
work."

"Which I do not regard as a terrible hardship, were it to be
even so," exclaimed Miss Fletcher; "but it would not be as
you say. We should always have servants, that is, helpers;
but we should have a higher class—sisters, not slaves; equals
whom we should be bound to treat with respect and consideration, and who would do their duties from a higher stand-point
than that which they hold now. This habit of disrespect towards servants, which we allow ourselves, does us as much
harm as it does them. The greatest curse of slavery lies with
the owners, not the owned."

"I wish I was like you," said Patricia impulsively.

"I hope you will be far better," answered her new friend,
patting her shoulder kindly. "But come downstairs; I must
not make you as sad a democrat as I am myself," she added
with a pleasant abruptness; "so let us go down. If we stay
much longer Mary Anne's tea will be cold, and she will find that
she has given her labour in vain; always a disheartening thing
for a worker."

The conversation during the evening drifted, not without intention, on Patricia's life at Abbey Holme. As there was
nothing to be ashamed of in it there was nothing to conceal.
Not that the girl entered into details. The great sorrow of her
life, how to reconcile humility and truth, and that other grief,
how to reconcile love with disapprobation, she left unnoted.
Her friendship was too new yet for full confidence. But the

Fletchers felt instinctively how sad it all was for her, and how difficult to remedy. In this house of emphatic rule and suppression here was a young creature entirely without guidance, and in all the dangers attendant on spiritual loneliness. Her energies, cramped on the one side, were wasted on the other ; her thoughts, becoming active and importunate, were without a centre or an object ; her self-education was necessarily fragmentary and incomplete, and there was no one to help her spiritually, intellectually, or morally. If only they might be of use to her—this fine-natured, noble girl, so lost and lonesome now ! Yet how could they help her ? They knew Mrs. Hamley's jealousy too well to hope that she would give Patricia into any one's hands ; while they, specially tainted in her sight with various moral heresies, of which that same servant-question was not the least, were less likely to win her than any other.

Still, if they might have her with them often, they knew they could do much for her. They could teach her how to think as well as what to learn ; they could open to her the marvels of science and the treasures of literature ; they could take her to nature for her joy and to humanity for her duties. Knowledge and love, knowledge and good work, knowledge and living out of herself for the benefit of others ; yes, the Fletchers knew clearly enough that they could help Reginald Kemball's daughter, and place her in the light if they were allowed. And it pained them both to feel that perhaps this bright, young, ardent soul would be atrophied in the sandy desert of conventional inaction, or stifled in the vapour-bath of luxury and the world, while they who might have led it up to greatness and delight were forbidden.

However, they made the effort. In a few days after this Miss Fletcher wrote up to Mrs. Hamley asking her permission to read German with Patricia. It would be a pleasure to her, and would help the girl who was anxious to learn the language ; with pleasant little personal words that were not without their due value. And Mrs. Hamley, because she was angry and discontented with her niece, consented ; with the feeling of abandoning Patricia to her own devices, casting her off and cutting her out of the inheritance of love. So Patricia began to read German with Catherine Fletcher, and to have " half-hours with

L

the microscope " with the doctor.   And when the lessons were
done she went with her new friend into the cottages of the
poor, where she saw life as it is without gloss or varnish, and as
she had seen it at Barsands.

This bold strong contact with reality did her good.   It
strengthened her for the better carrying of her own cross to see
the pathetic patience with which the poor bear theirs ; and in
thinking much of them she forgot to weary herself in trying to
find out the cause of her aunt's tempers and her own shortcomings.   But when Mrs. Hamley found that her niece " went about
with Catherine Fletcher," as she phrased it, she interposed and
forbade " anything of the kind."   Patricia would be bringing
home some horrid disease, she said, or something almost worse
than disease.   She would not have her made " as common " as
Catherine Fletcher ; she, Patricia, was quite enough inclined
as it was to be vulgar and democratic, and everything else undesirable.   If she went down to the Hollies—though why she
should go at all was a mystery unaccountable to plain people—
she must promise not to go into any cottage whatsoever.   Such
absurdity !   What good could she do ? and what did she want
with dirty children and coarse women ?   She was far better
at home among ladies and gentlemen.   And so on ; these being
the texts on which Mrs. Hamley preached her sermons of reprobation whenever her niece visited her father's old friend's.

By degrees, however, she broke up the girl's pleasant intercourse with the Hollies.   The German lessons went the way of
the cottage-visiting, and though the Fletchers often asked for
her, permission to accept their invitations became daily scarcer,
and when granted, drew down on her deeper displeasure.

Still Patricia had their counsel when she needed it. She was
to do the right thing ; there was never any doubt on that score.
She was to be patient and to avoid all causes of offence ; but
when the choice between right and wrong, truth and fair seeming, shameful obedience or noble dissent, came before her, she
was to hold by the higher law ; and if she had to suffer because
of her choice—well ! she must suffer, and bear her sorrow
bravely.

By principle.   There was no tampering with that precept
with them.   But then it was not always the best thing, they
said, to speak all that is in one's mind at all times.   The gold

of silence has its value ; and youth must learn to bear much that is unpleasant with shut lips, patience, and forbearance to oppose. They too counselled self-suppression as Dora had done, but from another stand-point. What was expediency with her was heroism with them ; and under their direction Patricia, though not changing a hair's breadth in her own truth and honesty, learnt so much of the wisdom of silence and the generosity of non-condemnation, as to become noticeably less prone to testify, and with fewer angularities of virtue.

Mrs. Hamley said she had grown indifferent and unaffectionate ; a state, however, she preferred to her former uncomfortable activity, though preference did not include approbation. But in truth Patricia was unable to please her aunt. She was out of harmony with the central point of the girl's character, and no method of life or action radiating therefrom seemed to be beautiful or fitting.

CHAPTER XVII.

LONG FIELD FARM.

THE country about Milltown had been originally noted for its large number of small holdings, in the days when the backbone of English manliness and liberty was supposed to exist in her yeomanry and peasant proprietors. In those days small farmers had possessed the greater part of the land ; the abbey lands which had been assigned by Henry the Eighth, at the dissolution of the monasteries, to the Lord Bareacres of the period, having been gradually disposed of by the descendants of that famous nobleman, field by field and farm by farm, till the greater part had, as has been said, been parcelled out into small tenements. The nucleus, however, had been always held together, for the final purpose of coming into the possession of Jabez Hamley, Ledbury's successful office-boy.

The progress of events had gradually changed the land-holding character of Milltown, and a new order of gentlemen owners had dispossessed the old. The change began about ninety years ago, after the great continental wars had enriched certain army contractors, and when the pagoda-tree was a shrub still worth shaking in India; and it had gone on ever since, till now only one or two of the original peasant proprietors remained in possession. And these clung tenaciously to their holdings, and resisted all the temptation of long prices and money down which the rich men of the place, and notably Mr. Hamley, offered to get them out.

No one indeed offered such advantageous terms for fancy-bits as did the owner of Abbey Holme. His land-hunger was the fever of a devouring greed, and never sated. It was a grief to him when a rood of ground was bought by any one but himself, and he held himself personally aggrieved for the loss. But he never confessed that he had been balked, and you could only judge of his mortification by the way in which he depreciated the value of the farm he had missed, and his loud asseverations that the concluding purchaser had given thrice its proper value, and that he would not have had it for half that sum. His schemes were always active. He had corners full fifteen miles off ; wedges that he had inserted in his neighbours' estates with the hope of driving them home to his own park gates ; and bit by bit he was creeping round the local map, colouring it so frequently with the Hamley crimson till now the very Quest itself had not such a large tract surrounding it as Abbey Holme. The brewer against the earl ; and the brewer had the best of it.

Perhaps even a greater grief than the occasional loss of a field or a spinney he desired to add to his estate, was the fact that he had no children to carry on his name and inherit his property. Man-like, the idea of founding a family was sweet to him ; and now that he had obtained and won other things he wanted, his wishes went all the more strongly in this direction. Sometimes he reflected for his comfort that he was only forty-five years of age all told ; that Mrs. Hamley was twenty years his senior ; and that Providence was often merciful, and removed to a better world elderly women who had begun to get nuisances in this. What ulterior objects he might have, should fate be kind enough to kill Mrs. Hamley, he never told to living soul. It was enough for him that he pondered on them in secret, and limed the twig for those birds in the bush of the future, which he had arranged with himself to catch. Mrs. Hamley had done the work for which he had bought her ; she had placed him among the gentry of the place, and taught him the alphabet of good manners. And having done this, now, like one who has fulfilled her life's mission, she was free to depart to her own place so soon as it should seem good to her, leaving the ground open to another.

Meanwhile, the land-hunger must be fed ; field added to field, farm to farm, and every corner of wood and meadow bought as eagerly as if each crooked elm had been a sapling oak, and all the worthless alders hereditary yews. Wherever he appeared competition was useless, because his final offer was sure to be in excess of the market value. This made it good for the seller ; if, on the other hand, the temptation of a fancy price induced men to sell who might have held on ; and thus made homeless wanderers, and sometimes ruined speculators, of those who might have continued in the old path of self-respecting independence and English proprietorship.

Also, if he was so far a benefactor to the world at large in that he was a good agricultural chemist and farmed high, to the small world near at hand he was by no means a blessing. He was a hard landlord, heart and hand, and if he gave employment he added sorrow to the wages. He beat men down at every point, and took advantage of all collateral depressions in the labour market. He grudged his labourers all but the bare life, and thought comfort, pleasure, education, refinement for "common people," not only foolish but positively wicked. He denied with his whole force the doctrine that the poor had rights. They were simply to him the pabulum, the footstools, the hands and energies of the rich, and capital was superior to humanity. Rights? No! "What is mine is my own," was a favourite aphorism of his and he acted on it.

One of the objects of his ambition—his ambition never extending beyond worldly things—had been to own a deer-park. There had been one at Abbey Holme long ago when the jolly old monks had preached repentance and poverty to the godless laity, but had taken care to pad their own crosses with silk and wool, and to live on the fat of the land while they eulogised the lean. And Mr. Hamley had determined that he would restore it. To do this he had dismantled a hamlet which had grown up on the old site of the deer-forest, evicting the cottagers with no more pity or scruple than if they had been so many rats which he had smoked out of their holes. His enforced exodus cost the lives of a few infants and aged folks. What did that signify? The poor are too numerous as it is : a little thinning is an advantage. He was famous too, for pulling down the cottages on his estate ; making his labourers walk to their work sometimes five or six miles out and the like distance in. Buildings, he said, were only so many drains on capital ; and as his highest idea of a man's life was the profitable employment of capital, duty to those under him had no place in his creed and formed no part of his practice. For duty is generally an expensive luxury ; and Mr. Hamley did not care for expensive luxuries which make no show, soothe no sense, and bring no renown.

In all these circumstances then, it cannot be wondered at if

Mr. Hamley, buying above market value every acre there was to sell, evicting his labourers like vermin, farming high but paying low, should be at once the most influential and the most unpopular man to be found in the district. He was even more disliked than Colonel Lowe ; who, if he let his tenants live like beasts in hovels that were not fit for beasts, and that stood at comparatively enormous rents, had a kind of excuse in that he was not over well off on the one hand, and on the other, that he was a gentleman and had thus an inherited right to treat the poor like beasts. It is a way some gentlemen have. But when it came to a man popularly supposed to possess millions—a man who, as a ragged, barefooted lad, had known what it was to want a dinner more often than to have one, who had been thrashed for stealing turnips as the stopgaps of his emptiness, and who had been fed by some of the very men, or their fathers, whom he now turned adrift—when it came to such as he grinding the faces of the poor to the earth, was it to be wondered at if he was hated ? And to do the Milltown labourers justice, they did hate him.

There was a certain farm at the north end of the Abbey Holme estate that had long been Mr. Hamley's Naboth's vineyard. It stood right in amongst his property, and was the thorn in his chaplet of roses, the poison in his cup of sweets. Long Field aggrieved him. It was a standing injury to the symmetry of his ring-fence, an enduring scoff at the wholeness of his ownership; and he coveted it. It never occurred to him that James Garth had inherited that land from his father and forbears ever since King Henry's time, and that it was he, Mr. Hamley, who had come in as the remover of old-time fences by his golden spade, not James Garth and his title-deeds that stood as the obstruction. When men are annoyed by circumstances they do not care to consider whether they have voluntarily put themselves in the way of those circumstances or not; but speak as if they had been hemmed round by them without their own assistance. In this case it was simply *Ote-toi que je m'y mets ;* and the refusal was accounted both an insolence and a wrong.

Things had not gone well with James Garth. His father had been a hard liver in his time, too fond of the hounds and too free with the bottle to succeed in his life's business, which

was to clean and crop his farm. Consequently the business he
neglected failed to do well by him. When he died he left a
handful of debts which came like a shower of hail about his
son's ears, and which had crippled his energies to pay off. For
James was a man with an immense amount of family pride. Not
pride of that flashy kind which thinks no one good enough for it,
but pride that cares to keep the family name unstained and the
family honour bright ; pride that is only another form of self-
respect, incapable of meanness and to which treachery is as impossible.

But beside this characteristic, James Garth had also more
than the average share of hope. He was sanguine by temperament, and always believed the better thing ; and so had borne
his heavy burdens with a gallant courage, a simple faith in Providence and the turn of the lane, that gave an almost heroic
flavour to his constancy. The two things which were as his
very life's blood to him were, to redeem his father's debts and
keep a good name. But just in proportion to his hope, his
energy, his pride, while things were well with him, would be
the collapse—if it came.

The struggle was an arduous one. He had a good wife and
a large family ; a wife who had wrought her day's work loyally,
made the best of everything, wasted nothing, borne him a
child every two years as regularly as the birds brought forth
their young in spring time, and given the children good health,
good food, and a bright example. These young ones would be
all of use by-and-bye, but most of them were mere infants and
children yet ; and only one or two had got forward on their
own account. James, the eldest, of course stayed with his
father, so did Robert, the next lad ; but Alice, the eldest
daughter, had gone out to service, and was now acting as lady's
maid to Miss Drummond.

This had been a little hard at the first to Garth, owing to
special circumstances connected with Mr. Hamley ; else he
would not have minded. His pride was not of that sort. He
was only a peasant proprietor at the best, and he aimed at
nothing higher. He scarcely saw the need. He did not care
to bring up his children on strawberries and cream like fine
ladies, he said, but would rather let them take the rough of the
world as well as the smooth ; and he thought it no shame that

Alice should take suit and service in a stranger's house, for all
that the title-deeds of his farm, lying in the old black chest,
were dated 1540. But it had cost him a struggle to let her go
to Jabez Hamley's; though in the end common sense had conquered prejudice.

Besides this large family and his father's debts, James Garth
had made a bad speculation. A man came down from London
and persuaded him that he had ironstone on his land, and that
he had only to set about with a pickaxe and a few charges of
gunpowder to make as much money as the owner of Abbey
Holme had made out of his brewing vats. So he set to work
and tore his land into holes here, and piled it into hummucks
there, and lost his money and his time for the better part of
six months. And when all was done he found that he had
been fooled, and that he had spent his strength in slinging
another millstone round his neck in addition to those made
out of his father's debts, his round dozen of children to feed
and clothe, and his want of capital to enable him to keep pace
with modern improvements; whereby he was ever at a disad-
vantage. For naturally the more a man puts into his land the
more he gets out of it. A year or two of bad harvests had also
made their mark; and the turn in the long lane in which poor
Garth so courageously believed seemed farther off than ever.

There was no doubt about it. Set in the midst of Mr.
Hamley's well-cleaned, steam-cultivated, lordly acres, Long
Field had a ragged poverty-stricken look that destroyed the
harmony of the landscape; and its dandelions and thistles
were an abomination. Nothing disguised, nothing extenuated,
it was a rough bit of country, and by no means farmed up to
its capabilities; but it was the man's own, and his all. And
Mr. Hamley had no philanthropic desire of adding to the
world's wealth in getting possession of it if he could. It was
merely that it stood in the midst of his own estate, and he
wanted his ring-fence to be symmetrical; besides having that
land-hunger on him, exaggerated to voracity, which nothing
short of inability to buy more would ever satisfy.

The creditors whom Garth had been obliged to make on his
own account were now pressing on him. It had been a glad
day for the poor fellow when he had cleared his father's reputation; and no Chinaman ever burnt incense before the tomb

of his ancestors with more hearty satisfaction to his conscience
than that which James Garth felt when he received the last
receipt in full of all demands on the outstanding accounts, and
brushed the last remains of dishonour from the old free-liver's
memory. But he had done this only at the cost of new lia-
bilities contracted on his own hand ; and with these and the
losses occasioned by short crops and the man who had talked
of ironstone and prophesied millions, things never looked
worse for him. Take it how he might, there was a sore pinch
before him, and he saw no way out of it save by borrowing on
the security of the land, which had enough to do to support
him and his without drawbacks.

All of which Mr. Hamley knew like the alphabet. Was not
Alice Dora Drummond's maid ?—and were the tears so often
in her eyes for nothing ? Besides, land-hunger is like any
other instinct, keen in scenting its food and absolute in its need
of satisfaction ; and Mr. Hamley's knowledge of the fields and
farms that would fall to the first bidder, and which he had
only to ride over to the house-door to secure, and of those
which must eventually come into the market and were to be
had for patient waiting, was almost like an added sense, it was
so acute and unerring.

" Well, wife, I shall have to do it at last !" said James, looking up from a dirty piece of paper that had done service for a
letter, and which his eldest son had just brought up from the
town. It was a letter from Cooper the wheelwright, who had
just lent him three hundred pounds, and now wanted it back
again without delay. And there were Jones and Martin and
Crace, all of whom had lent him money to go on with, and all
of whom would begin to clamour like birds in a nest, and to
press their claims in a body if Cooper got paid and they were
left out.

" What is it, James, my man ?" asked his wife. The two were
sitting in the kitchen at noonday while the boys were gathering in to dinner. Mrs. Garth, with one child at her foot in the
cradle and another at her knee, was knitting a coarse blue
stocking, while her husband smoked his pipe in the chimney-
corner and the pot bubbled and hissed over the fire. It was a
cold raw day, and the light and warmth of the kitchen were
pleasant.

"What will you have to do?" she repeated.

"Lay a mortgage on the land," said James, his eyes turned to the sanded floor, as if he could see his difficulties collected there.

"Aye? that sounds a bit awful," said Mrs. Garth.

"As bad as may be," her husband answered. "It seems just like a break; the beginning of an upset root and branch,"

"Why, James! that's not like you to look at the black side end foremost, and cry out before you are hurt!" said Mrs. Garth cheerily.

"Nay, it ain't," he answered back; "but somehow I am more down at this than I have ever been before. It seems as if it would never end, and I feel as if the place was slipping out of my hand somehow."

He sighed, and he seldom sighed, as he looked round with a kind of friendly fondness on all the things he knew so well and that were so full of old associations. His mother's samplers and his grandmother's, worked in silk with peacocks and quaint pyramidal trees, and "Anne Fletcher" signed to one in cross-barred letters, and "Alice Jones" to the other; things that he had always regarded as the highest efforts of creative genius in their way, sublime in industry and purely useless in intent; he would be sorry to part with them now, and suddenly they took a value in his eyes they had never had before. Then there was the old china teapot, and some blue Delft plates that had been brought over by his uncle who had been a seafaring man, and had visited foreign parts; and the sea-shells on the mantlepiece in among the flat candlesticks and teacaddy, with one delicate vase of Venetian glass with a twisted thread run through its stem, filled with small cowries, that had an almost superstitious value in the family eyes. There was the old Dutch clock that ticked as it had ticked when he was a boy, with the cuckoo that came out of the little door when the hours struck, and chirped them as loud and natural as the real thing. How he had wondered at that cuckoo when he was a little lad! —and how he liked to see his mother draw up the weights with a noise that made his flesh tingle with a pleasant sense of awesome fear, just the same as his own little ones felt now as they peeped behind their mother's skirts when she drew up the chains, and they saw the big old pendulum swing from side

to side as if it had life and a voice. The carved high-backed
oaken chairs, and the old carved bureau for which once a gentleman staying at Abbey Holme offered him twenty pounds—
he almost wished now that he had lost the chest and taken the
money ; the sanded floor where he and his brothers had bored
holes, and the father had called them worms ; the deep chim-
ney-place with a settle at each side, where the pot was hanging
with the dinner of potato-stew seething over the peat fire ; the
rack where the guns and whips hung; the shelves among the
rafters where the wife kept her stores out of the reach of small
marauding hands :—all these thousand trifles which make up
home seemed to come before him with more vitality, more
rooting power than they had ever had before, and to render
the possibilities of his position more bitter.

Just then came riding up Mr. Hamley of Abbey Holme. He
had been to his plantation ahead, and he thought he would look
in at Long Field on his way back. He had seen Cooper the
wheelwright yesterday, and had told him carelessly, as a matter
of common knowledge, that Garth was insolvent out and out ;
and that his creditors would not get sixpence in the pound if
they did not look sharp. Farming at a loss was not a good
groundwork for the liquidation of outstanding debts, he had
said ; and for his own part he was glad he had none of his
money lying among the Long Field weeds, for he should as
soon expect to shovel up last year's snow as to see a penny of
it back again if it had once got into James Garth's hands.

He had had no qualms of conscience in saying all this.
Garth would be forced to sell, he argued—for the good of the
Abbey Holme estate—and it was ridiculous his holding on.
Anything therefore that would hasten that necessity was so far
to the right side of the general account, if to the wrong of poor
Garth's, individually.

" But the world is made up of the individuals who succeed
and those who fail," said Mr. Hamley, flinging back his coat ;
" and every man has the power to choose which he will be. I
chose the first, and James Garth has selected the second ; consequently, I have purchased Abbey Holme and he will have to
sell Long Field."

This was an epigrammatic way of putting matters that pleased
him ; and Cooper thought that a man who spoke so sharp

must have a judgment to match ; as poor **Garth** found out to-
day when he came in from mending a few **fences** to his dinner
of potato-stew, and to exchange a loving **word with his wife**
and children.

Mr. Hamley rode up to the farm-house door, and **his man in**
his smart groom's livery took his horse as he dismounted.

" Well, James," he said, stooping **as he came through the**
doorway ; which he need not have done.

He was very spruce in his dark **blue overcoat with its broad**
velvet collar ; very clean about **his close-shaven** chin ; very
sleek and prosperous, **and well** got **up from head** to heel ; and
not in any way like **the lad** who had many a time held old
Garth's horse for a penny, and more than once **been fed at the**
farm as you would feed a tramp or **a** stray dog.

" My man," said Mr. Hamley, "you should keep your land
cleaner. Yon fields of yours are not fit **for pigs.** What with
stones and weeds, they are fairly a disgrace, and that's a fact."

" I see nothing amiss with them," replied James a trifle
surlily.

He was nettled at **the rich man's** superior manner. It always did nettle him.

" You want more capital," said Mr. Hamley pompously, but
with the carelessness of one to whom capital is plentiful ; speaking as if he had said that Garth wanted more chaff, more straw,
more sand.

"'That's sooner **said nor done,"** said James, his Saxon face
aflame.

He was a fair, ruddy man of forty-two or so ; in his prime ;
genial, openbrowed, frank ; a good-tempered fellow, but quick
too ; a man whose blood was not sluggish, yet more passionate
than rancorous ; but a man wanting mental fibre of a kind, and
to be overcome by an adverse fate.

" I was hearing at the town that **Cooper was coming on you,"**
continued Mr. Hamley.

" Ay ? that is strange now," said Garth.

" It will be a heavy pull to pay him off," said Mr. Hamley.

" Ay," he repeated ; " you are about right there."

" I wonder you don't sell the place for what it will fetch,"
said Mr. Hamley. " It's **worsening year by year,** and you'll go
under with it."

"I'll not sell, and I'll stick to the land," said James slowly.

"Well, you are your own man, and can do as you please; but I'd give you a tidy price for it if you liked to sell," Mr. Hamley said with a familiar tone and a broader accent than that which Mrs. Hamley had taught him to use. We're old acquaintances now, Garth, and I remember when your father was a man above my height. You'd rather see the land in my hands, I imagine, than in a stranger's; and I'd do justice by it and you."

"I'll hold on," said James.

"You will? Hold on to what? A bunch of weeds and a bed of thistles! What's the good of holding on to land you can't farm, man? I'd sell it if I was you, and could get my price."

"No, you wouldn't sell if you was me, if even you could get your price," retorted James. "What your father had left you, you'd like to leave to your son—as I do, and as every Englishman would, if he could. I'd liefer have a rood of English land than a dozen acres in a foreign country," said James.

"Stuff! you carry your country on your back," said Mr. Hamley. "A man's country is where he can buy the best coat and get the best dinner. Country! what signifies country, when they can speak the language like yourself? The Americans are English," he added with ethnological generosity; "and America's the place where a handy man like you would make his fortune."

"Mr. Hamley," said James Garth suddenly, "you've made your offer, and you've had your answer. I'll not sell till the bailies take me, and I'll not cry caught till the game's lost. Now, wife, if you'll turn out the pot perhaps Mr. Hamley 'll take a bit of dinner with us. It would not be the first, I reckon, he's had at Long Field, by many."

"Thank you; no. I shall partake of lunch at home," said Mr. Hamley, with a sudden return to his finer manner, and an angry flash in his small dark eyes. "I think you're foolish, James, but we have good authority for not meddling with a man's folly; and so I leave you to yours. Good day. Good day, Mrs. Garth."

"Good day, sir," said Mrs. Garth, with a curtsey. "And how's Alice coming on?"

"Oh, very fair, I fancy," answered Mr. Hamley condescendingly. "She's young yet, but she'll improve; and I don't hear Miss Drummond complain."

"I'm glad she suits," said the mother respectfully, as so much useful capital of which her daughter might have the interest. "My duty, sir, to your lady and Miss Drummond."

"Good day, Mr. Hamley," said James curtly. "Now, wife, the dinner."

"Curse the fellow's insolence!" muttered the rich man as he rode off.

James Garth repeated the same words as he sat down to his dinner with a heavy heart and a hot head, and the most passionate desire to break Jabez Hamley's.

And yet what had Hamley done? Literally a kindness, according to his way of putting it. He had offered a thousand pounds clear gain over and above the market value of a piece of badly farmed land—that is, he would have made a clean gift of the same to induce an insolvent landowner to sell what he could not keep. Garth, perversely perhaps, took it that his father's former charity-lad had traded on his necessities, and offered him a bribe to let go his cherished patrimony. It was common sense and feeling—the logic of wealth dealing with poverty according to material values and outside human emotions, and the passionate anguish of a luckless man rebelling against facts and logic, and asking only help and sympathy.

CHAPTER XVIII.

LATE FOR LUNCHEON.

INSTEAD of turning in at the Abbey Holme gates when he passed them on his way from Long Field, Mr. Hamley did violence to the domestic institution of luncheon, and cantered off to Milltown. He thought it best to take time by the forelock, and to have the first word with Mr. Simpson, the local lawyer, before Garth could put in his oar. So, grievously harassing that unfortunate gentleman by his untimely visit, disturbing him at his dinner, much to Mrs. Simpson's disgust, spoiling his food and deranging his digestion, he opened at once on his business.

He had no need to manage appearances with Mr. Simpson. He had long ago bought him, body and soul, and held him in his hand able to crush him at a moment's notice. The lawyer had nothing for it, then, but a flexible back-bone and a plastic conscience ; and to keep on good terms with his master and creditor, let what would stand in his path or be trampled out of it, was the only way open to him. Milltown, by-the-by, wondered that Mr. Hamley, who did everything in such a grandiose manner, and who never touched clay when he could handle gold, should employ Simpson at all. A low-class, second-rate man as he was, it was odd that the eminently respectable, self-made master of Abbey Holme should stand by him rather than by Mr. Perkins, who was at the head of his profession in these parts, and was a really honourable and worthy gentleman. But Mr. Hamley gave it as his reason that Simpson had once been kind to him in the days when he needed a friend ; " and I never forget a kindness and never forsake a friend," said Mr. Hamley of Abbey Holme, airing his gratitude ostentatiously.

" Simpson," said Mr. Hamley abruptly, as the lawyer, a sandy-haired, red-eyed, furtive kind of person, came sideways into the room, " you'll be hearing from James Garth, of Long Field, one of these fine days."

" Yes, sir, so I anticipate," said Mr. Simpson. " By all accounts, he's in a bad way, is James."

" Couldn't be worse," said Mr. Hamley. Then, after a pause; " There's Cooper pressing him for money, and the fool refuses to sell."

" Cooper pressing him for money and he refuses to sell; what a fool indeed, as you say, sir !" echoed Mr. Simpson.

" I have just offered him two thousand for his farm, and he says no," continued Mr. Hamley, in an injured tone.

" Two thousand, and he says no; he doesn't see his own interest ," repeated Simpson.

That's what I told him not half an hour ago; but Lord ! you might as well speak to a stone wall as to him ! He's blind and deaf and stupid, that's what he is ; and he can't see his bread when it's stuck under his nose buttered-side uppermost. He's the most of a pig's-head I've ever come across, and he'll have to suffer for his folly. Such men always do."

" No doubt, sir, no doubt. As you say, such men always do. I'm sorry for him, but if he *will* cut his own throat—why——" The lawyer spread out his hands, and shrugged his shoulders, intimating that he abandoned James Garth to that interesting operation, and washed his hands of all responsibility in the matter of sharpening the razors.

" Sorry for him !" said Mr. Hamley fiercely ; " how can you be such a fool as to say that, Simpson ? Sorry for a born jackass who won't take advice, and pocket a cool thousand when it's given him !"

" Well, not exactly sorry perhaps, but one would rather see him wiser," apologized the lawyer, bowing.

Mr. Hamley frowned. " I don't do much myself in the way of soft soap and sawder," he said insolently ; " I leave that to you, Simpson. And as for wishing him anyways different to what he is, you might as well wish a mole was a hawk and that geese didn't cackle."

The lawyer laughed and smoothed his hair. " He ! he! he! you'll excuse me, Mr. Hamley, but you are so very funny, sir !" he said. " As I always say, if you want to hear what I call a regular out-and-out good thing, there's no one that comes near

M

Mr. Hamley of Abbey Holme. **That's** the genuine article and no mistake !"

"Well, I always was accounted a droll dog," answered Mr. Hamley with a self-satisfied smile, stretching out his legs and running his fingers through his bushy black whiskers. " Many's the time I've kept them all in a roar down at Ledbury's when I was junior and hadn't what one may call so much to keep up as now. I was king of my company, that's what I was, and could cut a joke or sing a song with the best of them."

" That's what all Milltown says, sir !" cried Mr. Simpson enthusiastically.

" And Milltown has made worse guesses in its day and been further off the bull's-eye than here," said Mr. Hamley. Whereat they both laughed. This was one of the great man's witticisms : a fair specimen of the kind of thing which made him king of his company. " But I did not come here to crack jokes ; I came to talk business," he said, breaking off suddenly.

" And business be it," returned Mr. Simpson, grave on the instant, and assuming his professional manner like a mask.

" Garth **will** come here for a mortgage," said **Mr.** Hamley, checking off his first proposition on his finger.

" Just so."

" You must **find the money."** This was the second, marked off in the same way.

Mr. Simpson **made** two strokes on his blotting-pad.

" And you must lend it on your own hand, and give him rope. Give him twelve hundred if he wants it, at five per cent. That will be a tidy lot ; and when he has it, he's hooked."

" He is," said Mr. Simpson.

" And then one of the eyesores of the neighbourhood will be abolished," said Mr. Hamley, taking up his grand manner ; " and Long Field will be farmed as it ought to be."

" Which will be a public benefaction, Mr. Hamley," said the lawyer.

"I think so too, Simpson, I think so too," he answered pompously. " I think I may say I have deserved well of Milltown for the good I have done the land. It was weeds and rubbish, most of it, when I found it—a set of beggarly bankrupts, that's what they were—and I have made it, as one might say, a smiling garden."

" You have, sir ; and a beautiful simile it is."

" And yet that pig-headed brute would not sell !" said Mr. Hamley with his injured tone.

" Incredible !" returned the lawyer ; " most extraordinary ! "

" You may well say that," said Mr. Hamley, " Meantime see to the note of hand when Garth calls, and give him rope."

" I will, sir ; rope enough to hang him," said Mr. Simpson with an unpleasant laugh.

Mr. Hamley frowned, as he had frowned before ; this time from a benevolent motive. " I don't like such harsh expressions, Simpson," he said sternly. " They are unchristian, and not the thing."

" I am sorry I offended, sir," Mr. Simpson answered with a contrite look. " But one is apt to let one's feelings run away with one, even in office hours ; and a man who's no friend to one who has been, as I may say, the making of me and mine— why I can't be very soft on him, you see, sir."

" Yes, all that is proper enough," Mr. Hamley answered ; " but don't let your zeal get ahead of your discretion, that's all."

And the lawyer answered, " No, sir, I will not," humbly.

What good these two men proposed to themselves by this little transparent farce, it would have been difficult for either to have explained ; but it was the kind of thing they kept up together and each assumed that he deceived the other.

" By-the-by, Simpson, how about the last quarter's interest from Cragfoot ?" asked Mr. Hamley suddenly. " Paid yet ?"

" No, sir. Money's bad to get from the Colonel ; grows tighter quarter by quarter."

" Overdue how long ?"

" A week and two days."

" Give him a full fortnight, and then——" Mr. Hamley indulged in a little pantomime expressive of turning a screw.

" I understand, sir," said Mr. Simpson, with another hieroglyphic on the blotting-pad. " A fortnight's grace, and then the screw ?"

" Just so ; not too hard at first, you know. Gently does it, but fast hold all the same. You understand."

" All right, sir ; I know."

" Well then, I think I have no more to say ; so good morn

ing to you," said Mr. Hamley, flinging a condescending nod to
his tool, who bowed as low as if the master of Abbey Holme,
Ledbury's successful office-boy, was the Dalai-Lama in person,
and he one of his chosen worshippers. Then, mounting his
showy bay, Mr. Hamley cantered up the street, followed by his
smart groom also on a showy bay, luncheon waiting for him at
home—as he knew.

"Why whatever has kept you all this long time, Mr. S. ! '
was Mrs. Simpson's querulous ejaculation rather than question,
as her husband went into the dingy little back parlour where
his cold chop and flat beer awaited him.

"That beast Hamley !" was his reply. "I wish the dèvil
would wring his neck for him ! "

"Law, Simpson, how you do talk !" said his wife. "But I
don't wonder at your being in a wax ; it is rousing to be wanting one's dinner and it a-spoiling on the hob."

"It's more rousing to have to do that beast's dirty work,"
said Mr. Simpson, fencing with his conscience in that curious
way in which slaves and cowards compound for the evil they
commit by throwing the shame of responsibility on the man
who has bought them, and is now driving them to iniquity.

"Well, he saved us when we wanted a good turn," said Mrs.
Simpson, with a wife's natural contradiction and aggravating
gratitude for the benefits which gall her husband. "And it's
only natural he should be wanting his money's worth somehow.
If you didn't want him on your hands, you should have been
careful to keep him off them."

"Don't be a fool, woman, and hold your mag on things you
don't understand," said Mr. Simpson coarsely.

Whereat Mrs. Simpson tossed her head and said, "Well I'm
sure !" in a pet in which she continued to the end of the day ;
though it was uncomfortable, because she wanted to tell her
lord some Milltown gossip she had just heard—how that those
heathenish Fletchers were getting as thick as thieves with Miss
Kemball up there at the Abbey, and Miss Biggs did say she
expected soon to have an order, and she supposed they would
do it handsome.

When James Garth went down that night to Mr. Simpson's
he found everything as smooth as velvet. The lawyer happened
to have just twelve hundred pounds of his own to which he

was as welcome as the flowers of May ; **and he would draw** out
the note of hand as he stood there. This would pay off all his
creditors at one stroke, and give him a tidy little sum to put into
the land for better crops next harvest-time.   Twelve hundred
pounds !   It would set him square he hoped, both now and in
the future ; and he might take his own time to pay it off.

No, he would not put that into the bond, he said, when **Garth,**
with a peasant's natural acuteness where land is concerned,
wanted it expressly stated under stamp and seal, that the money
should not be called in before such a date, and then not until
due notice had been given.   There must be some kind of trust
between man and man ; and besides, it was not professional.
All he could do, or would, was to lend the money at five per
cent., and to promise verbally, that unless unforeseen accidents
should arise—which he did not contemplate, but for which he
would not hold himself responsible should they come—he would
not call it in while the interest was paid regularly, and the
I. O. U. looked safe.

And as need was pressing, and this was the best he could do,
James Garth took the loan on these conditions; and manfully
set himself to overlay a certain uneasy sense of insecurity with
the rose-coloured hopefulness of his buoyant temper.

As Mr. Hamley was riding smartly homewards, he said to
himself again and again what a remarkably easy thing it was
to be successful, and how pleasant life was to the man who
knew how to make hay while the sun shone, and to take time
and Mr. Simpson by the forelock!   He had no sympathy with
all those white-livered dyspeptic fellows who go about the
world shoes down at heel and coats out at elbows, unsuccessful and unhappy.   Look at him, how *he* managed !   Why, men
were so many puppets in his hand, and he was the master who
pulled the strings and made them dance to his tunes.   There
was Colonel Lowe now; he thought himself master of Cragfoot,
did he ?   Ah, he little knew that he was no better than a dog
in a kennel, and might be turned out at any moment!   He
swaggered and gave himself airs, did he ?   Well, let him swag-
ger.   If he came too near a certain forbidden subject, he would
simply have to learn his master before the week was out, that
was all.   If he behaved himself decently, and that cub of his
married money, well, he might drag on a little longer in Crag-

foot if he liked. It all depended on his, the secret owner's
mood, and what he wanted to do with the place himself. What
a glow of satisfaction that thought of power gave him! Perhaps—he didn't know—but perhaps, if Patricia married to his
liking, he might give her the Colonel's house as her portion.
It would not be unpleasant to his pride to have the world say
how generously he had dowered his wife's niece ; and it would
not be unpleasant to revenge himself on the Colonel for certain
well-remembered insolences of bygone times, when the smart
young owner of Cragfoot had cracked his whip over the ragged
lad loitering at Ledbury's door, and treated him as he would be
treated in his turn one of these fine days, if there was justice
on earth or in heaven !

Whenever Mr. Hamley spoke openly to men of his former
life, he spoke of it with the courageous confession of a wise and
brave man. Whenever he thought of it, he lost his inner self-
mastery. Those who had befriended him and those who had
insulted him, were equally in his Index of the future, and
equally to be punished. Colonel Lowe was of the latter ; James
Garth of the former ; and both had to bear the weight of his
hand now that this hand had power. He had them. He had
got both the big fish and the little one in his net, and he felt as
a good man feels who has fulfilled his life's highest intention.
It was odd how he had coveted that Long Field Farm! The want
of it had soured all the sweets of his other possessions ; but
now—he drew a deep breath as he mounted the hill whence he
could see Abbey Holme lying fair and stately amid its magnificent oaks and beeches, and his eyes wandered far over his own
estate—with the smoking chimney of Long Field to be soon
added to the rest.

But as he drew nearer to his own home, the image of what
was waiting for him there became more and more distinct, and
the effect sobering in proportion. He pictured to himself the
expression on Mrs. Hamley's face : he knew it so well !—and
the form of the punishment waiting for him became photogra-
phically distinct. He knew her way ; it was stereotyped. She
would remain immovable in the drawing-room after luncheon
was announced ; her ladylike work of many colours folded up
and laid aside ; her pale eyes fixed on the clock ; waiting with
crisped lips and voiceless forbearance until the truant should

make his appearance. Over and over again he had besought
her to give him just five minutes' law when he happened to be
late; which was seldom; and then to lunch without him. And
over and over again his wife had assured him, with the tart
submission of a deferential code grafted on to an aggressive
character, which was her way, that she should never dream of
failing so far in her duty to him. If he chose to forget what
was due to her, she used to say with the severe patience, the
antagonistic humility under which he had so often writhed,
she was not justified in following his example. He was the
master if she was the lady; and the master must be attended
to first of all things. It might not be good manners to keep her
waiting; but husbands did not always trouble themselves about
manners in their own homes.

He knew by heart the air with which she would take his
arm the instant he went in, and walk solemnly to the dining-
room, compressed and grim if her mood was confessedly warlike, or pathetically patient if she was in the humour to stab
through wool; as sometimes happened in her more subtle days.
He knew how they would sit down in funereal silence to their
sumptuous meal, with all the made dishes cold—and they could
so easily have been kept hot! he thought with a prophetic
pang; for Mr. Hamley liked good living—with the servants,
who had been kept hanging about in expectant state, cross
and hungry, and civilly showing the worst side of everything,
as servants can, all in the way of duty and their lawful service.
He knew how the disturbed arrangements of the afternoon
would be flung at him in a disordered heap, and the whole day
with some subsequent ones thrown out of gear, all for that
lost half-hour. He already heard the meekly-injured tone in
which she would refuse everything offered to her: " I cannot
eat that, John, It is spoilt with waiting;" the elaborate sympathy with which she would apologize to Dora and Patricia for
the uncomfortable state of the table; and, without a word of
direct reproach, how she would heap burning coals on his
recreant head, accepting his excuses with a frosty smile and a
stiff inclination of her well-attired body, her eyes saying as
plainly as words, " I know that you are telling falsehoods, but
you are the master and I am the slave, and I must set an example of wifely submission to the girls." For unpunctuality at

meals was one of the cardinal vices at Abbey Holme, where it
was held as an undoubted article of faith that life had been
given to man for the careful codification of conventionalities,
and not that conventionalities had been created for the better
regulation of life.

Visions such as these, with dear Dora's pretty face and dovelike eyes as his sunshine in the cloudy sky, her tacit but eloquent amiability, desirous to please both and careful to hurt
neither, flanked by glimpses of Patricia's directer endeavours
to show him that she at least was sorry for his discomfiture ;
which only made her aunt angry with her and more disagreeable
to himself—" the girl has a good heart, but she is deuced upsetting in a house, and as vulgar as you please !" was his
unspoken commentary on her honest sympathy—held the man's
pride a trifle low in the direction of home, to balance the
hunter's joy in having trapped his game so securely that whenever he chose to snap the lid he would hold his prize in his
hand, to deal with as seemed good to him.

And this last thought brought him to the Abbey Holme
door—with Mrs. Hamley waiting on the other side of it.

CHAPTER XIX.

PAYING VISITS.

MRS. HAMLEY was a regal kind of woman in her way, and like other royalties had a profound objection to all derangement of plans. She had appointed the carriage to be at the door at a certain moment, and her calculations founded thereon had been made with the exactness of a Chinese puzzle. As it was, everything was displaced. And this was an unpardonable offence. The days were short, and the visits which she had arranged to pay suddenly became of paramount importance ; after having been delayed for weeks innocuously, entailing no end of social misdemeanours now by being carried over into another day. There is no need to say that for the last hour life at Abbey Holme had not been joyous, and that the burden of human miseries had been heavy.

" Very sorry, Lady," said Mr. Hamley, coming out from his dressing flushed and flustered. Mrs. Hamley would not have sat down with him had he not been dressed—as he called it, " to the nines," but she, " as a gentleman."

" Your arm, Mr. Hamley," was the lady's curt response.

" I have been detained by business of the most important kind, else I would not have delayed you." he continued, still flustered, and louder than usual, more parabolic too than usual in consequence.

" Shall we sit down while you explain your affairs, Mr. Hamley, or shall we go into luncheon, which has been waiting a full hour ?" said Mrs. Hamley, withdrawing her hand from his own and looking at him sternly.

Mr. Hamley laughed uneasily as he picked up the lean long fingers and laid them on his coat sleeve ; glanced at dear Dora —looking discreetly another way, and at Patricia—looking in pained reprobation at her aunt ; and then walked off in silence to the dining-room, conscious that the time for propitiation had not arrived. And as they went, Patricia behind-backs took up

dear Dora bodily by the waist, and carried her for a few steps
with dreadfully rude ease, as her form of protest against the
dead dulness of the last hour and the sourness of the present
moment.   Had Mrs. Hamley looked round things would not
have been harmonious for Patricia for the next day or two.

Her iniquity, however, passed off without detection ; and as
Dora did not laugh or scream, being too angry with the girl
for the one part and too frightened of her sure share of Mrs.
Hamley's wrath should they be discovered for the other, and
as, moreover, deep indignation at Mr. Hamley's domestic sin
of unpunctuality had exercised so many of Mrs. Hamley's
faculties as to leave her none for suspicion, she noted nothing
of the little flutter that went on in the hall as that incorrigible
niece of hers affronted the *genus loci* once again as so many
times before, and scared the lares and penates as a kitten might
scare a cage full of white mice.

After an uncomfortable meal during which the carriage came
round—an additional log to the fire of Mrs. Hamley's anger—
they all set off to pay visits.   This, too, was one of Mrs. Hamley's regal ways.   She liked to do things in a certain cumbrous
state, and to be attended when she went out.   It was a rare
mark of social familiarity when she went with Dora alone to
any house.   As a rule she exacted Mr. Hamley's company as
the marital Goldstick whose duty it was to accompany her ;
and Patricia was now also part of her personal court.

To-day she especially desired to have all things decently and
with more than ordinary pomp and propriety.   She was going
to Cragfoot and the Rectory ; and more, she was going for the
first time to the Quest where the flag was flying—the family
having come down.   And Lord Merrian was a personable
young man who might—who knows?—thought Mrs. Hamley
with a critical look at the two young ladies who sat, discreet
and demure, facing her.

They were pretty girls, each in her own way ; and she would
not grudge the prize to one for the sake of the other.   For if
Dora won it—well, dear Dora was her own creation, as well as
her personal favourite, and she could say with pride : " Look
at the result of my training ! a coronet as the reward of learning lady-like deportment and self-suppression at my hands ! "
And if Patricia won it—Patricia was of her own blood, and she

could glorify herself in "My niece, Lady Merrian," or, please heaven to take the dear Earl from a sinful world to glory, "My niece, Lady Dovedale." Stronger brains than Mrs. Hamley's have woven as solid-looking romances out of as slight materials, and have been quite as sure of success—if only other people had not fingered the threads and broken in upon the pattern.

By way of parenthesis, it may be observed here that, because Mrs. Hamley elected to be accompanied by her husband when she was out doing her royalties, she was by no means blind to his deficiencies in the art of manner and the science of good breeding. Indeed, no one saw so clearly as she did when and where he failed ; no one knew so well the thinness of the veneer with which she had laboured so hard to conceal the inherent coarseness of the original material. But Mrs. Hamley was a clever social reasoner. She knew that courage and constancy are the only methods by which a conventional misdemeanour can be rendered respectable; and that when you have made an unfitting marriage say, the only thing to do is to carry your conjugal flag bravely to the front, and appear profoundly ignorant of rents and rags. To try to merge her marriage in her own personality was a mistake Mrs. Hamley was far too acute to commit. She had sold herself for a consideration, and she had so much more honour than usually belongs to women who marry for money, that she loyally performed her part, and never flinched from the obligations it entailed. Her husband was a coarse, showy snob ; she knew that well enough, and she knew the world knew it ; but the unwritten convention between them had been her social countenance and wifely loyalty in return for his money and conjugal respect ; and the bond had been faithfully kept. All the world believed that she did really love her black haired, florid, big-fisted Plutus, who was not a gentleman for all his acres ; and that he in his turn loved his faded, elderly, ultra-refined wife : and the belief counted as a medal of gold and a chain of silver in their honour. If they had quarrelled in public, or in any way allowed men to see that they confessed to a mistake, they would have been cut. As it was, union gave strength, and the success of the marriage commanded respect.

Consequently, when Mrs. Hamley went in state to-day to the

Quest, which represented Windsor Castle to the Milltown
world, she went with this marital Goldstick of hers by her side.
And though it was a trial that took all her force to bear with
dignity, it was one which she was conscious had certain solid
favourable issues not to be despised, and which must therefore
be borne bravely.

The first place at which the handsome ponderous carriage
stopped was Cragfoot. They found Mrs. Lowe at home, plaintive and taciturn as ever; tumbled as to her attire; dishevelled
about the head; wrapped in a rhubarb-coloured shawl, and afflicted with her eternal catarrh; taking mournful views of life
generally, and specially of all that pertained to that particular
day. She was a weak-spirited lady at all times, like some
middle-aged Niobe, the spiritual mother of tears and the heiress
of undesignated woe.

Miserable always, Mrs. Lowe would have been hard put to
it had she been obliged to crystallize her sorrows into a definite
shape. Everything afflicted her; from the decadence of England to the flighty manners of the maids; from the horrible
atmosphere of Milltown—of Milltown specially, more horrible
there than anywhere else in England—to the high edge round
one neighbour's garden and the low wall round another's. She
hated the country and she loved London. Once when, for his own
purposes, the Colonel had let Cragfoot for a year and had lived in
London, she had wept all the day and bemoaned herself all
the night for hatred of Blandford Square and desire to be again
at Cragfoot. When Sydney was born she refused to be comforted because he was a boy and not a girl; had he been a girl
she would have held herself accursed in that nature had denied
her a man-child. Whatever was was wrong with poor Mrs. Lowe,
the root and heart of whose misfortune was—her husband,
grafted on to a chronic disturbance of her digestion, and energies reduced thereby to zero.

While they were sitting with her, Patricia wondering why
she was so melancholy yet pitying her so much—and Dora with
her smiles, her downcast eyes and air of lovely amiability, doing
all she knew to charm Sydney's mother; and not succeeding—
Mrs. Lowe being sharper than she looked—the door opened,
and the Colonel and his son walked in.

The former was debonair, handsome, haggard, insolent as

usual; the gentleman's insolence, united with a perfect manner, a pure accent, and a charming voice: the latter pale, with that look of evil resolution about his thin lips and the fire in his dark eyes which those who knew had learnt to dread. He had made up his mind what to do, and he came prepared to act out his resolve.

Scarcely greeting the rest of the company, he made his way straight to Dora sitting on the ottoman, throwing flies of fascination for Mrs. Lowe, and shook hands with her in a familiar, half-tender, half-defying manner, which went like an electric shock through the room. Mrs. Hamley saw it and Mr. Hamley saw it; the Lowes saw it; and even Patricia's unsuspicious nature was enlightened with the rest. Each made his or her comment on what she or he saw, and all looked at Dora, to see how she would bear herself, and whether she would repel or encourage such an audacious advance.

She blushed for her first reply, and her eyes dropped for her second. She was frightened, not pleased; and wished that Sydney had not shown his hand so clearly, nor drawn her into the fray. She would have infinitely preferred that he should have gone into the battle alone—for there was a battle to be fought, and a hard one—and have only called her in to share the victory when he had won it. But the ordeal had to be passed; and it behoved her to be careful of her way among the ploughshares. One false step, and the whole thing would be over for her! And the first step she made was to answer the young man's daring address with her own dexterous power of conciliation; not angering him by her coldness nor the others by her warmth, but just accepting quietly what she could not disclaim, and making herself a party to no policy but the policy of peace. She was set between opposing fires, and she dodged gracefully.

"What a clever little baggage!" said the Colonel to himself as he read her with an accuracy of observation to be got only from a certain class of men who have studied in a certain school of women. "For all her softness that girl has the go of the devil in her! And this thing—what is she like?"

He turned his handsome, haggard face to the fresh and innocent one framed in its loose waves of brown hair watching

Dora anxiously; and from that moment the two girls were stereotyped in his mind as Brinvilliers and Joan of Arc.

The Cragfoot drawing-room opened into a conservatory.

"Have you seen our ferns?" Sydney asked abruptly, speaking to Dora without prefex or annex.

"No," answered Dora, with the sweetest air of modest unconsciousness.

This was another ploughshare dexterously avoided by the clever little feet, which understood wary walking.

"Come with me; I want to show you *my* maidenhair," said Sydney, looking full at the sunny little fringe meandering tendril-like about her temples.

The anonymity of his address was not lost on his hearers; and Mr. Hamley's face was a study that had its lessons for those who cared to read.

"We have a great beauty at home," said Dora simply.

Sydney laughed, "I know that," he said, still looking at her feathery curls; "but I will back mine against any other person's Come and see it."

He stood up and offered her his hand, and for politeness she could not refuse her own.

With a well-managed look of appeal to Mrs. Hamley, taking in Mrs. Hamley's husband by the way, she laid her dainty little close-gloved hand in his as she slowly rose from her seat. He drew it within his arm, and carried her off to the conservatory; speaking to her in a low voice and bending his face near to hers, as they walked across the room in this rather unusual fashion of going for two young people in an ordinary drawing-room filled with ordinary gentlemen and ladies. It was all done, however, more defiantly than tenderly—a challenge rather than a caress.

"Oh, do be careful, Syd!" said Dora in a frightened whisper over the maidenhair.

"No, Dora, I will not. I am going to bring things to a head," said Sydney. "I swear this shall not go on any longer. It shall be one thing or the other."

He spoke fiercely, like a flame of fire translated into words.

"It is one thing already, dear," said Dora with one of her most enchanting looks.

"If you look like that you will drive me wild! You know I cannot stand those eyes of yours, Dora!" cried Sydney.

"You silly boy!" lisped Dora, casting down her eyes and looking up from under her brows with the prettiest, most coquettish modesty. "I will not look at you at all then! Will that be right?"

"No, Dody; I should go mad then," said Sydney, with his hand on hers.

"Poor thing!—you are in a bad way!" she laughed. "Why, what will please you?"

"Not your ridicule, Dora!" he answered savagely.

He had a tindery kind of temper, whereon sparks were never wanting; the irritable temper of a selfish man who holds that the world and all within it were created for his pleasure, and who refuses to take his share of any of the disagreeables that may be afloat.

"Play is not ridicule, dear," said Dora gently. "You ought to know by now, Syd, that I would do nothing in the world to vex you."

But though she spoke with such delicious patience, in her own mind surged up the same contemptuous feeling that she had for Mr. and Mrs. Hamley when she obeyed, soothed, and tricked them. To her, inwardly so strong, outwardly so yielding, the men and women whom she managed were little better than children whom she deceived for their own good, while allowing them to consider themselves supreme.

"And nothing to please me," Sydney answered, his face darkening. "Temporize, temporize, wait, do nothing; that is your policy, Dora, and I am sick of it!"

"You will ruin us both if you do not follow it," said Dora earnestly. "Cannot you see, Syd, that we must have your father's consent before we can make a move? What would become of us if he refused as well as Mr. Hamley? I know that Mr. Hamley will refuse; but if Colonel Lowe consents we are independent."

"And why the devil should Mr. Hamley refuse?" cried Sydney in a rage.

Dora looked meek. "I am sure I don't know, she said; "unless he does not like parting with his money."

"Well, Dora, whatever happens I have made up my mind.

I will speak to my father to-night and to Mr. Hamley to-morrow."

"Not to Mr. Hamley unless your father consents," she pleaded. " We shall be no nearer if you do—only farther off than before."

" Then what do you propose, Dora?" asked Sydney insolently.

"Patience, dear," said Dora, raising her pretty eyes. " Patience and enough to eat ; not impatience and starvation."

"If you two young people have concluded with examining the flowers we will proceed," said Mr. Hamley behind them.

He spoke in his finest accent and with his deepest voice ; and Dora started as if a salvo of artillery had thundered over her head. They had not heard him come. He had taken good care they should not.

"We have quite done," she said, looking at him shyly. " Mr. Lowe was only showing me his ferns. Is it not a beauty, Mr. Hamley?" she continued, passing her fingers across a miserable little specimen which even Mr. Hamley, who knew nothing about flowers or ferns, could see was not worth the pot in which it grew.

" If that is what you have been admiring I can't say much for your taste. It seems to me a heap of time wasted in looking at them weeds!" he said coarsely, passion warring against grammar, and grammar getting the worst of it ; as it always did when he was excited.

" You cannot wonder at any one's forgetting how time goes in Miss Drummond's presence," said Sydney, gallantly as to manner, insolently as to intention, so far as Mr. Hamley was concerned.

Though it was a matter of vital importance to him as things stood to keep fair with Mr. Hamley, even to make him his friend if possible, he would not control himself to courtesy when the fit took him to be aggressive. And as the fit was on him now he indulged it. He hated Mr. Hamley, and he did not care to conceal it. He hated him partly because of his bad manners and his large means, but chiefly because Dora Drummond lived in his house—and he had power over her.

"Excuse me," said the master of Abbey Holme and Mr. Simpson's invisible client Jones, who had lent the money for which Cragfoot was mortgaged; "but if there is one thing more than another I think no gentleman should do, it is passing compliments on ladies when they are under another gentleman's protection."

"I was not aware that Miss Drummond was under any gentleman's protection—more than my own at this moment," said Sydney, looking at him straight in the eyes.

"Then I do," said Mr. Hamley, taking Dora's hand and pulling it roughly through his arm. "*I* am this young lady's protector, sir, and I wish the world to know as much."

"Miss Drummond must decide for herself," said Sydney, tossing up his curly head with an insolent laugh, "Which is it, Dora?"

"'Which is it'—what?" cried Mr. Hamley with a fierce scowl. "Can I believe my ears?"

"That is just what Midas said," sneered Sydney.

Mr. Hamley let fall a thundering oath. "Is it come to this —'Dora,' to *you?*" he said furiously. "Let me know what it all means, or by——"

"I am sure Mr. Lowe will apologize for his mistake; for he is not in the habit of calling me Dora;" said Dora, hurriedly interrupting the objurgation on its path. "I do not think you meant to offend either Mr. Hamley or myself, Mr. Lowe," she continued in her peace-making way, looking at Sydney and smiling at Mr. Hamley, whose arm she pressed tenderly and daintily. But she was treading heavily on the younger man's foot all the while; and Sydney understood pantomime.

"I certainly did not mean to offend *you*, Miss Drummond," he said half sullenly, half familiarly.

"Nor, Mr. Hamley," put in Dora. And there was another grind of the small high-heeled boot. "Mr. Hamley has been like my father all my life, and I owe him the love and obedience of a daughter." She looked prettily into his coarse, flushed face.

"Daughter be hanged?" said Mr. Hamley. "I hate rubbish, Dora, and you know it!"

"You surely do not mean to say that you regard Miss Drummond in any other light but that of a daughter!" flashed out Sydney.

"Mr. Lowe, sir, take my advice," said Mr. Hamley, measur-

N

ing him with his eyes from head to foot, and mentally wringing his neck as he would have wrung any young cockerell's
in his farm-yard: "take stock of your own goods and chat-
tels, and leave another man's alone."

Sydney's face and eyes flamed. "I suppose you know the
only interpretation to that?" he said. "As Miss Drummond
is not your wife, if she is your 'chattel'——"

"What she is to me has nothing to do with you," interrupted Mr. Hamley. "Keep to your own side of the way, Mr.
Lowe, and I'll keep to mine. There'll be mischief between
us else, and I flatter myself I am a trifle the heavier metal!"

An imploring look from Dora checked the angry reply that
rose to Sydney's lips. She liked it well enough that the two
men should hate each other, and be held back from flying at
each other's throats only by the force of conventionality, for
her sake. She was of the order of woman to whom, though
not personally cruel—quite the reverse—men fighting for her
smiles was supreme honour and enjoyment. What they suffered in the conflict troubled her no more than it troubles the
lioness who crouches, licking her lips and purring, waiting for
the bleeding victor, whether it is the black lion or the tawny
that lies dead under the forest trees. But too much was involved at this moment in the keeping of peace to allow her to pos-
turise as a prize for which men did well to contend; so literally as well as morally she brought pressure to bear on Sydney,
and being the wiser and the stronger, she conquered. He
ground his teeth together, but he kept the torrent of words
within them; and making that peculiar grimace which goes
by the name of a "sardonic grin," he turned to Dora, and
said aloud in French, "Ce soir, chérie?" as compensation.

"What's that?" cried Mr. Hamley angrily, "Who's
a-talking foreign tongues here?"

Sydney laughed unpleasantly. His laugh was naturally
unpleasant.

"French," said Dora with her tender smile. "Soit!"
with a look at Sydney; "it only means 'so be it.'"

"I think it deucedly ungentlemanly to talk your foreign lin-
go in society," Mr. Hamley answered, frowning. "Nowadays
gentlemen do rum things, and where you'd look for manners
most you find least. Now, Dora, come! We can't be here

all day, and it's my belief we've been here too long already."

" *Soit*," repeated Sydney, taking the hint.

Spreading out both his hands, with two fingers bent inward, he made a meaningless pull at his coat.

Dora's hat needed adjusting. She put up her hand and pushed in a hair-pin with her fore-finger. And the engagement stood for one o'clock that night; a meeting between them— where and how ?

Then they all took their leave; and when they were gone the Colonel said, but not unkindly; " Syd, my boy, come with me to the library. We must have some serious talk, you and I."

CHAPTER XX.

EXPLANATIONS.

"SHUT the door and sit down; and now tell me—what does all this mean?" began the Colouel.

" What does all what mean, sir? " answered Sydney evasively.

" Don't fence with me, Syd. We both understand each other so far. But what I do not understand is, your ultimate meaning—what you wish and what you intend."

" You are speaking in riddles this afternoon. If you will come to the point, I will meet you," said Sydney.

His father smiled. " You would have made a first-rate diplo- matist," he said.

" I wish to heaven you had put me into the service, or done anything for me but keep me knocking about at home! " cried Sydney impatiently.

" You are ungrateful," was the Colonel's cool response. " Your idleness is your own doing, not mine. If parents are to be blamed for all the wrongheadedness of their sons, their score will be a pretty heavy one in these days of liberty and equality."

" Who cares for what a boy wishes! " said Sydney. " Boys know neither their own minds nor their best interests. Of what use are fathers and mothers but to guide their decisions ? You should not have listened to me, sir ! "

" Perhaps not," said Colonel Lowe, playing with a paper- knife carelessly. " But if I should not, you are not the person to tell me of it."

"And if not I, who then pray? " answered Sydney. " I suppose it is more my affair than any other person's if my whole life is ruined that you may have had a plaything ? "

" Drop that, sir ? " cried the Colonel, turning round on him with sudden fierceness. " You ought to know by now what I can bear and what I will not, even from you. However, I have brought you here to reason, not to wrangle," he continued more quietly; "and wrangling is caddish. Tell me, what are you proposing to yourself with respect to Miss Drummond?"

"I don't know that I am proposing anything to myself with respect to Miss Drummond," answered Sydney sulkily.

"Then you are making a fool of her? All right I dare say, if a trifle cruel. She is probably worth nothing better at the hands of a gentleman—parvenues seldom are."

"Parvenue or not, she is worth more than all your Ladies and Honourables put together. Any man might be proud of Miss Drummond!" flashed out Sydney, falling headlong into the trap.

"All right on the other side," said the Colonel. "And you are not making a fool of her?"

"I am not," answered his son.

"In which case you are meditating an offer?"

"I did not say so," he replied.

"Perhaps have already made it?"

"Neither did I say that," said Sydney.

"I am glad of your disclaimers, my dear boy. As things are with us, any intentions—of an honourable kind—with respect to Miss Drummond would be decidedly mal à propos. For the rest, she must take care of herself."

"My dear father," said Sydney with an impertinent smile, "perhaps we shall come to a better understanding together if you will stick to facts and take nothing for granted. It is only women who jump to conclusions from insufficient premises."

"Thanks for the lesson in dialectics," said the Colonel. "Facts then it shall be : and I will begin with one I would willingly have spared you. I, and you in consequence, are both ruined."

The craven spirit of the man went down. He turned as white as Dora might have done, and his very lips were pale.

"Ruined ! you are surely joking, sir!" he gasped.

"I wish I was," said the Colonel quietly.

"But what am I to do ?" cried Sydney. Then, by the grace of an after-thought he added ; "what are we all to do ?"

"What you have to do is to marry money, by which we shall all profit," said the father.

"All very well to say marry money," said Sydney looking at his nails. "That is sooner said than done."

"Not at all : it is waiting for you. Julia Manley would jump at you. This I know for a fact ; and she has money enough in all conscience—five thousand a year."

"A woman like a camel !—with sandy hair and freckles ! " said Sydney in a tone of disgust.

" Golden hair, my boy, and beauty spots—with five thousand a year to gild them."

"Not to me, sir. She is hideous, and if she was Miss Kilmansegg herself she would be hideous all the same."

"Oh ! after a year's marriage all women are pretty much alike," said his father : " excepting indeed that the odds are in favour of the plain ones. They wear the best and want less looking after in all ways. Five thousand a year will make Julia Manley's camel's face prettier than Dora Drummond's wax-doll beauty, with not five-pence to give it consistency. You will see. A nice house and plenty of cash—and she will be quite handsome in your eyes before your heir is born. And good temper and habit will do the rest."

" All very well I dare say, if one entered into the thing quite free ; but—I had better confess it now—I *am* in love with Dora Drummond," said Sydney with a burst.

"Of not the slightest consequence, my dear fellow. Many a man before yourself has loved one woman by inclination and married another by necessity. I have not the faintest objection to your loving Hamley's pretty little girl, but I bar the banns. "Unless," he shrugged his shoulders and cut a sheet of paper carelessly, " you are prepared to turn into the world on your own account, without a halfpenny from me, present or to come."

" But why is Miss Drummond to be tabooed of all women ?" said Sydney. "She is pretty, lady-like, well-bred, and I am fond of her ; why is she to be thrust out into the cold ?"

"She is not tabooed ; it is only her want of money that won't fit. Let Hamley give her only two thousand a year, and I say amen with all my heart. You see I rate her, as woman with woman, worth three thousand a year more than Julia Manley ; which is ranking her high. But if, as I suspect, it is your pretty Dora and an empty purse, I say no, unless you have resources of which I know nothing."

"At least let me try," said Sydney dejectedly.

"Like Bruce's spider? By all means. And if you fail ?"
The young man was silent.

"Well! if you fail, what then, Syd ?" his father repeated.

"I am sure I don't know," he answered sullenly.

"No? I do. Your decision will rest then between two alternatives—marrying Julia Manley, or hopeless and irremediable ruin."

"I suppose Cragfoot will stand where it does ? " said Sydney.

"Probably ; but not for us. It is mortgaged up to the hilt. I tell you Syd," he continued earnestly, "we are ruined ; and I see no way out of the wood save by Julia Manley."

"At least, I will try old Hamley first," said Sydney, suddenly changing colour.

"By all means. You won't succeed. It's my belief he has his own reason for keeping that girl single."

"What the deuce do you mean, sir ?" cried Sydney irritably. "If I thought that I would break his head."

"You had better keep your hands clean," said Colonel Lowe. "Perhaps he is looking out for a title, and means to sell her only when he has made his market. There's Merrian. The old shoeblack may be ambitious of getting his name in Debrett ; or he may be looking forward to Mrs. Hamley's death. She is tough, but he's twenty years her junior if a day."

"Don't say that, father; it maddens me !" cried Sydney passionately. "I swear to you, if I believed that he had designs on Dora in the future, I would take her away to-night ! "

"Don't be a fool, Syd," returned his father. "Take the girl away to what ?—absolute beggary ! You would find no home here, and you have no income in your hands or your head. Let us understand one another. It is time. I have been an indulgent father to you, but everything has its limits. Mine is, your marrying a penniless parvenue. If you were to do so, I swear, in my turn, that you might starve before my eyes before I would give you a crust ; and if I came into millions not one sixpence would be left to you. You know, Syd, I am never violent, but I am determined. And now you have it."

"Your words are hard, sir," said Sydney, looking down.

With much bluster he had but little of the tenacity of a real fighter in him. A tyrant over subordinates, he was a coward when a resolute will opposed him ; and his father, who, to do

him justice, hated the task, knew he could bully him into submission whenever he chose to assume a certain tone which meant
he was not to be trifled with.

"If my words are hard my deeds will be harder," said Colonel Lowe.

"Still I have yet permission to do my best with that brute?"
said Sydney after a pause ; during which, handsome though he
was, he had a curious kind of likeness to a rat in a trap.

"By all means. And when you have done you best, come to
me and tell me the result."

"And if Mr. Hamley refuses?—father, I do love her!"

"I shall be sorry for you. But he will refuse ; and then you
must marry Julia Manley."

"If he consents so far as to give very little down, and to
make only a provisional settlement—you will not oppose me
then?"

The Colonel smiled, and yet half sadly. He thought his son
would have shown more pluck, more determination, than this
pitiful trying here and there for a way of escape. He was sorry
for him, but he was contemptuous too.

"I will say amen to any scheme you can propose, my dear
fellow, that will give you a gentleman's income and pay fifty
thousand pounds over and above your immediate wants," he
said. "Get even a thousand a year with your pretty
Dora, and I will not refuse my consent ; which is being liberal.

"I will go to Abbey Holme to-morrow," said Sydney ; but
he did not speak confidently, and his father knew that his
hopes were as few as his own.

"All right," he answered. " Now let us go and have a game
at billiards. Ah! if you could do everything as well as your
favourite hazard, you would not have far to go for your fortune."

"It is a pity you did not teach me something more profitable
while there was time," retorted Sydney, as they lighted their
cigars and strolled smoking towards the billiard-room.

While this conversation had been going on at Cragfoot, the
Hamley carriage, bearing its four silent occupants, had been
rolling rapidly to the Quest. It was by no means a comfortable
drive. Things never are comfortable when Fear sits on one
side and Nemesis on the other.

At the Quest they found the Countess and Lord Merrian

both at home. The Earl was out with his agent looking over the land. They saw him afterwards in the road ; a stout-legged ruddy-faced man, in a bulky shooting-jacket and leathern gaiters, looking like a well-to-do grazier rather than a man of fashion or an hereditary legislator consecrated by birth to patriotism and the public service. He was too well known by sight to the others for them to wonder at his unaristocratic look ; but Patricia was immensely astonished at his commonplace appearance. She had an idea that Lords and Ladies were of a different material from the rest of the world ; and that nature herself had delivered them visibly from the bondage of mediocrity and endowed them with their superior credentials.

But if the Earl was homely the Countess was superb—the typical countess of splendid attire, magnificent beauty, queenly manners, and looking about thirty when she was fifteen years older. Lord Merrian too, was delightful. He was a tall, poetic-looking, handsome young man ; well-mannered, superbly got-up, a trifle affected, but both clever and ambitious ; at this moment going through a temporary phase of intellectual rather than practical conscientiousness, by which he did honestly desire to know the truth and live up to the better thing, without having the moral thoroughness which would enable him to do either. He was an imaginative person, who took impressions for convictions and fancies for proofs ; not of strong character, and apt to be unduly influenced by his surroundings ; which gave him an undeserved appearance of insincerity. He professed to take mournful views of life and to be penetrated with a sense of the general hollowness of things. A mild sceptic on his own account, and with no definite creed on any side, he deplored the absence of faith in the masses ; a Conservative, holding to the righteousness of a privileged class, he deplored their degradation ; rich—at least absolutely, if relatively poor for a peer's son—titled, courted, and a social darling of the most cherished kind, he yearned for a crusade, he said, where men would go out to fight for some great stirring cause, flinging off the deadening fetters of society and the silken cordage of our modern luxury.

It was pretty and pathetic to hear him talk thus, lowering his soft voice and raising his handsome eyes in between the rare

Steinberger and the 'twenty-seven port ; his smooth young face
arranged with care, his costly button-hole bouquet shedding
sweet scents with every breath, the ball at his foot, and in his
hand every good gift by which humanity can be blessed and
life made happy. Women praised him for his earnestness, and
called him " a sweet fellow " and a " most charming young man
with such nice feeling " and " such good sentiments ; " men
laughed at him for his affectation and called him a humbug and
a sop. But he was not a humbug. He was theoretically in
earnest ; only practically he had not enough force to defy the
world, deny himself, and act out his higher faith in the face of
the society he affected to decry. His was not the stuff of which
martyrs are made ; and while he looked towards Pisgah carried daily sacrifice to Mammon. But it soothed his conscience
that he should talk ; and he did not feel saddened by the
hiatus between his word and his deed.

His manner of being and his style of conversation pleased the
Abbey Holme girls. Naturally he devoted himself to them
during the visit, the three sitting in a recess a little apart from
the rest—Lord Merrian holding forth. He was fond of drawing-room declamation, and especially fond of declaiming in a
corner with a few pretty women as his audience. To Dora he
was of course delightful. Was he not a young lord, well-looking and gallant? and did not his handsome eyes rest on her
with a kind of approving admiration that showed his cultivated
taste ? To Patricia, still in the age of candid credulity, he was a
nineteenth century Saint John. His second-hand Emersonian
turns of thought and modes of expression struck a chord in her
own heart that vibrated with a passionate echo. Her face
lighted up as Lord Merrian spoke of the valuelessness of the
individual and the grandeur of truth, of the need for self-
sacrifice and the sorrows of humanity. She felt inclined to
hold out her hand to him and call him brother. Had she been
a man she would have proposed a league between them on the
spot, by which they would have bound themselves like knights
of old to resist the world, the flesh, and the devil, and to devote
themselves to the good of humanity and the glory of God.
Being a woman, all she could do was to raise her large eyes,
dilated, dark, and tender, to his face, and to assent to his views
with an outflow of enthusiasm that partly stirred and partly

amused him. He thought what a grand creature she was; just the kind of woman to lead a man to the ultimate heights, and make him a hero or a saint, according to his bent and the development of his muscles. A little untutored perhaps; but too lovely not to be forgiven this or any other flaw there might be in her crown of perfection. He was charmed with her. She was so fresh, he said to his mother afterwards; so deliciously quaint and simple; a girl who reminded him of an early Christian martyr, or of Hypathia, or Vittoria Colonna; and he too added what Colonel Lowe had said—or Joan of Arc.

Of Dora he formed another estimate, but one as true in its own way. A clever, self-controlled woman, he said, leading an artificial life and wearing a mask, not a face; a woman to fence with, to play with, to be wary of; one of the felidæ—soft, silky, stealthy, creeping—but trustworthy? true? real? Scarcely!

Lord Merrian had not come to the mature age of three-and-twenty without learning a few facts of human life, and the Doras of the world of women were not unfamiliar with him.

Patricia on the contrary was a new study; and the young man's curiosity was roused, as Dr. Fletcher's had been before him. He mentally determined that he would see this noble creature again before long, that he would make himself a hero in her eyes, and rouse her enthusiasm as he felt it could be roused. After that he was conscious of nothing; save perhaps a vague idea that Mr. Hamley was popularly supposed to possess millions, and that Patricia Kemball was his wife's niece.

On the whole the visit was a success. The Countess was gracious in bearing and gorgeously arrayed; and Lord Merrian was pronounced a most distinguished-looking young man by Mrs. Hamley, and not so far amiss by Mr. Hamley. Mrs. Hamley felt when they left that she had made a decided step upwards, and had planted herself at last in the same hemisphere as her desires. She was convinced that they would be asked to the Quest this year; and when that was done, the last *huis clos* would be thrown down; the last stronghold of exclusiveness would have surrendered.

As they drove home she was quite gay, almost playful; and even Patricia came in for a share in the wintry sun of her smiles. Both she and Mr. Hamley had seen that Lord Mer-

rian had paid her just that extra amount of attention which
implies preference, and for the moment she was in the ascendant,
and had " the hands" usually accorded to Dora.

For the moment, indeed, the two girls seemed to have
changed places. Grim to Dora, Mr. Hamley was quite familiar
and jocular with Patricia. He " chaffed " her about her conquest, and called her " my lady " all the way home, till the girl's
burning indignation nearly choked her. He rolled his eyes
and wagged his head and smacked his lips as he said, " Oh! *I*
saw, Miss Slyboots, what game you were after !" or " Well, my
Lady Merrian, and when are we to order the bride-cake, eh?"
or " When a certain young lady's queening it at the Quest, I
suppose she'll be too grand for you and me, Lady," and so on,
with never a softening line in his face in answer to dear Dora's
shy eyes and tender smiles and pretty lisp, and all those subtle,
secret caresses of hers which generally had the power of putting
him into a good humour when he was cross, and of making life
very sweet and pleasant to him.

To-day he was impervious. Her tenderest looks fell on him
like dew on granite, and softened him no more than the dew
would have softened the granite. He had not got over the
scene at Cragfoot, and he had to have it out with her, as he
said to himself, before he forgave her. Besides, though Lord
Merrian had paid Patricia the most attention, to outsiders he
had looked at Dora admiringly ; and Mr. Hamley was well up
in the science of secret preference, and by what methods it
could be shown. Just before they came to Abbey Holme he
took occasion to say, speaking of Lord Merrian, " Yes ; I'm no
tuft hunter, I believe"—he was, though he did not acknowledge
it ; " but I could not help observing the difference between this
young man and that young hound, Lowe. I have lived pretty
long among gentlefolks, but hang me if ever I saw one as impudent as that jackanapes was to-day. However, you could
permit him to address you as he did, Dora, is more than I can
make out. It is that that gets over me. To call you ' Dora '
before my very face ! I should like to have wrung his neck
for him ! "

" It was very rude, very extraordinary!" murmured Dora
meekly. " I could not make it out ; he never did so before."

" And I'll take pretty good care he never does so again," said

Mr. Hamley. "I'll Dora him if he tries it on again, he may take his oath of that!"

"I am sure I do not know what possessed him to-day. He must have been out of his mind!" said Dora with a distressed face.

"He was drunk," said Mr. Hamley, coarsely.

And Dora turned her head out of the window, saying between her teeth "Wretch!" quite naturally.

"I thought he was rather free," put in Mrs. Hamley, looking kindly at her favourite. "But I don't see how Dora could have helped it. I don't think you encouraged him, my dear?"

"Oh, no, indeed I did not, dear!" said Dora pleadingly. "I was as much astonished at it as you could have been. I *never* encouraged Mr. Lowe, never!"

Patricia put her hand over her eyes. Her burning indignation at Mr. Hamley's ungainly playfulness to herself suddenly died out, and she became chilled, as if the air had grown colder than before, when she heard Dora's deliberate untruth. She knew that Sidney Lowe had been encouraged; did she not remember that walk, and all those long, half-whispered and wholly unintelligible conversations together? She wondered how Dora could have the courage—the bad courage—to say such a thing so unblushingly before her.

"I saw how much annoyed you were," continued Dora, turning her eyes meekly on her master;" "and I would have given worlds to have stopped him. But I could not! and I was so dreadfully distressed!" It was getting dark now. Leaning forward to impress her grief more closely on Mr. Hamley, Dora slid her soft, caressing little hand into his; and Mr. Hamley, squeezing it—forgave her.

"I think you were hard on Dora to-day," said Mrs. Hamley, as she and her husband sat before the fire in her dressing-room, waiting for the dressing-bell to ring. "It is only what we must expect; she is a pretty girl, and young men will pay her attention, of course. That young Mr. Lowe—I have often thought he admired her; and though Lord Merrian paid Patricia the most attention, still he looked very often at Dora, and he might have talked more to my niece as a blind. Young people will be young people; and though I do not encourage flirting, or anything undesirable, we must expect that the girl will be sought after!"

"I don't want young men about Miss Drummond," answered Mr. Hamley stiffly. "I have brought her up at great expense to be one of ourselves, and I do not relish the idea of having spent all that money for another man's advantage. We are getting old people, my dear,"—when Mr. Hamley wanted to please his wife he used to bracket himself with her, and deny his comparative youth in favour of her age—"and being old people, or on the way, Dora is useful to us. She makes a little life in the house, and she is nice in her ways, and so on."

"Good gracious, Mr. Hamley, we have Patricia!" said Mrs. Hamley sharply. "She is younger than Dora."

"And not half so entertaining," said Mr. Hamley. "Your niece may be a good sort of young person; I do not deny that, but she is horrid heavy on hand all the same. She can't do the things Dora can. I call her a wretched performer on the piano, and she has no manner as Dora has."

"She has not had Dora's advantages of course," said Mrs. Hamley. "No girl brought up as poor Patricia has been can possibly be equal to one cared for and educated by a lady, like Dora. For what she has gone through I consider her remarkable; and at all events she is a Kemball, which counts for something."

"She ought to be able to count something to the good," Mr. Hamley answered. "But make the best of it you can, you cannot make her a patch on Dora."

"I hate such vulgar expressions!" said Mrs. Hamley crossly.

"Well, it isn't quite the thing perhaps," apologized her husband; "but I mean to say you know what I am at."

"To go back to our starting point, you say you don't wish Dora to marry?" asked Mrs. Hamley.

She had her idea, and she was resolved to ventilate it before dinner.

"Certainly not. I can leave her comfortable," said the brewer decidedly.

"But I suppose you would not refuse a good offer; say such an offer as Lord Merrian for the girl?" Mrs. Hamley asked this loftily—lords were becoming her everyday acquaintance now.

"Wouldn't I just?—all the same as if he was that blackguard young Lowe yonder, or the stable-boy!" Mr. Hamley answered, a little more roughly than was usual with him when "conversing" with his wife. "Lord or no lord, I'll have none

of them here poking after the girl. I've paid for her bringing
up, and I consider I have the right to keep what I've paid for.
I've heard speak of pelicans, but I don't feel inclined to copy
'em."

" It is rather a novel way of looking at the matter, and I
must say a sordid one," said Mrs. Hamley. " I cannot think
with you that in adopting a child you are buying a slave."

"Don't you?" he answered coolly. "I'm sorry we cannot put
our horses' heads together in the matter. But whether we do
or we don't, I must be leader here, Lady; and if I leave you
full possession of your own to do as you like with, you have
no cause of complaint. If you are so anxious to get the young
ladies a husband with a handle to his name get him for Miss
Kemball. I'll give her as handsome a turn-out and make as
good a settlement on her if she marries to please me—and
you—as any girl need have. And I'm sure I can't say fairer for a young person as is no relation to me, and that I
don't especially admire."

" You are the oddest compound of generosity and tyranny-
Mr. Hamley, I ever saw! " said his wife, half pettishly, half
pleasantly; for they had their little conjugal flirtations togeth,
er when they were alone. At first for policy; but as time had
gone on, and Mrs. Hamley had followed the law of habit,
she had become both more oblivious to her husband's defects
and more tolerant of those she still saw, as well as personally more affectionate to him. His strength and vigour
seemed to stay her own failing powers, and she leant on him
more than she had done in the beginning; while he was
daily more conscious of the twenty years' gap between
them, if daily more careful to conceal that consciousness and
go through his appointed task creditably.

"Ah my dear," he answered, his thick lips parted into what
he meant to be a fascinating smile, and his small keen eyes
turned with such softness as he could command on his aged
wife, " I would do more for you than take your niece into my
house, and treat her like my own. What I did for my
cousin's child I can surely do for your brother's daughter; for
though I am but a rough diamond, Lady, I never forget
who you are and what I owe you. You have chipped me out
of the rough as I may say, and I don't begrudge my thanks."

" You are very good," said his wife softly, and stroked his thick hand almost tenderly with her long bony fingers.

Poor soul, she meant it well, though she did make his flesh creep !

" There ! I think I have settled the old lady's hash for a bit," was his unspoken thought as, the dressing-bell ringing, he stooped over her gallantly and kissed her powdered flaccid cheek. Then he went into his own room and stood before the glass, fingering his bushy whiskers complacently.

And standing there, large, florid, black-haired, showy, he smiled approvingly at the thing he saw.

" A fine figure of a man when all's said and done !" he said to himself. " I don't know a finer !"

CHAPTER XXI.

THE POSTERN GATE.

THIS conversation, wherein he had been able to lay down the law and set his foot on the budding head of the young scorpion—the thought was his own—restored Mr. Hamley to his wonted self-satisfaction. Perhaps that survey in the glass had something to do with it. The evening therefore passed off with an amount of cheerfulness not usual in the evenings at Abbey Holme. The three played their beloved bézique, and the good humour of the trio did not suffer by any of the accidents of the game. Patricia was "out," of course; but she was not snubbed as usual. Indeed Aunt Hamley made room for her to come and sit by her, and tried, as so often before, to teach her the mysteries of royal and common marriage, single and double bézique, sequences and tens and aces. And Patricia for very gratitude gave her mind to it, and did her best to understand it, but could not get beyond the length of thinking it all an incomprehensible muddle, and nothing in it when you got to the end of it. Still she was happy in feeling in favour; happy in thinking that a man in Lord Merrian's position, with his wealth and power, could hold such grand views and be so entirely noble-minded; happy in the remembrance of some poor people for whom she had given Catherine Fletcher a contribution out of her small store the other day, and to whom this timely help had been of infinite service; happy in having seen by a *Times* telegram that Gordon's ship, the *Arrow*, had got safely to her first station, and that she might therefore be soon expecting a letter; and in the general amiability of the time even Mr. Hamley thought her really a very nice-looking young person, and not so bad a girl after all.

As for dear Dora, she was so sweet and pretty, so animated yet so gentle, with such a lovely flush on her round, pink cheeks, and "so darling" altogether, he wondered how he could have been such a bear to her to-day. And yet when he remem-

o

bered Sydney Lowe, and that odd-looking scene in the conservatory, he did not find his bearishness so very remarkable. Of one
thing, however, he was quite sure—whatever that young jackanapes might feel, dear Dora thought nothing of him, and she
would not, even if she was asked, leave Abbey Holme: and
Mrs. Hamley

Abbey Holme was a large house, thickly carpeted throughout, and with well-oiled locks and hinges. Doors and windows
were all heavily bolted and barred, but neither bolt nor bar
made more noise than the piston of a steam-engine, and everything worked with a silent precision that was part of the Hamley luxury of living. Only one door was not barred with extra
bolts. This was a low-arched, oaken door, studded and banded
with iron in a fantastic mediæval fashion that looked formidable and was of no use; a kind of make-believe postern-gate,
opening on to the side shrubbery and for show only, for it was
never used. Indeed the key had been extracted from Mr.
Hamley's private drawer for nearly three years now; but he
had not missed it. Such a mere symbol as it was he had forgotten it had ever been.

But there was one person in the house to whom that key was
no mere symbol, but a thing of very positive use. Nearly three
years ago Dora had purloined it, and thus had held her freedom of nights, if not of days, in her own hands. And for the
last year she had used her freedom in company with Mr. Sydney Lowe.

Once a week or so, when the Abbey Holme household was
asleep, a little figure muffled up in a waterproof, hooded and
veiled, used to open the third door on the corridor and steal
down the broad staircase, with no more noise of swinging hinge
or falling feet than if a ghost had been abroad; used to glide
across the hall, every step counted till the nailed and banded
door was reached; used to feel with small pink hands for the
keyhole, putting in the key and shooting the lock with about
as much sound as the scratching and the falling of a pin would
have made; used to draw the key; stand for a moment on the
top step; and then on a cry which only her ear could have distinguished from the hoot of an owl, used to steal round the
angle into the dark walk where Sydney Lowe was waiting for

her. This had gone on as was said for over a year now, and no human being had the smallest suspicion of the truth.

To be sure, Alice Garth, Dora's maid, used sometimes to wonder how her young mistress's waterproof had got so wet when she was not out all yesterday ; but she had no theory to explain the wonder, and contented herself with thinking it queer and talking it over in the housekeeper's room   Twice, when she had spoken of it, some of the servants had set themselves to watch the young lady's door; but as each time it was on the night after she had gone out—when she was naturally safe at home—they had lost half a night's rest for nothing ; and the mystery remained unsolved.   If they had waited for a week or so, and had been as persevering as they were anxious, they might have been rewarded.

To-night it all happened just as usual.   Exactly at one o'clock Dora turned the handle of her door, and came out into the corridor.   She was dressed in her dark grey cloak, with her hood over her head and a thick veil over her face.   Brown woollen socks were drawn over her boots, and she had sacrificed high heels to the exigences of the expedition.   The moon shone brightly ; and she was always a little nervous in the moonlight. Indeed she was disturbed altogether to-night ; strangely so for her, generally so cool, so collected, and with no more nervous fancies than she had inconvenient passions.   She felt as if a crisis was at hand ; and she dreaded lest it should turn the wrong way and bring her ruin, not relief.

Besides, she was getting tired of her part.   More because of the dead weariness of her life than because she loved him with that intensity of passion which defies all law and conquers all obstacles, and more as her expression of revolt against the tyrannous domination to which she outwardly submitted so gracefully than as a matter of deliberate choice, she had entered into these secret relations with Sydney Lowe.   And now when she was irrevocably caught she was beginning to long for freedom. Lord Merrian had looked at her admiringly to-day ; and to be Lady Merrian, and later the Countess of Dovedale, was as a fool's bauble that jingled its bells merrily in her ears.   To be Mrs. Sydney Lowe by consent of the authorities had once seemed to her by no means a disagreeable outlook ; but she was getting weary of the uncertainty of that consent, and the first excite-

ment of her adventure had passed.   And again, in spite of all
that had happened, she did not so very madly love the Man;
she could have lived without him, had she tried, she thought!
His admiration had flattered, and his own love for her in the
fiery insistence had excited and carried her away.   She had
been dull and oppressed; always playing a part and always
humbling herself in submission; so she had oiled the bolts
and hinges of the postern-gate, and had used the key to more
purpose of late than when she had merely played at being
adventurous and secretly free in the beginning.

At the first it had been simply running half-a-dozen steps
into the shrubbery and back again, feeling awfully wicked, im-
measurably brave, and desperately frightened ; grateful too
that no big black man had come out of the darkness, and caught
her by the heels as she scampered up the steps panting and
trembling; and congratulating herself on her safety when she
had crept up into her own room again, and felt herself the mistress of the whole sleeping household.   These had been her
first experiences in the way of midnight sorties.   Then she had
ventured a little farther, and once right into the road over the
stile—the vulnerable point in the park—where, as ill-luck
would have it, she had met a real adventure in the person of
Sydney Lowe, himself out at that hour for no good : a meeting
to be henceforth continued by appointment, and on to the position in which affairs stood at present.   And they stood awkwardly enough ; could scarcely be worse, all things considered
—Colonel Lowe's ruin, and Mr. Hamley's determination not to
give dear Dora a farthing if she married against his wish, and
Sydney Lowe being of all men the one most decidedly against
his wish.

"Dora ! I have been waiting for you more than an hour,"
said Sydney, more peevishly than tenderly, as she glided across
the walk and ran into his arms.

"Poor dear boy ! I am so sorry! But I said one quite
plainly, you know.   I could not be sure of myself before," said
Dora prettily.

Not even to Sydney Lowe did she ever show temper or her
real self.   The concealment of her real feelings under a false
mask of amiability had come to be a kind of second nature with
her, and she liked the sentiment of strength and of an inner
unknown and unshared life that it gave her.

"But I wanted so much to see you, darling! I suppose that made me impatient," he said.

"Well, and now that you have me, what?" asked Dora.

"Dora, I and my father have had a jaw," Sydney began.

"You horrid boy—a what?" said Dora.

"Oh, never mind grammar, Dody!—let me say what I have to say in my own way!" cried Sydney. "My father has been talking to me, and it is all over with us!"

"What do you mean, Syd?—has he found out?" Dora cried, clinging to him in terror.

"Quite the contrary; he has no idea of the real state of the case, though I have told him something; but the game's up all the same. The governor has done something, I don't know what, but the upshot of it is—he is ruined and we have not sixpence between us."

"Sydney!" The pretty little head went down on to his shoulder, and Dora, whom this prospect of impecuniosity appalled, began to cry.

"Don't cry, darling!" he said soothingly. "What's done cannot be undone, and things may come right after all!"

"How can they come right?" she sobbed.

"I don't see exactly; perhaps old Hamley will come down handsomely. I am going to ask him to-morrow. That made me so anxious to see you to-night."

"Oh Sydney, you must not ask him!" she pleaded. "Things are bad enough as they are; this will only make them ten times worse."

"But why should it make them worse, Dora? I must ask him some day. We cannot go on as we are. I swear it makes me almost mad!—and we cannot live without money."

"And do you think he will give us a farthing? Not if we starved. Married or unmarried he will not help us with sixpence. I know Mr. Hamley!" said Dora lifting her head—the moonlight shining on her tears—and speaking with a bitterness rare in her.

"That is just what my father said I might do if I brought you without money," Sydney returned. "If old Hamley comes down as he ought he will receive you with open arms. He has taken quite a liking for you, Dora—and who indeed could help it, my beauty?—but he cannot give us what he has not got;

and he has not got enough to go on with for himself, still less
to set me up. The thing now is to get old Hamley to do it."

" Get him to set us up !—ask that stone, and you are just as
likely to move it as Mr. Hamley," said Dora. " He does not
want me to marry at all !"

" And why not ? " said Sydney passionately, unclasping her
hands from his shoulders and standing as if in another moment he would fling her from him.

He was not a brave man, but he would have fought for a
woman like a tiger or with one like a savage ; and he was
jealous.

"I don't know," lisped Dora. "How can I tell ? I am useful
to him at home, I suppose, and he does not want to part with
me ; still less with his money."

" If I thought it was anything else I would break every bone
in his body ! " flared out Sydney.

" What a silly boy you are, Syd !" said Dora.   " Cannot a
person be fond of one without being in love ? Why, Mr.
Hamley is old enough to be my father !"

" And his wife to be your grandmother," returned Sydney.

" Poor, dear, yes ; quite that," laughed Dora.

" Which is just the reason. It is you, Dora, who are silly."

" You are complimentary," she pouted.

"And you are unkind," he returned.

" If you have brought me out into the cold, such a frosty
night as it is too, only to quarrel with me, I shall go in again,"
said Dora, suddenly and strangely cross.

He stared at her. This was a new revelation to him. His
" little bit of swansdown," as he used to call her, cross ! his
soft sleek purring *felis femina* suddenly ceasing to purr and
showing her claws ! It was the beginning of a new order of
things and one that Sydney Lowe was not disposed to accept.

" Perhaps you had better," he answered coolly. "And perhaps I had better not come to Mr. Hamley to-morrow."

" How cruel you are, Sydney !" she cried.   " After having
got me into such a dreadful scrape talking like that !—and
when you ought to do everything in the world to get me out of
it again—as far as you can. It is too bad of you !"

" But you said it was of no use, Dora." His tone was still
that of an offended person.

"And if I did, does that say you are not to try? We cannot be worse off than we are!" she answered.

"Oh yes, we might," said Sydney significantly.

And Dora laughing, said : "Yes, a great deal worse, if it all came out, and we were forced to take up our position and keep to it. But Sydney," she continued, "what shall we do if Mr. Hamley will not give his consent, which means money?"

"Take French leave, Dody."

"I think we have done that already," she said demurely.

"Well, I am sure I cannot tell. We must go on like this, I suppose," Sydney said, biting his nails according to his habit.

"It is dreadful, dear, is it not?" said Dora; "but indeed I see nothing else for it. We cannot live on love and kisses, Syd; we must have a house to shelter us, and clothes to wear, and food to eat, and these are only to be had for money. And we cannot earn money—we must have it given to us somehow."

"Then I will come-to-morrow," said Sydney, taking her in his arms again as the last remains of their little tiff vanished.

"And be very sweet and nice," answered Dora. "You are a dear boy, but you were like a bear to-day—just a bear," pulling his curly locks playfully.

"I cannot help it, Dora. That man maddens me with his vulgarity. He is such a cad, and so insolently familiar to you! I feel as if I could thrust my fist down his throat when he calls you 'Dora' and speaks as if you belonged to him—conceited jackass!"

"Yes, I know all that; but he has the key of the position, dear, and there is no good to be got by making him angry. Our policy is to please him," was her sagacious reply.

"Little wisehead! when you are always with me I shall be a paragon of perfection."

Sydney said this with that curious mixture of banter and affection which belongs to a vain man in love when the woman he loves schools him. He did not like it, but he liked her, and so made the two fit in the best way he could.

She chose to take him simpliciter.

"Yes," she said, with her hands on his shoulders; "when you have me with you always, you will be different from what you are now."

"What the—what in the name of fortune do you mean?" cried Sydney.

" Just what I say, dear. Betting and drinking and smoking, and oh ! a world of other things—and swearing with them— all these will have to be given up when I am at Cragfoot."

" Do you want your husband to be a muff ? " he asked.

" Not the least in the world—only a gentleman," replied Dora.

" I must either quarrel with you or kiss you for that piece of impertinence," he said.

" Are you in doubt which ? " asked Dora, lifting her eyes shyly and lisping.

When Dora stole back to the house she was conscious of something unusual.   Lights were flashing up-stairs, and a sub- dued hum of voices told that the trim household was up and about, and that an event must have taken place in her absence. If it should be that she had been missed ! Quick as thought she drew off her socks and stole across the hall to the library, the door of which she opened, then came running up the stairs rubbing her eyes like one just awakened. She saw no one, however, until she came to her own room, where Patricia pale and tall as an avenging angel, met her at the door.

" Oh, my goodness ! what is the matter ? " cried Dora.

" Aunt Hamley has been taken ill and has been asking for you. Why Dora, where have you been ? "

" I went into the library to read a little bit of German I wanted to translate, and fell asleep. I am so cold—feel me," Dora answered, putting her benumbed hands into Patricia's.

" But how is that ?   I went into the library—I went into all the rooms for you," she answered.   " We could not find you anywhere ; and, Dora, I saw something that I know now was you cross the shrubbery path, and that horrid Mr. Lowe was with you. Oh, I am so sorry to say this to you," she con- tinued, as Dora started and trembled and looked as if she was going to faint ; " you know how much I love you ! Dora, I would rather have done a wrong thing myself than that you should ! I would rather have died than have seen this !—but I cannot live in falsehood, and what I know you must know that I know."

The tears gushed into her eyes and her lips quivered.

For just a moment Dora reflected ; then she took her deter- mination.

"Don't cry," she said. "Things look bad, but they are not so bad as they seem. You did see me with Sydney, but there is no harm in it—I am married to him."

"Married! Dora!—oh, it cannot be true!" said Patricia, putting up her hands.

The thought seemed indelicate, monstrous, almost criminal, sacrilegious. A married woman was a very different thing from a girl playfellow, even if she was seven years older than herself. A married woman was a person infinitely older, infinitely experienced, set in a different sphere, with thoughts and views and knowledge quite apart from all girlhood—a person to approach with respect; to wonder at while her wedding-ring was yet bright and fresh; perhaps to pity; perhaps to envy; maybe to regard as a traitress to the order of maidenhood; maybe as the fortunate chosen into a more beautiful existence—certainly not to treat with the foolish familiarity allowed to one of her own kind, and with which she had treated Dora. She drew back, shocked, chilled, terrified, revolted. She had loved Dora so much, and now to find herself so fearfully deceived!

"Don't be shocked, dear," said Dora, creeping up to her caressingly. "It was very wrong and silly, I dare say; but he made me do it when I was in London last autumn."

"No, Dora, no one can make you commit a crime," said Patricia, her head and eyes still averted.

"A secret marriage is not a crime, dear. Sydney is my husband," said Dora, humbly if emphatically.

"The marriage may not be, but the secrecy is. I ca' think how you can live with such a thing on your mind,' tricia answered, still turned away.

"It is horrible, but what can I do? There it is, and ¿ not get out of it; and the worst is, his father is ruined Mr. Hamley, I know, will neither give me his consent fraction. Colonel Lowe would like me well enough daughter-in-law if there was any money on either side; but, as Sydney says, we have not sixpence between us."

"But, Dora, this must come to an end now; you must decide on something. What are you going to do?" cried Patricia, suddenly looking at her.

The girl shrugged her should "What can we do?" said.

"Tell Mr. and Mrs. Hamley; and if you don't——"

"You will? No, Patricia, you will not," she said, putting her arms round her and looking up into her face. "I know your good heart too well for that. You would not ruin me; you are not my enemy, darling. I can trust you, and you would never be treacherous to me or take advantage of having found out my secret."

Tears gathered into Patricia's eyes, and fell slowly down her face.

"Would you?" said Dora, with a tender, suppliant, loving air; her arms still round the girl's waist, clinging closer and closer.

Patricia did not answer. She made a faint and ineffectual show of unclasping those beseeching arms.

"Patricia!" the soft voice pleaded again; "will you betray me? If you do, you send me out to simple beggary; and I have always been your friend here."

Still Patricia did not answer. She had covered her face now and was sobbing.

"Patricia!"—almost in a whisper—"Patricia, dear, will you betray me? If you think you ought you must—but I shall be ruined."

A step, or rather the rustle of a dress, was heard in the lobby. "Speak, darling—tell me!"

"No, no; I will not betray you!" said Patricia, turning to her, sobbing as if her heart would break. She carried the sacrifice of her truth to her love, and accounted herself accursed that her friend might be saved.

A light knock came to the door.

"Mrs. Hamley is wanting you, Miss Drummond," said Bignold the maid.

"Good gracious, Bignold! what is the matter?" said dear Dora through the closed door, tearing down her chignon and flinging a shawl about her to look as if she had just scrambled out of bed.

"Spasms, miss. Your aunt is very bad," said Bignold; and then Dora opened the door and slid out as if just awakened.

"It was only to say you need not be alarmed; and do not wake up Patricia," said Mrs. Hamley, feebly.

"No dear, I will not," Dora answered, kissing her forehead.

"It is quite enough that I am unhappy. How sorry I am to see you suffer like this!"

Mrs. Hamley smiled; she meant it tenderly, but the effect was ghastly—and Mr. Hamley, on the other side of the bed, thought it so.

"Dear, sweet child!" she said fondly. "What a comfort you are to me, love! Ah! if only Patricia, poor girl, was more like you!"

"She will improve," said dear Dora, generously. "She means well, and she is fond of you, dear."

"I hope so," answered Mrs. Hamley. "I have done my duty by her, but she is unsatisfactory."

It was a little tragedy in its way. The love and confidence and blessing—the blessing of Isaac to Jacob—bestowed on one whose whole life was a cheat, amiable and full of nice tact, but a cheat all the same; the reprobation given to the other whose faults were those of truth and loyalty, of conscience, love, and integrity. It was a tragedy in good sooth, but a common one.

Then Dora was dismissed and thanked for her prompt attention; and though Mrs. Hamley had herself desired that Patricia should not be disturbed, she had a sore feeling against her all the same, and thought she should have divined that something was wrong and have awakened of her own accord.

"It is so vulgar and heartless to sleep so soundly!" she said, peevishly, to Mr. Hamley; and Mr. Hamley, starting from sweet slumber and checking an incipient snore, replied, "Yes, it is, my dear; but she is horrid vulgar, you know, when you've reckoned her up, top and tail!"

On which Mrs. Hamley rebuked him for disrespect and maintained that her niece was perfectly well-bred if not always satisfactory.

CHAPTER XXII.

WHAT THE DAY BROUGHT FORTH.

IT is not the people who do wrong that are unhappy ; it is the people who have to see the wrong done and are unable to prevent it. Between Dora and Patricia, the one had a conscience void of offence, the other was as miserable as she felt guilty. No secret had ever come into her life before, and she did not know what to do now that she had one. It was a terrible secret too ; not a mere childish peccadillo of no great consequence to keep or to tell ; but a secret that involved a daily deception of the worst kind, and perhaps a crime : who knows ?

Poor Patricia ! What with her love for Dora and her sense of duty to her aunt, her loyalty to her friend and her faithfulness to her guardian, the young girl's natural excitement at so unusual an event and the modest maiden's shame at such a revelation, the overwhelming consciousness of the fact which made her feel as if she should be obliged to call aloud to the passers-by, " Dora is married ! " on the one hand, and as if every one must know it without being told on the other, her life just now was illimitably wretched.

Dora, on her side, justified herself. She was sorry for what she had done ; but she regretted, not repented. She thought she had been precipitate ; with Lord Merrian at the Quest ; and worse than precipitate now that Colonel Lowe was ruined and his consent or denial went for nothing. But though she saw no way out of the coil in which she was entangled, she was resolved not to make matters worse by an injudicious confession. She was glad that Patricia knew ; she could make her useful, very useful ; but she was quite determined that come what might no one else should know, unless Sydney came into the possession of enough to live on " nicely." She had but slender hopes that way. Still, even in these days, ravens do sometimes fly from out the darkness, and one might alight on

Syd. Miracles have been wrought before now and might again, but until such a one had been worked in her favour, she was resolved to remain the dove in the ark of Abbey Holme, and to enjoy the warmth and the wine, the soft carpets and the dainty attire, rather than go with her young husband into love and penury.

Penury was by no means to the taste of pretty Dora Drummond, To her way of thinking love in a cotton gown, with only cold mutton for dinner, was far more frightful than hate in velvet and contempt with diamonds in the hair. She would rather have the velvet and the diamonds than the love and the cold mutton; and Abbey Holme, with its subservience of habit and suppression of will—and the luxury and well-being that had become her second nature included—was to be preferred to Sydney Lowe ruined. She liked Sydney's love well enough, and she liked the excitement of their stolen meetings; they gave her a sweet sense of secret power and freedom that compensated for many disagreeables; but she would rather renounce the whole thing, deny her marriage now and for ever and become a second Lady Audley or Aurora Floyd, than keep to her bargain if it was for worse and not for better. And she believed that Sydney dreaded poverty even with love at its back, just as much as she did herself; and that if occasion offered she could make him amenable to reason, and induce him to renounce and deny in concert.

Meanwhile, she slept like a child and woke like a rose, and took care of her eyes and complexion as other people take care of their consciences and their love.

She came down to breakfast the next day sweet, fresh, delicate, dainty, and exactly punctual as ever. She inquired tenderly of Mrs. Hamley how she was, when she came in just the prescribed three minutes after her; inquired tenderly and devotedly, as if no graver care, no heavier weight oppressed her than the condition of an elderly woman's digestion. For Mrs. Hamley being of the grim order had struggled manfully with the remains of her last night's indisposition, and had straightened herself courageously for her daily duties, appearing at the head of the table, upright, lady-like, well-dressed, well-powdered, and with all her addenda and succedanea as accurately adjusted as ever, even to the hair restorer "which was not a dye," but

5

which nevertheless made grey hair brown at odd moments, and hung a veil before the hour-glass of Time so that its spent sand should not be seen.

Presently Patricia came in. She had kept awake half the night, now listening to hear if her aunt was astir and needing help—how it all reminded her of her dear uncle!—now fretting about Dora, and making her head ache between fear and pity, dread and horror; and thus had fallen asleep only when far into the morning—the "mouth of the morning," as the old Gaelic has it. Consequently she had been roused with difficulty, and had dressed herself hurriedly; with the inevitable result.

She came in when prayers were over; and this was her first offence. For Mrs. Hamley held by family prayers. They were respectable and might do the servants good, and they made the proper kind of roll-call whereby she might be sure of her domestic forces; and she was implacable when anyone was missing. And when Patricia did come in she looked tumbled and disturbed; her hair was not sufficiently smooth, her brooch was awry, she had forgotten her cuffs, and she had no bow to her band. And all these misdemeanors together filled up the measure till it overflowed.

"Are you better, aunty dear?" she said eagerly from the door, so soon as she had opened it.

Mrs. Hamley did not like people to speak to her from a distance, nor for the matter of that too near. Her hearing was just in that woolly stage when there is special need of distinctness; but it was an unpardonable offence to let the need be seen.

"Will you have the kindness not to speak to me at that distance, and not to talk so fast?" said Aunt Hamley stiffly.

Patricia went up to her. "Are you better this morning, dear?" she asked again in her loud, clear voice.

"Good gracious, child! you are enough to deafen one!" said Mrs. Hamley peevishly, putting her hands over her ears. "Yes, I am, I am obliged to you. Though I am sure I do not know why you should ask," she added with an offended kind of sneer. "You were not very much interested in my condition last night. I might have died, for anything you knew or cared. Sleeping through all that noise like a tired milkmaid! The place might be carried away, and you would not hear!"

"But I did hear and was not asleep," said Patricia.

" And if you knew that I was so ill why did you not have
the grace to come and see me ?" asked Mrs. Hamley sharply.

" Bignold would not let me go into your room," she said.

" And Bignold was quite right," returned Mrs. Hamley with
illogical severity. "But you might have gone to Dora. Dora
came to me; and you might at least have sent your love and
duty by her, and asked to know if you could be of any use."

" Dora——" began Patricia; when Dora raised her sweet
eyes, and said to Patricia—

" I did not like to disturb you, dear ; though I felt sure you
would want to know if you were awake. But I thought it a
pity to make you anxious for nothing, as you could not help.
I hope I did no wrong. If I did, you must forgive me; but I
acted for the best. So you see,"—gracefully to Mrs. Hamley,
and with a generous impulse shining through her timidity—
" if any one is to blame it is I; but I acted for the best."

" You always do, my love," said Mrs. Hamley kindly, and
Mr. Hamley wagged his head approvingly.

Patricia flushed till the tears were forced into her eyes. Her
position was becoming unbearable. More as a relief to her
own feelings than because she thought she would be welcome,
she put her arms around her aunt, and said affectionately—

" You must not think me unfeeling, dear, because I was kept
out. If you only knew, aunty, how sorry I was, and how glad
I am to see you in your old place to-day !"

" There ! that will do, my dear !" said Aunt Hamley throwing her off by a sudden twist. " You are late enough as it is.
Go and sit down, and eat your breakfast like a lady. I hate
such disorderly ways !"

She could never resist the temptation of snubbing Patricia.
She had that odd self-contradictory feeling for her which made
her impatient that she was not this and that which she was not,
and more impatient still when she did as she had desired. If
the girl left her alone, she neglected her ; if she paid her attention, she fussed her ; whatever she did was wrong, and she was
all that she ought not to be. Her image was reflected in a
crooked mirror where not a line was straight nor a form beautiful.

So Patricia went to her place ; passing by Dora, whom she
kissed with a new sensation and bashfully, as if she had been

kissing Sydney Lowe by implication ; and then to Mr. Hamley,
with her frank eyes a little clouded, and her head generally
borne so straight, a little drooped because of that mystery she
had penetrated.

Mr. Hamley rose pompously, shook hands with her noisily,
and asked her to have everything on the table in a hurried
heaped-up way, as if they were Israelites at the Passover, eating
with their loins girded for a journey and in haste. It was his
way of rebuke ; and effectual. All these were but small things
taken separately, and if they came only on occasions, but all at
once, and continually occurring, they were enough to sadden a
young girl of even as much cheerful courage as Patricia. So the
morning was melancholy for her ; and what with the burden of
her secret and the sore of her snubbing she **was** wretched
enough, and found herself more than once wondering when
Gordon Frere would be at home again, that her life might take
back its old brightness and freedom and love : more than once
wishing that, until this time came, she might be allowed to
find a home with her friends at the Hollies. If only this might
be, how happy she would be then, when now she was so miserable !

Just after luncheon Mr. Sydney Lowe called. He asked for
Mr. Hamley, and by his own desire was shown into the library
where the master sat surrounded by gorgeously-bound books he
never read, and could not have understood if he had ; gorgeously-bound books interspersed with lengths of lettered dummies
cleverly made by the carpenter, and quite as valuable to Mr.
Hamley as the realities. Indeed, being more ingenious, they
were more valuable.

The interview **was** not long. Sydney asked permission to
address Miss Drummond ; and Mr. Hamley replied cheerfully,
—with all his heart, if he could satisfy him about ways and
means. His present income ? his future expectations ? prosaic
things no doubt, but even a young gentleman in love must
remember that a butcher would demand payment once a year
at least, and it was as well to be provided with the means be-
forehand.

To all this Sydney was charmingly reasonable. He was quite
prepared to answer Mr. Hamley's questions, and he believed
satisfactorily. He mentioned Cragfoot with a flourish ; re-

minded Mr. Hamley that he was his father's heir and only child, and that his mother's jointure would come to him at her death. His mother, Mr. Hamley might be aware, was Lady Anne Graham's daughter, and his father's name spoke for itself.

"It all sounds quite first-rate," said Mr. Hamley; "but"— slowly, as if he was only reflecting; for he could afford to be gracious to-day—"I happen to know that Cragfoot is mort-gaged up to the chimney-pots, and that your mother's inalien-able jointure is two hundred a year, allowed by your father. Where the sixty thousand pounds she brought loose in her pocket has gone is more than I can tell; you had better ask your father; and if he tells you, pass the information on. It may be useful. I am afraid Mr. Lowe, sir, if you cannot show a better invoice than this, it will be no go for you."

Sydney set his teeth. The two men had grappled, but they were still making a feint of courtesy.

"I know that my father is in a little temporary embarrass-ment which he will soon overcome," said Sydney.

"When he has overcome it, I shall be happy to treat with you again," answered Mr. Hamley, politely. "Until then under-stand, that I take it on myself as a duty not to allow any engagement between you and Miss Drummond. Miss Drum-mond has been brought up quite the lady, and if ever she marries, she must marry where she will be kept the lady still."

"I hope, Mr. Hamley, you do not think she would forfeit her position as a gentlewoman in marrying me?" said Sydney with a flash of the old vicious passion.

"Oh, dear me, no! not at all, sir. Still, you have not means enough to keep her in what I call the lap of luxury, as she is now. And I would not bestow her hand on any one who could not put down pound for pound with me."

"Are the lady's own inclinations to go for nothing?" said Sydney warmly.

"They may go for everything, Mr. Lowe. I have no legal right over Miss Drummond. If she likes she can walk out of this house arm-in-arm with you or my groom, and marry to-morrow if it pleases her. But if she does, she and her husband will never see a farthing of my money; and I think I know her too well to be afraid of her."

P

"If you call that being good to a girl you profess to love like a daughter, I do not!" said Sydney angrily.

Mr. Hamley raised his eyes, and looked at him steadily.

"I didn't know that my being bad or good to the girl was part of the business between us," he said. "And what's more, I don't care a snuff whether you think me one or t'other. The business is, What money have you got to marry on ? and it's my say—Not enough."

"And I say I have, if you will give a sufficient income to the girl you have adopted as your daughter."

Mr. Hamley burst into a loud harsh laugh.

"Now that we've cracked the nut we've come to the kernel," he said. "Teach your grandmother ! Not a halfpenny, Mr. Lowe ! If you have her, you must take her in her shift ; unless you can give her the silk gown to cover her. I tell you again, I'll lay down pound for pound with you, and no man can say fairer ; but I'll not give her without an equivalent."

"The love of a gentleman counts for something," said Sydney disdainfully.

Mr. Hamley laughed even more disdainfully.

"Not on my ship," he said. "I'm a self-made man myself, and know what's what pretty well by now. I'd rather Miss Drummond married a man as could keep her as she ought to be kept, than a man as called himself a gentleman, and hadn't a blessed penny to play chuck-farthing with !"

"You speak as if I was a beggar, Mr. Hamley !" said Sydney, angrily.

"Do I ?" he answered with supreme coolness. "The remedy is in your own hands if I do. Show me Cragfoot without a mortgage on it, and a good thirty thousand to the back of it, and then I'll say my service to you. But," he added, suddenly changing from coolness to insolence, "I'm not a going to give my money to set you and your father on your legs again, with Miss Drummond forsooth as the decoy duck. Feather your own nest by your honest industry, as I have feathered mine, and then you can ask a gentleman for a lady's hand like a gentleman yourself, and not like a sneak and a swindler. No sir, not if I know it !" he cried, as Sydney caught up a heavy ebony ruler, and Mr. Hamley seized his arms just in time.

"You infernal blackguard !" exclaimed Sydney struggling in his grasp and hitting out savagely.

Mr. Hamley held him off with one hand, and rang the bell violently with the other. The servant came at the instant from the hall.

"Show Mr. Lowe the door, John," said the master of the house, releasing him. "And if he ventures to show his face in here again set the dogs at him. There!" he said, rubbing his hands as Sydney, with a horrible imprecation, was ushered out of the room, "that's the best day's work I ever did in my life! I have paid off old scores with interest, and I feel twice the man I did for it. He have Dora? No, not if he licked my foot for her, and I broke the whole boiling of them—as I will!"

CHAPTER XXIII.

CONSENTING WITH SINNERS.

IVING himself time to cool down a little, for he was flushed and rudely excited, into the drawing-room presently walked Mr. Hamley, with a high-handed masterful air, even more self-assertive and swaggering than usual. He found the ladies in their accustomed places and occupied in their accustomed work; that is, Mrs. Hamley was at one side of the fire knitting a coloured couvre-pied, Dora was at the other doing dainty modern point, each with her own special little velvet table by her side, and Patricia was in the bay of the window, at the remotest point, reading, or rather seeming to read, but in reality thinking of what she knew. The master surveyed his feminine belongings graciously. He felt grand and Eastern as he looked at them.

"I have had a visit, ladies, that will interest you like one of Mr. Mudie's green things there," he began.

They all looked up; dear Dora smiled in her gentle way.

"A love story," he continued.

He was doling out his news by bits; it was too precious to give entire and all at once.

"Indeed!"

This was Dora's exclamation; she was the only one who spoke.

"Indeed? Yes, it is indeed, I think. I have been well amazed, I can tell you. A young man has just been here asking permission to pay his addresses to one of you two young ladies. There now, the cat's out."

"But to which of us?" asked Dora, gaily.

"Well, which? Guess."

"Patricia," laughed Dora; "she is the youngest."

Her words made the girl start as if she had been touched by a hot iron. It was partly sacrilege, and partly an insult.

"What a shame!" she said, hotly.

"Calm yourself, my dear; so, so! be calm, I beg!" said Mr. Hamley, in an aggravating stable kind of voice. "Don't get so excited about nothing. It was not you; it was Miss Drummond."

"Me!" cried Dora, arching her eyebrows. "What an idea!"

"So I said, but I treated him as civil as if he had been a prince; that I did! I asked him his means, as one gentleman to another, and he said, 'Cragfoot.' Now you know him."

"Sydney Lowe?" said Dora, as if she had been guessing a riddle.

"You might have made a worse shot," answered Mr. Hamley.

"And Cragfoot is a lovely place, and Mr. Lowe comes of a good family," said Mrs. Hamley, crossly.

She had not the slightest desire that Dora should marry Sydney, but she did not like the whole thing to be regulated without her voice making itself heard in the councils.

"I grant you, Lady," Mr. Hamley answered, pompously. "Of the young man himself I will say nothing; he is not my mark exactly; but Cragfoot would not be bad even for a young lady out of Abbey Holme, if it was Cragfoot, and not as one may say a mere shell with a name tacked to it. I have reason to know that it is mortgaged body and bones, and that the colonel is neither more nor less than a bankrupt. What he and that precious son of his have would not keep Miss Drummond in shoe-leather. Was I wrong, then, to refuse him her hand?"

"How can you ask such a silly question?" said Mrs. Hamley tartly. "How could the child marry a young man without any money to live on? It was an insult to ask for her."

"Was I wrong, Dora?" he continued, turning to Dora and watching her narrowly.

"Certainly not," she said steadily. "As dear Mrs. Hamley says, I cannot live on nothing."

"Is this your only reason?" he asked again.

"Why, yes," she answered lightly.

"You would not have liked it if he could have laid down a clean bill? You are not what is called 'in love' with him?"

Patricia's heart stood still. By her face it would have seemed as if her own love, not Dora's, rested on the answer.

Dora raised her eyes. "In love with him? No!" she said, with the faintest little movement of her round shoulders.

"And at those times when he has tried to make himself agreeable to you, you have held him off?" again asked Mr. Hamley, still searching her face.

"Yes, indeed I have," Dora answered, her sweet face the very ideal of frankness if also of tender modesty. "I have never encouraged him; he knows that."

Patricia gave a shuddering kind of gasp and dashed from the room like a storm passing through it. This was consenting with sinners indeed; and she staggered under the burden of her cross. Her whole nature revolted at the false position in which she stood, and the sin to which she was so unwillingly a party. She felt that she must get out of the house, shake off the influence of this strange, cold, lying life, else she should suffocate and die. She ran up-stairs and locked herself in her own room, and bathed her face in cold water to get rid of a kind of cobweb that seemed to have come before her eyes. Her pulses were beating tumultuously, but she was trembling as if in an ague-fit. Heat and cold, poverty and hunger, she could have borne, and cheerfully; but this continual presence of evil to which she must give a tacit consent, this awful confusion of thoughts and feelings, this terrible uncertainty of duties, this love without honour, this pity without sympathy that she felt for Dora, nearly maddened her. She was like one carried away in a torrent where was no help and no hope.

She flung herself on her knees and laid out her sorrows in passionate prayer; but no angel came down to tell her what she ought to do, and though her prayer carried the blessing of present soothing with it, it brought no solution of her difficulties.

Flushed, yet still with this ague-like trembling on her, she dressed herself for a walk and went back into the drawing-room. She wanted to get out of the house, first of all things, and she wanted to go down to the Hollies. If she could find peace anywhere, it would be there.

"I am so feverish, dear aunt; do let me go out for a little while?" she pleaded in answer to Mrs. Hamley's look of astonished rebuke.

Dora rose from her seat and went up to her caressingly.

Patricia trembled more than ever, and turned away her head. Acting, which was as easy as breathing to the one, which was indeed a pleasant pastime, was agony to the other; and having to control herself at this moment was an added pain she felt Dora might have spared her.

"You are not looking well, dear," said Dora kindly. "How I wish I was as strong as you and able to face the cold as you do! I would go with you." In a whisper she said pleadingly, "Do not think harshly of me, dear!"

"Please may I go, aunt?" said Patricia, not answering Dora, not returning the pressure of her hand—she whose frank love had hitherto leapt so gladly to meet the faintest sign of tenderness her friend had ever shown; but her own heart only knew how hard it was to steel herself against that pleading voice, how desperate the pain to have to judge harshly where she loved so warmly!

Mrs. Hamley was vexed by her request. She disliked being made a fuss with when she was ill, but she liked to be the central consideration of the house—to have her little court standing at respectful attention, waiting on Providence and her humour, watching for time and her pleasure. It seemed to her the most heartless, the most shameless thing that could have happened; but she said, "Certainly, Patricia, you can go," coldly, with the feeling of a martyr generously sacrificing her rights for another's pleasure.

"I will be back before dark," said Patricia.

"May I ask where you are going?—or am I presuming too much on my position as your guardian and the mistress of the house?" said Mrs. Hamley with cold formality.

"I want to go down to the Hollies," answered Patricia. "I want to see Miss Fletcher."

"May I suggest, Patricia, that this continual going to the Hollies is rather odd and not very delicate?" said Mrs. Hamley, still in the same cold and formal manner.

"How not delicate?" asked Patricia. "Miss Fletcher wishes me to go. I do not force myself on her."

Mrs. Hamley glanced up at her contemptuously; she was about to say—"Dr. Fletcher is an unmarried man?" but when she saw the child-like face that looked down with frank inquiry into hers, the better part of her womanhood prevailed over the worse and she conquered her spite for the sake of her involuntary reverence. Undoubtedly Patricia was a fool, she thought; but she was an innocent one, and it was not for her to enlighten her.

"Go, if you like," she said crossly. "What you and Catherine Fletcher can find to say to each other is more than I can make out. You are the dullest companion possible at home. I suppose, like many other people, you reserve your liveliness for strangers and give your home only your ill temper."

At that moment the door-bell rang, and Lord Merrian and Dr. Fletcher were announced. They had met at the lodge-gate, the one riding, the other walking, and so had come up the drive together. As if by magic Mrs. Hamley's sour face changed its expression and became placid and well-bred. She could have dispensed with the doctor; but the coming of the young lord so soon after their own call gratified her immensely. It must have done so to have made her so suddenly amiable.

"I hope you do not consider me intrusive," said Lord Merrian with his fine smile and gracious manner; "but I fancy this belongs to one of you ladies, and as I was riding past I undertook to deliver it for my mother; else," smiling again—and what a pleasant smile it was—"I should scarcely have ventured on such an invasion."

It was a mere nothing that he gave to Mrs. Hamley, wrapped up in a little tissue paper parcel—a rather tumbled crape bow, one of the mysteries of Patricia's dress that, as she phrased it, had gone adrift in the drawing-room at the Quest. It was not an unusual thing for Patricia's ornamental trimmings to go adrift, and Mrs. Hamley often found it necessary to lecture her on the righteousness of needle and thread, and the value of that stitch in time which saves nine. This time, however, she condoned the offence for the sake of the visit it had occasioned, and handed it over to her niece with a smile that was more friendly and compassionate than usual.

Patricia blushed, of course, when she received her truant property, and looked very pretty, even through all her trouble of mind; but she was not disposed to take any share in the conversation to-day, or to profit by Lord Merrian's visit in any way, so drew a little apart and sat down on a sofa standing diagonally like a barricade between the table and the window, by which Dora was left mistress of the situation; and as Lord Merrian could not have indulged in any of the heroics of yesterday, with so many critical ears to listen to him, he contented himself with the small talk of ordinary society, which suited "the fair girl" better, and showed her to advantage.

In the midst of an animated monologue on the music of the future, of which neither he nor his audience knew more than that its high priest was Richard Wagner and that it was excessively odd, Henry Fletcher went over to Patricia in his sloping, lazy way, and subsided on the sofa by her.

"Are you going out or coming in?" he asked, glancing at her hat and jacket.

"Going out," said Patricia. Then in a hurried unhappy voice she added: "I so much wish to see your sister to-day; I have just asked Aunt Hamley if I can go, and she says I may. May I go with you?"

His thin, brown, leathery face lighted up, and he looked quite young because so glad.

"Certainly," he said; "we shall be delighted. My sister was speaking of you this morning and saying that she wanted to see you again. Indeed I called now with a message from her, hoping to induce you to come."

"How good you are!" said Patricia, lifting her eyes gratefully to his. "I will tell aunty, then; and as she said I might go, whenever you like I am ready."

"Perhaps I had better give her my sister's message," he answered smiling. "Mrs. Hamley is particular, and she may think I ought to do my business *selon les convenances*. What an old father she thinks me!—just an umbrella!" he thought to himself with half a sigh. "And yet she is right; I am only an old father to her."

The request, made with that quiet taking-it-for-granted which so often gets what it asks, was successful, though Mrs. Hamley was not over well pleased with Dr. Fletcher or his object. She was indeed anything but pleased that her niece should leave at all during Lord Merrian's visit, and more especially was she annoyed that she should leave in company with Dr. Fletcher. But the Fletchers were people who had a peculiar power over Mrs. Hamley; she was always finding fault

with them behind-backs, but to their faces she did not resist
them. She considered the one the son of perdition and the
other the daughter of folly; nevertheless, strong in her own
righteousness and wisdom as she was, she let them have their
will of her when they chose to ask it, and while she affected
to contemn did really respect them too much to gainsay them.
As now, when she would rather have kept her niece to look
beautiful in the eyes of the future Earl of Dovedale, but felt
herself constrained to let her depart with Henry Fletcher
because he had begged for her in the name of her sister, and
had come up to carry her off.

So Patricia went with her friend, leaving Lord Merrian
secretly disgusted and sore with the feeling of having been
" sold; " but still discussing the music of the future, and the
respective merits of Wagner and Verdi, as if he really enjoyed
the conversation. He might have done so had not his interest
been forestalled ; for Dora was putting out all her little coquet-
ries and fascinations with supreme indifference to the fact that
another man called her wife, and that how much soever she
might make Lord Merrian admire her, he could not advance
her fortunes one jot nor abate by a line the difficulties of her
present position. Wise as Dora was, and far-seeing, she had
not always the best kind of wisdom ; and because she was deft
in undoing knots she was not always sufficiently careful to keep
her runnings clear. Like many clever people she enjoyed a
complication wherein her talents could be exercised ; and got
herself into danger for the pleasure of getting out of it again.

" How I like being with you and Miss Fletcher ! " said
Patricia, drawing a long breath as she and Dr. Fletcher walked
briskly down the avenue, and her load seemed already lessening from the mere contact with one whom she respected and
who was true.

" Do you ? " he answered, looking down at her kindly.
" That's right ! And we like to have you. Though this is
more natural than that you should care to spend your time
with two such elderly fogies as ourselves."

" Don't say that, Dr. Fletcher ! Besides, if you are old, you
remind me of my dear Barsands home more than any one else
does," said Patricia simply. " Though you are so unlike him,
I feel somehow when with you the same as I used to feel with

my uncle. Only I had no Miss Fletcher then," she added a little sorrowfully. "I wish I had had."

Dr. Fletcher turned his eyes on her. She was looking up at him frankly, affectionately, as she used to look at her uncle when he spoke to her. In a minor degree truly, less tenderly, less demonstratively, but in the same spirit.

He smiled.

"I take that as the highest compliment you can pay me," he said.

Then he turned away and the smile faded from his face.

Miss Fletcher was glad to see her pet, and half surprised that leave had been given her to come. Knowing Mrs. Hamley she was very sure it was a "tight pattern" for poor Patricia from first to last. She pitied her with her whole heart, and often said to her brother how much she wished they could take her away bodily, and bring her to the Hollies for life. Perhaps her saying this so often had made him think of ways and means. But the one which seemed most natural was just the way which was most impracticable; and as yet the woman's loving wish to protect, guide, and bless the girl, had no issue in any plan on which it was possible to act. To-day she was even more than usually tender to the poor child. She saw at once that the young soul was ill at ease, and that something had gone wrong; and Catherine Fletcher was not a woman of that kind of motherliness which cares only for the body. She knew in her own person what sorrows and difficulties lie in the heart and mind, in the affections and in the thoughts; and the strong and generous hands which cared to give good gifts to the poor cared also to bring consolation to the sad and surety to the doubtful.

Presently Patricia began to talk about the perplexities of life, and the need she at all events—she would speak for no one else—had of superior direction; how she envied the Roman Catholics in being able to go to a man learned in righteousness and spiritually wise who could tell them what to do and disentangle their contradictory duties so that they became clear and simple.

"And if you had a director, what would you say to him, dear?" asked Miss Fletcher, who saw that her words had a personal meaning.

"Oh, many things," she answered. "But I do not want to

talk of myself. I only want to know what ought to be done,
whether by me or by any one else."

"Give me an instance."

"Well, this," said innocent Patricia, feeling quite diplomatic,
and sailing as near to the wind in the matter of honesty as was
possible for any right-minded person. "If you knew of anything wrong going on in the house where you were, would you
think it your duty to tell what you knew to the head of the
house ?"

"That depends, my dear, on two things ; one, if my keeping
silence involved my being mixed up in anything unworthy, the
other if keeping silence did harm to others. If the first, I should
think I owed it to my own self-respect to keep my hands clean,
and if I could do that only by public protest, I would make it."

"But I am not mixed up in it, except by knowing it and
keeping it secret—consenting by silence," interrupted Patricia.

"You see, dear, as I do not know the circumstances, I cannot answer you very satisfactorily," returned Miss Fletcher.
"This is not saying that you are to confide in me. If the secret,
whatever it is, is not your own you must not tell it even to me ;
but none the more can I give you a clear answer."

"No one can answer difficult moral problems or vague hypo-
theses," said Dr. Fletcher, in his calm way. "What I should
say, is this. If you have personally nothing to do with the
circumstances to which you are alluding, leave it alone, unless
it is injuring others, and then I think you are bound to tell it.
As a rule we are not obliged to be detectives or informants ;
though most young people who care for truth and justice
think they are consecrated to this task before all others. But
there is a world of difference between action and negation,
sharing and silence."

"Yes, I see ; but it is so dreadful to know that things are going
wrong and people being deceived every day, and under one's
own eyes !" said Patricia. "When one hears things said that
are not true, it makes one feel as if one told stories oneself by
not crying out that they are untrue."

"If what you know hurts your uncle and aunt, you ought to
tell them," said Miss Fletcher. "If it implicates you, you ought
to tell them also. But if it does not hurt them, and is only a
wrong done by some one to his own conscience, his own sense

of right, leave it. Don't you see? You ha. 'e either been told in confidence or you have found it out by chance. If the former, you are bound to secrecy; if the latter, you need not constitute yourself the police of morality. Are you any clearer now?"

"Just a little," said Patricia with a heavy sigh. "At all events I will not speak, at least not yet."

Neither Dr. Fletcher nor his sister took Patricia's perplexities to mean more than a discovery of some of those domestic peccadilloes which are inevitable in a household as tightly held as Mrs. Hamley's; human nature rebelling against undue bondage, and rebellion having the trick of expressing itself in ugly forms and crooked ways. They were a little afraid of her fearlessness and strong sense of right; and thought it better to curb rather than to spur her on. In fact they took her fears to be probably exaggerated; and as they did not want to see her become meddlesome or officious in her quest after the noble life they put her off with an anodyne rather than a solvent. But if they soothed her, all the same they heartened her; and she went back to her prison with a braver will, setting herself to bear the burden of Dora's sin with as much courage and equanimity as she could command, and hoping for both relief and solution in times not too distant.

"The zeal of the young is so apt to outrun discretion," said Dr. Fletcher, when she had left. "But what a noble nature it is!"

"Yes, rarely so!" his sister answered. "It is what Montalembert called a true 'bath of life,' to be with Patricia Kemball. She is the most perfect creature of the natural kind I have ever seen. She reminds me of the old classic nymph, or of the ideal savage princess, clothed but not converted to our odd conventionalities of life."

Dr. Fletcher smiled and said yes, but made no further remark; and then Catherine looked for a moment at the picture of a young knight after Albert Dürer hanging on the wall, and her soft brown eyes became dreamy and mournful as she looked. It was an old print picked up at a broker's in London, which had reminded her of Reginald Kemball; and for that reason had been hung where she could always see it. For there had been certain love passages between Catherine and

Reginald in olden times ; love passages interrupted in the bad old way of jealousy and misunderstanding when Colonel Lowe, then a dashing young officer with laurels freshly gathered in the Crimean trenches, had come down to set the world of Milltown womanhood in flame, and to devote himself to Catherine Fletcher in especial. Reginald, self-doubting, jealous, sore, poor, had taken Captain Lowe's attentions as Catherine's acceptance. No distinct understanding had been come to between the unsuccessful artist and the squire's daughter ; and from the time when Captain Lowe's fancy had turned that way, he took care that none should be possible. He appropriated Catherine in that quietly determined manner in which some men contrive to dominate women and public opinion ; and Milltown put its wisest heads together and settled everything to its satisfaction. Some of them even knew the price of the bridal gown and veil, and where they were bought ; and a few scented wedding-cake in a certain clock-case which came from London. There was nothing more positive than that Captain Lowe and Catherine Fletcher were to make a match of it ; and while all the world waited for the wedding, Reginald Kemball went off to London, and in a fit of despair married Patricia's mother—a pretty and affectionate little girl who was badly treated at home, and who fell in love with the handsome artist at sight.

But Captain Lowe did not marry Catherine Fletcher. He was deeply in debt, and Miss Graham, Lady Anne's daughter and heiress, had a dower that would not only cover his deficiencies but set him well before the world for life. So he married where he did not love, and only "for money ;" as his poor wife found out when too late. And he had no scruple in proving to her that what she had found out was correct. He always used to say that the only woman he ever really loved was Catherine Fletcher ; and he passed a great part of his time in bewailing the untowardness of circumstances which had prevented his marrying her. When he had done anything specially bad, he used to excuse his sin to himself by saying that he would have been a different man with her. He would never have got into his present bad habits of drink, debt, and the race-course ; but he would have gone out in his profession, and by this time would have been a General. He would have made a name ; and he would have deserved what he had made. All

the potentialities for good which poor, weak Matilda Graham
had had power to render abortive, according to him, would
have bloomed and blossomed into the stateliest growth, the
goodliest fruit, had Catherine Fletcher taken him in hand.

With only a germ of a conscience, with no sense of justice,
and with the moral coward's need of self-justification and a
scapegoat, Colonel Lowe laid the burden of his sins, which
were heavy, on the shoulders of the woman whose life he had
ruined. It is the way of the world; a habit belonging by nature to the average son of Adam with whom Eve is always the
teterrima causa, and the woman who did tempt him. Catherine
Fletcher, however, would not have married Colonel Lowe had
he asked her; so his unfortunate wife carried more blame than
she deserved on this side as well as on others; and the Colonel's
bewailings were as baseless as those of a child who runs after
a rainbow—and fails to catch it.

CHAPTER XXIV.

BETWEEN TWO FIRES.

IT was not to be expected that the Lowes would let such an insult as that which Mr. Hamley had just offered to the heir of the house pass without some kind of notice ; though Sydney, wisely enough, made the least, not the most of it. But the question was, what could be done ? It was a disagreeable position as things were, but how could it be bettered ? As Colonel Lowe said, sagely enough, the ruffian would not fight if he was called out ; and there was no case for a summons— scarcely one for a thrashing. A man's house is his castle, and if he chooses to be king on his own door-step, and to shut the door in the face of intruders, there is no one to gainsay him, and the law upholds his right of expulsion. The case was certainly difficult ; and Colonel Lowe confessed that he could not see his way clearly.

On the one hand he felt, as he had always felt, that he had condescended too low in receiving Mr. Hamley as a guest on an equal footing. A man who had worked his way up from sixpence a day and been lashed in the street for a bare-footed beggar, even if he had ultimately come to the possession of Abbey Holme, was not like a man born in the purple and wrapped in its golden fringes from the beginning. Yet, on the other hand, Mr. Hamley was rich, and Cragfoot was mortgaged up to the chimney-pots ; and from information received the Colonel had reason to believe that the master of Abbey Holme knew more about that mortgage than any one else, save himself and the lawyer. Then, Sydney was evidently deeply attached to that pretty piece of waxwork, Dora Drummond ; and, such being the case, there seemed to be no way of making him take kindly to the idea of Julia Manley, even with her five thousand a-year to gild her freckles and beautify her homely camel face. It was odd how tenacious and unselfish the boy was ! thought the father, wondering. He did not believe that he could have been so hard hit, and so disinterested. Though he was sorry for it, and quite capable of being immovably severe and furiously angry if Syd still went on persisting in his folly, all the same he could not help honouring him in his own heart—he who had always thought his boy selfish, forced now to rate his power of disinterested love as superior to the charms of competency for life !

Yet none of these thoughts answered the one grave question: What was to be done? The gentleman's blue blood boiled, but the embarrassed man's necessities froze it back to calmness ; the father's natural wish to see his son happy plucked him by the skirts, but the aristocrat's disdain of mud, however thickly mixed with gold, held him by the sleeve; while over all flamed the fiery man's angry passion and instinctive desire to lay hands on his foe.

In the midst of his perplexity the Colonel bethought himself of Henry Fletcher, and went off to consult " the wisest man in the parish." He went just as it was getting dark, at about five o'clock, while Patricia was there taking counsel for herself. But when the two men were seated in the library—the keen mobile face of the one contrasting so strongly with the thoughtful serenity of the other—what could the one say that the other did not know? The idea of Mr. Hamley fighting a duel with Sydney Lowe was as absurd as that of his playing Harlequin in a pantomime. If a challenge was sent he would simply refer the thing to the gentlemen on the bench, his brother magistrates, stating how it came about that the young man was thirsting for his blood—because, not being able to make proper provision for his adopted daughter, he had therefore declined his proposal of marriage. And the bench would applaud him, and gravely censure Mr. Sydney Lowe, with public ridicule to follow. No ; that was not to be thought of for a moment.

To be sure, he might have told him more delicately. Dr. Fletcher allowed that ; but "what can you expect from a snob like that ? a beggar on horseback—a self-made cur ! " said the Colonel disdainfully ; with a moral lunge at his friend and host, who at this moment stood in some sort answerable for Mr. Hamley's insolence. For was he not a " confounded Rad," and thought snobs as good as gentlemen? And are not all who uphold the rights of the poor, and who preach the fra-

Q

ternity of men, answerable for the sins and shortcomings of
their plebeian brethren !

Dr. Fletcher was accustomed to these moral lunges, and never
cared to oppose or to return them. He passed them quietly by,
and went on to the second head of the subject under consideration ; the love-affair between the young people, of which the
Colonel had just made pathetic use, appearing as the tender
father, the sympathetic witness, with a very creditable display
of the softer emotions.

"Well, as for the love affair," said Mr. Fletcher, "that of
course rested in the hands of the young people themselves. They
were of age, and might manage that as they chose. If their
love was as strong as Colonel Lowe had said, could not something be done to set them up in hope, if not in present means ?
Was it so utterly impossible for Sydney to do anything whereby he might gain an honest living ? In fact, would not a sincere love for a portionless girl give an incentive to exertion,
such as nothing else could supply ? Might it not prove to be
one of those blessings in disguise which sometimes come into
men's lives, like angels unawares ? Sydney Lowe might do
worse, perhaps, than engage himself to Dora with the determination to make a home for her, and discover the means of
supporting her by his own manful work."

" Good heavens, Henry, don't talk of such a thing ! " interrupted the Colonel angrily—sympathy with young love scattered to the winds. " Marry Miss Drummond ! that would
be the crowning misfortune—the most infernal mischief of the
whole lot ! "

Take it all round, then, and from above and below, Mr.
Hamley was master of the situation. He always was master
of the situation, whatever it might be. For what else had he
cultivated his will as he had done ?—for what else lived through
those early years in toil and penury, preparing the ground for
his present greatness, if he could not stand four-square now,
dominating circumstances ?

The Colonel felt, he said, " like a race-horse haltered by a
boor ; " and he backed up the simile by a quantity of bad language that affected the matter at issue about as much as the
snorts of the race-horse would have affected the haltering by
the boor. But as oaths and imprecations do not clear a man's

brain, Henry Fletcher brought him back to the subject in hand, and discussed it afresh ; till they both came to the conclusion—nothing was to be done.

"And I might have saved myself the trouble of asking your advice !" said the Colonel ill-temperedly.

"Unless talking a thing over makes it clearer," said Dr. Fletcher. "I think, too, it is always satisfactory to know that another mind sees things in the same light as one's self ; for two people, and one an unimpassioned spectator, will scarcely be blinded or warped in concert."

"It is not much of blinding or warping, if by that you mean friendly partisanship, that any one will get from you, Henry," said Colonel Lowe pettishly.

And Dr. Fletcher thought, not for the first time, that, whatever men may say, women are not, after all, the exclusive possessors of the folly lying in undisciplined tempers.

There being nothing, then, to be said on the subject beyond the three words "Leave it alone," the two men went into the drawing-room, where Colonel Lowe drew a chair close to Miss Fletcher, and began to talk to her in a low voice, being in that mood which makes a man long for a sympathetic auditor—a creature with soft eyes and expansive faith—to whom he can tell the fact of his grievance while keeping back the form of the truth.

He always went for sympathy to Catherine when things went wrong. True, he had behaved ill to her ; he liked to believe that. He liked to believe that he had nearly broken her heart, and that it was because of him she had never married ; but that did not trouble his conscience or make him shy of seeking her sympathy when he thought he wanted it. She was his sanctuary, the refuge to which he fled when he was unlucky on the turf, or more than usually discontented with his unhappy wife ; or, indeed, when he was only idle, and wanted amusement. And as all women nourish a certain tenderness for the man who has once been in love with them, she gave him the sweet pity for which he came, and generally did really soothe him. He was always "poor Charles" to her ; and she held it as an article of faith that he had thrown himself away on Miss Graham, and might have done better had his wife been a woman of more character. She was wrong there. Men of Colonel

Lowe's stamp are impatient of superior women as their wives.
Slaves suit them better, seeing that they must be tyrants, not
only masters. Better keep such men as friends only, not take
them as husbands. Friendship with a dash of sentiment in it
gets the wine of life, where marriage soon comes to the lees ;
and had poor Charles and dear Catherine married they would
have been as miserable in their own way as were now the
Colonel and that frightened tormented Matilda of his.

While Colonel Lowe sat by Catherine and played at sentiment and melancholy, but thinking all the same, " Poor dear
Kate, how stout she grows !" and while Demeter took him
into her honest loving heart and pitied him vaguely, Dr. Fletcher
was talking to Patricia on that sentence of St. Paul : " For I
could wish that myself were accursed from Christ for my
brethren."

"I think," he said, "if we cared more about others and less
about ourselves—more to do that which is good for our neighbours and less merely to save our own souls—it would be better
for the world and a higher state generally of spiritual life. The
great art of righteous living is to live for others and the ad-
vancement of the truth, rather than for our own individual
moral culture. Herein I stand against Goethe and with Paul."

He said this with intention. He had an idea that Patricia
was in danger of drifting into a state of rigid selfhood and
moral hardness, virtuous enough, but not the highest virtue ;
and he wished to save her from the danger. He missed his
way. Her danger was in excess of sacrifice, and the fire he laid
the altar kindled more than was needed.

"Yes," she said warmly, "I will remember that."

But as she spoke, she turned a troubled face to Colonel Lowe ;
and Dr. Fletcher, though he had not the key to the riddle,
noted her look. Was it possible, he thought after a while, still
watching the troubled face, that her perplexities were connected with this love-affair between Sydney and Miss Drummond ? Had she been entangled in the meshes ? dragged into
complicity ? The more he thought and the keener he noted,
the more he seemed to see light ; but he resolved to keep his
suspicions to himself, and not to share them even with his sister.
Was it possible, too, that this love affair had gone farther than
was known ? He had no idea how far, and his mind stopped

short of real evil. He imagined nothing worse than a secret understanding between the two young people ; but a secret understanding of which Patricia had been made free, and of which her honesty felt the burden grievous.

He was sorry if she had been implicated in this matter, and he wished he could help her to clear her feet from the snare into which she had run. But what could he do ? Just as he was powerless in counsel with the Colonel, so was he unable to be of use to Patricia. He could not ask her to confide in him ; and she would not have done so had he asked her. It was one of those miserable passes in life when sorrow is unavoidable and help is not to be had ; when the soul must walk through its own dangers unaided and those who could make the way smooth must stand by inactive.

Presently the maid came in with the information that the Abbey Holme servants had come for Miss Kemball. The lengthening February days were still too short to allow her to return alone ; for the twilight had come by now; so Mrs. Hamley sent one of the footmen and her own maid to bring her back, not choosing to let Patricia be seen alone with a man even in plush and with a powdered head, and thinking Bignold, unaccompanied, insufficient protection for a walk of twenty minutes in a place where everybody knew everybody else, where fustian doffed its cap and said " Good night" to broadcloth as if class homage was the eleventh commandment, and where all the grandees were of the Lord's anointed to the little people. The whole country round Milltown was as safe as the Abbey Holme drawing-room ; but Mrs. Hamley sent a man and a maid, meaning a rebuke, and to show her niece how troublesome and upsetting she was.

To-night, however, she was trebly protected, for as the Colonel's way home lay in the same direction—Cragfoot standing on the London Road, past Abbey Holme—and as he was walking he insisted on going with her. His quarrel was with Mr. Hamley, not with Mrs. Hamley's handsome niece ; and he enjoyed the idea how angry it would make the old ruffian to know that he had so little regard for him as to deny him the triumph of annoyance, and that he was so profoundly indifferent to anything this other could say or do as to be able to treat one of the family with his customary condescension.

So Patricia walked off with her companion, followed by her two guardians, whereof the one was grim and the other impudent, devoutly wishing herself back in the wilds of Barsands where were neither gentlemen nor powdered footmen, and where she could come and go as she listed with no one to protect her and no one from whom to be protected. She would not have minded so much, she thought, if Dr. Fletcher had been with them ; but it was a terrible trial to be thrown suddenly alone into the hands of Colonel Lowe, knowing what she knew, and instinctively dreading him as she did.

The Colonel got little good out of her companionship. Her frank face was clouded ; her loud, clear, argentine voice subdued ; he could talk of nothing that interested her, of nothing that could pull her, as it were, out of the enchanted wood of her thoughts ; and " Dora is married to your son" was so entirely the one dominant phrase which her mind kept on repeating to her, that she was in terror lest she should unwittingly say it aloud. What he asked of her she answered ; but shyly, awkwardly, like an underbred school-girl. He threw her countless balls of conversation and she did not pick up one. Certainly, she was the most stupid, the most uninteresting young woman he had ever met with, he thought ; and talking to her was simply a waste of good material. He lapsed into silence, and she was too grateful for the respite to disturb it ; when, turning round on her, he said with an affected little laugh :

" Have you heard anything, Miss Kemball, of this silly affair between my boy and Miss Drummond ? "

Patricia felt as if he had struck her somewhere about the heart.

" Yes," she said in a low voice.

" What do you know ? "

What was she to answer ? Truth certainly ; but was the whole truth part of her duty ? Her uncle's last words, " Never betray a friend," flashed into her mind. Come what would, she would not betray Dora.

" That Mr. Lowe came to Mr. Hamley to-day about Dora," she answered, after a pause.

" Mr. Hamley told you that ? "

" Yes."

8

"With comments?"

"I do not understand you," said innocent Patricia.

"No?" The Colonel smiled with a bland, superior kind of smile. "Did he make any remark—tell you anything but the mere fact that my boy had asked him for Miss Drummond's hand?"

"He said he had not money enough to marry on," said Patricia.

"And Miss Drummond assented?"

Another pause, during which the downcast face took on itself all colours and all expressions.

"Miss Drummond assented?" repeated the Colonel.

"Yes," said Patricia.

"She allowed that my boy had not enough to marry on?"

"Yes," she said again.

"Did she acquiesce quietly, or did she cry or rave?" laughed Colonel Lowe, as if it was a farce he was rehearsing.

"Acquiesced quietly," said Patricia, but in so low a voice he had to bend his ear to her lips; and even then he made her repeat the words more distinctly.

"And she made no scene, you say?"

He went over the ground again like the Christy-Minstrels.

"No."

"Did not cry?"

"No."

"Took it quietly?"

"Yes."

"Quite agreed with Mr. Hamley that the thing was absurd? not to be thought of? insane?"

"I don't know that she said all that," said Patricia, looking up.

"Still, she did agree with him?" persisted her tormenter.

"She said they could not live on nothing," said Patricia.

"And she is prepared to give him up?"

Patricia was silent.

"Why not answer me, dear Miss Kemball? The question is surely not so difficult. Is she or is she not prepared to give up my boy?"

"I do not know," said Patricia. Then with the courage of desperation she cried, "It is scarcely fair to cross-question me in this manner, Colonel Lowe. I have nothing to do with the affair, and do not want to have anything to say to it."

" Your resolution comes rather late in the day, my dear Miss Kemball," replied the Colonel maliciously. " You have given me all the information I required, and," laughing, " I must say that you have made the most surpassing witness. Transparency is an inestimable quality. Good evening, and ten thousand thanks. You have made my way so clear to me? I doubt though," laughing again, " if your friend Dora, as you call her, will be so much obliged to you as I am."

Lifting his hat, the Colonel turned sharply away, leaving Patricia with the feeling of having betrayed her trust and done her friend some mysterious mischief—she who would have done anything in the world but dishonour to have served her.

There was no time to speak to Dora before dinner, for in truth Dora avoided her. She knew that she would some day have to " fight it out" over those little answers of hers to Mr. Hamley, but she was not in the mood now. She wanted her faculty of invention and all her brains for a graver purpose than convincing a stupid girl, as she mentally called her friend, that deceit was virtuous and lying a better thing than truth. So the dinner came, and Patricia had been able to give no hint.

" What an extraordinary companion you chose for your walk home!" said Mrs. Hamley, when the servants had left the room after dinner. Bignold had enlightened her as to the young lady's nefarious proceedings.

" I did not choose him; he chose me," said Patricia.

" And you had no power of rejection?" returned Aunt Hamley. " Pardon me, that is the privilege of all ladies, and one that can always be exerted. When it is not used, it is presumably because it is not desired."

" If you mean, aunt, that I wanted Colonel Lowe to walk with me, I did not," said Patricia hastily. " I do not like him well enough."

Her aunt put on her smile of frosted graciousness ; Dora looked up with a rapid glance of anger and astonishment ; Mr. Hamley's colour deepened, and he turned his keen eyes on his wife's niece viciously.

" So!" he said ; " you tramp about the country with that blackguard bankrupt, do you? Upon my word, young lady, your tastes are not remarkably refined for an admiral's grand-daughter."

"I do not know what you mean," said Patricia, lifting her head defiantly. "I meet Colonel Lowe at the house of friends and I go with you yourselves to his own house. I do not see that I am unrefined, or anything else that is bad, for speaking to him civilly and walking on the same side of the way with him."

"Don't be impertinent, Patricia," said Mrs. Hamley. "Your uncle has a right to remonstrate with you. And in the present condition of affairs between the two houses I must say I think your conduct both unfeeling and indelicate."

"Aunt, how could I possibly help it?" cried Patricia with warmth. "How could I, a mere girl as I am, be impertinent to a man of Colonel Lowe's age! He said he would walk home with me when I got up to go; what could I say to prevent him?"

"I wish you were always so considerate to the superior claims of age and understanding," said Mrs. Hamley. "As I said before, Patricia, you are one of those who carry their virtues abroad and wear only their faults at home."

"Was Lowe at Fletcher's?" asked Mr. Hamley.

So soon as he got on the trail of facts he left the badgering of the girl to a future occasion.

"Yes, he called while I was there," said Patricia.

She was almost grateful for the diversion.

"Did he say anything about to-day's pretty kettle of fish?"

"Not there, that I heard," she answered.

"Not there; then he did elsewhere?"

"Only to me."

"Oh! ' only to me,' did he? And what might he have said 'only to me'?" asked Mr. Hamley with a mixture of mockery and banter.

"Not much," answered Patricia.

It was the most diplomatic answer she had ever given. But it did not succeed. Mr. Hamley rose from his seat, large, parabolic, majestic. He walked over to Patricia, took her wrists in one hand, and turned up her face by the chin with the other.

"Look me in the face, young lady," he said in a deep voice; "no subterfuges—I'm not the man for them. What *did* this bankrupt, this beggar, say to you to-day ? Answer straight, or"——

" Leave the girl alone, Mr. Hamley, you frighten her," said Mrs. Hamley.

"No, aunt" answered Patricia proudly, "he does not frighten me. I have done nothing to be ashamed of. Let go my hands, Mr. Hamley. While you hold them I will not open my lips."

He unclosed his thick fingers.

" Now tell your tale," he said.

" I have none," said Patricia, looking at her aunt, not at Mr. Hamley. " Colonel Lowe asked me if we had been told of his son's call to-day, and I said yes, we had. Then he asked if Dora cried, and I said no"—(" You vile wretch !" said Dora under her breath, looking at her with a sweet little smile)— " and if she acquiesced in the decision, and I said yes."

" You are the most detestable animal I know ! I will repay you for this," said Dora, *in petto* again.

" You spoke like a sensible girl," said Mr. Hamley aloud.

" Then you might have spared yourself the trouble of coming over to me, and me the indignity of your touch, Mr. Hamley," cried Patricia, with a sudden burst of angry contempt that was like anything in the world but herself, as she started to her feet, wiping her hands and wrists as if from the soil of his grasp.

" You should not have provoked him," was Mrs. Hamley's reply to her ; but to her husband she said, " You ought not to have touched her, Mr. Hamley. She was not a thief who was going to run away."

And she spoke as tartly to the one as to the other.

But Patricia did not hear her. For the first time in her life she was madly passionate, for the first time felt insulted and outraged. As she stood there flushed and rigid, her head thrown back, her nostrils dilated, her eyes large and fixed, and her bosom heaving, she became suddenly a new person among them all. Hitherto she had been just an innocent, amiable, clumsy, and guileless child whom they had bullied and ridiculed at their pleasure—whom, indeed, they had found it rather amusing to bully, she was so sorry, so surprised, so candid and responsive ! Now she was a woman whose self-respect was fairly roused—an antagonist prepared to defend herself.

Mr. Hamley saw he had gone too far.

" Friends, my dear ?" he said offering his hand.

Patricia folded hers within each other, and kept a scornful silence.

" Don't be silly, child ! " cried Aunt Hamley crossly. " I declare this violence of yours, these vulgar noisy scenes, will make me quite ill. Shake hands I say ? "

" I cannot ! " flashed out Patricia. " I have not forgiven you, Mr. Hamley, and I cannot pretend that I have."

" Do you know what I would do with you if you were my niece ?" asked Mr. Hamley quite gravely.

The girl made no answer at first. Seeing that one was waited for, she said, still in the same excited, passionate voice : " I do not know, and I do not care ; and thank heaven I am not your niece ! "

Mrs. Hamley looked aghast, and Dora's face mirrored hers. But Mr. Hamley burst into a coarse laugh.

"Bravo, my dear !" he cried. " Splendid. What a performer you would have made ! Well, thank heaven too on my side, as I may say, that you are not my niece ! I'd as lief have a tiger cub ! But if you were, I'd kiss you well, and see if you would not forgive me then ? "

He made a step forward as if to put his threat into execution, when Patricia caught up a knife. It was only a silver dessert-knife ; but she did not know that.

" If you touch me I will stab you !" she said. And she looked what she said.

The scene was never forgotten. . From that hour it became a Hamley tradition that Patricia only wanted opportunity to develop into a murderess, and that her temper was simply fiendish. But strange to say Mr. Hamley seemed both to like and respect her more than he had ever done before ; and many times privately expressed his opinion that the girl had something in her if it could only be properly brought out. And he was the man to do it.

The next morning, however, the night having brought good counsel, Patricia went up to him at breakfast, and held out her hand. Very pretty she looked with that frank penitence on her fine face, and her eyes a little moist with shame and the effort she was making.

"I am very sorry, Mr. Hamley," she said, "that I was so cross last night ; and I hope you will forgive me."

"Oh, don't mention it I beg," answered Mr. Hamley with magnanimous acceptance. "We all get put out at times. Even I myself am not always up to what I call high-water mark. But you certainly did take me a little aback, a-wanting to stab me with a dessert-knife ! " He laughed noisily, and struck out his limbs as his manner was.

"I thought it was steel," said Patricia simply.

Then she turned to Aunt Hamley.

"And I ought to ask you to forgive me too, dear aunty," she said tenderly ; "I had no right to make such a scene before you."

"No, you had not, Patricia," returned her aunt. "A young lady, my niece, talking of stabbing her uncle indeed ! What is the world coming to, I wonder, when such horrors as this are tolerated ? "

Patricia looked down. She did really look very sorry for her sin, and her child-like confession touched Mrs. Hamley's heart. It was the kind of thing she liked ; a moral bending of the stiff young neck, and putting it under her own feet, that just suited her.

"Well, my dear, now that you are sorry, we may as well say forget and forgive—hey, Lady ? " said Mr. Hamley, who did not want for a certain coarse good-nature, especially towards women. "Come, give me a kiss, and make up."

"I will make up, but I will not kiss you," said Patricia gravely.

"Absurd ! why should you not kiss your uncle ? " cried Mrs. Hamley, who yet was angry with her husband for asking this grace, and who would not have been more pleased had Patricia obeyed than she was now when she refused.

"I have never kissed any man but my own dear uncle," said Patricia, her voice sad and low ; "and," lifting her eyes, "Gordon."

"Gordon ! Who is Gordon ? " cried Aunt Hamley.

"Gordon Frere—my Gordon," she answered.

"Oh ! " said Aunt Hamley wearily, "more complications ! Here is a love-affair now ! Go to your place, child, do, and don't keep the breakfast waiting any longer ! How I wish you

were as sensible as Dora there. It is a positive relief to look
at her, so quiet and amiable and well-bred as she is! You will
be the death of me before I have done with you, and then I
suppose you will be satisfied."

This was the first time Aunt Hamley had heard of Gordon,
and she took care not to enquire more. If she should ever have
favourable views for her niece, it would be the better policy to
know nothing inimical to them ; and she dreaded rather than
courted information and confession on the subject of an undesirable young man—for he must be that if Patricia had picked
him up of her own motion at that awful Barsands !

CHAPTER XXV.

A MYSTERY.

THE next meeting between the two young lovers was a stormy one. Dora had written to Sydney to tell him how she had wept when Mr. Hamley told her what had happened ; how she had besought him to be more merciful ; how she had expressed her determination to be faithful unto death :—and Colonel Lowe took back Patricia's version, which somehow sounded like truth, and carried with it conviction.

So that when the next meeting came there was but little love to cheer them in the darkness of their circumstances and the blackness of the night. Sydney made Dora responsible for Mr. Hamley's insolence, and she made him responsible for his own failure. He reproached her with her double dealing—playing into the hands of the enemy, according to the account given by Patricia ; she tossed her small head disdainfully, asked him how he could be so dense as not to see that this was a blind to be adopted merely in public ?—and assured him, with the half reluctance of virtue wrongfully accused and too proud to vindicate itself, that she had really wept and besought as she had said, but in private and to Mr. Hamley alone.

" Do you think I would have made a scene ?" she asked with a fine irony ; " that would not be quite like me ! "

But Sydney was not satisfied ; and they walked in the cold dark shrubbery, and quarrelled without ceasing ; and when it began to rain, they went into the shelter of the conservatory and quarrelled there. They were like creatures caught in a net, both the one and the other ; and the thing they had called love, which had brought them there, had suddenly turned bitter in their mouths and heavy on their hands. Sydney had but one cry, " Money—I must have money ! " and Dora but one answer, " I cannot help you."

Then Sydney flung Miss Manley and her five thousand per annum in Dora's face, and claimed her gratitude for the sacrifice ; and Dora brandished the potentiality of my Lady Merrian in his, were she free to encourage those who only asked leave to seek. But when she said this Sydney became furious, and vowed he would take her away in the sight of all men carry her to a garret in London and slow starvation, rather than have any one else trenching upon his rights, and paying atter tion to the woman who was his property.

And when he said this he frightened her, and made her cry ; the threat of confessing their marriage being, of all the misfortunes possible to be encountered, the one most formidable to her, the most terrible. Things were bad enough as they were, with that compelling service at St. Pancras last October and Lord Merrian riding over to Abbey Holme to discuss the Music of the future and look admiringly into her eyes! Things were bad enough indeed, with the leisurely repenting closing up so sternly on the hasty marriage. All that could be done, however, to mitigate the disaster into which they had plunged themselves was to maintain silence and secrecy ; to keep their own counsel absolutely unshared ; and to trust to chance and time for their better direction.

Dora did not tell Sydney that Patricia had found out their secret. She reserved this for an occasion when it might be of use to her. She knew as well as any one the value of a stone in the sleeve, and she was an adept in the art of keeping hers unsuspected and always handy.

So they quarrelled and made up again ; talked and pouted, and then kissed each other ; and Dora now cried and now lisped, and sometimes drove Sydney frantic with her seductions, and sometimes just as frantic the other way with her provocations. But before the young man left, the main object of his visit had been accomplished ; Dora had gone back to the house, had look. ed into Mrs. Hamley's work-table drawer where she knew the lady had placed a rouleau of ten new bright sovereigns received from Mr. Hamley that morning, and of which drawer she had a key that would fit ; had come out again, and had put that rouleau into Sydney's hands, half laughing and half crying. The cleverness of the trick amused her, but she resented the screw under the pressure of which she had made herself a thief.

"There will be an awful row when this is found out!" she said to Sydney. "I cannot think how it will be got over."

"Oh, you are so clever, you can devise something," he answered.

"I don't see why I should devise anything!" she said. "Mrs. Hamley will not suspect me, why can't I leave it alone?"

"I leave the ways and means to you," laughed Sydney; "only don't risk your own dear little neck!"

"Much you would care if I did!" she said petulantly.

"Oh, yes I should, Dody! Little fool, as if I did not love you," he answered tenderly.

But Dora was in no humour to be coaxed. She drew herself away from his arms, saying: "Don't, Sydney! I don't like it!" as if she was quite unused to his methods, and found his love-making reprehensible as well as strange.

"You cross little thing, I'll be hanged if I ever come to see you again!" said Sydney rudely.

"And I am sure I wish you would not. I don't see much pleasure in coming out such weather as this to be quarrelled with!" was Dora's snappish answer.

And with the word she hurried away and ran back into the house; and Sydney nearly got them both into trouble by the loud voice with which he called "Dora!" and which struck upon Mr. Hamley's ear just as he awakened.

As he heard nothing more, though he sat up in bed to listen, he concluded that a dream had played the usual trick of dreams with him, and turned himself round with a smile on his sleepy face.

"Little beauty, my life would be a blank without her!" he said, just as Dora crept up the last flight of stairs, and stole along the carpeted passage to her own room; revolving in her mind how she should act to-morrow when Mrs. Hamley came to the knowledge of her loss—whether to prepare the way for suspicion or let things take their course without intermeddling. By the time she was undressed she had matured her plans, and to-morrow would see them executed.

The next day Alice Garth was in the drawing-room with the two girls, settling some work for her young mistress. Mrs. Hamley had gone into the housekeeper's room to arrange the day's commissariat; for she was her own head housekeeper, with cook to help rather than to rule; and her work table drawer was standing about a quarter of an inch open.

" Patricia, dear, will you just open that drawer and give me
a skein of blue silk I believe you will find there ?" said Dora.
" I am sure Mrs. Hamley will let me have it."

" You are sure she will not mind my touching her things ?"
asked Patricia half reluctant. Her fear of her Aunt Hamley
was deepening to quite a wholesome extent; and in her state
of earnest desire not to offend again, since her outbreak over
the silver dessert-knife, she was learning a tact almost as nice
as Dora's own.

" Oh, certain !" lisped Dora. " Of course not, else I would
not have asked you," laughing ; " it is just in front, I know."

Patricia opened the drawer and removed one or two things
discreetly.

" I see no skein of blue silk, Dora," she said.

" You dear little blind eyes !" laughed Dora, whose fair
face was rather flushed this warm spring-like day. " Here,
Alice, do you go and help Miss Kemball to find it."

Alice flung her work over her arm and went to the drawer ;
lifting a few things also discreetly, but perhaps a little more
with the tips of her fingers than Patricia ; but neither could
she see the skein of blue silk ; and then Dora said good-humour-
edly—she was such a pleasant young lady to serve—

" Never mind, then. I must say you are one as blind as the
other, but it does not signify ; and perhaps Mrs. Hamley has
taken it away."

So the subject like the search dropped, and presently Dora
found the skein in her own work-box, and laughed lightly at
the incident.

Then Alice left the room with her patterns and her instructions, and Mrs. Hamley returned from the offices, her duties as
the châtelaine ended for the day so soon as she should have
paid cook's bill, for which she had the money ready packed.

She opened her work-table drawer and looked in, specially
moving a black and gold needle-case which Dora had made for
her years ago ; the child's first piece of well-conducted fancy-
work, and for which she had the maternal fondness that hallows
the early work of children. She looked twice, thrice, and all
about the drawer ; then she muttered, " How extraordinary !"
and looked out into the room as if considering.

Dora watched her furtively without seeming to do so.

B

Patricia, to whom the drawer and the skein of blue silk and
the black and gold needle-case had no more significance than
so many unnumbered dominoes, had her head in the French
grammar; covering the lines with her hand, which she brought
down a step gradually as she repeated in a whisper to herself,
"Je souffre, tu souffres, il souffre," and so on. Mrs. Hamley,
still with her look of deep consideration, of searching back in
her memory and general bewilderment of mind, left the room
silently, but after a time came in again and once more turned
over the things in her drawer.

"How extraordinary!" she murmured again, and looked
with a kind of perplexed ill-temper at both the girls.

The two tranquil faces she scanned so curiously told her nothing. Dora, with a pretty little smile of loving recognition
on her small fresh lips, looked up from her work as guileless as
the dove that was her favourite emblem. Patricia was staring
vacantly at the ceiling, repeating with praiseworthy diligence:
"Je souffrirai," and "nous souffrirons."

What had either to do with the mysterious displacement or
loss out of the little work-table drawer? What could either
have to do with it? Mean and irritating in small things, Mrs.
Hamley had a certain dignity of action on large occasions. Her
temper was more in fault than her heart; and though she did
not scruple to make her house-mates unhappy, she would not
willingly have wronged them. It seemed to her an insult she
could not possibly offer to ask either, such good girls as both
were, if they knew in any way of her loss. How could they?
She remembered now that only Dora was in the drawing-room
yesterday when she put the roll away; what then could Patricia possibly know of it? Besides, was not the one as absolutely
clear as the other?

She was perplexed and distressed, and on Patricia's going
out of the room to get a dictionary, she looked at Dora wistfully—Dora, her dear child, her consoler in all her little afflictions—and Dora went over to her at once, and kneeling by
her, said prettily:

"You look disturbed, dear. Have you lost anything? or
heard any bad news?"

"The most wonderful thing has happened, Dora!—I cannot

make it out!" answered Mrs. Hamley. "I put a roll of gold in here yesterday, and now it has gone."

"Gone! Oh! how strange. Why, how can it have gone?" said Dora, putting the tips of her fingers into the drawer as if they were magnets, and the missing sovereigns stray filings. "You surely must have overlooked it, dear."

"No, I have not. I have moved everything—searched thoroughly," she answered.

"I never heard of anything so odd. What can have become of it?" said Dora, moving thimbles and reels to make sure that the roll of gold had not lost itself in the shadow. "Do you think it can have got behind the drawer? Let me take it out and look. No!" she cried, as she peered carefully into the hollow, "there is nothing there. How very odd!"

"Who can have taken it?" said Mrs. Hamley. "No one ever goes to my drawer, and it is always kept locked; and we have no one in the house that I could possibly suspect. To be sure there's the new kitchen-maid, but she could not know of it."

"No, no one could know of it," said Dora, reflectively. Then suddenly, as if the remembrance of an unimportant event which might have important issues had just struck her, she told Mrs. Hamley how Patricia and Alice Garth had looked in for a skein of blue silk which Alice wanted for her work, and which she thought was there. They did not touch the things, she went on to say with a fine earnestness of advocacy that pleased Mrs. Hamley. They did no harm; she was sure of that; and they could not have interfered with the roll at all. It might by some strange chance have caught in their fringes or sleeves; but then it would have fallen on the carpet, and she and they must have heard it. It was not there too, as she found by moving the chairs and footstools, sofas and tables, to the remotest corner of the room. She was indefatigable in her exertions, and Mrs. Hamley thought how good and sympathetic she was.

"Well, I don't suppose either of them took it on purpose— stole it, in fact," said Mrs. Hamley sharply. But she said in her own heart, "How I wish Patricia had not left the room as she did!"

"No, I suppose not," said Dora quietly. "Of all three,

Patricia, Alice, or myself, I should as soon suspect one as the other."

"But in any case I will not allow my things to be touched," Mrs. Hamley said with temper. She was getting cross now, and Dora's diligence in search was losing its effect. "You ought to have prevented them, Dora; you know how particular I am, and how much I dislike to have my things interfered with and pulled about."

"Yes, dear; I know I was wrong; I should have stopped them," said Dora. "But I assure you they did nothing more than just look into the drawer."

"We will say no more about it," said Mrs. Hamley, with a sudden greyness on her face. "It is one of those mysteries I do not like to think of, and that no thinking can make clear. Tell me though, who went to the drawer first?"

"Patricia."

"And then Alice Garth?"

"Yes, then Alice."

"What can that girl be about?" said Mrs. Hamley irritably.

"Who, dear?" asked Dora.

"Patricia; where is she?"

"She went out of the room for a book, I dare say. She was learning a French verb, I know."

"I wish she would come back!" said Mrs. Hamley, and fretfully re-arranged the work-table drawer.

"Shall I go and call her?" suggested Dora.

But Mrs. Hamley said "No," and re-arranged the things with redoubled energy. Suddenly she said : "Go to the maids' room, Dora, and ask Alice if she has found anything in her sleeves or hanging about her anywhere. Do not tell her what I have lost, but just ask her."

"Yes, dear," said obedient Dora, gliding swiftly and noiselessly from the room.

While she had gone, Patricia came back, holding on by a huge French dictionary which she was carrying in the old cushion and kitten fashion, under her arm.

"Where have you been, child?" asked Mrs. Hamley very sharply.

"In the library, aunt, looking for this," said Patricia, startled at her tone.

" What a time you have been! Come to the fire—getting cold in this way!"

" I am not cold at all, aunt, thank you. There was a large fire in the library," she answered pleasantly.

" Come here, I say!" reiterated Aunt Hamley in an authoritative manner.

And Patricia, wondering, went.

" Not cold, your hands are like ice!" said Aunt Hamley, touching her as she passed ; " and, good gracious, child, what do you keep in your pocket?" she added. " It bulges out like a schoolboy's. What have you in it? stones or nuts and apples, or what?"

" Something of everything," laughed Patricia colouring.

" Let me see," said Aunt Hamley in a low voice, trembling.

" Dear aunt, yes, if you like. I have no secrets," said the girl, tumbling out into her aunt's lap a heterogeneous collection of the most extraordinary odds and ends a girl could possibly get together ; string, wax, a foot-rule that folded in three, a screw, a few white pebbles which Gordon had given to her as possible agate or white cornelian, a huge buckhorn-handled knife of the kind called in the north jackylegs, or joctelegs, two pocket-handkerchiefs, and a pair of garden-gloves. No wonder her pocket bulged!

For the unwomanliness of the collection, and its disorderly character, Patricia got a severe lecture ; but Aunt Hamley found not a trace of what she sought. It was horrible to have had even this momentary suspicion, but what could she do? She was confronted with the undeniable fact that her ten sovereigns had been abstracted and that no one had been near the place where they were save Patricia and a steady, good, modest girl, the daughter of a yeoman farming his own land, who was almost as far above suspicion as her niece. If she had allowed her mind to wander into the depths for a moment, who could blame her? A rouleau of gold cannot go out of a drawer without hands, and the police always say : " Look for the thief where you least suspect."

So she reflected and tried to soothe her conscience for having dreamed of suspecting her niece only to fall on to the other horn of the dilemma, when at night she told the whole circumstance to her husband, and asked him what he thought.

"Alice Garth," he said. "Make your mind easy, Lady, that young woman is the thief. I am not a magistrate for nothing, and I know the whole rat-hole of them pretty well by now. Keep your eyes open, Lady, and I'll wager my best that you'll find her out before long. She's no good, that girl; and my word is 'Troop.'"

"You might express your word with a little more refinement, Mr. Hamley," said his wife primly; "your counsel is always valuable, but I cannot say I always admire the manner in which you give it."

"Matter goes before manner," said Mr. Hamley sententiously; "and them as has a rough diamond need not be ashamed of it because it ain't polished. A diamond's a diamond, rough or smooth; that is what I say, and I think I am not so far out."

"You might attend a little more to my instructions, I think," said Mrs. Hamley. "'Them as has'—'ain't'—how often I have told you of these errors!"

"Beg pardon, Lady; won't do it again till next time," Mr. Hamley answered jocularly. "He is a bad boy, I dare say; but he isn't bad to his missis."

Mrs. Hamley made no reply. She was weary and distressed; glad to have no shadow of case against her niece, but sorry that Alice Garth should have presumably failed so fearfully; perplexed what to do between want of proof and strong suspicion. She held the crime in horror, and wished to banish the criminal forthwith, but she was haunted by the dread of accusing the innocent; and yet, if not Alice, who could it have been?

Mr. Hamley, however, cut the matter very short. He was not sorry to make James Garth eat dirt in the face of the congregation; and to dismiss his daughter without a character and at a moment's notice was as good a means to this end as any that occurred to him. The next morning then, he summoned Alice into the awful sanctuary of his library, and without a word of reproach or explanation, handed her her wages, salary, and board wages, calculated to a fraction, for the next month, and told her to pack up her boxes and be off before the clock struck twelve.

She was a pretty, fair-haired, delicate girl, with large light-grey eyes and large pupils; a nervous girl, with a spirit proud of her honesty, proud of her fair fame, and a lady in her degree.

She was warmly attached to her good-natured young mistress, and passionately fond of her father; a girl as pure in mind, as refined in feeling, and as incapable of low vice as if she had been a duke's daughter; and this sudden dismissal struck her at all points. What would her father say ? What would the world think ?

Quivering with nervous pain, she asked in a suffocated voice: " What is this for, sir ?" her poor hands clasped in each other and her sensitive face blanched and drawn.

Mr. Hamley waved his hand. He did not look up. He did not like to give pain to women, especially pretty young women, so he did not care to look at the pitiful face which he knew was looking so beseechingly into his. Had she been a lady indeed, he could not have done it; but a maid-servant—that was different. Mr. Hamley was not the man to fly in the face of Providence and blaspheme caste ; and it was scarcely necessary for the master of Abbey Holme to trouble himself about the sorrows or the wrongs of a yeoman's daughter, his paid and hired servant. Still he did not care to look at her.

" I make no remark," he said ; "I say nothing. We may have suddenly resolved to alter our establishment ; a thousand things may have happened. The upshot that concerns you is —here is your money and you must go."

It was beating against a stone wall to stay then and try to soften Mr. Hamley ; he had set his face like a flint, and had he been Rhadamanthus in person he could not have been more impenetrable, more immovable.

One eager gaze into the coarse fixed face convinced her. Gathering up her pride through all her sick despair, without a word she turned away with a dazed expression like one suddenly brought from darkness to the light, and went out staggering. Patricia was crossing the hall as she came out of the study, holding on by the wall and creeping round, almost unable to drag herself along.

" Alice! what is the matter ?" she cried, laying her hand on the girl's arm.

Alice looked as if she did not understand her ; and Patricia seeing that something was gravely wrong, and frightened at her face, took her upstairs into her own room, more than half carry-

ing her, and placed her in the easy-chair she herself so much
despised ; then she bathed her face and made her drink some
water, and by degrees got the story from her.

Story indeed there was none ; simply the bare uncompromising fact of a sudden dismissal without cause of complaint or
reason assigned.

" It is an infamy ! " cried Patricia warmly. " Mr. Hamley
is a monster! But you must not mind, dear Alice, good Alice !
You will find friends, and he will never have a blessing !
Here ! " she said, as a sudden thought struck her ; " take a
note to Miss Fletcher and see what she says. Whatever she
says will be right," she added, with the relieved look of one
who has found a way of escape in a difficulty, and a sure guide
in danger.

She sat down and wrote a rapid little note to her friend,
begging her to see Alice Garth and to talk to her and comfort
her ; saying that she was, a good girl and had no faults, and
ought not to have been sent away. After which she emptied
her purse into the lap of the disgraced maid, who hated to take
her money for many reasons, but was fain for the greater good
there is sometimes in compliance than in self-assertion ; and
for her farewell she put her arms round her neck and kissed
her as she might have kissed a sister ; which opened the founts
and sent poor Alice into a fit of crying that culminated in
hysterics, and taxed both Patricia's skill and patience.

If Aunt Hamley had only known that her niece had kissed
a servant ! Of a truth Miss Fletcher's democratic example was
bearing fruit !

But Mr. Hamley had his own trial to bear after this sudden
assumption of domestic power. Mrs. Hamley, who never allowed interference in her kingdom, made his life a burden to
him for days and weeks. Bignold, her maid, who had to work
double tides—dear Dora being utterly incapable of dressing
herself, and Patricia with the best will in the world not being
sufficiently deft to help—in her turn made her mistress's life a
burden to her ; and all Dora's tact and self-control, and natural
good nature were taxed to the utmost to keep the tiring-woman
tolerably civil or efficient. It was a hard time for them all, the
innocent as well as the guilty ; but Mr. Hamley took care not
to show he felt the ground-swell that he had raised, and, in

his malicious glee at having wounded James Garth through his daughter, bore with the Lady's pin-pricks like a stoic. They were cheap at the price, he thought. Perhaps if he had known that Catherine Fletcher had taken Alice into her service out of hand, not letting her go home even for an hour, but adopting her then and there without enquiry as to why she was dismissed, and without the formality of asking for her character, he would not have thought his daily annoyances so cheap. There would be a breeze, as he phrased it, when he came to know it.

Not that Miss Fletcher much regarded the chance or the reality of a breeze, when the question was one of kindness or conscience. She believed in Alice whom she had known from childhood; and when the girl told her with tears that she was entirely ignorant of any cause whatever why she should have been dismissed, that she had done nothing, said nothing, been just as she always was, and that the whole affair was a mystery from beginning to end, that no shadow of reason had been assigned, and no complaint of anything wrong in the house which might have been fastened on her made public, Catherine accepted her statement implicitly.

"Take off your bonnet," she said, " and stay here. You have come at the right time. I am wanting a cook, for Jane is to be married soon—is only waiting indeed, till I am settled with her successor. You cannot cook, you say? Never mind! I will teach you. Lady's maid or parlour-maid or whatever you may be, Alice, you are a woman first of all, and therefore ought to know how to cook," she added smiling. "A woman who cannot cook is like a man who cannot handle a tool ; a helpless creature with only half her faculties. There is nothing like being able to do everything; so now, my dear, you are engaged here as cook, and you can go home this evening and tell your mother of the change."

CHAPTER XXVI.

BIDDEN TO THE QUEST.

MILLTOWN society, such as it was, always profited by the advent of the family at the Quest—" the Dovedales," as certain of the upper people called them, with a fine assumption of elemental equality, and a public announcement that they considered themselves of the same flesh and blood as even an earl and countess ; or " my lord and lady," as others styled them, with a reverential abasement of the inner man, and a humble confession that a nobleman has different physiological constituents from plain John Smith, and that in all the qualities which make up womankind my lady the countess is not the same kind of creature as Joan the drudge. Well, the Dovedales being human and not silly, were neighbourly people in their way, and placed a good deal of their religion in the exact performance of their social duties. Hence they stirred up the society about Milltown and the adjacent parts, and gave œcumenical entertainments to which all the visitable people were generously invited.

This did not prevent their being the proudest people on the face of the earth for their own parts. But their very pride enabled them to condescend with that perfection of art which conceals itself ; and as no amount of condescension could raise others or lower themselves to the same level, they were always gracious because never afraid.

They gave weekly dinner-parties, and had their sets rigidly arranged. And among others they had one set of which the Lowes and the Fletchers formed part, and in which this year, for the first time, the Hamleys were invited. This was the most democratic thing the Dovedales had ever done ; but even they felt themselves compelled to float with the incoming plutocratic tide, and pay their homage to wealth when they met it. And as Mr. Hamley had the reputation of being even richer than he was—furiously rich, some one said—and as Mrs.

Hamley at all events was a gentlewoman by birth, the democracy involved in the invitation was reduced to a minimum, and what was left was exalted into a virtue by that sacred shibboleth, "the obligations of our position." Wishing, however to get as much pleasure out of their virtue as might be, they formally asked the two pretty girls as well as the elders, and took care to have their particular Milltown set on a day when only a few nobodies were staying at the Quest; who nevertheless were nobodies with names and places, and thus made a show for the dazzling of the natives. Generally the fine ladies staying there, not being bound to condescension by any exigencies of local position, took no active part in these democratic feasts of sacrifice. They looked critically at the women, whom they invariably pronounced bad style; and though they might have been friendly enough over the vol-au-vent and the chartreuse with the gentlemen belonging, kept aloof in the drawing-room when they had to remember their dignity and what was owing to themselves. But this is the way with women. They will flirt to shamelessness with Dick, but they will not know Mrs. Dick. "The men might pass, but it is those badly-dressed women who are so dreadful!" they say among themselves when discussing their social inferiors. And they are right, according to the register of their standards.

It was the fine gentlemen who did all the work; who overlooked the immorality of an exaggerated pattern or a last year's mode, and brought down their finery to the lower level, like so many Apollos among the goatherds, or Crishnas consorting with the Gopias. Still there was fun, if of a mild kind, to be had out of certain of the provincial Sampsons; and it was anticipated to-day that Mr. Hamley would be a rich mine. For all the outside varnish with which his wife had so diligently sought to overlay him these fifteen years, the stuff beneath was as coarse as ever; and the varnish had the habit of not sticking, but of coming off in bursts and showing the original grain as clearly as if it had never been brushed on at all. The owner of Abbey Holme was notorious in his own way; but gilding goes farther than varnish in these days, and even the Dovedales condoned the coarseness of the grain for the sake of the gilt.

It was not a pleasant surprise to either when the Lowes and
the Hamleys met in the drawing-room of the Quest. Hitherto
Colonel Lowe had regarded this as the one inviolable temple
which the old shoeblack of Abbey Holme would never be permitted to penetrate. If he, as one of the leading men of the
district, had felt bound to recognise him, as a superior being
might recognise the inferior, that was a different thing from
being classed with him as equals together by one who was
superior to both—bracketed as social equivalents, and fit com-
panions in the same harness. He felt the invitation of his
enemy as an insult to himself, and hoped some blessed chance
might occur which would give him the opportunity of putting
a spoke in the wheel of the Hamley car of triumph, and bringing him to the ditch and the dust.

On his side Mr. Hamley would rather that Colonel Lowe
had only heard of his invitation, not been there to witness his
acceptance. Not that he cared much about him ; but, all
things considered, it was awkward, and we do not go out to
dine with earls and countesses to be annoyed. If we are to
have a helping of gingerbread, in mercy's name let us have our
share of gilt undefaced ! Nevertheless Mr. Hamley bore himself with commendable propriety ; and when he came up the
long drawing-room with his wife on his arm, and the two pretty
girls at his heels, and made his parabolic bows, the coolness
with which he ignored the Colonel and his son would have
done credit to the most veteran diplomatist.

Perhaps the young people suffered the most. Some weeks
had elapsed now since Mr. Hamley had given his ultimatum so
distinctly to Sydney, and husband and wife had kept apart since
Dora's last secret issue with Mrs. Hamley's roll of ten bright
shining sovereigns in her pocket. Twice had Sydney thrown
gravel up to the window, and hooted with such artistic perfection as to madden the neighbouring owls; but Dora never
"showed." She was getting frightened since Mr. Hamley's
seizure and Patricia's discovery. She was getting frightened,
too, of Sydney himself, now that he had begun to press her for
money ; so she did the best she could to keep him quiet and in
good humour by writing pretty little notes which she smuggled
into the post somehow, generally only after she had intrigued
and manœuvred to an extent that might have saved a kingdom.

And above all, she and Patricia had seen Lord Merrian some three or four times ; and she had taken to herself the several accidents which had brought them together, and had spent much time in brooding on possibilities, could the past be undone or safely denied.

The meeting, then, was by no means pleasant for any one ; and it took all the tact and good breeding of the belligerents not to show that Cragfoot and Abbey Holme had "cut," and that the Quest was less a nest where doves were cooing than a field where dogs would fight if they dared.

It would be useless to give an Homeric catalogue of the guests, or to designate their places. It is enough to say that Mr. Hamley was in the second place of honour by the Countess ; and that Sydney had been told off to Patricia, but had on the other side of him Miss Manley with her indefinite hair, her weak eyes, her freckles, and her camel's lip, her long waist, thin shoulders, and five thousand a year. Immediately opposite, Lord Merrian, between Mrs. Lowe and Dora, ●presented youth between duty and inclination ; but he was too well-bred not to give the chief honours to the elder lady who belonged to him by right ; in which he showed himself a better gentleman than Sydney Lowe, who turned his shoulder to Patricia persistently and left her to Dr. Fletcher while he devoted himself to Miss Manley. He and Dora were having a silent duel across the table, whereby Lord Merrian and Miss Manley benefited.

Never had Dora looked so pretty or behaved with such a perfect imitation of real breeding. She was the belle of the table, not even excepting the gracious Countess, a woman of the mature siren type, who in last season's dresses, magnificent if no longer fresh, looked at forty-five no more than thirty, and who might well have passed for the daughter of her husband and the elder sister of her son. To be sure her maid and the morning saw what the world did not ; but Tongs was a discreet young woman whose sympathies were with pearl-powder, and the Bond Street bills were never published.

As for Patricia, hers was beauty of a kind which does not harmonise so well with the state and glitter of a fashionable dinner-table as with heathy moors and whitening seas. She was a nymph, not a belle ; and was more at home in the wild

free country than in an assemblage of jewelled dowagers whose
estimate of social fitness is about as sharp as the bridge over
which Mohammedan souls walk to Paradise—Gehenna yawning
below.   Set in the midst of the gorgeous array that surrounded
her, she shone conspicuous by the simplicity of her manner and
her dress, which last however was neither meagre nor ungrace-
ful.   The Countess was in a millinery marvel of blue and gold ;
one of Worth's masterpieces in decadence, deftly caulked and
repaired.   Dora was in white silk—she looked best in white—
cut very low on her shoulders, with lovely little outbursts of pale
pink in unexpected places, suggestive of a blush rose—a maiden
blush—the white petals of which close round yet just reveal its
tender, flushing heart.   She wore a single row of large pearls
round her throat, and a few blush roses peeped out coquettishly
from among the gold of her shining hair.   At Colonel Lowe's
her costume had suggested bridal ; here, by Lord Merrian's
side, it emblemised wooing.   The rest of the ladies were in the
various shades of mauve and silver grey, pink, blue, maize and
peacock-green, usual to age and complexion ; while Patricia was
in a thin black material made high to her throat, where it was
ruffled with white.   No scoldings and no coaxings could induce
her to hang herself about with chains, submit to have her ears
pierced, pile up her head with false hair or underlying tow, or be-
dizen herself in any of the ways fashionable at this time.   All
she could be induced to do was to allow a white camelia to be
pinned into her rich brown hair, and to wear another on her
bosom.   For the rest, her dress had been made by the redoubt-
able Biggs according to Mrs. Hamley's instructions.   Hence it
included all the due mysteries of frills and puffs with which
modern millinery assails art.   For these things she did not
care.   So long as she might discard ornaments and wear her
gowns up to her throat, she let them manage the rest as they
would ; and even Aunt Hamley had to be content with a com-
promise.

Perhaps the girl's instinct was right after all, thought Mrs.
Hamley ; for she certainly looked very distinguished, even at
the Quest, and a different stamp of girl from the rest.   There
really was something wonderfully noble about her, she thought
again, watching her from the extreme end of the table, half in
admiration of her appearance, half in fear of her behaviour.

She might have spared herself her pangs, for Patricia was not sufficiently at ease to be spontaneous, so sat with a kind of North American Indian's stillness and dignity of bearing which to the superficial seemed the perfection of good breeding, but to the observant showed her unaccustomedness to the full as much as the soubrette's flush and flutter would have done. She was troubled in more ways than one. She did not like to sit by Sydney Lowe, knowing all she knew ; and she did not like to see Dora look at Lord Merrian as she did. She had certain absurd notions about the sacredness of marriage which this kind of transferred fascination did not suit ; and she felt as if she was responsible for all she knew, and knowing, condemned. Then she had an uneasy consciousness that certain mysteries, of which she was ignorant, were connected with the arbitrary choice of spoon or fork ; and that she was not so well up in the accidence of the dinner-table as might have been. To be sure, she had been well-drilled at Abbey Holme ; but to a girl accustomed to eat hunches of bread and meat standing on the deck of a yacht, with the tiller-ropes in her hand, the nice minutiæ of a perfectly-arranged dinner-table are troublesome to learn and difficult to practise.

For one part of her present discomfort however, she had but little reason. Sydney, as has been said, turned his shoulder to her from the beginning of the meal to the end ; and Miss Man ley's pale dun face lighted up under his darker fires as it had sel-dom lighted before. She took quite cheerful views of things for the whole two hours the dinner lasted. In general she was of a desponding turn, and thought life had but little to recommend it to a wealthy, young, unmarried woman, morbidly conscious of her own plainness, haunted by a dread of sharks, deficient in hæmatine, and longing for love but fearing lovers. To be taken possession of by some good, kind Christian soul, who would ad-minister her fortune favourably, treat her personally with chiv-alrous devotion, take interest in her mild pursuits, and walk with her through life hand in hand—a man to whom a little bad art, a little desultory reading, and a little imperfect botany, were quite sufficient recreations—that was the sum of her ambition, the highest point to which her visions reached. She had not found such a one yet, and Sydney Lowe had not quite the out-side look of her ideal ; nevertheless, he drew her magnetically,

and she expanded under his attentions like a crumpled, half-
dead insect reviving under the sun.

But the person who was decidedly the happiest of the whole
assembly this day was Mr. Hamley. To be invited to the Quest
had been for years one of the secret points of his not too elevated
ambition. He remembered, as if it was only yesterday, when
he stood among the obsequious throng crowding the gates at
the home-coming of the young earl and his bride. He was out
of the barefooted stage then, six and twenty years ago, but he
was still only a clerk in the concern whereof he was so soon to
be sole manager and the prosperous proprietor. And he remembered, as he sat there with my lady's gorgeous blue and gold
every now and then rustling against his knees, how this house
had been to him like a Paradise, where, could he be once admitted on terms of equality, he should be satisfied. It would
be his version of the *Nunc Dimittis*, and he would ask nothing
more from fate or fortune. Indeed, neither fate nor fortune
could give him anything more. Let them but grant him this
one crowning grace, and he would feel that he had drained the
golden cup to the last luscious drop, and left no flower in the
Elysian Fields unplucked. So he was satisfied in the present
as well as in the past; unctuously, fully satisfied; as he would
himself have said, replete with happiness. He knew too, that
his being here was disagreeable to the Cragfoot people, over
whom it gave him a prospective advantage when the fitting
time should come; which would not be long now. He had a
bill against Colonel Lowe; it had been running for many a
year; but he thought he saw daylight and the payment of his
pound of flesh; and he was pleased, now that the first awkwardness had worn off under the influence of the wine and his pleasure at being seated near the Countess—a higher place than the
Colonel had !—that they had met as equals at the Quest before
he had to give his enemy that lesson he had been waiting so
long to deliver. The possession too, of a ladylike, if aged wife,
and of "the prettiest girls out" as his maiden satellites, was
not without its value. Taken all round, his lot was a grand one
this night; and he had courted Fortune with good effect.

Mr. Hamley was a self-made man who had a good deal to
say about native worth and all the rest of it; but he believed
in a lord all the same; and he loved him. As he sat by Lady

Dovedale and flourished his large hands, with their large diamond rings sparkling and flashing in the light, expanded his
broad chest with his elaborately-embroidered shirt front, used
his finest words, and showed his long white teeth, he was altogether radiant and contented, supple and subjugated.   Had
my lady asked him to commit any baseness in the world not
penal, he would have wiped his lips and done it. All the same
he was trying to impress her with the sense of his own worth
as a man and his solidity as a money-bag—to edge his big
shoulder under the delicate fringe of her feathers, that he might
force her to recognise his claims to equality.

His version of the family to those of his friends who were
not admitted to the heaven of the Quest, was, that lords and
ladies were just like other men and women when you came to
know them.   And he said it in the tone of a discoverer. A deal
of nonsense was talked about the aristocracy, he said, by them
as had never conversed with a live lord.   Those as had got behind the scenes knew better, and he for one could say there
was no difference between them and other people when you
came to know them.   Take the Dovedales, now ; my lord was
as free and hearty as his own brother—not a bit of nonsense
about him, and with his head screwed on the right way ; and
my lady was not only a splendid creature to look at, but as
affable and simple as a child.   He could do anything with her
—just the kind of woman he could manage, like he didn't
know what, and twist round his little finger.   He mentioned
"young Merrian" with approbation, though he did not quite
like his manner to young ladies.   Still, the lad meant well, he
dared say, and at the worst he was but young yet and would
improve.

In spite, however, of his own exceeding glory, he was not
over well pleased at the young lord's evident admiration of dear
Dora. Why could he not tackle Patricia ? he thought, as he
every now and then came down from his heights and watched
them across the flowers and lights.   If Patricia now could
catch Merrian, he would say grace over that meal ; but Dora,
—no, he could not part with Dora ! She was his one ewe lamb,
and not even for the right of calling across the street, " Hi
there ! Merrian my boy, how are you all ?" could he give her
up.

Had he watched a little more keenly he would have seen that, though Lord Merrian flirted with Dora, he was watching Patricia—Patricia talking to Dr. Fletcher with something of her natural animation as the dinner was drawing to a close, and therefore the difficulties of manipulation were lessening, while Sydney's persistent neglect reduced him to the rank of a circumstance only.

Lord Merrian cared nothing for pretty Dora Drummond, but . Patricia had touched him deeply. She was the first woman who had appealed to his nobler aspirations, his higher being —who had stirred his soul rather than his blood, captivated his conscience and imagination rather than his vanity or his senses. He had seen the girl many times, by that lucky kind of intentional accident which befriends young people on the lookout, and though always more demonstrative to Dora, had given his mind most to Patricia. And the more he studied her the more she fascinated him. Nevertheless, he played with Dora ; and Dora did not see through the feint. As for Patricia, she understood no more of the meaning there was in the young lord's eyes and tones than she understood the meaning of Hebrew. She talked with him freely, and accepted him in a fraternal kind of way that was delicious in its innocent unconsciousness ; but the world cannot judge of what it does not see, and Mr. Hamley judged only like the world.

Three conversations, each having an esoteric meaning deeper than their words, were going on at the table at the same moment. Of the one, Lord Merrian, speaking quietly, took the lead.

" Do you and your cousin ever ride, Miss Drummond? I have only seen you driving."

"Sometimes ; not very often ; not this winter at all, since Patricia came ; but I used to ride with Mr. Hamley."

" Walk ?"

" Occasionally."

" Are you a good walker ?"

She laughed. " No."

" Is your cousin ?"

" Oh yes, magnificent ? She can walk as far as a man. She is immensely strong."

" What a splendid place for botanizing the Long Field Lane is !" said Lord Merrian innocently.

"Yes ; but there are no flowers out yet," answered Dora, just as innocently.

" Do you think not? I am going to look for some to-morrow," he returned in the same simply indifferent way. "Are you fond of botany?"

" Passionately," said Dora, who called all hawkweeds little dandelions, and who did not know that dead nettles do not sting.

"You had better join forces with me to-morrow, you and your cousin," said Lord Merrian. "We may find some good specimens."

She smiled with the sweetest, most ingenuous little smile in the world. No one could have suspected that it ratified an assignation.

"That would be very nice," she said.

" Agreed?" asked Lord Merrian.

"If you like," answered Dora.

Opposite, Sydney, with his shoulders well turned to Patricia, had brought his conversation with Miss Manley on to the theme of marriage. He was angry with Dora for her looks and lispings to Lord Merrian, and he had a kind of fierce desire "to pay her out."

" I should not like to marry any one with money," he said to Miss Manley, a shade of melancholy on his handsome vicious face.

" No ?" she answered, playing nervously with her bread.

At this moment she wished that she had not five thousand a-year, but that it stood in Sydney Lowe's name—he looking at her as he looked now.

"No, indeed ! I should like the woman I married to be sure of my disinterestedness. If I loved one with money I should like her to put my affection to some stirring test—to drop her glove into the lion's den——"

" Oh ! like De Lorge?" interrupted Miss Manley with animation. She was a sentimental young person, and fond of poetry and romance.

" Yes, like De Lorge," said Sydney, casting his intellectual bread on the waters without the faintest idea where it was floating.

"But perhaps she might believe in you without such a test."

Miss Manley spoke hesitatingly. It seemed almost too bold a thing to say, with her heart beating as it did against her gaunt ribs, and her pale-dun cheeks flushed—not becomingly.

"That could be only one who knew me well," said Sydney.

Miss Manley was silent; but Dora read her poor, plain face with tolerable accuracy, just as she herself said "If you like," to Lord Merrian.

At the upper end of the table Mr. Hamley was discussing politics with the Countess.

"Yes," she said, arranging her lace tucker with graceful art; "Merrian will stand for the borough at the next election. I do not anticipate failure; do you, Mr. Hamley?"

Mr. Hamley fidgeted. It had been his secret intention to contest the borough himself at the next election; but how could he say this to her ladyship at her own table, when she had honoured him too, as she had done?

"Me, my lady! anticipate failure!—by no manner of means. I should think his lordship safe to succeed," he said with over-acted heartinesss.

"He comes in on the right side," said the Countess; "at least," she continued with her sweetest smile, and she had a very sweet smile, "I trust *you* will say so, Mr. Hamley. A Liberal-Conservative, he is prepared to accept all good reforms, but resist mere innovations which would only do harm; and he will keep down with a strong hand noisy agitators who have no one's good at heart save their own."

These were safe platitudes. They defined nothing and bound no man's conscience; but the Countess said them with unction, and as if they were a programme of the exactest character.

"Bravo, my lady! we must have you up at the hustings. You would take the conceit out of us men if you were to make a speech to the people just as you spoke to me now!" cried Mr. Hamley, overflowing at every pore with oily approbation.

"You flatter me," the lady said, smiling; "and I am glad to find you on our side. An intelligent person like yourself is a host at an election, and such a gain to the right cause!"

" I will do my best to secure Lord Merrian's election," said
Mr. Hamley proudly. "And I think I have a little influence
in my native town. A self-made man as I am, my lady, you
see I understand both sides. I know the poor because I remember them when I was one of them ; and I know the rich,
seeing that I have become what I call a rich man myself. I
shall consider it a honour to work for your ladyship's son, and
we'll carry him in among us, no fear."

"That is very nice of you," the Countess answered. "Do
you know, Mr. Hamley, I had heard that you were such a dreadful Radical I was almost afraid of you ? I thought that probably you would not come to the Quest at all, if we asked you ;
and you know we poor sinful aristocrats cannot help being born
with titles."

"Heaven forbid you should help it if you could !" exclaimed
Mr. Hamley. "And who could have told your ladyship such an
infamous lie as that I was a Radical ? I assure your ladyship I
yield to no man in my love for the respected institutions of our
venerated country, and I would not see one of them destroyed ;
least of all the institution which the Earl and Countess of Dovedale adorn."

" Neatly said," was his own unspoken comment.

"I am sure *now*, you never could have been a horrid Radical;
why you are quite a courtier ! " said the Countess graciously.

Mr. Hamley laughed and spread out his feet under the table
and his hands above it.

"Try me when the election comes on," he said, tossing off his
wine.

"I thought he would have been more difficult," was the
lady's comment to her husband when the dinner-party was
broken up. "But he was too easy. He is a dreadful creature ;
no bait is too transparent for him, no flattery can be too
coarse."

" He is a beast," was the Earl's vigorous reply.

Nevertheless these aristocratic personages did not disdain the
promised assistance of the beast, and thought his hand, however coarse and unclean, as good as any other for a political leg-
up to their son.

On his side Mr. Hamley swelled with satisfaction. He had
been singled out by my lady for special honour and distinction,

and the carriage seemed hardly large enough to contain his
jubilant pride.   All during the ride home it was one incessant
round of what my lady had said, and what he had said, and how
she looked, and how he had tried to impress her by his looks
back, and what he had eaten, and the beauty of the " set out "
—but the wine was inferior to his own, he thought, and the
cheese was not ripe enough.

" We'll show them how to do it, Lady, when we have them
out at Abbey Holme," he said to his wife, rubbing his hands.
" I'm a self-made man, earned sixpence a day once upon a time
and lived on it ; but I'll give my lord a glass of wine he can't
match for all the cobwebs in the Quest cellars."

He was quite frisky in his lumbering elephantine way, and
complimented his ladies enthusiastically all round. He was
gracious beyond measure to Patricia, to whom he said pater-
nally : " But you should have talked more to my young lord
than you did, my dear, mewing yourself up with those old
Fletcher birds !   I do not approve of boldfaced jigs in young
ladies ; but Lord Merrian deserves a little nice attention."

He did not add that he had taken occasion to inform Lord
Merrian, when the ladies had withdrawn, that he intended to
dower his wife's niece handsomely if she married to his liking ;
but that he had only left his own cousin provided by will ;
which he thought was doing the thing as it should be done—
the correct card outside and in!

CHAPTER XXVII.

THOROUGH.

"WHAT a lovely afternoon !"

It was Dora who spoke, standing by the drawing-room window after luncheon ; her enthusiastic admiration directed to a grey sky with flying lead-coloured clouds, and fitful gleams of a watery, greenish-yellow sunlight.

"A lovely day? my dear, you are surely dreaming!" said Mrs. Hamley. "It is as cold as Christmas, and looks as stormy as November."

"But it is a nice fresh day for a walk," said Dora.

Mrs. Hamley stared at the girl, who in general was content to sit close "into the fire" through the winter ; and who, when she went out, went out only in a close carriage, well wrapped in wadded silks and dainty furs, with a hot bottle for her feet and a wolf-skin for her knees, and who even then shivered and said : "How cold it is!"

"Has Patricia infected you with her odd liking for snow-storms and east winds?" she asked.

"Perhaps she has!" laughed Dora. "Evil communications, you know, dear. But I cannot tell why, I have quite a longing for a walk this afternoon. I heard you tell Jones you did not want the carriage, else I should not have asked you. But if you are not going out, and have nothing for me to do at home, may we take a walk to-day?"

"Yes, certainly, if you like, my dear," said Mrs. Hamley. Yesterday's dinner at the Quest had sweetened her temper divinely. "Does Patricia want to go?"

"Yes, that is why I have asked you," said Dora, without blushing.

She and Patricia had not spoken of it.

"Well, have a nice little walk then—not too far ; and come home blooming," said Mrs. Hamley : "my blush-rose and my —I am sure I don't know what to call Patricia—my hollyhock, I think, she is so tall and straight!"

"You clever dear!" said Dora. "I never knew any one so clever as you are. You are so bright and original."

Mrs. Hamley looked pleased.

"There was nothing very clever in that, pussy," she said.

"Oh yes there was!" cried Dora.

"Ah. that's because you love me, you see, and are prejudiced in my favour," said Mrs. Hamley.

And Dora assented, and said yes, that was true for the one part, but not for all; and love or no love, she was clever and original, and a darling all the same.

"Am I not good to get you this nice walk, you cross old pet?" asked Dora, clasping her hands round the arm of Patricia whom she dug out of the dark depths of the library.

"Yes, very good, Dora," said Patricia, gravely.

"'Yes, very good, Dora,'" laughed Mr. Hamley's fair-haired cousin, mimicking and exaggerating the girl's rather sorrowful voice. "Why, where have all your smiles gone of late? You are as grave as a judge, and as cross—oh! as cross as the cats, as my Irish nurse used to say."

"I am not cross, Dora."

"Yes, you are; you are so cross you do not know how to look like a Christian, not to talk of behaving like one! Well, never mind! Let us go and get our things on now, and we will talk as we go. I say, miss," she added, turning her gracious head half over her shoulder, "you are quarrelling with your best friend, and very ungrateful to her too, when you go on like this to me! There is no one in the house who cares so much for you as I do, or who tries so hard to make your life pleasant and to smooth down your thousand and one difficulties. I am always getting into little troubles for your sake: and for my reward you sulk with me as if I was a monster."

"I don't, Dora!" cried Patricia earnestly.

Dora made a little grimace. Had Patricia been a man it would have been a challenge for a kiss. As it was it only made the girl take hold of her by her two shoulders, and look down into her face sorrowfully and lovingly, while she said; "Oh, Dora, you might be an angel if you chose!"

"And I am, I suppose, a—" she coughed—"instead!"

Patricia smiled, and then she laughed.

"Perhaps an angel with one black feather!" she said; and

Dora gave her a playful push; whereat they both ran upstairs to dress, convinced that life was very good, and that a country walk on this grey March day was the most charming thing the world could give.

Long Field Lane was not far from Abbey Holme; about a mile perhaps; which, though a mere "step-over" to Patricia, was an expedition for Dora. Moreover, the one dressed in simple single garments which allowed her to keep cool or get warm as she liked; the other in multifarious devices of fur and eiderdown, quilting and wadding, which, though making a pretty picture, were hindering. As the time was at hand when Lord Merrian said he should be botanizing about the bare hedges, Dora was anxious to make way; yet by no means anxious to keep her tryst heated or disordered. For the matter of that she never looked either, even when on rare occasions she felt her golden feathers ruffled, and her various artistic arrangements out of gear. And to-day the pretty pink flush on her cheeks, induced by the wind and the walk, only made her the lovelier. Patricia too looked beautiful. She was still sorrowful—that was the set character of her face now; but the little playful brush with Dora had brightened her into gladness; though still and ever the secret unhappiness of her soul broke through the temporary sunshine; and hers was a face, noble always, to which sorrow gives even a nobler expression.

As they turned out of the main road into the lane they saw at a little distance the tall, well set-up figure of Lord Merrian coming leisurely along, not botanizing.

"Dora, there is Lord Merrian—how odd!" said Patricia, suspecting nothing.

"So there is!" lisped Dora. "How odd, indeed, as you say."

But Lord Merrian, who was not naturally rusé, for all he made Dora Drummond his stalking-horse from behind which to observe Patricia, showed so little surprise at seeing them, met them indeed with such an expectant if more than gratified air, that even Patricia was struck by it. Why did he seem as if he knew they were coming? as if he had been waiting for them? That Dora should have made an assignation never occurred to her. She would have thought such an underhand manœuvre bad even with Sydney, and knowing all she knew; but for

Dora to plot and arrange to meet Lord Merrian ? Dora!
Had she suspected this she would probably have abjured her
society for ever, and have made herself miserable ; between
hating the sin of the friend she loved, and lamenting her absence, torturing herself far more than the cause or the person
merited. As it was, she simply wondered at that quiet air of
expectancy in the young lord, and thought that perhaps he had
seen them in some miraculous manner from a distance, and so
knew that he should meet them.

"You were right, Miss Drummond ; there are no flowers,"
he said, after the first greetings.

"I thought none were out yet," she answered.

"Only two," said Lord Merrian.

And Dora laughed, while Patricia looked up and down the
hedge and into Lord Merrian's hands to see which two he
meant.

That inquiring look delighted him. Dora caught it too, and
thought "how dense"—and took honour to herself for her
superior quickness ; but Lord Merrian translated it—"how
innocent ; how perfect in its sweet unconsciousness ;" and—
"how knowing ; how far too clever !"

Nevertheless he smiled at Dora, a little too familiarly perhaps for perfect breeding ; and then he looked at Patricia, and
spoke to her with a certain respect and homage of tone and
manner very noticeable in its difference.

Dora would rather have had the familiarity. She did not
understand the other, and called it coolness ; but she thought
Lord Merrian full of friendliness and admiration to herself, and
she was glad that she had showed so well. She scarcely knew
what she was proposing to herself in all this. She knew that
she could not marry if even she was asked ; but it pleased her
to sail in troubled waters, managing her little craft with such
consummate grace and skill that no one should suspect her seas
were not halcyon. She had always been an adept at untying
knots, and her mechanical aptitude emblemised her mental
cleverness.

After a while the ball seemed to pass somehow from Dora's
hand to-day. In the most natural manner possible Lord Merrian brought the talk round from conventional inanities to
deeper things—from literary small talk to moral principles,

from newspaper politics to historic meanings. **And here Dora** was distanced. All she knew of life was its material **well-be-** ing, its dainty food, its soft attire, the position you held in your society, the dinners you gave, the carriages you kept. She thought it was as well to keep out of doing wrong if you could, and if you could not, then to be careful not to be found out. She liked peace, and she supposed truth the right thing to cultivate when possible. But as it was not possible for the majority, she thought the art of telling lies with coolness and cleverness the most important of all to learn betimes. She blamed those who made the lies necessary, not those who did not dare to tell the truth ; and when she had come to this, and going to church on Sundays, and speaking softly to her inferiors, and laying herself out for the perpetual propitiation of the authorities, she had her code complete, and held that those who wanted more were inconveniently earnest or stupidly intense.

But where Dora was lost Patricia found herself. Also the thoroughness which Lord Merrian lacked she supplied. Lord Merrian was a man with thoughts higher and nobler than his life. He yearned for the millennium, and was dissatisfied with the present worship of false gods ; but he was not one who would go forward to chain the devil, though he faintly cheered on those who did ; and while he vilified the ritual, he nevertheless carried his daily sacrifices to Mammon with the rest, contenting himself with lamentation that the world was so bad, and that so few were found to make it better. All this was very fine to listen to, but very unsatisfactory to the man's own conscience and to the more earnest of his friends. He felt the weakness of his position, and wished it were otherwise ; but the world had him fast in its golden fetters, and he was not strong enough to break them—at least not alone.

Patricia's nature was fashioned on a different plan. With her to believe and to be were identical. She could not lament a wrong and give in to it. The tongue to speak and the hand to do must be in harmony ; and no golden fetters that the world could forge would be found strong enough to bind her back from the upward path, however difficult, if once her face was set that way and she knew it as her duty. So that when Lord Merrian, speaking especially to her, began some of his well-expressed and well-worn jeremiads on the injustice of society and the sorrows of the poor, Patricia turned to him with her strong practical impulse.

" But Lord Merrian," she said, her bright eyes lifted to his face, " you have power to prevent all this misery and injustice on your own estates. If you like you can make your tenants prosperous and happy ; it all depends on your own will, and how you choose to employ your money ; is it not so ? But you will, when you come to reign at the Quest ; will you not ? "

" Ah, that is just the difficulty ! One person can do so little," he said. " And besides, we must not interfere with the natural self-adjustment of the labour market," he added, adopting the current phraseology to excuse the half-heartedness whence it takes its rise. " Say that my father, or I, or both, agreed to lower the rents, give higher wages and better dwellings than our neighbours—than indeed we find regulated by the condition of supply and demand—we should be doing an injustice to those of our brother landowners who would not, or let us say could not, do the same as ourselves, and we should be opening a door to all sorts of encroachments from our tenants."

" I cannot see the first, and I do not believe the last," returned Patricia. " If you choose to do what is right, that cannot be wrong to any others. They may not like it because of the contrast ; but surely that does not signify ! And I can- not believe that the poor would ask for what they ought not to have, because they had given to them what they ought."

" I know all this sounds the right thing in theory, and it is what one's own heart dictates ; but the difficulty is in reducing one's aspirations to practice," said Lord Merrian.

" No, not so far as your own tenants are concerned," said un- compromising Patricia. " Look at Miss Fletcher's houses ! There you see it put into practice ; and what a pleasure it is to go and see the people there ! "

" But do you hear what the other Milltown landowners say of the Fletchers ? " asked Lord Merrian.

Patricia looked up. " No ; and I should not care whatever I heard," she answered calmly. " Do we not know that the world always speaks against those who do the real right ? We know for ourselves, at least I do, how good the Fletchers are

—they are like angels—and what can it matter what others say?"

" You are an able advocate, Miss Kemball," Lord Merrian answered.

He did not know whether he was quite pleased to hear her praise of the Fletchers ; but as she looked very beautiful when she spoke, and her eyes were honest and tender with her thoughts, and looked into him as if he was the cause and not merely the object, he made the best of her enthusiasm, and accepted it—transferred.

" Am I?" A smile broke over her face. " I should think I was, if I could make any impression on you, Lord Merrian."

" You have," he said in a lowered tone ; " a very deep impression."

" And your tenants will benefit? You will do as the Fletchers have done, and make them happy by better treatment than your neighbours give? You will, Lord Merrian?"

" Ah !" he said, and he sighed as he spoke ; and sighed sincerely, believing in the phantoms that he conjured up for himself ; " If only I could! You do not know how we are fettered ! Bailiffs and stewards, and leases and conditions, and above all, that self-adjustment of the labour market with which it is more than doubtful whether we ought to tamper—one's will is so strong, but one's power so weak !"

Patricia shook her head.

" No," she said earnestly. " No one's power is small—it is the will to use it that is wanting. Men in your position, Lord Merrian, can surely do as they like. No good can be done without trying—now can it? and does not trying always cost trouble? and doing what is right when the world does what is wrong—why ! it must be hard and painful ! But if one will not, and another will not, how can reforms come?"

" Yet it is not always possible, even with pain and trouble, to do the right which one would," he answered.

She looked at him, and tears seemed near her eyes.

" Do you know what you remind me of?" she asked.

" No ; what?" he answered, looking down into her face.

" That young man in the Bible who went away sorrowful because he had large possessions," said Patricia.

There was a pause. Her words had struck a little rudely on

the secret sore of her companion's conscience, and he winced
under them.

" Perhaps you are right," he said at length, and it cost him
an effort to accept the blow so magnanimously ; " but I think
I know how my halting will could be strengthened." He said
this almost as if to himself. " But am I really such a half-hearted,
halting sinner in your eyes, Miss Kemball ? " he asked appeal-
ingly.

" I was wrong perhaps to say what I did," stammered
Patricia.

Truth was all very well, but even truth need not be offensive,
And had she not been a trifle priggish ?

" I must say, dear, I think you are *very* bold," put in Dora,
who had sauntered a little way ahead, knowing that her dark
blue dress and chinchilla trimmings made a pretty bit for the
foreground, and that the wind had blown a tiny lock of gold
as a point of colour against the grey fur. She had been listening to this dull talk between the two, and wondering greatly in
her own mind at Lord Merrian's odd choice of subject and
Patricia's unabashed speech.

" No, you are quite right," Lord Merrian said ingenuously.
" We may not like it, but a true, brave word does every one
good. The precious balms, you know," smiling to Patricia.

" You are very good to take me so kindly," she said, looking
down.

" That, however, is not answering my question ; do you
think me so halting and half-hearted as you seemed to say ? "

She did not like being pressed, but she was too brave
to deny the truth when put to it.

" I think you have less determination to do the right thing
than you have clearness in seeing the wrong," she answered.

" Which comes to the same thing," said Lord Merrian.

She blushed.

" I suppose so," she replied. " But indeed I ought not to
speak as I do ; " she then said, with an eager, apologetic tone.
"I sometimes feel as if I did know something of right and wrong,
and then again as if I was the merest child, ignorant of everything."

" Not of everything," he said, in a soft voice. " Do you
never think you have a mission yourself ? "

" I ? a mission? no, indeed !" she cried. " On the contrary, I feel a mere useless encumberer of the ground, an excrescence belonging to no one, and of no use anywhere."

Lord Merrian flushed like a girl. In general his pale, finely-formed face showed but few changes of colour or expression. It was always a slightly sad face ; statuesque, and cast in a tragic mould of the first degree ; and he cultivated stillness ; but now it became rudely coloured, while every part of it seemed to speak.

" You will find your mission some day perhaps," he said in a low voice. " The mission of strengthening a weak will and making a half-hearted life a whole one. Found any flowers yet, Miss Drummond ?"

" No," said Dora, turning round with a pretty smile. " Have you ?"

By this time they had wandered as far as the gate leading into the farm enclosure. A stout lady in black was standing by the furze stack talking to Mrs. Garth.

" Oh, there is Miss Fletcher !" cried Patricia.

Without thinking of what she was doing—if she had thought perhaps she would have done it all the same—she started off running.

" My own dear ?" she said, putting her arms round the kind, broad, handsome woman. " How glad I am to see you !"

" Why, where have you come from, child ?" said Miss Fletcher laughing.

" Lord Merrian and Dora," answered Patricia, looking backwards.

Lord Merrian and Dora, yes ; but some one else too ; for riding down the lane, examining again, as so often before, the fields which were so soon to be his own, Mr. Hamley suddenly appeared on the scene and joined the two just as they were passing through the gate.

" Heyday !" he said jocularly ; but he was not quite pleased at what he saw ; " are the skies a-going to fall ? Miss Drummond out on her ten toes so far from home, and you too, my lord—morning, my lord—padding the hoof ? Have you got any of the carriages hereabouts, Dora ?"

" No," said Dora, with a graceful little greeting by which she managed to convey to Mr. Hamley her exceeding pleasure at this chance meeting, and yet not cast in her lot with him visibly to Lord Merrian, who, she was aware, detested him. "We came out for a walk, Patricia and I, and met Lord Merrian in the lane."

"I am sure it is very good of his lordship to escort two such troublesome young ladies," said Mr. Hamley, still jocular. "Did you find them very bad to manage, my lord? I'll go bail you did for one!—but this little mouse, she gives no trouble to any one. That is why she is so useful at home, and why we are never going to part with her, hey Dora?"

"I have found both charming," Lord Merrian answered, coldly.

"Ah! and there's Miss Fletcher I see talking to Goody Garth. Why, all Milltown has made its comether at Long Field? I'll ride in and pay my compliments. Coming, my lord?—after your lordship."

Mr. Hamley would have done better to have stayed outside the farm gate, for Mrs. Garth was just then in a burning state of indignation against him and his, which Catherine Fletcher was doing her best to soothe. She had known of her daughter's going suddenly from Abbey Holme to the Hollies, but not until last evening of the reason why the exchange had been made. She had thought the ladies and Alice had cooked it up among them, she said, partly to oblige Miss Fletcher, and partly because she supposed Alice had been bitten with a sudden mania for the spit and the stewpan; and it was only last evening that she had got the whole story out of the girl, founded on her unsuspicious question: "Well Alice, and when did you see the old lady and Miss Drummond last?"

She was furious; as perhaps was only natural. A mother who had brought up her daughter in the way of honesty and virtue, and whose temper was as hot as her pride was strong, was not likely to accept very quietly a method of dismissal which of itself was as damaging as any accusation. Indeed, more damaging; inasmuch as it was an intangible injury—one that could not be met, and consequently one for which there was no redress and against it no protection. She talked of taking the law of Mr. Hamley; of suing him for libel and damages; of making him prove his words; and all the rest of it. She talked passionately, unreasonably, wildly, like an angry woman and an insulted mother; and Miss Fletcher's wiser words at first fell unheeded. She was burning with too fierce a fire of wrath to be able to receive them. By degrees however, the clearer brain took the customary power over the excited one, and Mrs. Garth's passion began to moderate. She was quite calm now, discussing her barn-door stock by the furze stack, when Patricia ran in, and immediately after Dora Drummond and the young lord, followed by Mr. Hamley on his prancing bay.

And then the old fire burst forth again, and the outraged maternal instinct woke up to renewed fury. There was a stormy scene. Mrs. Garth lost her temper, and said a few hard truths crudely; Mr. Hamley kept his dignity. The one demanded to know the reason why her daughter had been dismissed so summarily; the other refused to tell her.

"I have the right to know!" said Mrs. Garth.

"And I have the right to refuse," replied Mr. Hamley.

"Is there no law for the poor against the rich—no justice in heaven or earth?" cried the mother, flinging up her hands passionately.

Catherine Fletcher touched her on the shoulder.

"Dear Mrs. Garth," she said kindly, "you have no such heavy cause of complaint on the whole! Be reasonable. Your daughter passed at once from Abbey Holme to our house, and I do not think any one would consider that a degradation. She has not suffered, and will not, if you do not yourself noise the story abroad. Then indeed she will."

"Oh! passed to you, did she?" said Mr. Hamley. "I never heard of that. Pray, does Mrs. Hamley know?"

"Not that I am aware of," said Catherine quietly.

"You engaged her without a character?"

"Surely! I knew her too well to need one."

"Peculiar conduct!" sneered Mr. Hamley. "Consistent with your school, I suppose?"

"With the school of justice, and doing as I would be done by, Mr. Hamley?—I hope so," was her answer.

"I appeal to you two young ladies—to you Miss Drummond—had you any complaint against my girl?" cried Mrs. Garth excitedly.

Dora lifted up her blue eyes.

T

"I know nothing about it," she said quietly.

"Yet she was your maid, miss!"

"But Mr. and Mrs. Hamley are the master and mistress," said dear Dora with the sweetest little air of loving submission imaginable. "It is not my place to inquire into the reason of anything they choose to do; still less to object. They sent Alice away, and as they did not tell me why, it would have been very unbecoming in me to ask."

"That is right," said Mr. Hamley approvingly. "If all ladies were as amenable as Miss Drummond, things would progress a vast sight better than they do now."

"Did you know nothing, miss?" Mrs. Garth continued, speaking to Patricia.

"No, nothing." she answered with girlish tenderness. "I only saw Alice in trouble, and I told her to go down to the Hollies."

"*You* told her, did you?" repeated Mr. Hamley fiercely. Then he looked at Lord Merrian and checked himself. "You did right, my dear," he said with an effort. He thought it would never do to humiliate his wife's niece in the sight of the future Earl of Dovedale; "but you should have consulted your aunt before you took such a step. Good impulses, I make no doubt; but good impulses have to be ridden with the curb, not given their head, what say you, my lord?"

"I do not understand what all this discussion is about," Lord Merrian replied, and looked at Patricia.

"I will tell you when we go away," said Dora confidentially, as if she was speaking to her chinchilla muff. "And do let us go, Lord Merrian!—this mad woman is dreadful!"

Doubtless she was. A farm-house Constance, with her cotton gown bearing the stain of poverty, the soil of service, is of no interest to refined folk who yet would probably weep quite genuine tears at the sorrows of a stage Constance simulating royal grief cleverly. Royal grief is a respectable kind of passion, and royal madness has its especial power of pathos; but a rude and homely woman of the people pouring out her sorrows and her wrongs in unclassic English—refined folk see no pathos there, and only think "how dreadful!"

"I am in a maze," said Lord Merrian; "pray enlighten me." And he and Dora moved towards the gate.

Then the disintegration of the close-set group began. Mr. Hamley rode after Dora, not caring to let her linger alone with my lord, saying as his parting shot : "I am sorry to see you in such a taking Mrs. Garth, at what was a duty—a disagreeable but meritorious duty—on my part."—Miss Fletcher shaking hands and giving a few last words of comfort; and Patricia shaking hands too, and adding her fresh young sympathy to her friend's.

"Don't grieve so much, dear Mrs. Garth," she said kindly. "No one thinks a word about Alice to her disfavour—no one can ; and she is better off where she is !"

Which Mrs Garth in her own heart knew to be true.

Lord Merrian watched Patricia's leave-taking with the farmer's wife. He felt a certain odd distaste mingled with admiration for her friendly action.

"She is gloriously thorough," he said to himself; "but—I wonder if I should like it in my wife ! Surely things can be carried too far, and we ought to draw the line somewhere. Ladies and common women are not equals!"

When they reached home Patricia had more to bear from her aunt than Mr. Hamley's mild expostulation at the farm. She was really as angry as Mrs. Garth had been ; but she expressed herself in better English, and she did not gesticulate so much.

"That girl is always doing something to irritate and upset me !" she said to Dora peevishly. "Just now, when I was so well and cheerful, to be annoyed like this !"

And Dora purred a soothing assent ; by no means seeking to defend or justify Patricia, by which she would have merely made Mrs. Hamley angrier than before, to the inclusion of herself in the roll-call of the disgraced ; but when the fitting moment came she led the conversation on to Lord Merrian ; telling Mrs. Hamley of the attention he had paid Patricia to-day ; and how she was sure he liked her ; and, with a smile dimpling her fair face and her blue eyes watching keenly, what a delightful thing it would be if he really did take a fancy to her and make her Lady Merrian !

The ruse succeeded ; but only partially ; for even while Dora spoke Mrs. Hamley caught herself wondering why Patricia had shown such friendliness for Alice, who was not

her maid Why indeed ? Had she compunctions ? It seemed
like it ; and the thought shook the poor lady, heart and brain.
She went on to reflect however, that, whether Alice was innocent
or not, Catherine Fletcher had acted with an unpardonable
want of ladylike feeling in taking a servant discharged by her
without a character ; and " I will tell her of it," said Mrs.
Hamley, stiffening her back to the brunt. She was of the
nature of those who must have a scapegoat when things go
wrong ; and it not being quite politic, with the Quest in view,
to snub Patricia over much, she turned against Catherine
Fletcher, who could bear it.

So far Dora dealt kindly by her friend, and stood between
her and her aunt's displeasure. She was an artful little woman
and abominably untruthful ; but she was kind-hearted, and
always ready to scheme and manœuvre to save Patricia as well
as herself; provided she did not burn her own fingers in the
fire, or suffer in any way by her advocacy.

CHAPTER XXVIII.

PASSING IT ON.

THE wolves were pressing round Cragfoot, and Sydney's more expensive enjoyments were fain to be flung one after the other as successive sacrifices wherewith to stave off their worst attacks. When debts of honour—losses on the turf and the like—swallowed up all the available cash, and money was wanting for interest and house-bills, it was only to be expected that the younger man should have to share in the general discomfort, and be asked to contribute his tale of surrenders with the rest. But this was just what he would not do. He was one of those men to whom happiness consists in personal pleasure, and without money he saw no good in living.

Life at this time was thorny for Sydney Lowe. He was as passionately in love with Dora as he could be with any one ; but he was most of all in love with himself. And of the two he found it harder to give up his own pleasure than her. Since things had taken their present untoward turn he bitterly repented his rash step, and longed, as the weak and wilful do, to be able to unravel what he had so thoughtlessly knit up, to destroy what he had so firmly built. It was to no good, however, that he fumed and fretted. Dora was his wife by the laws of both Church and State ; and neither his father's ruin nor Mr. Hamley's close-fistedness could alter that fact, undo that tie.

And now, to make matters worse, there had sprung up a certain coolness between himself and his wife which robbed him of all the good of his folly. It made his heart beat with an odd exultant pride when he reflected that this pretty creature, the pride of Mr. Hamley's life, watched and guarded and desired and coveted at all points, had laughed with him at the close defence-work set about her, and that he had carried her off out of their hands and from under their very eyes. But over this exultant pride of late had come a kind of consciousness that something was amiss, that Dora was not as she had been.

There had been no meeting between them since the dinner party at the Quest, and already the lengthening days had brightened into spring. There were no means of communicating with her against her will ; and he could not make their relations public, even for the gain of making them open and continuous, at the cost of ruin ; which would be the price he should have to pay. She was growing mysterious too ; hinting at better arrangements if they had never met at St. Pancras, and writing melancholy little notes, which distracted him on more accounts than one, and set him thinking of many things. He had not the slightest suspicion that she was alluding to herself in these potential better arrangements, had they never repeated those fatal words behind the caryatides. He was too young to be doubtful of his own ability to keep the woman he had won ; that kind of mistrust comes only with experience ; and though jealous he had no self-diffidence. No, she meant for him, not for herself; of that he was quite sure ; and, judging of her feeling by his own knowledge, she meant Julia Manley.

Julia Manley! Bad as the exchange would be, woman for woman, how heartily he wished, now that his father's impecuniosity was pressing personally on him, that he could make it ' —how sorrowfully he was obliged to confess that, as Colonel Lowe had said, money does indeed make the homeliest visage beautiful, while the want of it leaves Venus herself undesirable!

Still, with all these drawbacks, he wanted to see Dora again. He yearned for the old fascination of her words and ways and looks, and wandered about the Abbey Holme grounds at midnight, to the imminent risk of being taking for a burglar by the gardeners when they went to look after their stoves, or for a poacher by the keepers watching the preserves.

But more than for the pleasure of looking into her pretty eyes and hearing her sweet voice, being coaxed while scolded and petted while rebuked, he longed to see her for a graver reason. He had been scheming something in that busy brain of his, and he had decided that Dora should help him. So it came about that she too, wishing to keep him in good humour, fearing last he might divine her thoughts respecting Lord Merrian, met him as usual one night in the garden; and heard his scheme.

They were sitting in the little summer-house where they had so often sat before, he holding her in his arms lovingly while he whispered his grand idea into her ear. Apparently it was one that distressed her greatly; for she shrunk and cried, and said she could not and she would not, and now tried indignant refusal, now pathetic appeal, and now coaxing persuasion, to make him alter his determination of implicating her.

Sydney was immovable. To all her beseechings he answered only in the one strain: "You are so clever, you will not be found out; and even if you are you will not be punished. Hold your tongue and do as I tell you, and no harm can come to you."

"You are the most cruel wretch I ever saw," at last said Dora with energy; "and I hate you!"

Sydney took her by the wrists, twisted her round, and looked into her face.

"If I thought that I would throw everything to the winds to-morrow!" he cried fiercely. "You are my wife, and your place is with me; and if I have to commit a crime, I would rather kill you than be put in prison for bigamy!"

"You will be put in prison for forgery, which is worse," said Dora.

"If you betray me, yes," he answered, looking down into her face intently. "If you do betray me however, remember you will go to prison too as an accomplice, and have the pleasant name of a forger's wife pinned to your back for life."

"Sydney, I believe you are a fiend," said Dora passionately. "You frighten me sometimes, I declare you do, with your violence and wickedness."

"Come Dody, this is nonsense," said Sydney, suddenly changing his rough manner to one of caressing softness. "Our lives are one now, and we have to stand or fall together. Money I must have and mean to have; and you can get it for me, and shall get it for me, else you will repent it," he added, the fierce old intonation ringing in his words; for his moods were as changeable as a sick child's, and he was not to be counted on for stability in anything—save self-indulgence.

"I perfectly dread the sound of your voice," Dora said pee-

vishly. "You are getting associated in my mind with everything that is painful and horrid. At one time it was the joy
of my life, my only happiness, to meet you like this; now we
never see each other but you quarrel with me, or ask me to do
something disgraceful for you. First I have to get you ten
pounds, and poor Alice is turned away on suspicion of having
taken it, and I am sure Patricia is suspected too; and now I
have to get you money on a forged cheque! Where will you
end, Sydney?"

"On the gallows perhaps," said Sydney lightly.

"There is many a true word spoken in jest; and if you go
on like this you will end on the gallows," said Dora viciously.

There was no good to be had, however, in quarrelling.
Sydney was determined; and he had more resolution of the
active kind than Dora. In a real contest between them she
would inevitably give way; and before they parted she had
given way, accepting after a short pause of rapid consideration,
a piece of paper whereon was written an order to the local
banker to pay to bearer the sum of £100—signed "Jabez
Hamley."

"Mind Dora, gold!" were Sydney's last words. "Gold
cannot be traced; notes can."

The next day was a fine, bright spring day, but Mrs. Hamley
kept the house. She had not been well for these last few
weeks, and the spring seemed to find out her weak places.
She looked more pinched and worn than usual, and she was in
a depressed state generally. But she would not have a doctor,
and was annoyed if any one seemed to think she was failing.
She complained a good deal to Dora of her disappointment in
Patricia, and to Patricia herself had always a headache. Dora
was, of course, sympathetic and soothing, and agreed with her
in her low estimate of "poor Patricia," and said she was certainly an infliction; but nevertheless she had always her little
word of kindness to add as the sweetener, and more than once
brought Mrs. Hamley into a favourable state of mind out of
one cankered and unfavourable.

As Mrs. Hamley was not going to drive to-day, Dora proposed to take Patricia in the pony-carriage which Mr. Hamley
had given to her on her last birthday; a pretty little blue Victoria, with two mouse-coloured ponies with blue and silver hare

ness, and a pyramid of bells topped with blue tufts hung about the neck-gear.

For their personal attendant they had the page boy, at Dora's request. She told Mrs. Hamley she did not like to take one of the men out of the house while she was in it—it scarcely looked respectful. "Dora has such nice feeling!" said the lady, relating the anecdote to her husband. And, having permission to take Collins, she put a handful of apples into her beadwork carriage-basket for him. She wanted to talk to Patricia, and she knew that if the lad was eating apples at the back he could not hear what was being said in low voices in the front. She could scarcely have bribed a man so innocently; so perhaps her nice feelings, on which Mrs. Hamley had expatiated, would have left a rather different residuum had they been analysed.

To the boy of course the condescension, kindness, thoughtfulness of the gift were immeasurable; and from that day forward he was her devoted adherent who would have gone to the stake for her had there been the need. If the true motive of all ladies' smiles could be made known, how many loyal knights would be left?

As they got into the little pony-carriage, with the butler and footmen at the door, and Mrs. Hamley looking at them from the side-window of the ante-room, it was almost like a royal departure; and when they drove off down the avenue even the dull old butler thought they made a pretty turn out—for young ladies not of the real aristocracy—and Mrs. Hamley was quite proud of them. Both the girls looked back and waved their hands to her as they drove away; but it was Dora who waved hers first. Simply because the other did not know that her aunt was there. But the little incident made the lady sigh, and wish that her niece had been as satisfactory as her husband's cousin.

Then they drove through the gates and into the road, and presently Dora, turning round, said graciously to the boy; "Here, Collins, here are some apples for you. I like to please children, and Collins is really only a child!" she added apologetically to Patricia, who needed no apology for an action to her mind full of grace and sweetest womanliness.

It was but a little action; but it set the measure in the girl's mind, and disposed her to more than her usual admiration for

her graceful, fascinating friend—the model ever held before her
as the supreme excellence to resemble which she ought to devote all her energies.

Presently Dora, looking into her face, said tenderly : " I
don't think you are quite well dear, are you ? "

" Yes, quite !" answered Patricia ; " what makes you think
I am not ? "

" You are so much more depressed than you used to be.
You seem to be so unhappy ! "

" So I am," said Patricia, tears coming up into her eyes. " I
am more unhappy than at one time I thought it was possible
for me to be.   When I was quite young I felt as if I could not
be unhappy, as if I must conquer circumstances ! "

" But what is there to make you so unhappy ? " asked Dora.

" Knowing what I do, how can I be anything else ? " she
answered.

" About me ? "

" Why, yes."

" Why should you let that disturb you so much ? " said Dora
quietly.   " You do not suffer by it if I am in a scrape."

" Is that your idea of life, Dora ?   Do you think one does
not suffer when a person one loves is in trouble ? " asked Patricia quickly.   " It is worse than if it was oneself."

Dora made her favourite little grimace. . " I don't think so ! "
she said.   " And it is all very well for a person who is not implicated to say so, but we who have to bear the reality know
how light the mere sympathetic reflection is ! "

" Ah, Dora, it is not light ! " Patricia cried, a world of pathos
in her voice.

" I think it is," persisted the other.   " Look here now, Patricia.   You say you love me, and feel for me, and all that,
and make yourself miserable on my account ; but just see what
you do—you make things ten times worse for me by fretting
and looking as if you were always sulky, or so miserable no
one knows what to do with you.   I have to be brave and
cheerful, I who really suffer : and you who have nothing to do
with it, have given way, I must say, both childishly and sel-
fishly."

" I do not want to be either. Dora ; but indeed, the knowledge that you are living in all this deception has nearly broken
my heart," said Patricia as humbly as earnestly.

" Patricia, be reasonable ;" remonstrated Dora. "What earthly good do you get by breaking your heart, as you call it, except spoiling your complexion and making everybody talk and suspect something ? Grant that I have been wrong, foolish, stupid —anything you like, what is done cannot be undone ; and my only wisdom now is to make the best of it."

" Making the best of it would be to tell," said Patricia.

" Well, let us see what that would do for me," said Dora, quite calmly. " I should, first of all, be turned out of the house ; the Hamley's would not give me sixpence, perhaps not my clothes ; Sydney would be discarded by his father, who is moreover ruined ; he would have no money, as he knows nothing by way of a profession by which to earn a loaf of bread. Now, what could we do ?"

" You would not starve, Dora ; you can teach. If I were in your place, I would do anything rather than live in falsehood."

" I cannot teach ; I have never taught ; I have no connection ; and pupils do not come for the mere saying you are ready to have them."

" But other people get on by their own exertions ; why not you ?" said Patricia.

" I should hate teaching, for I hate children," said Dora.

" Dora, don't !" cried Patricia, who loved them.

" Well, dear, I will tell stories and make up a face as girls do, if you like that better, and say that I adore the dear little wretches," said Dora coolly. " I thought you liked truth."

" So I do ; but I like the truth to be good and beautiful," Patricia answered.

" Ah, you see I am neither moral nor sentimental, Patricia ! I know nothing of beautiful truth or ugly truth. I know only of an inconvenient discovery, and the wisdom of keeping one's own counsel."

" Well, we are different !" sighed Patricia. " I could not act as you are acting now to save my life. And I feel that I am sinning against my own conscience to consent to it, even as I do."

Dora smiled to herself. She thought the sin against her conscience and her consent to evil doing would be greater before this drive was over.

" Your conscience !" she said, flicking her ponies with an

off-hand air. "I have always noticed that when people want to do anything particularly bad, like betrayal or selfishness, they talk of their conscience. I don't pretend to be very truthful or very conscientious, or very anything that is grand; but I think I would stand by a friend, such as I am and have been from the first to you—ask Mrs. Hamley if I am or not !—to the very death. And if I knew of her being in such a dreadful scrape as I am, I would not talk of my conscience, or doubt whether I ought to betray her or not, but I would help her to the very utmost of my power."

"You know I would not betray you, Dora, and you know that I cannot help you," said Patricia.

"I am by no means sure of the first, and you can do the last," Dora answered. "You can help me very much—even to-day—if you chose."

Patricia shrunk back.

"I ? no !" she said.

"Oh, don't be alarmed," laughed Dora, with a certain mockery in her manner. "I am not going to ask you to hurt that precious conscience of yours ! I only want a cheque changed, that is all."

"I will do that, of course, Dora. But why cannot you do it yourself ? "

"You inquisitive little puss !" she laughed. " Well, I will tell you why. I have some money in the bank, and I want to draw it out for poor Syd. He is so dreadfully hard up, poor boy, and I want to help him. You know he is my husband, Patricia, and it is my duty," with a sorrowfully subdued and loyal air.

"And you do not want the Hamleys to know that you have taken it out ? "

"Of course not—not for worlds. I should be ruined indeed if they knew. Syd will put it back again some day, and it will never be found out if you take the cheque. Of course it would if I did."

The mysteries of banking were by no means clear to Patricia ; and she accepted Dora's reasoning.

"I am sorry you have to give the money," she said.

"But it is my duty, is it not ? " said Dora sweetly.

Patricia hesitated for a moment.

"Yes," she then said ; " it is."

Dora gave a great sigh of relief; then she smiled pleasantly.

"I must say this, Patricia, you are a most good-natured girl," she said looking into her face prettily. "I am going to turn down the London road now, and we will pass through Milltown on our way home. I will stop at Martin's; I want some muslin; and you can walk into the bank and get the cheque changed. It's for a hundred pounds, and you must bring it all in gold."

"Very well," said Patricia.

"And you will be sure, dear, not to tell?"

"The Hamleys? Of course not."

"Not if they ask you? Suppose they get any suspicion of it, you will never betray me?"

"Certainly not," was Patricia's answer.

"You swear?" with strange earnestness.

"Yes. I swear."

"Join hands on it!" said Dora.

And Patricia took the little well-gloved hand in hers and pressed it.

"You may trust me, dear," she said. "When I promise, I hope I always perform."

After this the conversation turned, and Dora seemed as if she could not show enough tenderness and sweetness to her friend. She was everything that was most charming—playful, grave, affectionate, earnest; full of the freshest sympathy for Patricia's troubles with her aunt, and eager to point out where and how she could mend her position; she spoke respectfully of the Fletchers, with whom there had been a break on account of Alice Garth, much to Patricia's pain; with a matronly appreciation of Lord Merrian; tenderly of the poor; with wonder and regret at the whole mystery of Alice Garth. There was not the slightest fibre in the swansdown nature of her that curled the wrong way, and the remainder of the drive was simply what she intended it to be, enchantment. She was a Circe in her way; and blinded if she did not brutalize her lovers.

But to do her justice, all the time she felt the deepest hatred for Sydney, who was forcing her to this sorry part, and a kind of reverential pity for the credulous affection of the girl on whose loyalty she was trading; while disagreeable gushes of self-accusation forced themselves in between her shallower thoughts like bitter waters welling up through surface pools. But self-accusation was not much in her line, and as a rule she was more inclined to throw the blame of her own wrong-doing on others than accept it for herself.

At last they reached Milltown, and Dora drew up at Martin's. Collins jumped out to the ponies' heads.

"Will you go now, dear?" Dora said to Patricia, putting a folded piece of paper into her hand.

"Yes; what am I to do?"

"Just hand that across the counter as it is. You need not open it. The man will say, 'How will you have it?' and you will answer, 'Gold.' Don't be persuaded into notes. It must be gold."

"Very well," said Patricia and went off on her errand.

In due time she returned. She had a small canvas bag in her hand, containing a hundred sovereigns, bright and fresh. Never was a felony committed with so much ease, so little doubt, so little delay. Sydney had reason to be proud of his wife's ability, and Dora of her own power. Poor Patricia was the sacrifice on to whom they bound the burden of the sin ; a burden she bore so innocently, with such simple unconsciousness of its true meaning, such a faithful desire only to do what was right and kind and loving. But so it ever is in this strange life of ours. We are punished more for our virtues than our vices ; and those of us who succeed best in their generation are for the most part those who sin beyond the average, but with more than the average craft and cleverness.

The next month passed like wedding-bells. Everybody was in good humour, consequently every one was delightful. Sydney, freed from his immediate embarrassments and set afloat for a time, was again dear Dora's devoted lover, and their relations were of the most harmonious kind ; for she too, disillusioned as to the possibility of the great prize had things been different, thought Sydney Lowe better than no one, and made herself happy in her consciousness of power and a secret.

Lord Merrian came frequently to Abbey Holme ; but he let it be seen he came for Patricia, and no one could doubt that he was "paying her attention." Apparently Lord and Lady Dovedale were not averse to their son's choice, for the two girls were as often at the Quest as Lord Merrian was at Abbey

Holme ; and the countess took especial notice of Miss Kemball, and sought to train and draw her out in every possible direction. She was not the girl she would have chosen ; but she knew her son, and—knowing him—adopted the silken and not the driving rein, taking care never to oppose him when she wished to guide. If Patricia Kemball was richly dowered she would put up with her unformed habits for a while, trusting to her own future power of perfect modelling. So she cultivated Lord Merrian's Joan of Arc assiduously, and by the look of things she was pleased at the result of her studies. On her side, though Patricia never liked the countess as she liked Miss Fletcher, and never got to feel really at home with her, she was too affectionate and responsive not to open her heart when so graciously entreated ; and as she suspected nothing beyond what she saw, and showed that she did not, she was at least unconscious, if not always unembarrassed.

The Hamleys watched this growing affair with intense satisfaction. As Lady Merrian, Patricia's greatest faults would become shining virtues, and every defect would be a splendid jewel. Her aunt would feel then that she had been bountifully repaid for all her care, her endeavours, her annoyances, her headaches ; and Mr. Hamley would bow down to her as one of the divinities by whom he had been borne upward. He was prepared to give her a really magnificent portion ; one quite up to the mark set by the earl and countess ; and he would never grudge the outlay, he said. It would be money well laid out, he felt, and he did not care how soon he had to write the cheque.

So the sunny days of May came in with hope and serenity all round ; save perhaps to Patricia herself. She did not feel so joyous as the rest, and she missed the Fletchers. For them, they looked on a little sadly ; but they did not discuss the present state of affairs even between themselves. All that Henry Fletcher said when he had seen the young people together was : " I question if our Patricia will be perfectly happy in that sphere ; and I doubt if Lord Merrian is strong or true enough for her !"

CHAPTER XXIX.

THE ORDEAL.

MR. HAMLEY'S making-up day with the bank came round, and his books and cheques were sent up to Abbey Holme as usual. He sat in his private study; not the larger library where Patricia used to go for big books and brain-bewilderment, and where he was wont to receive his more special visitors when he wished to impress them as a man of culture as well as of substance ; but in the smaller " Growlery," as he used to call it, which the upholsterer and the gilder had made as fine and shining as a newly-minted sovereign. He himself, clad in his gorgeous Oriental morning gown, clean, perfumed, his hair well oiled, his whiskers curled and lustrous, every point of him prosperous and every line of him magnificent, was a fit inmate of that gorgeous, glittering, florid little room.   As he sat in his big arm-chair and balanced his counterfoils and his cheques, his payings-in and his drawings-out with method and satisfaction, he looked the type of vulgar affluence, of sensual, social contentment.   There did not seem to be a crook in his lot anywhere ; not one invading fly to disturb the sweetness of his fat and fragrant ointment.

Cheque by cheque, and voucher by voucher, scrip and warrant, dividend and rent, all was exact and all satisfactory ; when suddenly he gave a surprised snort and jumped with an undignified kind of bound in his chair. A cheque which was none of his, but which was signed with such a perfect imitation of his handwriting that he could scarcely disbelieve its evidence, came out from among the rest, and for a moment staggered him.   " Pay self or bearer one hundred pounds ;" signed Jabez Hamley, and dated about three weeks ago. He might look at it till his eyes ached, he could make no more nor less of it than a cheque with his name to it, and a hundred pounds written off his balance. It was a forgery, but so neatly done that he had to be quite sure of his unvarying exactness not to be forced to accept it as his own.

After examining it all round, balancing his figures again and again, hunting through and through his books and papers with no better result than at first, he wrote a hurried note to Mr. Wells, the bank manager, and sent off a man on horseback to Milltown at hot speed ; which note had the effect of bringing up that gentleman, also at hot speed, with a scared and troubled face.

"Here's a mystery somewheres, Wells," said Mr. Hamley, flicking the cheque with his forefinger. "Here's a bit of paper that I never put pen to—that I'll swear!"

"Surely, sir, surely!" said Mr. Wells in a deprecating tone. He thought the prosperous brewer a little out in his objection.

"I suppose I may be allowed to recognise my own hand-writing!" said Mr. Hamley haughtily.

"Certainly, sir; but when a member of your family presents a cheque signed—or apparently signed, let us say, for argument's sake—by yourself, and asks for it specially in gold, one is not likely to suspect any mistake ; especially with such a signature," Mr. Wells replied ; "I happened to be in the bank at the time, and I remember the circumstance perfectly well."

He took up several of the cheques, one after the other, and compared them with the one which Mr. Hamley disowned. Not the cleverest expert could have told the difference between this and those acknowledged. The method of filling in was precisely the same, and the "Jabez Hamley" was fac-simile. Like many men of his kind, Mr. Hamley had never been able to conquer satisfactorily the mysteries of caligraphy. He spoke pompously, but he wrote meanly ; an uneducated, rude sort of hand, both pinched and illegible. His signature, however, was his strong point. With infinite pains he had elaborated a special cipher which he considered inimitable. The way in which the H joined on to the z was to his mind a marvel of ingenuity; but because it was so ingenious it was also the easiest thing in the world to copy. One "Jabez Hamley" was just like another "Jabez Hamley;" and the flourish at the end, with the loops intersected at precisely the same point, and the three spots in the middle, was always done as exactly as if it had been lithographed. It was a signature no more difficult to imitate than so much print, and so far was charac-

U

teristic of the ordinary knave, inasmuch as it imagined itself inscrutable and was patent.

"Which member of my family?" asked Mr. Hamley in a tone of surprise. "Oblige me with the name."

"One of your young ladies," said Mr. Wells. "And I do not know her name."

Mr. Hamley's florid face grew several shades paler. For a moment he did not answer. Was he on the track of a mystery? beginning with that roll of ten sovereigns, had it gone on to this daring deed of iniquity?

As Dora was out of the question, was it possible that Patricia Kemball, with all her directness and apparent honesty, was in reality only a thief? a forger? and if so, why? and under whose instruction? "She was far too big a fool," he said to himself, "to do this thing alone. Who, then, was her confederate? Who egged her on? Who backed her up?"

Mr. Hamley was not a cruel man, save to his early patrons or fore-time tyrants, and he was truly sorry for Patricia, supposing it to be she; for his wife, too; but he was a magistrate as well as a host and a husband, and he had his duty to society to perform like a man and a citizen. And he had also his duty to perform to Dora. He thought of all this rapidly. He must have it made quite clear to Mr. Wells that the member of his family, the young lady of whom he spoke, was not his cousin, Dora Drummond. It was bad enough as it was, whoever it might be. Had it been indeed the other? Even to Mr. Hamley, prosperous, affluent, well oiled, and trimly brushed, life would have lost its savour had Dora Drummond proved a failure. No, he must have no suspicion rest on her pure head. It was a sad alternative, truly; and he pitied that misguided young person, Patricia, profoundly, supposing she was to be convicted; but justice compelled him.

He rang the bell.

"My compliments to the two young ladies, and beg them to step this way," said Mr. Hamley to the servant.

In a few moments the girls appeared, both looking as was their wont, save that Dora was just a little paler than usual. Graceful, self-possessed, and yet not in the least assertive, she came in with her pretty bending action and sweet amiability of face, followed by Patricia, tall and upright, with her large inquiring eyes and child-like unconsciousness, looking half-amused and half-amazed as to what Mr Hamley could possibly want with them.

" Be seated, young ladies," said Mr. Hamley, waving his hand magisterially.

The girls, greatly wondering, sat down—at least, Patricia . wondered and Dora feigned that she did. In reality she knew the whole thing by heart, and was aware that Patricia's ordeal, and in consequence her own fate, were both at hand. One glance at the bank manager, at the open cheque-book, and the cancelled cheques—at *that* cheque lying uppermost, more than all—told her the name of the mystery, and why they had been summoned. But she took her chair peacefully, and sat with meek attention on her face, waiting.

" Which young lady ?" said Mr. Hamley, not without a secret hope that there had been a mistake, and that the person who presented the cheque might be found to have been only a servant in her holiday clothes ; and, of course, the ruin of only a servant was but a trivial affair.

" That one," answered Mr. Wells, pointing to Patricia.

Patricia looked frankly into his face ; Dora by a side glance seeing what she did, turned her pretty head also, and looked up like Patricia at the manager.

" You are sure ? " demanded Mr. Hamley ; and, in spite of himself, his voice trembled.

He did not like Patricia over-well ; but to find her guilty of forgery was rather different from finding her too full of energy, more direct than he considered lady-like, and not half as pliant as she should be.

" Ask the young lady herself," said Mr. Wells.

" Did you perform this action, Miss Kemball ? " asked Mr. Hamley.

He called her by her surname purposely, that Dora's might be held clear.

" Perform what ? " asked Patricia.

At that moment the door opened and Mrs. Hamley came in. She had no idea of a conclave in which she had not her place ; and where the girls were she felt she had a right to be also.

" Come, this is too strong ! Did you present this cheque to the bank on the third ? " said Mr. Hamley.

"I took a cheque to the bank, certainly ; but I forget if it was on the third ?" said Patricia; "and I do not know if it was that one or not."

"Then you did not do this yourself?" Mr. Hamley demanded.

"Do what ?—I do not understand," she answered.

"I will be explicit. Did you or did you not sign a cheque with my name—a cheque for one hundred pounds, made payable to self or bearer, signed Jabez Hamley in imitation of my usual signature ?—that is, did you, or did you not commit this forgery ? "

Patricia started to her feet.

"Commit a forgery!—No. Are you mad, Mr. Hamley!" she cried.

"Are you ?" he answered significantly.

She turned towards her aunt, and holding out one hand cried, "Aunt!" Her voice and attitude meant, "Protect me from this man's insults ! "

Mrs. Hamley came forward and laid her hand on the girl's shoulder.

"The child is incapable of such an action," she said.

Patricia threw up her head with its old free gesture and kissed the long, lean hand fervently.

"Thank you aunty," she said, and looked at Dora.

Dora was looking down, and keeping silence.

"So I think, Lady," said Mr. Hamley, with not ungenerous promptness ; "your niece does not possess enough knowledge of business to enable her to have played this trick ; but she may be the tool of some one else, and I believe she is. I want to get to the bottom of this, and to know whose hands she is in. The person who gave her that cheque must have known it was a forgery."

Slowly the truth began to dawn upon Patricia.

"You say that cheque is a forgery?" she asked, turning her eyes down to the table and speaking to Mr. Hamley without looking at him.

"It is so ; a forgery," he answered.

"And any one but myself would have understood this ?"

"Any one," said Mr. Hamley, emphatically. "I should say that no one well out of the egg-shell but Miss Kemball would not have discovered that fact."

Again she looked at Dora. Her face had a kind of agony in it, but it was firm too. Dora was gazing tenderly at Mrs. Hamley, her soft voice murmuring sympathetically, " Poor dear, how I pity you ! "

" But you presented this cheque ? " continued Mr. Hamley, after a short pause. " So much you acknowledge ? "

Patricia's eyes went back from Dora to the table.

" Yes I gave that cheque, or one like it ; what I gave I never saw," she said.

" You got the money for it, however ? "

" Yes ; I got a hundred pounds in gold for it." She spoke slowly and distinctly.

Mrs. Hamley withdrew her hand.

" You say you did not see the cheque ? " continued Mr. Hamley in the manner of a cross-examination.

" No ; it was folded up when I had it, and I gave it to the man folded."

" And you received your hundred pounds in gold ! "

" Yes."

" What has become of that sum of money ?—a considerable sum of money for a young lady to lift ! "

" I cannot say."

" Did you make use of it ? "

" No ! " she said indignantly. " Do you think it was for myself ? "

" Then who had it ? who benefited by it ? "

" I will not tell you, Mr. Hamley," she answered.

Dora wiped her short upper lip daintily with her embroidered handkerchief, and drew a little sobbing kind of breath.

" Did you hand over the money to the person who gave you the cheque ? "

" Yes," she said.

" And you had no idea of its being a forgery ? " asked Mr. Wells.

" A forgery !—I ? No, indeed ; quite the contrary," said Patricia, with energy. " It was given me by a person who said the money was their own ;" with intentional bad grammar : her own would have betrayed Dora, his would have been a falsehood.

" But how came you to be asked to do such a thing ? Good heavens ! who could have asked you ? " cried Mrs. Hamley.

" That I shall not tell," answered the girl. " I promised to keep the secret, and I shall not break my word."

" I think," said Mr. Hamley with unpleasant but yet kindly pomposity, " if I could convince you, my dear young lady, of the injury this piece of paper has done me, you would consider it your duty to deliver up to me the name of the delinquent."

" I am very sorry, Mr. Hamley," Patricia said, not in any manner defiantly, humbly indeed and sorrowfully, yet quite steadily ; " but I promised that I would not."

" And, if failing your confession which I have the right to demand, I assume that you are cleverer than your words—that you have concocted this story to account for the forgery—and that you yourself have forged my name, trusting to my respect for my wife, your aunt, not to prosecute you—what then ? " asked the master of Abbey Holme loftily.

" I shall have to bear the burden," said Patricia in a low voice. " I did not know that I was doing wrong or being mixed up in anything disgraceful. Still, as I promised, I must keep my word whatever happens to me."

" It all seems to me like a dream ! " said Mrs. Hamley. " A forged cheque presented by Patricia, and she owning to it, with some wild story of its having been given to her by some one, and she promising not to tell. It is like a nightmare ! " The poor lady put her hand to her forehead. " Can you understand it, Dora ? "

" No, dear," said Dora softly.

" You cannot guess at anything to help us ? "

There was a tone of anguish in the thin voice that was infinitely tragical.

" No, dear," again answered Dora.

" Let us refer back and see what you were engaged in that day," said Mr. Hamley, turning over the pages of a diary. " Where were you Miss Kemball, may I ask, on the third of last month ? "

" Driving with Dora," answered Patricia.

All eyes turned on Dora, who met the glances innocently ; then turned her face towards Patricia, as if listening like the rest to a story she did not understand.

" Driving with Dora," repeated Mr. Hamley. " Good, to commence with. Driving with Dora! where?"

" To Green Lanes first, and then to Milltown," answered Patricia.

" And at Milltown what may have occurred, pray?"

" I left Dora at Martin's, and went on to the Bank for the money," said Patricia quite steadily.

" Dora! do help in this horrible mystery!" said Mrs. Hamley angrily.

Dora raised her eyes and looked at Patricia.

" I cannot," she said, " All I know is that Patricia left me at Martin's, and went up the street by herself. When I asked her where she had been, she said to the Bank to change a cheque. Of course I made no further inquiries. I could have no kind of idea that any thing was wrong in the affair, and to say the truth I never gave it another thought till this moment."

During this speech Patricia stood like a statue.

She neither moved nor spoke, neither looked nor sighed. She might have been struck to stone for the absolute rigidity of her face and bearing. The whole thing suddenly became clear to her, and she understood for the first time the real nature of the girl she had loved and pitied and put before her as a model to be imitated—if at such a humble distance, yet always loyally.

" But you said you did not know anything about it," said Mrs. Hamley irritably to Dora.

" Nor do I, dear. I know no more than I have said," she answered deprecatingly.

" You should have told us that Patricia went to the Bank," said Mrs. Hamley. " A girl of her age and ignorance should not be suffered to do such things unknown."

" Perhaps I ought—I know I ought." said Dora coming close to Mrs. Hamley and speaking with caressing humility; " but I thought nothing of the fact at the time, and never once remembered it since. Believe me, dear, the whole thing is as dark to me as to you. I knew and suspected nothing!"

As Dora came nearer to Mrs. Hamley, Patricia drew away. She felt it as an infinite dishonour to seem to canvass for her aunt's good favour while Dora, that false friend, was by her side. She was not willing to put herself in any kind of competition

with her ; rather, with the passionate self-immolation of the
young, she felt, let them suspect her of a crime and praise
Dora for her truth and goodness ; the consciousness of her innocence was enough for her, let what would else afflict her !

"Well ! I do not see that I can do more in this affair," then
said Mr. Hamley turning to Mr. Wells. "You will please to
forget this household scene, this little domestic drama as I call
it ; and observe, Wells !—I accept the cheque. There is a
mystery about it ; but hang me if I can find it out ! and I am
not a going to prosecute Mrs. Hamley's niece to get hold of it.
Keep a close tongue in your head of what you have seen if you
please, and now, good morning."

So Mr. Wells bowed himself out, and went from the presence
of the great man burdened with a secret of bigger dimensions
than he had ever had before.

And when he had gone Patricia's worst time began.

Mrs. Hamley, whose family pride and natural sense of womanly justice were no longer called into action by the presence
of a stranger, took her in hand, and dealt with her as severely
as she had hitherto been lenient. She seemed to forget that she
had just now claimed for her innocence against her husband,
and turning round on her, told her that she had disgraced herself, her father's name, and her uncle's memory ; in any circumstance, and put it as mildly as she would, she was still a
disgrace to the family and a shame to herself. It was her
duty to tell. If she had not really done this thing herself, and
had been, as she pretended, the dupe of some one else older
and more designing, it was still her duty to tell. In keeping
it secret she was making herself a party to the fraud, and was
in point of fact as bad as the person, whoever it might be, who
initiated the crime.

Mr. Hamley followed on his wife's track by talking largely
of his " ward's"—if she would allow him to give her this appel-
lation—at all events his " guest's" duty to the state as a citizen ;
of the obedience due by all citizens to the law whereof he was
an unworthy dispenser ; and of the consideration due to
himself personally, as her host and the husband of her aunt.

To all of which Patricia listened respectfully enough ; her
dilated eyes filling now and then with tears which never overflowed the lids, wondering when her lecture was to be over ;

wondering at Dora's infamy and shame in suffering her to bear
all this without coming forward to defend and exonerate her ;
but, while her intelligence was broad enough to take it all in
from their point of view, and to see herself as they must see
her, clinging to her own higher sense of truth and loyalty, and
preferring to bear all rather than betray her trust.   Since Dora
had spoken as she had done, disclaiming while seeming to explain so far as she could the mystery she herself had created,
Patricia had not once looked at her, nor had Dora looked at her ;
so far the latter knew the grace of shame ; and she gave but
one unvarying answer to all their threats, their entreaties
to tell—" I cannot," or " I must not."

Then said Aunt Hamley in a rage,

" I tell you what it is, Patricia—you did it yourself.   It is
absurd to think that a girl of your age could have been made
such a mere catspaw as you pretend.   You knew what you were
about, well enough.   You forged your uncle's name, or you knew
that your accomplice had done so.   You stole that ten pounds
of mine in the beginning ; and now you have gone on in your
wickedness till you have done this awful thing."

"Aunt, don't ! don't !" cried Patricia covering her face.
Then holding out her hands beseechingly, " Say you don't believe
this, aunt ! Say it, aunt—dear aunt !—for my uncle's sake, for
my father's sake ! "

" Confess, Patricia ! If you are in earnest, confess !" said
Aunt Hamley's harsh metallic voice.

" I cannot! I must not, aunt ! Oh, believe in me ! indeed I
am innocent !   Dora! tell them I am innocent ! "

" How can I tell them that ? " said Dora with sincere regret
—yes, her regret was sincere enough ; but she spoke with meaning all the same, to recall Patricia to herself and the remembrance
of her promise.   " I believe that you are innocent ; in my own
mind I feel sure ; but how can I tell them positively ? "

" Oh, it is hard ! " murmured Patricia, as with a heavy sob
she turned away to the window, where she stood looking
vacantly at the sunshine lying on the grass and budding trees,
thinking how green everything looked, and what a lovely day
it was out of doors, and oh ! if she could only escape into the
freedom and peace of nature once more !

They left her to her own meditations for a moment, and then

Mr. Hamley went up to her and took her by the hands in a friendly way enough.

"Better-minded, young lady? will you inform us now, and confess all you know about it?" he said.

She looked into his face pathetically.

"I must not!" she sobbed, and hid her face on his shoulder.

"Dear! dear!" said Mr. Hamley, whom the action conciliated, patting her head. "I would give that hundred pounds twice over that this had never happened! Poor young lady! How came you to be such a fool, my dear? I am sorry for you, by George I am! but you are too big a fool to live; you positively are!"

And then he put her away. He did not like to pet her before his wife, and when she had been such a wicked girl too; nor to let Dora feel, as he phrased it, "as if her nose was put out of joint." So he lifted up the miserable face and dropped the poor nervous hands; but he sighed and was very sorry, and somewhat ashamed.

"Go to your room, Patricia," then said Mrs. Hamley severely. "Let me never see your face again till you have confessed, either that you have committed this sin yourself, or who is your accomplice. Go, I say. Dora, leave her alone; she is not fit for you to touch."

For Dora, weeping real tears, frightened and remorseful, but not brave enough to own to the truth, had made as if she would have gone nearer to her, caressingly

Patricia shrank from her visibly.

"Yes, leave me alone," she said in an altered voice.

Her aunt and Mr. Hamley took the change of manner and accent to mean so far a confession of guilt in that she felt the stainless purity of Dora as her punishment; and it thrilled the poor lady like an electric shock. But Dora, flushing to her temples, drew back—her eyes bent on the ground. She made a beautiful picture at the moment of innocence blushing yet pitiful for guilt; while Patricia was that guilt, conscious of its own enormity and respecting innocence. So it seemed to the two looking on; and not an angel from heaven could just then have shown them the reverse of the shield.

"Good-bye, aunt; you have misjudged me. I am innocent of all knowledge, all offence in this," said Patricia, preparing to leave the room.

"Leave me silently," said Aunt Hamley, rising and waving her away. "Do not dare to come into my presence again till you are invited ; and consider yourself regarded as a thief—do you hear the word ?—as a thief, Patricia, till you have confessed and made restitution."

Without another word Patricia went ; and when she had gone Mrs. Hamley's courage of anger gave way, and she fell fainting into a chair.

"That cursed girl ! she will be the death of her aunt !" said Mr. Hamley savagely.

Providence might take the old lady in an orderly manner as soon as it liked, but he did not want her to die in a sudden muddled-up way like this. When she went he hoped to have all things done respectably and with befitting state—a doctor in daily attendance and a physician for special consultation ; a nurse sent from the best training school in London, and daily inquiries at the house by all the neighbourhood ; Mrs. Hamley's health the talk of the place, the topic of the hour. To go off in a fit of rage because her niece had forged his name to a cheque was by no means the kind of exit he had at heart for his aged lady-wife ; wherefore he said again "That cursed girl !" and Dora was too much scared to put in a word of conciliation. Then he looked at Dora and almost whispered, his voice was so soft: "Oh, you best and dearest ! what should we do without you !"

"Dear thing !" was Dora's oft-repeated formula as she leant over Mrs. Hamley crying.

"Don't cry, Dora," said Mr. Hamley ; but he himself was moved. He had felt deeply the whole affair, and hated the part he felt compelled to play ; but he was curiously torn between anger and pity, and scarcely seemed to know his own mind somehow. "She is not worth one of those pretty tears of yours ; you are too good to pity her, and yet—heaven forgive me for my weakness !—I am sorry for her too;" he continued, turning away his head. "She is a fine young woman, if a trifle rough ; and I cannot think how she came to do such a dirty trick, or who could have put her up to it."

"It is all a mystery, and we might as well give it up—it will never be found out," lisped Dora sobbing, as Bignold came hurrying in to attend her fainting mistress.

CHAPTER XXX.

UNDER HOME ARREST.

THIS then was where her love for Dora, and her loyalty to her promise, had landed Patricia—into actual if innocent complicity with a crime ; and with the accusation of having committed that crime herself fully justified by appearances. As she sat in her own room, mournfully trying to understand something of the position in which she found herself, but only more and more bewildered by the contradictions of life and teaching, the old question forced itself once more before her : what was right ? She had lived but a few years in this world as yet, and of these few, but a little while in an artificial state of society, yet she had seen enough to know that society and elementary morality are at war together, and that conventional virtue is not the virtue of the law, nor the prophets, nor yet of Christ. She had been taught to revere truth, loyalty, and uprightness; and she found herself disgraced for her adherence to her old lessons. She saw how Dora had made her place soft and warm by suppleness, untruth, disloyalty ; how she was loved and praised through the very sins which she herself had been always taught to hate and shun ; how her faults had prospered with her, and how by them she had made herself happy and been the cause of happiness to others. She knew quite well that for her own part she had disturbed the quiet ordering of the Hamleys' home ever since she had come into it ; and that her very faithfulness to her sense of right had been a sin and an annoyance.

What then was true, what was right, in this strange world of ours ? Christian practice ?—surely not ! at least in the estimation of Christian professors. Truth and sincerity ?—truth and sincerity had alienated her aunt's affection from her from the first, and had finished by landing her here. Constancy, courage, magnanimity, whatever virtue she had learnt in early youth from her uncle—whatever had stood foremost in a good man's simple code—she had proved to be all wrong in practice; and if Dora was right and if Aunt Hamley was right, wise living for men and women means the practical denial of all the righteous lessons taught the young. And why then, she thought perplexedly, are people taught when young things which the world will not let them practise, when grown up? and which if they do practise, they get themselves and others into trouble, and are blamed all round for folly or for fault?

The day wore on with a scarcely conscious passing of time. The girl had not moved from the place where she had first sat down. All her old life passed like a series of pictures before her, and her uncle's words came back as the pages of a closed book which she was reading again. She seemed to almost see him as he had looked and smiled when he lived. She seemed to hear his voice calling to her so cheerily, " Hi there, my love !" with the wind off the sea blowing through his silver hair and freshening the ruddy tinge on his kind face. And Gordon too how vividly he stood out from the mists of distance in his young man's strength and wholesome beauty, his love, his faithfulness, his courage, his high sense of honour, and his ready submission to the better law of discipline ! How she loved him ! how she felt to stretch out her hand to him now in her affliction, as if she could have called his spirit to her by the very force of her yearning, the very need of her love ! True, for all these months she had had no word from him; but she did not doubt him. Her letter had miscarried, or his had missed its way. She longed with a child's longing for home and mother to hear from him, to make sure that he lived : that he loved her if he lived she had no need of outward assurance. She knew that ; but oh ! if she could but hear from him, hold his letter in her hands, and read the words his hand had traced, how comforted she would be !. Yet nothing of her longing sprang from or was mixed with doubt or fear. It was only the yearning of love strengthened by loneliness and sorrow.

Amidst all the grief and dismay, the mental perplexity of her state, Patricia had however a strange feeling of freedom. Her body was in prison but her soul felt free. She was as if restored to herself and the past. Banished from the life of Abbey Holme, she had gone back to the old days at Barsands ; yet had gone back with a difference. She was no longer the Patricia who had lived like bird in bower, merry, unsuspecting, fearless, and ignorant. She had tasted of the bitter fruit of knowledge since those young days of hers, and no one who has once done that can re-inhabit the old self. Nevertheless she was free; and gradually, as has been said, her mind warped away from the tangled speculations of her first mood to the loved images, the sweet remembrances of her uncle and Gordon, and her childhood's happy life by the dear old rugged Cornish coast.

So time passed and the hours crept on, but no one came to disturb her. She did not herself know how the day was passing till the evening began to fall; and then, as she had had no food, she began to get hungry. Hitherto the kind of trance in which she had been had stopped all physical consciousness. Now, however, she came back to herself and reality, to find herself not at Barsands with her uncle and Gordon, but sitting by the window of her own room at Abbey Holme, with her arms and hands numbed by being so long clasped in each other as they rested on the window-sill, and her neck and forehead stiff from the long lying of her head on them—to find herself, not the loved of old and young, but deserted and in disgrace, a prisoner on parole and a presumed forger.

Aunt Hamley it was who had ordained this penance of the senses. She thought it might have a salutary effect on the proud, rebellious spirit; and she calculated on her girlish fear when Patricia should find herself deserted by the whole family, and left as if she was no longer one of them. Perhaps that would bring her to her right mind, she thought, and induce her to confess. Had any one suggested to the properly-intentioned lady that she was simply torturing her niece, she would have denied the accusation indignantly. Torture meant the thumbscrew or the bootikins, the rack or the wheel, not merely trying to break down the spirit of a naughty girl by fasting and desertion.

On his side Mr. Hamley would have sent her food, and would have even added a generous glass of wine to help her to bear her disagreeable position better. There was a certain hospitable openhandedness about the man which would have prevented his adding hunger to his punishment of a delinquent, especially if a pretty girl; but Mrs. Hamley was a woman, and small indignities come easier by nature to a woman than to a man—

adding pin-pricks to sabre-cut not being out of the feminine line, speaking by majorities.

Patricia, wakened up to herself and her sense of discomfort, nevertheless stayed loyally where she was. True ; she was cold and hungry. She had no light, no food; but if she had been left to starve, she would have starved rather than have disobeyed her aunt's command and ventured into the forbidden quarter of the house. So the hours passed and the evening stole on into night. The stars came out and the moon rose up. She knew that by the reflection on the blank white wall which was her sole window prospect. Then she heard the softly-falling bolts and bars ; the sharp double bell summoning the servants to prayers—"and forgive us our trespasses as we forgive them that trespass against us," one of the clauses ; with perhaps St. Paul's chapter on charity for the reading, or the story of Ananias and Sapphira. After which she heard the rustling of her aunt's rich black silk sweeping majestically through the passage and past her own disgraced door, and Mr. Hamley's lordly step striding after it. And by this she knew that the Abbey Holme household had gone to bed, and that she should see none of them for this night—the servants had evidently been told not to go to her room—and that Dora too had gone to rest peacefully like the others ; Dora, quiet, amiable, sympathetic, a little mournful perhaps to suit the sombre mood of the moment, but making the life and charm of the evening as usual, blessing and blessed, and secretly rejoicing in her escape from a disagreeable position at the price of her friend's ruin and on the calculation of her devotion.

And at this thought it seemed to Patricia as if she should die of shame and heartbreak. It seemed to her so infinitely shocking that Dora should have done this wicked thing. The one she had so tenderly loved, had worshipped with all her girlish power of admiration as excelling in womanly loveliness and grace, to have proved herself this treacherous Delilah ! Had it been an accident, a chance thing the real issues of which had been unknown to Dora as to herself, she would have borne the burden of it better ; but it was the plot, the premeditated cruelty and treachery that seemed to her so frightful, so inconceivably hideous ! It was not for herself she was breaking her heart ; it was for the destruction of her ideal, the death of her love.

After all this was the tragedy, not her own disaster. Time would repair that ; and even if it did not—she was innocent, and no appearances could alter that blessed fact. But time would not restore what had fallen into dust to-day. The graciousness, the love, the beauty, and all that grew out of these in her own heart—all had gone into ruin together ! No wonder she felt as if her heart would break. It was a wreck more pitiful than the wreck of the *Mermaid*—a death as real as and almost more sad than the death of her uncle !

Presently the door of her room softly opened and Dora came stealing in. She had coaxed Bignold to bring up some food for the poor prisoner; which the maid, knowing only that Patricia was in disgrace and thinking it " an awful shame that she should be left to starve like this," was glad enough to do. So Dora stole into her room wrapped as usual in her soft luxurious furs and cashmeres, with her golden hair loose on her shoulders, and her small hands holding a tray laden with good things ; a very fair enchanting picture, but one which had no more fascination for Patricia.

Patricia shook back her falling hair, cleared her dreamy eyes, and rose to her feet. She felt more humiliated to be visited thus by Dora as her good angel than at any other circumstance of this dreadful day.

"Oh, dear, dear child ! how sorry I am for you and for everything ! How cold you must be, and how hungry ! " began Dora, setting down the tray and gliding up to Patricia who was standing by the dressing-table. " See dear, I have brought you something to eat ; why, you must be half-starved ! "

" I will not eat it," said Patricia, turning aside her head and putting off Dora's hands which she had clasped round her arm.

"Not eat, Patricia !—why not ? You have had nothing all day ! Are you going to starve yourself to death ? "

" I am my aunt's prisoner ; I will not eat, nor go out of my room till she allows me to do so," said Patricia. " And, Dora, I do not want you to come and see me," she added. " You come secretly, against aunt's wishes; and I have done with secrets now, once and for all."

" You are cruel ! " said Dora beginning to cry.

They were not sham tears—she was really very sorry for the

pass to which things had come; but what could she do ?
Patricia would not be killed ; after a little while she would be
taken into favour again—as much favour as she could ever
receive at Abbey Holme—and all would be forgotten and forgiven. And she, Dora, would do her best to put her well before the authorities, and to give a fine-sounding name to her
delinquency. But if she were to tell the truth, what would be
the result ? Simply ruin! Wise little Dora reflected that
Patricia's temporary discomfort was to be preferred to her own
everlasting destruction ; and if the girl would only be amenable
to reason, and like any other sensible creature, her 'erm of trial
would be shortened and its bitterness sweetened ; and she
might—who knows ?—come out as a heroine when all was over.

But Patricia was not like any other sensible creature. She
had her own Spartan code which was quite opposed to Dora's
favourite worldly wisdom, and she chose to stand by it, hard
as it was, rather than be guided into her former friend's softer
ways.

" I am not cruel, Dora ; but I understand you now—I never
did before to-day," she answered ; and by the dim light of the
little chamber-lamp that Dora had brought in she looked almost
heroic in her power and sorrow, her steadfastness and her stern-
ness—like a maid of another race and time.

" You are doing me injustice," said Dora, feebly fencing with
her rebuke.

"Can I ?" asked Patricia. " After you have led me into
a crime by my love for you, by my sympathy with your difficulties, and by your own falsehood, Dora—led me into a crime
and left me to such disgrace as this—can I be unjust to you ?
What can I think of you ? and what may I not call you ! "

" Hush, Patricia ! you frighten me !" said Dora cowering.

" Let your own conscience frighten you, not me; if only it
could frighten you into doing the right !" said Patricia.
" How can you live in such a state as you must be in ! That
is the wonder to me !"

" You are mad, Patricia ! how can I act differently ? " cried
Dora. " Do you want me to be ruined ?"

" No, I want you to be saved—to save yourself out of this
sea of deception into which you have got. You are being ship-
wrecked in it, Dora, for time and eternity !"

v

" I dare not tell !" she said ; and then the coward fear that
always possessed her came uppermost, and she gasped out
piteously ; " Are you going to betray me, Patricia ? You had
better kill me!".

Patricia looked at her with a steadfast, sorrowful, and yet
half-scornful pity.

" Can you ask me ?" she said. " Do you not know me
better than that, Dora ? If I were left here to die by inches
you need not be afraid of me."

Dora flung herself against her bosom, and threw her arms
round her. " You are so good and brave !" she said, sobbing
passionately.

But Patricia put her away with resolute quiet strength.

" Don't, Dora ! I cannot bear it ! I would rather you did
not thank me, please ; it is too shocking to me," she said in
broken sentences.

She could bear her own humiliation better than Dora's—her
own wound better than her former friend's craven cowardice.

" Oh, how you hate me !" said Dora half pettishly, half
pathetically.

Patricia did not answer. She felt the falseness of this
attempt at softening her, and let it pass. The two girls had
changed places. It was the adorer who was now the judge,
the adored who besought.

" Now, Dora, go ; I do not want to see any one, to have anything done for me till my aunt orders it," said Patricia. " I
tell you I have washed my hands of all secrets for ever ; and if
you come in to see me again, though you do it in kindness, I
shall tell my aunt. What I know I will keep sacred to the last,
but nothing more—nothing new."

" I believe you are mad !" said Dora, rather angrily for all
her gratitude and shame and late emotion.

It was a new experience to her to be repulsed, and she did
not like it.

" Yes, I am beginning to think that truth and loyalty are
looked on as little better than madness by you all here," said
Patricia ; " but it is a madness I choose rather than the contrary. So good night : thank you for your good intentions ;
but I will have nothing."

" And I am to carry this ridiculous tray back again ; and it is so heavy, and hurts my hands!" said Dora with a helpless look.

" I am sorry I cannot carry it for you, Dora—it *is* heavy for your little hands," said Patricia sympathetically and in her natural voice and manner.

" I can get round her in time!" thought Dora smiling to herself.

But she calculated on insufficient data. That something which when it once breaks is irreparable, had snapped in Patricia's heart ; and her love had died, and was buried in the same grave as her belief and her respect.

So Dora, making a sorrowful face, took back her burden ot good food ; leaving her door ajar to catch Bignold on her exit from her mistress, to tell her to try her power with Patricia and make her eat something.

But Bignold failed as entirely as herself ; though the maid did what the friend had not done—made the prisoner cry like a child. She was brave and strong and steadfast, but she was only a girl yet ; only nineteen ; and the day had tired her terribly ; and most of all Dora and this last scene had shaken her very soul. And then she was desperately hungry, poor child ; and feeling a little faint and sick for want of food. But she held to her word " Not until aunt allows it ; " and Bignold determined to face her mistress's displeasure to-morrow, should this cruelty continue another twelve hours, and tell her how she had herself tried to induce Miss Kemball to eat something, and how, though she was half-hungered and owned to it, she would have nothing till her dear aunt sent it.

" And if that doesn't touch the old witch nothing will !" thought Bignold indignantly,

For though Patricia was no great favourite with her—she was too little " the lady " according to the definition of the lady's-maid to be thoroughly liked—yet she was a nice spoken young person in her way, and at all events a woman.

Bignold had her humanities lying like diamonds in quartz among her professional crotchets ; and just now she thought her mistress the bigger sinner of the two, whatever Miss Kemball's offence had been. To treat a poor motherless creature in this way—Bignold held it heathenish ; and scoffed at the family prayers as possessing any power of good for hearts or lives.

" Better act like a Christian and leave the prayers and the Bible alone, than bother them all, night and morning, as the old lady did, and behave worse than a heathen the day through," said Bignold to the housekeeper.

She was an impenitent kind of person ; one of those who respect good morals but make no account of spirituality. She despised the religion which is made up of strictness in the matter of pious observances, flanked by an unlimited accompaniment of bad temper and uncharitable feeling ; and often used to say that she would rather folks did what was right, though they had no " gifts," than talked beautiful and did what was wrong.

CHAPTER XXXI.

THE OFFER OF FORGIVENESS.

KNOWING nothing of the pitiful little domestic drama, as Mr. Hamley called it, which had just been enacted at Abbey Holme and which was even now going on, Lord Merrian rode up to the house as usual one day during the term of Patricia's home arrest—lengthening now into three weeks. He had been absent from home for nearly a fortnight; on a visit to some friends of his own conventional rank and standing; where he had seen among other charming people a bevy of pretty girls of suitable degree—Ladies Maud and Victoria, Ethel and Ada, girls of good style, well-bred, aristocratic, and of finished training.

But somehow he had not enjoyed himself as of old. At one time he would have been supremely happy in these circumstances. They would have just suited him. He would have talked his fluent Young England radicalism, while conscious in every fibre of his exalted position, his honourable title, his glittering prospects, as also of the paternal earls and dukes of his fair audience; and he would have lamented the sorrows of the poor and the inequality of society with a pathetic intonation in his sweet voice, while wearing the best fitting coat Poole could turn out, and with the most exquisite little bouquet of choice exotics in his button-hole to be had from the stove-houses. He would have spoken eloquently of the need for some grand crusade against the half-heartedness of the age, and how he longed to see some stirring protest made against our habits of demoralizing luxury, our damning love of pleasure, with our poorer brethren helpless and degraded at our gates; and then he would have gone to the opera and given his guinea for his stall as a young nobleman should, and may be, he would have calculated his distance to a nicety, and taken his hansom cab the "long mile" which means no extra fare. All this was of the nature of the man; a nature of kindly thoughts and a lack of earnest resolves; with good intellectual abilities apt to exhale themselves in words, and the fatal mistake of accepting emotional thought for purposeful endeavour.

And the young ladies—the better gifted among them at least—would have listened to him sympathetically: and some of them, to whom his fine eyes and distinguished air counted for virtues, would have thought him a consecrated leader of men and one of the future saviours of society. They would not have foreseen him as he would become in a few years' time, a contented, easy-going father of a family, who had sown his wild oats betimes—and those wild oats of principles only, not vices; a portly, good-natured kind of man, thinking the world a jolly kind of place after all for one who had kept his digestion in order and his banker's book well in hand ; and as firmly convinced as Mr. Hamley himself, that those were successful who ought to win, and that when men fail it is because they have not the stuff in them to succeed; an hereditary legislator who would look back to his enthusiasm for freedom as a craze honourable to his heart but young, very young ; and who when the time came for radical reforms in Parliament would shelter himself behind constitutional policy and the difficulties of statesmanship, for the one part—when the rights of labour were urged by those who laboured on his own land, would put forward his steward and his agent, for the other ; who would be ever and always the Spenlow of good intentions who would, but for that ubiquitous and immovable Jorkins who would not. Alas ! that so many bright flames should burn down into such fat darkness as this ! that prosperity should prove such a benumbing Circe, and that maturity should so often drop the heroic parable of youth !

As it was however, this visit of his, though he was surrounded by nice girls of his own caste and made much of as the future Earl of Dovedale, did not please Lord Merrian. He found himself incessantly comparing his pretty but colourless audience with the girl whose enthusiasm stirred his own so powerfully, whose sense of truth and wholeness of nature seemed made to be the spur of his weaker and more lagging soul. He had got into the habit of thinking of Patricia as his Egeria. He once spoke of her to Lady Maud as his Egeria ; and when Lady Maud asked " Who is Egeria ?" he laughed

and said, " Was ! a nymph ;" and would **give no farther ex-**
planation.

He was really and honestly in love with **her ; and it was**
with the best part of him that he loved her. He felt that
clearly enough ; and as he had at last won the consent of his
father, and of his mother the countess too, after a longer struggle—should Mr. Hamley give the dower **for which they stipul-**
ated—he had only to be quite sure of himself to take the final
plunge.

This visit to the Duke of Burton **fixed his convictions.** He
was in love with Patricia Kemball ; no one else delighted him,
no one else appealed to him as did she. He would make her
the offer of his hand and his life, and he did not anticipate that
he should be refused. But before speaking to her he would address himself to Mrs. Hamley. Lord Merrian was a gentleman
emphatically, from head to heel ; and moreover he was so sure
of his game he could afford to deliberate and to do things in
good style.

It was then with more than the intention of paying an ordinary morning call that he rode up to Abbey Holme to-day ; and
with more than ordinary exultation that he saw himself once
more in the gorgeous crimson and gold drawing-room of the
prosperous owner.

Mrs. Hamley and Miss Drummond were alone. Lord Merrian's eyes looked round in vain for his Egeria ; only the tall,
thin, pinched, but perfectly lady-like figure of Mrs. Hamley and
the gracious presence of pretty Dora met him ; but the clear
eyes and noble bearing of the woman he loved were not to be
seen.

He spoke a few words to Mrs. Hamley, and she was conscious
at the first glance, the first sound of his voice, that something
more than usual animated him to-day, and that his visit was
not merely one of ceremony. He looked half-embarrassed and
half-important ; and there was a wistful expression about his
eyes that seemed to presage confession and emotion. He was
almost tender in his manner to her : had not she too something
of his darling to glorify her ?—and he seemed to forget that
Dora Drummond was a young woman, and a pretty one, to
whom he had once paid marked attention, in the general family
benevolence with which he classed her as part of Patricia, as he
had classed Mrs. Hamley.

Was it really true that the grand *coup* for which she would have given a handful of her best remaining days was on the point of accomplishment? thought Mrs. Hamley. Should she live to see her niece Lady Merrian, future Countess of Dovedale, and the mistress of the Quest? How trivial this last little misdemeanor of hers had suddenly become! A child's credulous complicity: a child's mistaken loyalty! She had been punished as a child, but she should be forgiven as a woman. My Lady Merrian might do worse things than present a forged cheque and refuse to tell for whom, and yet be forgiven!

Presently Lord Merrian asked for Miss Kemball, with a delicate but delicious lingering on the name that was like the softest music to the ears of Mrs. Hamley.

Her pale and peevish face looked up with almost a light on it as she answered : " I am sorry to say the dear girl is not very well, and keeping her room at present."

" Nothing serious ? " asked Lord Merrian anxiously.

"No, nothing serious, thank God!—only a cold. Girls," with a ghastly smile, " are always taking cold."

" I hope it is nothing worse," said Lord Merrian uneasily. " She is too precious to all of us to be suffered to fall ill," he added.

" You are very kind, Lord Merrian," Mrs. Hamley answered with a little inclination of her head ; and Dora, knowing that her best policy now was self-effacement, quietly left the room ; and in so doing took credit to herself on Patricia's side, and held herself to have all but atoned for the misdeed which had borne such terrible fruit.

And when she had gone Lord Merrian opened his case, and formally proposed for Patricia Kemball's hand through her guardian and next of kin, Mrs. Hamley.

To which Mrs. Hamley, carefully concealing her exultation, gave her assent with a certain womanly dignity that struck the young lover as " excellent form," and promised to convey the news to Patricia, who would doubtless be well enough to see him personally to-morrow, when he proposed that he should call again. It was all done with good breeding and good taste ; and Mrs. Hamley's share in the transaction showed the fact that the brewer's wife was by no means objectionable, if the brewer himself was. Lord Merrian called himself a Liberal, but he was glad that Patricia—his Patricia—had her aunt's blood and not her aunt's husband's in her veins, and that she, not he, would be his relative by marriage.

The momentous visit then passed off with brilliant but subdued success, and Lord Merrian rode home satisfied if disappointed. Like all weak-willed men, he felt happy now that he had irrevocably committed himself, now that his will had, as it were, the support of external circumstances ; but he was desperately sorry he had not seen Patricia. He longed to see her great grey eyes look into his with their candid love, half frank half shy, and to hear her earnest innocent confession, " Yes, I love you." He had been so much occupied with making up his own mind he never reflected that perhaps he might have missed his way—that perhaps she had only the sister's love for him which would neither satisfy him nor impel her. It had been his own difficulties with which he had struggled—his difficulties of self-certainty and diversity of social position ; but he never doubted that his path with her would be smooth enough when he had absolutely defined it and made sure of his own intentions. Handsome young English noblemen scarcely look for obstacles when they condescend to women of an inferior grade. The redundancy of which we hear so much would alone be sufficient to give them confidence ; and where the old, the unpersonable, and the mediocre can choose very much as they like, the young, the well-looking, and the highly-placed may surely think themselves secure. Add to this, the respect for rank ingrained in the English character and so ingrained as to be accounted a virtue, and Lord Merrian may stand acquitted of all charge of foppishness if he believed in his success, and took counsel of his love rather than of doubt.

So he rode home disappointed but happy ; and while lamenting the trial of his patience, and that long delay of twenty-four hours before he might hear the dear assurance his whole soul was desiring, he was all aglow with the anticipation of his delight when he should have secured it. How tenderly he would love her when he should have gained her, he thought ! What a life of happiness, of mental help, they would have together ! It would be no sickly honeymoon of vulgar endearments ; it should be a life worthy of a man and woman who had higher objects than those of sensuous pleasure—of a man and woman

who would give the world an example of noble living and of
moral thoroughness. She should be his Egeria and she would
make of him her Numa—prophet, king, and leader of men!
Sweet thoughts; bright visions: and the reality that stood
like the angel in the way, with drawn sword barring the gates
of that fair Eden!

Just now the reality was being transacted with a distinctness
that left no margin for mistakes; and in a manner who could
have foreseen? thought Mr. Hamley, watching Patricia curiously
as a kind of *lusus naturæ*, if indeed she was not one of those
only too common whom science and the world call mad.

After Lord Merrian's visit was brought to an end, Mrs. Hamley sent for Mr. Hamley and dear Dora; to both of whom she
detailed what had passed: namely, that Lord Merrian had
made a formal proposal for Patricia's hand, and that she had
granted him permission to ask the girl herself to-morrow.

"I did right, Mr. Hamley?" she then asked with unwonted
meekness.

It pleased her at this supreme moment of success to affect
womanly submission and wifely inferiority; it gave a zest to her
triumph and was the pleasant burden of her golden crown.

"Yes; you did right, Lady," was Mr Hamley's reply, made
pompously but with condescension.

He had caught her lead and followed it.

"And now, I presume, this poor misguided child may be
forgiven?" said Mrs. Hamley. "She has been punished sufficiently for her offence; not too severely, considering its magnitude, but sufficiently. What do you say Mr. Hamley?"

"Certainly Lady, certainly; let her be forgiven," said Mr.
Hamley. "It would hardly do to keep my Lady Merrian confined to her own room like a naughty child. My Lady Merrian!" he added, rolling the words like a delicate morsel under
his tongue. "My wife's niece, my Lady Merrian—the future
Countess of Dovedale.

How he blessed Providence and the old admiral's wiry constitution that Mrs. Hamley had been graciously pleased to live
until now! Once let this marriage be celebrated, and the poor
conjugal moth, having then indeed completed her mission, might
fold her wings and leave her work for the kindly hatching of
time and good chances.

" Go to her, Dora," said Mrs. Hamley.

And Dora obedient, rose.

" We must not forget our Dora though, in our pleasure at this great success, this proudest moment of our lives, as I call it," said Mr. Hamley looking at his cousin with a strange expression on his face. " She is always our first, hey Lady ? "

" Come here, child," said Mrs. Hamley ; and poor Dora, with tears of jealous disappointment in her eyes—they looked beautiful, and like tears of sympathy—knelt down by her cousin's wife.

Mrs. Hamley put her arms round her bended neck and drew her pretty head to her bosom. She smoothed the golden hair, and her lean hand lingered lovingly on the fair round face, while she gazed at her with maternal tenderness. Then she kissed her with what was for her a passionate affection.

" I am glad of this good fortune for Patricia," she said in a moved voice. " It is very natural ; she is my own flesh and blood, my brother's child, and she has no one in the world to look to but myself ; and I may not last long ; but she can never be to me what you are, my little girl—never take the daughter's place that you have filled from the beginning. God bless you, my Dora ! the light of my life, and dearer to me than even my own ! No, we can never forget our Dora even on this or any other day of triumph. And please God, we shall see such a day some time for her."

" Amen," said Mr. Hamley ; with the unspoken proviso, " I, but not you."

Patricia had now been nearly three weeks under home arrest, and for all this time had seen no one but the housemaid who came to arrange her room. Dora had not appeared again ; and as Mrs. Hamley had ordered a scanty kind of breakfast to be taken to her the next morning, Bignold's advocacy had not been needed ; so, wisely enough, the maid had forborne to intermeddle in a matter where help was not needed, and whence she would be sure to bring away but burnt fingers for her pains. The solitude and confinement, the insufficient food, and the sorrowful thoughts that had possessed her for all this time, had told on Patricia's appearance ; and there would be small difficulty in convincing Lord Merrian to-morrow that she had been, and indeed was still ill. Looking at her through the lustre of

her coming honours Mrs. Hamley was shocked and startled to
see how ill ; and more than all she was startled to see how unutterably sad she looked.   Was this indeed Patricia, that bright,
spontaneous, fearless girl who had come into their quiet life
like a whirlwind ; whose very grief for her beloved uncle had
been unable to subdue her young energies, and whose breezy
activities had reduced the subdued, staid household to general
despair ? Not that there was anything drooping or craven
about her even now. Her head was carried as straight, her
slender figure was as upright, as before ; but all colour had
faded from her hollow cheeks ; her eyes were pathetically large
and lustrous, and there were dark rings round them that made
Mrs. Hamley's heart ache. Her hands too, which had once
been so large and strong, were fine now and slender ; and the
black dress, which had been cut for the best advantage of her
figure, hung in loose folds and creases about her waist and
shoulders.

A pang of self-reproach seized Mrs. Hamley. Had she over-
stepped her duty ?   Had she done really what she ought by this
unprotected girl ? Could she meet her brothers as a faithful
sister should, and pointing back beyond the grave to the charge
that had been assigned her, claim from them, and God, approbation of her work ? Still, it would not do to give in. The
curse of spiritual pride clung like a weed round the woman's
soul. No, it would not do to give in, or to confess by word,
deed, or look, that she had been wrong or over hasty.

Not rising from her chair, she held out her hand as Patricia,
following Dora, came silently but steadily forward. Patricia
went up to her and put her hand in hers. Something in her
throat choked her voice so that she could not speak, and even
Mrs. Hamley found it difficult to say: " Good morning, Patricia."

" Good morning, young lady. I hope I see you in the enjoyment of good health, though I cannot say you look it," was
Mr. Hamley's salutation, made with many flourishes of his hands
and some plunges of his well-developed limbs.

But he meant it good-naturedly, and so Patricia took it. It
made a little diversion too, and a healthy one. Sentiment and
Mr. Hamley did not go together quite harmoniously.

" Good morning, Mr. Hamley," she said naturally ; and
looked at her aunt, including her.

"Take a chair, Patricia, and sit down quietly," said Mrs. Hamley. "I have sent for you to have some grave talk with you."

Patricia took a chair and sat down.

How large the room looked, she thought, and how bright and full of gold and colour! The mirrors and the gilding and the upholsterer's magnificence all through quite oppressed her. She would have preferred a fisherman's hut or the poorest den of a cottage at this moment to all this showy glitter. Since her banishment up-stairs the present had become dark to her, and she had lived so much in her memories that Barsands and the cottage had become almost more real to her than Abbey Holme; and this grandeur and excess quite pained and dazzled her eye-sight. Nevertheless, she sat down quietly, and looked at her aunt, forcing her attention which was loose and a little wandering.

"I have had a most unhappy week, Patricia," began Aunt Hamley clearing her throat. "I may say indeed that we have all had a most unhappy week; and I suppose yours has not been much better?"

"No, I have been very very miserable," said Patricia simply.

"Are you prepared to do what you ought to have done at the first?" asked Mrs. Hamley.

"Do you mean tell for whom I took the cheque, aunt?" said Patricia after a pause, during which she seemed to be searching back in her memory. "No!" shaking her head.

Her aunt frowned.

"Come now, Lady," said Mr. Hamley, seeing that she had begun on the wrong tack, "shall we not let bygones be by-gones, and no more said about it? Let us suppose that your niece has some reason for her obstinacy. It will do us no harm if we suppose that she has some good reason—some what I call valid excuse; and, believing this, let us shake hands all round. There are times and seasons for everything; and the time of forgiveness has come now. Am I right?"

"You are kind, Mr. Hamley; you always are," said his wife. "Well, Patricia, we will do as your uncle has suggested—offer you our forgiveness."

"Thank you, aunt; thank you, Mr. Hamley," said Patricia lifting her eyes.

She did not smile. She took their grace with a certain serious simplicity that was grand in its own way. Even at this moment, when she should have been penetrated with the sinner's contrite gratitude, she bore herself as an innocent person, and expressed neither pleasure nor shame, neither gratitude nor contrition.

"I confess," said Mrs. Hamley a little tartly, "that I am mainly induced to do this through a matter that has occurred to-day."

Patricia gave a quick glance at Dora. Had the truth come out? No; dear Dora was bending over her modern point with her usual placid amiability. Whatever it was that had happened, it surely had not touched her; and Patricia, checking a sigh, turned back to gaze at her aunt again.

"Lord Merrian has been here," said Aunt Hamley; and then she stopped and watched her niece.

"Yes aunt," said Patricia unconcernedly.

She liked Lord Merrian very well, but she was too far down in the depths at this moment to be lifted out of them by the simple intimation of his having called.

"And he has done you the honour," said Mrs. Hamley slowly, "of demanding your hand from me."

"Demanding my hand?" repeated Patricia, who at the first moment did not catch the drift of the phrase. "Does that mean," she then said suddenly, "that he wants to marry me?"

Mrs. Hamley was a little disconcerted at this abrupt method of inquiry; but Mr. Hamley, disposed to see in a favourable light all pertaining to the young person by whom he was to be related to the family of the Dovedales, rubbed his hands and thought this simplicity delicious. It was so like Patricia; and so far better than humbugging about the bush to go straight ahead and hit the right nail home!

"Yes, it means that Lord Merrian wishes to marry you," said Mrs. Hamley firmly.

"But I do not wish to marry him," said Patricia quite quietly. "I like Lord Merrian very much indeed, but I do not want to marry him."

Mrs. Hamley raised herself up in her chair and looked at her niece. She looked at her curiously, as if she was something

odd and wild and strange; and also as if she doubted her
senses somehow. Mr. Hamley's jocund smile .became a trifle
fixed and ghastly; and Dora laid aside her work, and looked
at Mrs. Hamley with sympathetic astonishment.

"You do not want to marry Lord Merrian?" slowly repeated
Mrs. Hamley.

"No aunt," said Patricia.

By the faces before her she saw that she had again committed
one of her usual sins; but, though she was sorry, this was a
matter in which she must rouse herself and be firm. Like the
forged cheque, it was an affair of life and death, and involved
her loyalty to others as well as her truth to herself.

"Not want to marry Lord Merrian?" repeated Mr. Hamley
after his wife.

"No," said Patricia in a low voice, but distinctly.

"And why this extraordinary disinclination, may I ask?"
said Mrs. Hamley with a polite smile.

"Because I do not love him, I suppose," replied Patricia
colouring. "I like him very much, very much indeed; but I
do not love him so as to wish to marry him—and," turning
pale, "I do love Gordon."

"This is the second time I have heard that person's name,"
said Mrs. Hamley, still speaking with that dangerous smooth-
ness, that deadly politeness which to those who knew her best
was the most formidable weapon of her rather large armoury.
"May I be permitted to know who this Mr. Gordon is?"

"Gordon Frere," answered Patricia.

"And who and what is Mr. Gordon Frere, pray?"

"Third lieutenant on board the *Arrow*," answered Patricia.

The name and style were as proud to her mind as those of
Viscount Merrian, son of the Earl of Dovedale at the Quest.

"And are you engaged to this very promising young gentleman, this third lieutenant on board the *Arrow?*" asked Mrs.
Hamley.

"Yes, aunt. Dear uncle, the last night, just before he died,
engaged us. But we were always fond of each other—ever
since I can remember," she added.

"Now Patricia, this childish folly must come to an end," said
Aunt Hamley, suddenly changing her tone to one of severe determination. "I am your guardian and I absolutely refuse

my consent. I forbid the whole thing. You are not engaged
to Gordon Frere. Do you understand? I have forbidden it;
and I have the legal as well as the moral right to do so. You
are no more engaged to him than you are to—to whom shall I
say?—Mr. Sydney Lowe; and I command you to accept Lord
Merrian."

"I am very sorry, aunt, to be always offending you," said
Patricia humbly but firmly; "but it is not my fault if I am.
As for saying I am not engaged to Gordon, you might as well
say that I am not alive. While I am alive I must love him,
and only him; and I could no more be false to him, and
marry Lord Merrian, than I could betray any other trust or
break any other promise." This she added in a lower voice.

"You hear her, Mr. Hamley!" cried the poor lady, turning
with an appealing gesture to her husband.

"I hear her certainly, and I see her," said Mr. Hamley;
"and, hang me, if I can make her out. Is she mad, Lady?
Have you anything"—he rapped his forehead—"in your family?"

"Why do you call me mad?" said Patricia speaking earnestly. "Is keeping my promise being mad? Is refusing to marry
one man when I am engaged to another madness? I think I
should be worse than mad if I acted differently—I should be
bad."

"And how am I to convey this insult to his lordship?"
asked Mrs. Hamley. "How—with what face—can I tell him
that a ridiculous little school-girl like yourself has had the au-
dacity to refuse such a magnificent proposal?"

"Lord Merrian would be the first to understand me, and to
say that I was right," said Patricia warmly. "Do you think
that he, good and clever and noble-hearted as he is, would want
a girl to marry him who loved another man, and had promised
to be that other man's wife?"

"Why need you tell him anything?" said Mr. Hamley.
"Take my advice, my dear young lady," he went on with his
soothing voice, " keep your own counsel and we will help you.
Do nothing but wipe your mouth and say, ' I will my lord,'
and so bring all your troubles, and ours for you, to a happy
conclusion."

"No, Mr. Hamley; you mean well, but I cannot do that,"

said Patricia. "If I ever see Lord Merrian I shall tell him the exact truth ; and I know that he will not blame me."

"And after that what do you propose to yourself ?" asked Mrs. Hamley smoothly.

Patricia looked at her aunt.

"I do not know," she said. "I must leave that to you. If you like I will leave the house, or I will live as you are making me live now, or I can go back to Barsands—dear old Barsands !—and live there. I don't care what becomes of me," she said with a heavy sigh, "till Gordon comes home. And then "—a light came into her face as she lifted it up and raised her eyes—"it will be all over, and I shall be in the sunlight again !"

"Now my young lady, hear me," said Mr. Hamley rising, planting his legs wide apart, and with his thumbs in his arm-holes preparing himself for an address. " Whatever happens things cannot continue as they are ; they are too cursedly un-comfortable. I don't like to feel that Abbey Holme is turned into a jail, and that a fine young woman like yourself is mewed up in her bedroom like a state prisoner. But neither can I have a forger, or at least the associate of a forger, set at loose as one may say in my establishment. So you see where you are—in a cleft stick, unless you get out of it by my lord's help. Marry him, and you shall have the best turn-out that has ever been seen in the county, and I'll give you as handsome a fortune as if you were my own child. There'll be something left for a rainy day and this little one here, after that ! I can't say fairer than this. But, by George ! if you refuse my lord, you may go hang yourself! I'll not turn you out of my house—you are my wife's niece and the admiral's grand-daughter ; but you'll understand that you stay here only on sufferance, as a kind of genteel pauper, a stray dog fed from charity on scraps, a thing too mean and paltry to be kicked out. There, I have said my say, and I'll not say I've made it too hard."

"Go to your room again, Patricia," said Mrs. Hamley severely. "Think of what your uncle has said. He is master here and I cannot act beyond or against his wishes. Put it clearly before you : Lord Merrian and honour, Lord Merrian and happiness, or this immodest infatuation—for I call it noth-ing else—and disgrace. As Lady Merrian all will be forgotten and forgiven ; as Patricia Kemball, with this infamous young

W

man in the distance, you are the companion of a forger and banished from my heart and esteem for ever. Now go ; think of what we have said, and pray God to turn your stubborn heart, and soften your wilful wicked temper."

"Dear aunt," said Patricia rising, " I am sorry to distress you so much, but I am fixed in this. If you kill me for it I cannot say to Lord Merrian that I will marry him ; and I would rather be killed than prove false to Gordon."

" Go ; leave the room this instant. I will not have Dora's ears polluted with such immodesty ! " cried Aunt Hamley angrily.

And Patricia once more went back to her prison, feeling that surely now the measure of her sufferings was complete.

" Could any one have believed it ! " cried Mr. Hamley when she had closed the door and gone. " I tell you Lady she is mad."

" No more mad than yourself Mr. Hamley," said his wife snappishly. " She is simply wicked and wrong-headed. But how to tell Lord Merrian when he calls to-morrow I do not know ! What shall I say ? What can I do ? " She rocked herself backwards and forwards in her chair moaning.

" Do not see him at all, dear," said Dora's soft voice. " Let Patricia see him herself."

She did not often make a suggestion, but this was so obvious she could not refrain.

" True ; that is it," said Mrs. Hamley. " You are right dear ; always right ! Yes, she shall have it to do herself ; but oh, I feel that I could just lie down and die for despair ! "

" Hard-mouthed young jade ! " muttered Mr. Hamley. " To refuse Lord Merrian !—positively to disdain to be made Countess of Dovedale ! A mad-house is the only place for her ; and if I had my will she should go there. Maybe she'd find her senses then ! To decline to be made Countess of Dovedale ! Was there ever such a maniac ? And all for a third lieutenant in the navy ! Good Lord, the world is turning upside down ! "

CHAPTER XXXII.

THE AIR CASTLE.

THE next day was a warm and tender May-day ; a day full of hope and sweet presages of a lovely future ; a day in joyous accord with the gladness and the love that filled the young man's heart as he rode quickly between the blooming hedge rows, and thought how good a thing it was to live, to love, to be young, and to be loved. No shadow of mistrust dimmed the brilliant sunshine ; no little cloud no bigger than a man's hand foretold the coming storm. As he rode through the lanes humming to himself snatches of *l'Elisir* and *Cenerentola* in a very exuberance of joy, handsome, loving, sure, he looked as if he had conquered once for all doubt and sorrow, those old enemies of man, and had come into the Eden where he would be.

The birds sang greetings from the trees as he passed, and the skylark overhead poured down its shower of melody like an epithalamium to his honour ; the meadows, bright with sun and brilliant with flowers, seemed like a royal carpet for his lover's feet ; and the crimson twigs of the maple and the hawthorn looked as if they ran with blood that blushed like her fair face. There was no loving simile, no tender conceit that did not flow like music through Lord Merrian's brain as he urged his horse onward, while his thoughts went like messengers before him. His imagination coloured all he saw, attuned all he heard ; so that earth and heaven seemed to have come together in his soul, making both one world in which only love and happiness existed and where Patricia Kemball was the queen.

It was the hour and the man ; the supreme moment which comes to us all when we have conquered.

So he rode through the lanes and park and avenue, always humming his snatches of song, now passionate and now jubilant, till he drew bridle at the door of Abbey Holme. And then he was ushered obsequiously into the drawing-room.

It was untenanted. Neither Mrs. Hamley nor Miss Drummond occupied each her accustomed place, and there was no Patricia to meet him with her glad shame and bashful love. It chilled him to see himself face to face with emptiness in the place of welcome. His nerves were so highly strung they vibrated to every influence, and this cold unresponsive room struck the first note of discord.

Presently the door opened and she came in. He went hurriedly forward to meet her, but stopped half-way, and his smile and the sunlight faded out of his face. There was something about her he could not fathom. True, he had heard she was ill, and she looked what he had heard; but there was more than this. There was a depth of sorrow, of strangeness even in her face and manner, that seemed like the beginning of a tragedy, the announcement of a mystery. The strangeness was due partly to the long duration of her home arrest; so that leaving her room, and being free to walk across the hall and through the passages, had almost a bewildering effect on her, making her scarcely know where she was and whether in her old circumstance of union with the family or in her new condition of isolation. Moreover, she was sorry for what she had to say.

It was no blushing bride, yearning if trembling, who came up to her expectant lover prepared to accept as much blessedness as she bestowed; no happy maiden rejoicing in her love and glad that the term of doubt was past, it full of sweetest tremors at the unknown certainty for which it was exchanged; but a pale, sad girl in some deep trouble come to give the death blow to his hopes and his joy. No; it was no bride who came up to him as he stood shocked and chilled midway between the table and the door, with one hand grasping nervously the back of a chair, the other half held out and half withdrawn.

At the first glance of her large eyes raised to him with such steadfast mournfulness, Lord Merrian read his answer before he made his request. He knew his doom, though he would not acknowledge it to himself; but went through the formula prescribed, and tempted Providence in the old wild way.

He spoke to her; but how differently from the manner in which he had anticipated as he rode along the lanes and pictured her shy face with its unspoken confession, which would make his words so few but so eloquent! Now he had something of the feeling with which a man leads a forlorn hope—a feeling of desperate determination and more resolve than belief—when he told her how much he loved her, and how ardently he desired that she should be his wife.

She listened to him with downcast air, tender, sorrowful, but not responsive. And when he had finished and had asked her for the one word which would be the confirmation of his flickering hope, she put her hand into his with a frank kindness that was not love, and said, looking into his face:

"Dear Lord Merrian, I am very, very sorry, but I cannot marry you."

It had taken Lord Merrian some little time and thought to be quite sure he loved Patricia Kemball well enough to wish to make her his wife. He had many doubts and a severe struggle, not only with his parents but also with the more conventional part of himself; but now he felt as if he had determined on this from the first, that she had known it from the first, that she had encouraged him, and that consequently her refusal was cruel and undeserved. And he felt too, that he must break down that refusal at any cost. The prize he had doubted whether he should or should not reach out his hand to take when it stood as he thought within his reach—now that it was denied suddenly became the one thing in his world which he would devote his life to gain. It is the way with men in almost all things; but chiefly their way with women, as the wiser among these last know, and act on.

"I cannot take that answer," he pleaded; "I will not believe that you mean it."

His handsome face looked with a heart-broken kind of appeal into hers, and her own heart ached to see it. But what could she do? There could be no paltering with truth, no irresolution. She was going to make him as unhappy as she herself was. She was sorry; heaven knew how sorry! but she could not help it. She must be firm, for his own sake as well as for Gordon's.

For a moment she did not speak; and then Lord Merrian poured out on her a flood of passionate beseeching and more dangerous pleading. He told her how, if she married him, she would help him to be his best self; how she would bring

out all his highest nature ; how she would strengthen his hands
for good, and give meaning and life to his resolves. With her
by his side he would live as a man with an ideal should live ;
and the world would be all the richer and cleaner for the
example their lives would afford it—an example rooted in her
and her only—due to her and her only. He besought her to
reflect on the power of good which she was putting from her ;
she, whose enthusiasm was for good ; whose heart went out to
humanity, and whose whole soul was filled with the desire to
make men happier and better. Married to her he would devote
himself to the sacred cause of humanity and progress : without
her he would be wrecked—a purposeless drifting wreck of all
that makes man noblest. Had this no compelling influence
with her ?

He said all this and more ; with scarcely conscious craft
taking the line of argument that he thought would have most
weight with her ; lover-like wanting her on any terms so that
he might but have her, and trusting to himself to make those
terms all that would best content him in the future.

His words for a moment dazzled her. To be of this great
value in life seemed to her such an infinite good ! It would be
bought by her personal sacrifice ; she neither desired to be
Lord Merrian's wife nor the possessor of a title. She loved
Gordon, and she was a democrat by nature who could never be
at home among the aristocracy ; but to do good—to be the
motive force which impelled a man of Lord Merrian's future
place and influence to turn his energies into the right direction
—it was a temptation just for a moment, the sophistries natural
to enthusiastic youth coming into her mind like voices bidding
her to accept this offer as her sacrifice of self carried to the
gain of the world.

And then she thought of Gordon ; of that last day, and their
long life-love ; and she felt that to hold fast by simple integrity
was better than to be led away by any false reasoning on the
value of sacrifice or the greater gain of complex virtues.

Looking once more into her friend's face, she said : " I cannot indeed, dear Lord Merrian ! How can I when I am
engaged ? "

There is no circumstance in life in which a man shows of
what stuff he is made so much as when he is in love ; none

wherein the difference between a gentleman and a boor is more distinctly proved. That chivalrous obedience to his lady's will, however painful to himself, which marks the gentleman, is just the quality wanting in the boor. The one waits on her desire, the other enforces his own ; the one sues, as for a grace granted by crowned weakness, what the other compels by the force of brute strength.. Patricia had judged her friend rightly. He loved her ; more than ever at this moment when he felt that with her was gone all the light of his life, all the hope and glory of his youth ; but he would have scorned to have pressed now for what she so courageously denied. He was a gentleman : and he respected the rights of his rival. Perhaps too a feeling of wounded pride helped to stiffen his shoulders to bear their burden with the quiet dignity of a true man. He, Lord Merrian, knowing his full value, knew that socially he was far ahead of a nameless third lieutenant in the navy without family or money. Man for man too he did not fear any comparison that could be made between him and any one else. He knew how he stood there ; with what good gifts nature had endowed him when she sent him into the world a nineteenth-century Antinous ; so that even on this lower personal ground he was aware that he stood too high for any possible humiliation.

"I have no more to say," he said after a long pause, during which he had stood holding her hand in his ; "you have been frank and true, like yourself. I cannot, even for my own happiness, urge you to act against your feelings or your principles. If it was only a case of waiting I would wait for you as long as Jacob waited for Rachel !—I would wait years on years till you took pity on me and said come! Is there no hope of this ?"

He bent down and looked into her face.

She shook her head.

"While Gordon lives I could love no one else," she answered simply and gravely ; "and if he died I think I should die too ! He is all that is left to me now of my only real life ; for this life is not mine, and not real."

"You seal my lips," said Lord Merrian turning away ; "and you have broken my heart !"

She stood up by him and laid her hands on his arm.

"No! no!" she said ; "you will find some one of your own

class who will be better fitted for you than I am : and we shall
always be friends. Shall we not ?—brother and sister together ? "

He smiled in the sorrowful way in which men do smile when
they are offered this pale comfort of fraternity where they had
looked for the warmth of a life-long love.

" Yes," he said in a broken voice ; " we will be friends
always."

Her hands lay heavily on his arm. He unclasped them
gently ; kissed them as if he was standing by a death-bed and
this was the last leave-taking ; and then murmuring some in-
distinct words that sounded something between a farewell and
a blessing, he left the room hastily ; and soon after Patricia
heard the sound of his horse's feet thundering down the
drive.

She did not know exactly how the next few moments passed.
She remembered nothing but an aching at her heart and a sense
of confusion in her brain. She scarcely knew where she was,
nor what had happened, nor what was to come, but sat with
her eyes fixed on the carpet, not thinking, only feeling.

" Have you seen his lordship ? "

It was Mr. Hamley who said this, as he and Mrs. Hamley
stood before her. They had come into the room in the noiseless way characteristic of Abbey Holme, and she had not heard
them till the unctuous voice of her aunt's husband broke the
silence and her reverie together.

She looked up and pushed back the hair from her forehead.
She had a bewildered and startled expression that seemed almost to justify Mr. Hamley's supposition of latent madness.

" What did you say ? " she asked, looking from one to the
other.

" Have you seen his lordship—Lord Merrian," repeated Mr.
Hamley, pronouncing the words very distinctly as when one
speaks to a foreigner or a deaf person, a child or an idiot.

" Yes," said Patricia fetching a deep breath.

" And what have you told him ? " asked her aunt.

In spite of herself the poor lady trembled. There was just
a glimmer of hope left alight.

" I told him that I could not marry him because I was
engaged, and loved some one else," said Patricia.

" And he accepted this excuse ? " said Mrs. Hamley in that dangerously smooth voice of hers. She had better have spoken roughly, so far as Patricia was concerned.

"He thought of course that I was right, and went away," Patricia answered. " We are friends," she added anxiously, as if to reassure them ; " we shall always be friends."

Husband and wife looked at each other. Mr. Hamley beat the devil's tattoo on his chest, and softly whistled a few notes of the " Ten Little Niggers." Mrs. Hamley's bitterness of disappointment exhaled itself in a few angry tears, which she concealed in the best way she could, under cover of a sudden cold.

" Well Patricia," then began Mrs. Hamley, " you are so far your own mistress as to be allowed the liberty of rejection. I cannot force you to marry Lord Merrian, or any one else, how much so ever I should like to do so, foreseeing your future, and judging for your good. But if you choose to decline such a chance, you must. All I can say is, that I wash my hands of you now and for ever. I do not know what your uncle's designs for you may be. He is a kind man, but a just one too ; whatever he proposes, to that I shall assent. If he says that you are to be turned out into the streets to starve, you must go. I cannot plead for you. And if he says that you are to live here as you are living now, in solitary confinement till you are twenty-one, you must do it. He is the master, and you yourself have tied my hands."

Mr. Hamley came forward.

" I said last night if I remember correctly," he began oratorically, " that I would neither turn you out of my house nor prosecute you for the crime which you have been guilty of as principal or accessory ; nor yet maintain you a prisoner in your own room. You are my wife's niece, the grand-daughter of an admiral and a K.C.B., and though about the biggest fool for a young lady with all her senses that I have ever met with, still a young lady as I feel bound by family circumstances to look after so far. You are free to remain here as long as you like. I do not grudge you your diet ; it won't break me ; no more will an occasional new gown or bonnet when absolutely required ; but, like your aunt, I have done with you. I take no more interest in you I don't care a hang what you do or what becomes of you, so long as you don't disgrace this house. You are as free as a bird for me; for I would as soon give myselt the trouble of poking after the sparrows in the hedge, and seeing what they were a-doing of in the mornings, as give mysel, the trouble of regarding you. You are wiped off the slate—done with. And now you know where you are; so make the most of what is left you, for it's precious little I tell you!"

"I scarcely understand what you both mean or how I am meant to live here," said Patricia, looking vaguely from face to face of the two stern judges who stood before her and condemned her. "Do you ever mean to speak to me, aunt? am I a prisoner? or what?"

"You are free, Patricia," replied Mrs. Hamley. "What you have desired you now possess. You will live with us apparently as usual. Mr. Hamley is not one to wish our private affairs to be made public property, nor do I desire to create a scandal. The world shall see no difference."

"Only I shall know it?" she asked.

"Only you shall know it," repeated her aunt grimly. "You will not be punished, and you shall have enough to eat, and be occasionally seen out with us to keep up appearances. But you will understand that all my love for you has gone, all my care; and that, as your uncle says, you are as free as a bird in the air because of no more consequence. You have an asylum here, not a home. You will soon know the difference, and be better able to estimate the worth of what, in your wicked folly, you have thrown away."

"But I cannot live like this!" cried Patricia a little wildly.

Aunt Hamley smiled and spread out her hands.

"It has been your own doing!" she said.

"Aunt! dear! what would you have me do?—marry Lord Merrian while I am engaged to Gordon? Could you counsel any girl to so base a thing!" she cried, with something of her old energetic sense of right, something of her old directness and abhorrence of crooked dealings breaking out through the maze and the deadness, the strange confusion and oppression of her present state.

"We will not go over the old ground again, if you please," said Mrs. Hamley frostily. "We discussed that last night. A theme becomes tiresome when continually repeated."

Patricia put her hand up to her head, and the fire burnt itself out of her eyes and brain.

"I seem to be in some horrible dream," she said wearily. "My whole life has been a dream since that night!"

She sat down on the sofa with a heavy dazed look, but neither Mr. nor Mrs. Hamley was in the mood for pity. Nothing short of the absolute agony of death would have softened them at this moment. They were too sorry for themselves to be able to be sorry for her.

"If you are not well, Patricia, you had better go up-stairs," said Mrs. Hamley coldly. "The drawing-room is not the place for a girl's hysterics."

"Uncle!" cried Patricia holding out her hands and looking up.

It was to the dead she called; but Mr. Hamley took it to himself, albeit she never called him uncle, and always made an internal protest when her aunt so spoke of him.

"Poor young woman; we must not drive her too hard, hey Lady?" he said, taking both her burning hands in his.

He was a man with his soft places; women found them out though he was a good husband. Pleased vanity and a pretty woman together found those places very soft.

"Come come, rouse up!" he said, patting her hands; "we can't have you go on like this, you know! You have disappointed and injured us, but you shan't come to harm. Look about you and pull yourself together; this kind of thing won't do, you know. Water, Lady! get some water! By George, she is going to faint!"

"Don't make a fuss with her, Mr. Hamley," said his wife; "it is the worst thing in the world for hysterics. Lay her down and open the window. She is just a little overcome; and no wonder; but there is not much the matter with her. Girls are always fainting when things go wrong with them."

But Patricia did not faint, or, as people call it, "go off." She was only benumbed and overwrought; and after a few deep sighs and bewildered movements, she came to herself again, and painfully staggered to her feet.

"There! sit where you are till you are fit to walk straight instead of staggering about as if you had I don't know what," said Mrs. Hamley peevishly; "and here are my salts. How silly you are to go on like this, Patricia!"

"Now you know a little of what we feel," said Mr. Hamley

with a rather hazy idea of sequential reasoning, as he sat down
by her on the sofa and fanned her with his wife's large
French fan, telling her all the while how wicked she had been,
and how bitterly he had been disappointed in her, and how she
had cut her own throat and no one could help her now the deed
was done; [with more to the same purpose; Patricia hearing
his voice as a far off kind of mill stream which sounded but did
not convey much meaning. But though he lectured and talked
big words—big words and bad grammar—he did not speak unkindly. That pathetic cry of "Uncle" had touched him; and
he was disposed to regard this recalcitrant sinner with something like human kindness; which to him seemed extraordinary generosity.

For the matter of that, however, both Mr. and Mrs Hamley
felt that they were wonderfully generous all things considered,
and that they were doing their duty with heroic magnanimity towards one in no way worthy; more than their duty indeed,
and far beyond what could possibly have been expected of them.

So they were, judging by their own lights and from their own
stand-point. To forgive so far as not to prosecute her for a
forgery in which she had been confessedly an accessory, as Mr.
Hamley said, and then to forgive, so far as not to banish her
from the house, the severest social disappointment she could
have inflicted on them—in both these acts they were generous;
and they glowed with the conscious satisfaction of the virtuous
as they reflected on their good deeds.

What an outsider might have said was another matter.
Could rough old mother Jose, or even prim Miss Pritchard or
any one of the simple fisher-folk who had known Patricia in her
Barsands days have seen her now, her health and mind breaking
down under the iron despotism of her aunt's rule—that unlov-
ing, cold, and contradictory rule which allowed no freedom, no
expansion, no power of growth to youth or character—what
would they have said? Something very different from Mr. and
Mrs. Hamley's concluding talk that night, when he threw out
as a fine fly to which she was expected to rise; "I think, Lady,
no one after to-day can say I am a hard man or an unjust one?"
and she had answered; "No, Mr. Hamley, you have been
more patient than I dared to anticipate. We have both acted
as Christians, I hope; which must be our consolation and
support!"

CHAPTER XXXIII.

ADDED TO THE ESTATE.

NEVER had life been so prosperous with James Garth. That twelve hundred pounds had surely carried a blessing with it ! It had fructified in his hands so that it had done him the good of twice its amount, and had mended the grievous rent which ill-luck and an evil inheritance had made in his affairs as if the stitches would never give way, and all was as good as new. It was a pleasure to see him with his honest face beaming with satisfaction, and his step as light as his heart, when he set out on his day's work ; and how he held his head high and seemed to congratulate himself on his state as one that could not be bettered, as he passed from field to fence and from yard to fold. And yet how sad it was to those who knew that his prosperity had no more root than a cut flower blooming in a vase, and that he was virtually Mr. Hamley's serf, held on during the great man's pleasure, to watch his exultant satisfaction and childlike forgetfulness that nothing of all this was really his own since the day when he had accepted Simpson's loan.

Still he had used the money well ; and for a rootless thing it all looked clean and vigorous. Not a penny had been wasted. He had paid up all his creditors, save the most dangerous, the man who had consolidated his debts into this one huge millstone ; replenished his small farm stock which had dwindled into a mere nothing, worse than none at all ; set up his children in boots and his wife in crockery and house gear ; got one or two loads of "strengthening" for the land, and hired labour for a bit of fence work here and a yard or two of drainage there. Yes, he had used the money well, and had made every pound of it pay. But he had used it. And of the loan not more was left than thirty pounds to meet the first half year's interest. But he calculated on a tidy little sum for the small croft of hay that would be ready for cutting in another three weeks or so, and the crops looked well so far.

To be sure every now and then flashes of an odd kind of doubt came into his mind ; but a doubt perfectly unreasonable, and, as he would try to convince himself, ungrateful as well. But he could not quite get rid of it. The fact was he had never really liked Mr. Simpson ; though he was the poor man's lawyer thereabouts ; a man who took up land and legacy cases, and suits for lapsed rights on speculation and the terms of no gain no pay, but if success then half the amount fought for and obtained. It was a bold way of doing business that sometimes succeeded when the law of the case was too strong to be set aside by technicalities, but that as often failed ; the longest purse making the best fight of it in the law courts as elsewhere, and, whatever may be said about justice being no respecter of persons, the peasant rarely getting the better of the gentleman. In spite however of this professional class-philanthropy, and in spite of his unconditional loan which had such a look of off-handed generosity with it, Mr. Simpson was, as has been said, no favourite with James Garth ; and he looked anxiously to the time when he should be able to pay off his debt and be a free man once more. He recognised the lawyer's trust and kindness and all that, he said ; but he preferred to be his own man and to owe nobody anything.

As he sat in the kitchen one evening painfully making calculations and adding up sums on dirty scraps of paper, for head-work was not much in James Garth's line, he made it clear to himself that, with such and such a profit on the hay and the barley and the handful of wheat in the angle, the patch of roots, the calf, and the litter of thirteen born that very day —as fine young pigs as could be seen in a day's walk ; thirteen ; not one missing or moiled, and of which Mrs. Garth, like a true farmer's wife, was as proud as if they had been her own children and about as anxious that they should be done well by—with all this in hand, he made it clear to himself that he should be able to pay off so much of the loan by the back-end of the year. It was a fair-looking calculation, as comforting as Alnaschar's, and as real. For though the figures stood well, nd proved like a sum-book, yet granting them true as they tood, at the best nothing had been allowed for a bad season and spoilt crops, and the margin, say for sickness or extra expenditure of any kind not tabulated, was merely x, no more.

It was just the kind of bright-looking bubble which hope and a sanguine temperament fashion between them, the momentary will o' the wisp which fortune in her crueller moods flings out to mislead men before she destroys them.

This was emphatically true of James Garth and his prosperous future; for while he was sitting at home, putting down his rows of exact but obedient figures and beguiling the evening with pleasant but fallacious Q. E. D's., Mr. Hamley's last words were ringing in Mr. Simpson's ear; "Call in the loan at once. No humbug, no delay. Down on the nail it went and down on the nail it must come back. Send up a man to-night; twenty-four hours; not a minute more; and d'ye hear? sharp's the word."

The blow fell hard and heavy. It came unexpectedly and it came cruelly. When everything looked so well, everything promised so fair, it was hard to have the whole fabric shattered for a rich man's greed—the possibility of success that was so probable destroyed for a stronger man's selfish will! Perhaps it was extrinsically better that the acres owned by James Garth should be taken by Mr. Hamley who would farm them more completely than that other could. But it was a life's ruin all the same; and some one once said that the life was more than meat and the body than raiment. But these are old-fashioned words, which the world has gone a long way past in this nineteenth century of ours!

Still, economically right as it might be, the thing seemed a pity all the same. Even the clerk who brought the notice was sorry for the errand on which he had come. The place looked so clean and bright as he came in out of the soft May evening twilight! There were such pleasant evidences of homely sufficiency in rack and shelf and dresser; in the cheerful little handful of fire crackling on the hearth for the boiling of the supper pot hanging from the chimney crook; in the tidy clothes of man and wife, and the contented faces of both as they turned their eyes to the door when it opened and bade the visitor step in and come to the light and the fire.

The man, Simpson's clerk, was the son of a peasant himself. He knew the signs, and he felt for one of his own kind; as was but natural. Moreover he hated Mr. Hamley whom he feared, and had no more love for Mr. Simpson whom he despised. He would rather it had fallen to any one else, he said, to do this thing; but he was hired for Simpson's work; and subordinates cannot afford to keep either feelings or a conscience. The great food question is king over all others, and poverty makes its victims of soul as ruthlessly as Jaganâth of bodies.

There were no loud words, no swearing, no exclamation even when James Garth opened the letter and read the notice. He took it with absolute calmness. It might have been a mere circular telling him the upset market price of beasts, or a notice of a sale to be held to-morrow in Milltown, for the quietness with which he received it. He only flushed a fiery red for a moment, the veins in his neck and forehead suddenly starting like cords; and then he paled to a dead white which left his face like that of a corpse, as the whole thing suddenly revealed itself. He had walked straight into the snare that had been laid for him, and there was no way of escape, look where he would. The twelve hundred pounds required of him before twenty-four hours were come and gone, and Mr. Simpson confessing that the money was not his own but Mr. Hamley's, and that all entreaties for time would be just so much labour lost—why the thing was self-evident! He had been entrapped; and Simpson had simply been Jabez Hamley's tool and decoy.

It was neatly done. Cruelty of the worst kind always is neat. Mr. Hamley had never done anything with nicer precision or more heartless inhumanity. He had marked his game, covered him, and now had him safe; as safe as if Long Field Farm was already mapped out on the estate plan of Abbey Holme, and the old title-deeds of the Garths locked up in the fireproof safe let into the walls of the "Growlery." Yes, it was neatly done. No one could have shown more patience in stalking his prey, thought Mr. Hamley rubbing his hands; and now he had the reward of patience. A grand quality! To know when to hold and when to strike—is not half the meaning of success to be found herein?

While he thus congratulated himself on his method and held himself to have deserved well of men and the science of agriculture, as practised in the country round about Milltown, James Garth sat in the house which was substantially no longer his own, conning that text which had been assigned to him out of the popular lesson of the day—the weaker man must lose, and Might is Right.

"It is not only that I want the land for personal purposes—I could have disappointed myself easy enough if that had been all," said Mr. Hamley to Mr. Borrodaile, getting the first word with the rector, knowing there would be more words than one on the transaction when it became known, and anxious to make himself appear a public benefactor in his private dealings; "though I don't deny it will fit in very well with the rest—no gentleman likes to have a bit here and a bit there among his own that ain't his own; but when it comes to a bit of weed-ground, as this Long Field is, why it's a disgrace to the neighbourhood, and a nuisance too, to every gentleman as desires to keep his land in good condition. Thistles and dandelions—that's about the size of it. And who wants to have his fields stocked with them, I should like to know? Not for as many James Garths!"

To which the rector said—no, certainly not; no man spends his money on guano and top-dressing, to have his careless neighbours ruin his labours; and if James Garth could not farm the land properly it had better pass into the hands of one who could and would.

Unfortunately it happened that at this moment both Dr. and Miss Fletcher were from home, else may be James, knowing how good they were to their poorer brothers, might have gone down to them with his row of figures and his story. But they were away in London; and time was too short for letters to pass between. Had not Mr. Hamley foreseen all this, and had he not waited until "yon hound Fletcher" was clear off the premises for a few days? A child of the generation as he was he would have scorned to have committed the blunder of leaving the back door open. No; he had James safe in the toils, and in Dr. Fletcher's absence there was neither man nor mouse in Milltown who could gnaw the cords asunder. So the fiat went forth, and Long Field Farm was sold to Mr. Hamley, standing crops, house, stock, land; and Garth had a full hundred more than if any other man had bought the lot. Mr. Hamley wanted to have it said that he had done the thing handsomely. And he did it handsomely too, according to his code; leaving the dispossessed farmer with a clear hundred in hand, when all

x

expenses were paid and the whole thing ruled straight between them.

Garth was strongly urged by his friends to go abroad with this sum, and try his fortune in Australia or America. He let men talk ; and either did not answer at all, or, when their words roused him, bade them shut up with an oath, and a savage look not like his old self. But then he was not like his old self any how. He might have been another person altogether. The James Garth men had known these five and forty years and more, active, industrious, hopeful, cheerful, had died and left the mere shell as his representative. He did nothing, would do nothing ; and while food was set before him, and he had a place where he could creep like a dog to sleep in when he came home, he neither cared nor knew what was behind. The present and the future were alike swallowed up in the vanished past, and he lived only in regret and remembrance.

His sorrow had broken him down, and had turned him, if not to absolute madness, yet to something that was very near it. People looked after him and shook their heads when they met him ; and little children, who had always loved him, shrank from him in fear. Unshaven and neglected, and though his clothes were whole yet leaving on you the impression of rags and sordid misery, he wandered about the Long Field lanes, never speaking even to his oldest friends beyond a hurried good day ; or may be it was only a sullen nod that he flung with a slouching air and a downcast, side-long glance. Never resting, never working ; muttering to himself ; sometimes to be heard laughing wildly and sometimes with his face buried in his crossed arms weeping just as wildly ; or standing by one of the Long Field gates looking with burning eyes and blackened lips on to the land that the master of Abbey Holme was breaking up into harmony with his own—and he a trespasser on the ground where he and his forefathers had been owners ; not drinking, but having so much the look of it in his unsteady gait and confused air that even his friends held he must " get it on the quiet," and all thought he was never better than half sober at the best ; this was how he lived and looked from the hour when Simpson's clerk brought up that notice, and he knew that he had been tricked and sold.

But there was nothing bad about him, poor fellow! neither was he mad ; no more at least than any other heart-broken creature is mad. The world called him so for want of a finer distinction, and it answered Mr. Hamley's purpose to set the report well afloat. It prevented too much sympathy for his victim. We do not feel real sympathy for mad folks. We are theoretically sorry for them and express ourselves shocked ; and if we can bring it out clearly why they have gone mad, and make a well-rounded domestic history of cause and effect, we are satisfied. All the same, we keep away from them ; and our precious balms would be of the kind to break their heads if we administered them. At the best too, we think it deplorably weak that they should have lost their wits for sorrow. When half Milltown said James Garth had gone out of his mind because he had lost his land, the other half, which listened, thought that he was showing a contumacious and undisciplined spirit which deserved less pity than reprobation. Man is born to sorrow, and he should take his inheritance patiently. Besides, it must be so very unpleasant for poor Mr. Hamley, they said. He had put money on the estate, and of course he had a right to have either his loan or his land. He had behaved nobly to the poor fellow ; and see what an improvement it would be to all that bit of the road when the farmhouse and its pigsties and the dirty old sheds were all taken down and carted away, and those ill-kept fields in as good order as a garden! So far from blaming him they thought he had done both well and wisely ; and they were only sorry for him that his good work had wrought such havoc with that half-witted fellow. For he could never have been worth much if his mind had given way at the first little trial like this ; and it was not a nice thing for poor Mr. Hamley to feel that he had been the cause of such an awful upset.

Mr. Hamley represented society, success, and the law. To a law-abiding people legality is a tremendous backstay, and sanity and success are so much more pleasant to contemplate than insanity and ruin ! Besides, take it how you will, it was better for the world at large that Long Field should be owned by a capitalist who could farm it up to its capabilities, rather than by a peasant proprietor who, doing the best by it he could, grew more weeds than worts and took less off than he put in.

All this good economic reasoning, however, did not mend matters for poor James Garth. But what did it signify? Between the more symmetrical rounding of a rich man's property, and a peasant's holding on to the land of his fathers, who would hesitate which is the better thing to see? And if the dispossessed break their hearts or lose their heads for grief, they but confess their own weakness thereby. The stronger must take the crown of the causeway as his right, and the weaker must go to the wall as his sorrow. The law of nature has crystallised this fact ever since the first wolf eat the first lamb; and there are those who deny any difference between men and wolves—with lambs.

Mr. Hamley and James Garth represented the righteous supremacy of strength, and the inevitable overthrow of weakness, and only a few washy enthusiasts on the one hand, and godless democrats on the other, would maunder about a law of duty imperative on the rich and strong, or uphold the doctrine of rights on the side of the poor and weak. It was an insignificant little transaction save to the persons immediately interested; but it was a type; and for the occasion Long Field Farm was as a microcosm where the tremendous facts of the universe were being transacted unhelped or unhindered by the love or good conscience of men.

The Garths had moved into lodgings in Milltown. This of itself was a change of no mean magnitude. The farmhouse freedom and rough plenty that had made part of the rule of life at Long Field, the ceaseless activity, the interest in work never ending and always changing, the open-air life for man and boy and child were all gone now—exchanged for cramped lodgings in a confined back street smelling of stale fish and foul sewers, in the heart of a town. For though Milltown was nothing but a large-sized village to those accustomed to metropolitan centres, it was like a metropolis, a closely-packed human ant-hill, for these poor folks, accustomed as they had been to the breezy uplands and the unconfined air of moor and meadow.

Mrs. Garth, good soul, battled with all these untoward circumstances bravely. When women are brave they make a divine fight of it, and when men give way the collapse is generally complete. The wife, however, was so much better off than her husband in that she had her children to think of, the place to keep tidy and appearances to maintain. Her mother-hood and housewifery remained the same now as at the farm, but his occupation was gone. And then again, though she had loved the place well it had never been to her all that it was to James. She was a woman of strong instincts and keen affections as well as of sound good sense, but she wanted just that dash of sentiment which had expressed itself in him in the pride of family proprietorship. If he would have put his shoulder to the wheel and have gone out to one of the colonies with the money he had in hand, she would have been quite as well pleased, had they prospered and the children kept their health, as if they had kept Long Field. This does not say that she did not grieve for the loss of the farm, or that she failed in tenderness or sympathy, only that she had more objects of interest left to her than he had, and less sentiment to make her suffer. Still she did make the best fight of it incomparably ; and when people saw the difference between them they said she was doing her duty like a Christian, but as for James, the wreck he had made was disgraceful, and the way he let things go by the board a shame.

All these things were remembered in the days to come when a motive had to be found for a deed that thrilled society at Milltown as it had never been thrilled before ; and a theory had to be constructed that would fit the facts for the one part and hold together for the other. It was then found how much a man may damage himself by not taking his inheritance of sorrow cheerfully, and what evil results may follow on not acknowledging the divinity of that law of the strongest by which the weaker is destroyed.

CHAPTER XXXIV.

THE CLEFT STICK.

IF Mr. Hamley had come down on James Garth, he was so far impartial in his dealings with man and man as to come down on Colonel Lowe as well. He had to make it evident to Milltown that he, Ledbury's office-boy, had bought up one of the local aristoi, a "swell" who had married Lady Anne Grahame's daughter; and bought him up as easily as he had covered a poor paltry peasant. Besides, he had that need of action which comes after a disappointment; and, failing marriage and Lord Merrian, turned to Cragfoot and revenge. So it came that Colonel Lowe, being far behind-hand with his quarterly interest, received a notice from Mr. Simpson—all due legal forms being complied with—that his client who had lent the money had given notice to foreclose. Unless then, he could find some one else to take up the mortgage, his bad quarter of an hour was at hand, and his turn at the Hamley grindstone had come round.

Six months wherein to settle his affairs—six months wherein to find another capitalist who would lend sixty thousand pounds on a decaying property, with the quarterly interest always in arrears and getting yearly more difficult to find. It was a bad look-out for the Colonel; but to do him justice he faced the gloomy prospect manfully, and gave way to no weakness of hopeful gilding by which folks so often make bad appear good and present ruin look like future fortune. He only cursed his evil stars, and that fatal luck of his which had landed him in this hole. Had any of the thousand and one fortunate probabilities come off which never do come off for the gain of amateur gamblers, or any of the unfortunate accidents not happened which always do happen to overwhelm those who are tempted to their destruction on the Turf, the Colonel would have stood to win ever so many hatfulls. But all his bets turned the wrong way; and instead of bringing himself home,

as he had hoped, he had plunged heavily—each time more
heavily than the last—losing with a persistency of miscalcu-
lation that should have warned him had he been of the kind
to accept warnings, and that as it was looked like Nemesis.
The upshot of it however was, that he stood now on the very
verge of ruin, with only one chance left—Sydney's marriage
with Julia Manley and her hundred thousand pounds. ·

If the boy would not marry her—and he had not made a
move that way—they were all done for; but his father had
not kept him about him all his life not to know something of his
nature; not to know, above all, that poverty was just the thing
Syd would not accept, let what would be the means by which he
would creep out of the net, and that when the fix came he
would get money somehow, by any act of treachery or dishonour compatible with his position as a gentleman. He had no
fear of the result when affairs pressed seriously ; and the day
after he received the notice he resolved to make a final appeal
to his son's good sense and right feeling, and having done this
to abide the issue—of which he had no doubt. Once convinced
that his only course, as a man and a gentleman, was to marry a
woman utterly distasteful to him in every sense but that of a
convenient banking account—and the thing was done. To be
sure, he was hard to convince ; but then he was young; and
young men are self-willed at times and the elder and wiser
must have patience.

Colonel Lowe had never himself shown to greater advantage
than he did to-day, when, for the second time, he went thoroughly
into his affairs with his son, and placed the whole condition of
things clearly before him. Nothing could exceed the delicacy
with which he stated the only chance of escape left them, unless
it was his manly frankness, his paternal tenderness. Sydney
was selfish, insolent, ill-tempered, weak—had a thousand faults
for one virtue ; but he did really love his father, and the difficulties of his own position were increased by the desire he honestly had to help the Colonel, and set him free from his embarrassments. Had he not been Dora's husband he would have
been Julia Manley's within the month ; but what could he do ?
He was in a cleft stick, and there was only one move which
could free him. And that one move—would Dora consent to
it ? Before he compromised himself here he must be quite

sure there. He believed that she would release him; for she loved poverty no better than himself; but until he was assured he must fence off a promise, and fall back on his personal reluctance as his safest card to play. He thought he could compel her; he felt convinced he could when he had once made up his own mind, just as his father felt convinced about himself; but between love and doubt, that vacillating mind of his was not made up as yet, but was tossed like a football now by his affection for his father, now by his hatred of poverty, now by love for Dora, then by doubt of her acquiescence, and then by his repugnance to the alternative.

"I loathe the woman!" he said passionately. "Of all the women I know Miss Manley is the most detestable in my eyes."

"Poor Julia!" said his father. "She is no beauty I confess; but she is very amiable, and she has a hundred thousand pounds at her disposal."

"It is frightful," said Sydney covering his face. "But I will think of it. I can say no more If I can I will; but the sacrifice is maddening!"

"I only ask you to think of it, my dear boy," replied the Colonel gently. "I am so sure of your good sense that I have no fear of your decision when you have once given your mind to it. I do not think that you could bear to see the old place sold and given over to that shoeblack, as it will be if we cannot raise the money somehow. Nor do I think you will like to begin life on your own account as a clerk in some office, with not as many shillings a week as you have been accustomed to have pounds. And yet—I see no other chance for us."

"Why the deuce did you ever go on the Turf?" cried Sydney with a sudden outburst of insolence.

His father shrugged his shoulders.

"Ah, yes," he answered tranquilly. "But if the favourite had won?"

"If!" cried Sydney; "a man ruins his family for an if!"

"A little hard but smart, my boy," said the Colonel quietly. "Of what consequence a few ill-tempered splutterings," he reflected philosophically, "if you can carry your point and get the main thing ruled to your liking? Syd might be as insolent as he chose poor boy, if he would marry Julia Manley at the

end. It amused him, blew off the steam, and hurt no one else
—just the play of the fish before he was landed; a thing for
which experienced anglers must be prepared." Still the
Colonel did not like his insolence. He would not quarrel with
him for it, because it is impolitic to fall out with your tool ; but
he would stop it. So, rising, he laid his hand on the young
man's shoulder, saying kindly in his very best manner—frank
yet dignified, paternal yet friendly—

"Don't worry yourself now, dear boy Time is valuable of
course, but we are not going to be sold up to-night. Think it
over, and see what you can do. If you feel that Julia, poor
soul, is really impossible, well—we must face our ruin like
men and gentlemen, but if you think you could marry her
with some reasonable prospect of happiness after—and you
know my belief on the subject—why then we are saved, and
old Hamley's triumph is cut from under him. I confess I shall
be sorry if you decide against my wishes ; but if it is for your
happiness old fellow, I shall not grudge my share of the bill
we must pay."

"Curse Hamley and all his crew !" cried Sydney savagely.

"Yes, so say I too ; curse Hamley !" repeated his father.
"I would sit here and swear at him till all was blue, if that
would do any good ; but as it will not, we might as well save
our energies for useful things."

On which he lighted his cigar and strolled away, very sorry
for poor Syd, but decidedly of opinion that the best thing he
could do was to get out of his presence as soon as possible, and
that solitude was the safest condition for his son at the present
moment.

After a little while spent in useless thinking and vain regrets,
Sydney Lowe, also lighting a cigar, strolled away as his father
had done ; and, ordering his horse, went for a ride, to see if a
hard gallop through the leafy lanes and across the moor would
clear his brain so that he could discover how to make two and
two five, and in what manner it would be possible to put back
the hand of time and cut the knot that could not be untied.
And while he was riding he found himself in the Long Field
lanes, and came suddenly upon James Garth standing with his
chin resting in the palms of his hands, staring fixedly across
the fields where Mr. Hamley's men were working, and where

had he ventured he would have been warned off as a trespasser.

A sudden thought seemed to strike Sydney as he passed the man. His wild and haggard face put a vague and misty idea that had been passing through his brain into tangible shape. Here was a man who, as well as themselves, had wrongs to revenge ; a common peasant, therefore a creature without a conscience, and to be either bought or impressed. He rode forward for a short distance, then turned back and reined up as he came to Garth still standing where and as he had left him, his elbows on the gate and his chin resting in the palms of his hands.

" Good-morning, Garth," said Sidney briskly. -

The man looked up with a sidelong, quick, suspicious glance that had become habitual to him. He flung the young fellow a nod, but did not answer. Nothing disturbed him more than to be spoken to. He wanted to be left alone in the world, and to have no interruption to his mournful broodings.

" That's a sad sight, Garth," said Sidney, pointing with his whip to the fields. " I don't know when I was so sorry for anything as I was for this trouble of yours."

" Eh ? " said Garth.

" I call it a damned shame," continued Sydney speaking with energy ; " a cruel scandalous injustice."

Garth looked up. The passionate speech and accent of the gentleman struck him as odd. It was kind of him to feel so keenly for him, a poor man ; but what call had a gentleman to take the sorrows of a horny-handed working-man to heart ? It jarred him somehow ; and yet it was kind.

" He laid his lines and he took it," said Garth slowly.

" Yes, I know all about that ; and how you can stand there and see it all I can't make out," said Sydney. " If the fellow had done as much by me, or half as much, I would have broken his head before now."

Garth's eye blazed out with sudden passion and his wan cheek flamed. He clenched his right hand and muttered something between his teeth. Sydney did not hear the words, but the look and the action were significant enough.

" That's what I say," repeated Colonel Lowe's son in a lower voice, and with a vicious kind of distinctness in his words. " If he had done as much by me, or half as much, I would have broken the fellow's head ; and broken it so that it would not have been mended again in a hurry."

"It would be a good job done," said Garth as if to himself.

"A very good job !" said Sydney. "The fellow is the pest of the neighbourhood ; a low-lived cur ! He has neither the manners nor the feelings of a gentleman. If he got knocked on the head some dark night there is not a soul in the place but would feel that a nuisance had been got rid of, and would be right thankful to the hand that had done it."

"A rich man and few friends," Garth muttered.

He still spoke as if to himself, as if Sidney Lowe had passed out of his sphere altogether.

"A blackguard without one friend," said Sidney. "Why ! how did he treat that nice girl of yours ?—sent her off at a moment's notice because his wife had lost a pound or two ! He did not dare to say why, but I ·happen to know that was the reason. What can you say of a man like that ? "

James Garth made no reply ; his face was still turned to the fields, his hand strongly clenched, his lips set, his eyes fixed and burning. A vision passed before him. He saw his enemy, the man who had tricked and sold him, walking before him in the evening darkness. He noted his jaunty stride, his chest thrown forward, his shoulders set square, his head well up, as a man who had conquered fortune and beaten all round in the game of life. He saw himself creeping after him with a stealthy step—a shadow dogging him as revenge dogs crime ; he saw the distance gradually lessening, he gained inch by inch upon him ; he was creeping up to him, always in the shadow, till he was close—close ; and now—

There was a cry that startled Sydney and made the men in the fields throw down their picks and spades and come hurrying to the gate.

"No ! no ! not murder ! Good Lord ! not murder ! " shrieked James Garth, struggling and foaming. He had had an epileptic fit once before in his life ; this was only a recurrence.

"Who said murder ? " asked one of the men looking darkly at Sydney.

"And what's to do here, sir ? " asked another.

"I do not know what it all means," Sydney answered. **As**

he spoke his face changed, and his eyes had the look of a quick
thought in them. "That poor fellow," he then went on to say
with an air of charitable disdain—he was a gentleman now,
speaking of a boor to his fellow-boors—"that poor fellow there
seems to have had a bad kind of thought. We were talking of
Hamley, and he said how infamously he had been used, and
then suddenly shouted 'murder!' I hope he was not thinking of doing for Mr. Hamley," with a slight smile that had a
ghastly look in it.

"That's a hard word to say, sir," said one of the men sullenly. "James ain't the man to take life."

And Sydney, with a careless "Well, I hope not; but murder
has an ugly sound with it," rode away revolving.

That night he and Dora had an unreal kind of interview;
but one in which he was defeated. Each wore a mask, and
both fenced cleverly, with more feints than threats; but she
was the stronger of the two and spoilt his game. He told her
of his difficulties, his father's ruin, and the foreclosing of the
mortgage; she sympathised with him in the dearest way, and
complained of her own perplexities in the Hamley resolve to
keep her as a kind of state prisoner at Abbey Holme for ever;
and what could she do to help him? Between too little money
and too much love, she thought life very hard and people very
queer, she said, with a pretty shrug of her round uncovered
shoulder—one of her nice little tricks that Sydney admired.
He asked for her counsel as to what he should do, as she could
not help him; and hinted at Miss Manley and her hundred
thousand pounds; but she was too wise to take up his hint.
She was determined that what he wanted her to know he should
say in plain terms, leaving no loophole by which to creep out
should things turn ill. Not that she wanted their marriage to
continue, as things were, could it be safely broken. She would
if she could have torn her marriage lines as she might have
torn a milliner's bill that had been paid and done with. As
she could not do that, she was not minded that Sydney should
have any advantage she could not share.

She was so full of innocence and high-mindedness to-night
no man could possibly have proposed to her a crime to which
she must give her assent—so full of sweetness and love, no man
could have told her he meant treachery and desertion. He

was foiled at every turn. She would not understand his hints, and he could not quarrel with her. How can any one quarrel with a sweet, amiable, lovely little girl whose every accent is a caress, every word an endearment ?—a soft, purring creature, sympathetic and responsive, and offering no more resistance than a ball of swansdown ? The thing is impossible ! You might as well try to play fives with that same ball of swansdown as cross swords with a woman of Dora Drummond's type when she has set her mind to yield and to fascinate, to guide by a silken thread—yet to hold with an iron hand.

Ever since Sydney had made her take that roll of ten sovereigns Dora had begun to hate him, and to hate him all the more because she had begun to fear him. She did not know what horror he might not force her to commit, if his necessities urged ; and she did not like the unhappiness of which he had been the cause. Soft, sensual, self-indulgent women never do like to see unhappiness ; it disturbs and annoys them ; and for all her capacities for cruelty if she was pushed to it, Dora was essentially good-natured when it did not cost her too much. Nevertheless, though she hated him to-night, she held him and she fascinated him, never having been more delightful, more endearing. Not that she would at any time have suffered herself to sink into the ordinary groove of English wives—that groove wherein they do not think it necessary to try to please their husbands ; having got, not caring to retain. Had she detested the man who owned her she would have made herself none the less pleasant and coquettish to him. She might have poisoned him, and probably would, but she would have been careful to have handed him his dose of quietness with the prettiest little smile and the most becoming little cap in the world. Ten minutes before she had eloped with her lover, she would have put her arms round her husband's neck and have called him a dear, and would have asked him if her dress was not pretty, and, smoothing her flounces, just the thing for a journey ? Her creed was, that if disagreeable things had to be done, there was not the smallest reason why they should not be done pleasantly ; and if jalap has to be taken, in the name of humanity smother it well in jam.

Sydney understood nothing of all this. He saw her as she chose he should see her, and took her at her own valuation.

Had things gone well with them, he would never have seen
her other than as the sweetest and most amiable little girl the
world had ever produced; he would have been even a better
man through the soothing influence of her assumed virtues, just
as the Hamleys were both happier and better through that
same influence. He would have lived and died and have never
learnt the truth to the last—not when he kissed her hand as
she gave him the poisoned cup, and blessed his friend for whose
sake she had given it. These women—soft, fair, and false—
have ever been the women men love best. They have their
uses; and one is that they sometimes avenge their honester
sisters.

When they were about to part, Sydney said half-jokingly,
half-seriously; "What would you do Dody, if I was forced to
marry Julia Manley?"

"Syd!" she answered, her cheek on his shoulder. "As I
cannot imagine anything so dreadful, I cannot say what I would
do."

"You would scarcely give me in custody for bigamy?" he
laughed.

"Why not, dear?" asked Dora, innocently.

"Why not? Because you would not like to be the wife of
a felon, in the first place; nor a poor little lost love, turned out
of house and home and having to work for your living, in the
second," he answered.

"As if I should mind what became of myself in such a
horrible position as that!" was her reply. "There are two
things for which all women, who are real women, would sacrifice
themselves, Syd," she went on to say with her pretty professorial
air; "love and revenge. I have gone far enough, as things
are, for the one; I don't want to find out by experience how
far I could or would go for the other."

"Not to your own ruin, though perhaps to mine," he said,
smoothing her hair caressingly. "You might not care about
me, but I am sure you would about yourself."

"I think I would sacrifice myself too, if I wanted to punish
you," she said in the sweetest way.

And then he laughed and kissed her, and said she was a
dear little transparent darling, and good fun to humbug—she
believed everything he said to her.

To which Dora, smiling and showing her small white teeth, said—Why, of course she did! What were women for but to believe in and love their husbands? If—pouting—he humbugged her, that was very wrong,. and very wicked of him. She never humbugged him, and she thought he ought to be as loyal to her.

"Well, then, I will!" said Sydney. "So I may not marry Julia Manley?"

"If you do I will kill you and your Julia Manley too!" said Dora with the most enchanting assumption of viciousness.

He laughed again, and pretended to be afraid of her; and then he vowed he would be a good boy, and so on; with a dozen varieties of falsehood and folly. But when he went away he wondered to himself what Dora really would do if he were to marry Julia Manley; as he must —he knew that well enough. It was horrible, detestable, but he must! She could not betray him, let her threaten as much as she liked. The same reasons which had kept them both from confessing their marriage would keep her quiet when it was broken; and for the far-off future—if the day should ever come when she should be poor and he rich; a not very likely contingency, but if it should come—why then he must trust to the chapter of accidents, and hope for a miracle; as weak men and bad men do.

But what a dear she was!—his fluid thoughts went that way now. How could he ever give her up? What a perplexing pass he was in! What could he do—how could he save himself from pain and annoyance? How warmly he would have welcomed the Mephistopheles who would have got him safely out of this cleft stick in which he was held, even by the payment of that shadowy thing he called his soul! And this thought brought him once more to the remembrance of James Garth and *his* soul; and what a blessed solution of all present difficulties it would be, could that half-mad fellow be induced to break old Hamley's head one of these dark nights, and so end the coil once and for ever! What would become of him, the murderer, afterwards was a thing of no consequence. He was played out; and whether he died in the workhouse or a madhouse, of starvation or on the gallows, his life was done for and the manner of the end signified but little. How could he tempt him? he thought; how get the idea into his poor feverish head? Probably the old ruffian had left Dora well provided for. If only he could be swept out of existence at this juncture, how smooth the road would be!

Meanwhile Dora, on her side, resolved never again to meet as of old Sydney Lowe, her lawful husband. What he intended to do, she thought, let him, without counsel or consent from her. If she wished to keep him in her power, as she did, he must tie his own nooses and slip his own head into them without help or hindrance so far as she was concerned. Her rôle was innocence coupled with devotion ; and she must be careful of both the properties and business belonging to her part. This was her resolve, as she crept back into the house, and locked up the key of the postern gate in her most sacred drawer. The plot was thickening unpleasantly ; and she was quite acute enough to know that her safest place was one to the side, where she could observe but where she was not included

CHAPTER XXXV.

ABANDONED TO HERSELF.

MRS. HAMLEY was not a woman to do things by halves. What she said she generally meant, and she had not that kind of nature, morally severe and physically tender, which promises hard things and does soft ones. On the contrary, if her words were severe her actions ran them close ; so that when she told Patricia she was cast out of her love and abandoned to herself—given her freedom on the one hand, but receiving desolation on the other—she said what her heart dictated ; and she acted up to it.

Patricia was in very truth abandoned to herself. She was never scolded, never thwarted, never denied, because absolutely ignored. She came and went, and no notice was taken of her; no one asked where she had been or what she had done. She took her place at the table, and the servants attended on her with the rest ; but she was not included in the inner kingdom, and if she made an observation, which was not often, her words fell flat and without response. Had she absented herself, no one would have asked for her until the thing had begun to look serious ; and once when she was late for luncheon and made her excuse in her old frank, hurried way, her aunt answered coldly : " Pray do not give yourself the trouble to apologize. It really does not signify the least in the world whether you are late or not."

Abandoned to herself ; cut off from all family communion ; denied even the friendliness of rebuke ; it was infinitely worse than being coerced and herded as in the older days ; and Aunt Hamley intended that she should feel it worse. To add to Patricia's troubles, there was not only "a cut" between the Abbey Holme people and the Fletchers, owing to their taking Alice Garth without a character—which cut perhaps Patricia might have ignored in any circumstances, and more especially in these present ones—but they were away. Had they been at home,

Y

poor Garth would not have been ruined. So that she was utterly alone at home and without a friend abroad.

Dora would have been kind to her in secret, and, to do her justice, always tried to put in a conciliatory word for her when she could without hurting herself, and which Mrs. Hamley, even while she rebuked, treasured up as evidence of her favourite's sweet and lovely nature ; but Patricia would have none of her. Her heart had turned against the Dora of the actual, and she refused to be caressed back to belief. The Dora she had loved had died, and had left behind her nothing but a memory and a regret. The Dora who remained was a mere show, a mask, an unreality ; and she would not join hands again with one who had deceived her as she had done. Her self-respect, too, was outraged at having been made a tool wherewith to work iniquity, and her sense of honour had been revolted. She had touched pitch and she felt defiled. And yet perhaps, Patricia in future years would develop sufficient passionateness to be able to touch pitch voluntarily in certain circumstances—as the offering of her soul to the good of a cause. But if this might be true of the future it certainly was not of the present, when the law of girlish righteousness allowed of no deviation from the right line, and when she was both too young and too straightforward for casuistry ; and when, take it how she would, supplying Sydney Lowe with money stolen from Mr. Hamley was scarcely reason enough why she should have been dragged into the mire of a crime, innocent of all criminal knowledge though she was. So there she stood amidst the wreck of more than home and fortune ; like some worshipper of the old-time gods taken by the initiated into the secret places, and shown the tricks by which the awful holy thunderings were made, and the glorious beauty of the Divine revealed, and the kneeling crowd held captive to the faith it never proved.

Night and day she thought of all this—of the Dora she had loved and believed in and of the Dora she had found in the place of her ideal ; of the good success of baseness ; and then of her old life at Barsands ; till she scarcely knew which was real, the present or the past, and whether her uncle's teaching had been right or her aunt's commentary wrong. Her mental condition was in truth for the moment slightly clouded. Her brain had been overtaxed, and was fogged like an imperfect photographic plate. She had to fight through it alone. It was a bad pass for a girl given to singleness of mind and purpose and belief, but it had to be gone through; and there was so much good in it that the struggle would make her all the stronger, and she would be a nobler woman at the end of it than she was in the beginning.

The warm spring days were mellowing into summer. There was no earthly reason, thought Patricia, why she should not sit out of doors under the shade of copper beeches and elms and horn-beams, as well as in the heavy rooms of the magnificent mansion. And as no one asked, though Mrs. Hamley always took care to know, where she was, she did sit out of doors the whole day long; which was just the best thing she could have done. Had she exhausted her strength at this time she would probably have fallen ill. All she wanted was quiet and fresh air, and to be left to regain her mental clearness undisturbed by any outside influence whatever.

The poor girl bore herself with signal patience and dignity all this miserable time of undeserved disgrace; and with as signal loyalty. Knowing that her aunt disliked her going about alone, she would not have left the immediate home-grounds under any temptation. She always sat in one place in the shrubbery, out of sight but not lost, and within the range of the meal-time gong. The day when she had been late she had fallen asleep, but she never let herself be overtaken again; and even her aunt, disposed as she was to see her in an unfavourable light in which way soever she was facetted, could not but acknowledge that, without the smallest attempt to re-instate herself, she did not take a rebellious advantage of her freedom, but ordered her life with as faithful a regard to rules as if she benefited by their observance.

Mrs. Hamley almost wished she had not been so loyal. It cut the ground of displeasure from under her own feet, and made the girl's conduct about the cheque only the more inexplicable. For who indeed could understand such a strange mixture of qualities? she used to say peevishly; so good in some things, so bad in others, and so tiresome in all! Perhaps it was wrong, she would add, to wish that she should be more wicked than she was; but it would be more comfortable and more harmonious. These composite characters were trying to deal with, and gave her a disagreeable sense of unrest.

So she grumbled, as was her wont, and watched with a strange confusion of mind, half anxiously, half fearfully, for signs of greater iniquity or for symptoms of repentant subjection. And when neither came she resented her disappointment as an offence. This was one phase of mind; another was a very real unhappiness about the girl's condition—when she did not remember that she was angry. She used to watch her wistfully enough when Patricia was not looking, and ever with a heartache which neither her pride nor her anger would suffer to be seen. She noted how the healthy appetite which had so much distressed her in the first days by its unlimited appropriation of dry bread, had refined now into a sick indifference to food altogether. She saw how thin she had become, how listless in her movements, how feeble in her gait; how her once responsive face was fixed and rigid, and her once bright eyes veiled and dreamy. She sometimes longed to take her to her bosom, to scold her viciously, then to cry over her and forgive her, and consent to accept the whole affair as a mystery wherein she was not blameworthy. And then she remembered Lord Merrian, and hardened her heart like an English Pharaoh. Besides, Mrs. Hamley's temper could not brook mysteries in the minor world about her. She claimed to be supreme pontiff to whom all things should be known; and if she felt at one moment an impulse of tenderness she was able to damp it down into manageable displeasure the next when she put it clearly before her that Patricia had dared to have a secret, and to keep it from her.

In the midst of all this, Patricia's daily dress got shabby; and a letter came from Gordon.

For her own sake as mistress of Abbey Holme, also· for a certain womanliness of feeling still left for the girl amidst all her displeasure, Mrs. Hamley must keep up appearances to high-water mark. She could no more allow her niece to be ill-dressed now, in the days of her dire disgrace, than if she had been foremost in favour. She was spiritually the Cinderella of the family, seated among the ashes weeping, but her body must be clothed with decorous magnificence as befitted the mansion in which she had her place.

Wherefore one day at breakfast Aunt Hamley said in a cold voice—

"Patricia, oblige me by not wearing that gown again."

Patricia started, and looked up as if awakened from a dream. It was so strange to be spoken to again! Dora glanced up with a friendly little congratulatory smile which swept from Patricia to Mrs. Hamley, and on to Mrs. Hamley's husband in an impartial way, excluding none.

"Yes, aunt," Patricia exclaimed.

Mrs. Hamley smiled sarcastically.

"You are ready with your promises," she said. "Pray what will you wear instead?"

"I don't know, aunt," she said. "Have I any other?"

"What a question to ask!" cried her aunt crossly. "A young woman of your age not to know what gowns she has to wear! Is it stupidity or affectation, Patricia?"

"Stupidity I am afraid, aunt," said Patricia quietly.

Mrs. Hamley hesitated for a moment. The girl spoke with such touching simplicity; her sorrowful face, which had lightened up under the address, was so full of ingenuous humility; she looked so glad to be spoken to again, and yet was so little self-assertive, so unaffected, that her aunt did not know whether to call her to her and kiss her and forgive her, or scold her for being so wicked when she was so nice. She was so angry with her for her stupidity—putting herself into this miserable position when she might have made such a brilliant alliance, atoned for her mysterious crime, and done them all so much good! And yet she was so sorry for her!

Her momentary little struggle ended, however, in the maintenance of her old attitude of displeasure, so she only answered as coldly as she had spoken before :—

"Well, never mind what you have or have not. You will find a new gown in your room to-day; so pray condescend to attend a little to mundane things, Patricia; give the one you are wearing to Bignold to put away, and do not let me have to speak to you about your personal appearance again. You are going about like a cinder-wench!"

"I did not know I was shabby," said Patricia looking at her dress.

"Then you know it now," snapped her aunt.

"Mrs. Hamley has given you such a pretty dress!" said Dora pleasantly.

" I have done my best for a most ungrateful subject," said
Mrs. Hamley with her martyr's air.

" Thank you, aunty, very much," said Patricia turning a tender face towards her ; a moist-eyed face, with the curved lips
slightly quivering.

" Thank your uncle whom you have wronged," said Mrs.
Hamley severely.

" Thank you, Mr. Hamley," repeated Patricia.

" Ah ! " said that gentleman plunging and fingering his
whiskers, and not sorry to see the bonds relaxed a moment ;
for though he too was angry at the fault, he was sorry for the
person, and would gladly have joined hands over the mystery
weeks ago, and have accepted it and reinstated the delinquent ;
but the Lady was mistress, and he found it best to follow her
lead when once within the four walls of Abbey Holme.   Still
he was pleased at this little break so far.   " To return good
for evil, eh ?—heaping coals of fire ?   I told you that you were
welcome to your diet and your clothes, and I am a man of my
word.   I don't promise and when the time comes cry off, and
don't perform, do I, Lady ? "

" No, Mr. Hamley ; you always fulfil your promises," said
Mrs. Hamley ; " which is more than can be said for every one."

At this moment the butler brought in the letter-bag, which
was opened and the letters distributed by Mr. Hamley as usual,
Among them came that long-expected, long-desired ship-letter,
with its many official notifications, its signs of travel, its promise of abundance.

" For Miss Kemball," said Mr. Hamley, throwing it across
the table.

She took it.   A mist came before her eyes.   She forgot her
aunt and her late more mollified mood, Dora's pretty little congratulatory face, Mr. Hamley's ostentatious graciousness ; she
forgot Abbey Holme and her present misery and all that was
her life now—she had Gordon's letter ; Gordon was alive ; he
loved her ; he would come back for her some day ; he believed
in her and would trust her.

She held the letter in her hand, breathless while she looked
at it and took in the fact that it was really from him—his
hand-writing—paper he had touched—words into which he had
put his life ; unconscious of the cold inquiring eyes that were

looking at her, weighing and measuring, judging and condemning. She was called back from her memory of the frank, fair, honest face, the clear voice resonant and yet so tender, and bright blue eyes that had never been ashamed to meet man face to face and that would not be afraid to meet death and the Eternal—she was called back from her vision of the dear future when he should come and take her hands in his before the whole world, and lead her from darkness to light, from imprisonment to freedom, from degradation and despair to life and love, by her aunt saying in her harshest manner; "When you have quite finished staring at that envelope, Patricia ; perhaps you will attend to your uncle saying grace."

They had never had breakfast grace at Barsands ; but they had thanked God more through the day.

Then the vision faded away, and she was once more Patricia the reputed forger, or at least the guilty accomplice ; once more a dependant in disgrace ; the truth living among lies, which they had had the power to make appear the blackest lie of all.

She stood up with the rest, and walked out of the room with the rest ; but though the brief moment of the loosing of the spell had passed, and her aunt had hardened herself against her once more, and she was only Cinderella among her ashes again, she felt as if she had a talisman now which could change all things, and that even Aunt Hamley would have to yield to it.

She went into the garden to her usual seat, and read her letter. It was a long, true, and loving one ; the second Gordon had written though the first she had not received. It said all that words could say, and expressed more than it said. It spoke of courage, faith, constancy, patience, and of the reward which comes to true love in the end. It told her how she was his hope, his dream, his beloved ; but it was the letter of a man as well as of a lover, and of a sailor above all ; a sailor full of professional ardour and a not ignoble ambition, rejoicing in the life to which he had devoted himself and glorying in his work. It came like one of the old Barsands breezes into the dull and stifling fog of Milltown, and seemed to clear the horizon of her life. It roused her as nothing else could have done, and seemed to give her new energy and to bring her back to herself

and the need of action and a purpose. It was like the lifting
up of a material veil from her eyes, the taking of a weight
from her hands. She belonged not only to herself and to her
aunt, but to Gordon. Was she living now as his wife should
live? Was this dull and clouded patience under injustice the
noblest thing she could do, or was there a better way? Ought
she for his sake to remain where she was so misjudged, so hardly
punished?—or ought she not rather to withdraw herself from
Abbey Holme, and, ever keeping loyal silence, refuse to undergo more humiliation? Patience and humility are grand virtues
truly ; sweet and true Christian graces ; but the old, heroic,
pagan self-respect, which also was integral to Patricia's nature,
was a virtue too, and just now was in the ascendant. Hitherto she had proved her patience, now she must justify her self-
honour.

It was on the fourth day after she had received this dear
letter, and when she had heard Mr. Hamley say how he had
met that precious pair of Tom Noddies, the Fletchers, in the
Market-place that day, that she went to her aunt sitting in the
drawing-room as usual. with her many-coloured worsteds in
her hands, with dear Dora still busy at Venetian point and
butterflies for the hair by her own little especial table. It was
a sunless sultry day, but only one window of the room was
open about a couple of inches from the top.

" Aunt," said Patricia coming in and going up to her aunt
very quietly and with the sadness always on her now, but with
a strange look of determination in her face and manner ; " May
I speak to you? "

Her aunt looked up at her curiously.

" Certainly," she answered with a surprised kind of condescension. " What is it you wish to say? "

" I cannot go on living like this," said Patricia with quivering
earnestness.

Mrs. Hamley bowed her head.

" And what do you propose to do to alter it? " she asked.

"Let me go away," she cried.

" Willingly. Where?—to do what? "

"Let me earn my own living," said Patricia.

" Willingly again. But," with Mrs. Hamley's special smile,
" to come from heroics and generalities to common-sense details

—how do you propose to earn your own living? As a governess? What can you teach? For my own sake I cannot allow you to go out as a servant; besides you cannot wait at table, and I could scarcely recommend your honesty," she said cruelly; "and ability to steer a yacht on to the rocks, or even to ride barebacked, will not I fear get you a living. This last might indeed do for the circus; but I see no other opening. I am willing to discuss any scheme with you, but it must be a rational one."

All this was cruelly said; with intentional harshness and insolence. Patricia turned pale and her hands clasped each other with a nervous pressure. She held her breath for a moment; and then as if she had cast her anger from her as a meaner thing, raised her eyes and said with a sweet and touching dignity, a noble patience that was the maturer fruit of her former girlish cheerfulness; "I know that I am very ignorant, but I would indeed rather go out as a servant, earning my own bread by my own labour, than live like this."

"Are you so very cruelly treated here?" returned Mrs. Hamley as if asking an honest question. "Who offends you? Dora, do you do anything to offend Patricia?" Dora shook her head. "If you have any complaint to make, Patricia, pray make it. It seems to me that you are left very much to yourself and have no cause to grumble. I do not interfere with you. To be sure I would not like you to disgrace the house by any wild or wicked ways; but, failing this, I really do not see how you are coerced or what cause you have to complain."

"Ah, aunt, you do not speak as you feel—as you know," said Patricia.

"Thank you, Patricia. At my age it is not quite usual to be told one tells falsehoods." Mrs. Hamley said this with ominous quietness. It was merely an argument she was holding, not an offence she was resenting.

"I did not mean that exactly," returned Patricia; "but you want to try me. You will not come to my point, and when people do that——"

"They do tell falsehoods?" she said.

"In a way, yes," answered Patricia bravely.

Her aunt smiled disagreeably.

"Are you adopting exactly the right method to make things better for yourself?" she asked. "Shall we, for your sake and before you commit yourself farther, go back to the starting-point? What do you purpose to do if you leave Abbey Holme?"

"I see nothing now," she said with a candid throwing up of her cards. After a pause, she added, in a pleading voice—"Aunt, will you let me go to the Fletchers for a little while? I know they are at home, and I am sure they would take me."

"As a dependant?—if you please. Why not? It will be simply a change of place not circumstances," said Mrs. Hamley quietly.

"Aunt, don't!" cried Patricia in a kind of agony. "Well!" she then said, pressing her hands over her eyes, "let me go. Miss Fletcher will understand me and believe me."

Dora flushed a little, and glanced upward. She was very sorry for the necessity, but she did not exactly want Patricia to be understood. Mrs. Hamley flushed too.

"I know you love Miss Fletcher better far than you have ever loved me," she began in a level tone that soon rose to the graver accent of displeasure, and that finally deepened into anger. "Go to her if you wish it. I should be sorry to keep you. Carry your false tales out of the house, and make out that you have been ill-treated when you have only been too kindly considered. Ungrateful, disobedient, untrustworthy girl, you leave me as you came to me, a creature I have been utterly unable to improve, and, with all my kindness, as utterly unable to make love me. Not another word. Leave me, I say. If the Fletchers, or any one else, will keep you till you are of age, when I can wash my hands of you for ever, I shall thank them. Go! *Will* you go, Patricia? I want never to see you again!"

"Will you not say good-bye, aunt?" said Patricia, standing before her, holding out her hands. "I did not mean to vex you. I do not like to part in anger."

"No, I will not say good-bye," answered Aunt Hamley. "The word means a blessing. I cannot bless you. Go!"

"Aunt!"

The depth of anguish in the girl's voice made Mrs. Hamley's every nerve quiver; but she was not minded to yield to her weakness. She looked resolutely away from the pleading face, the beseeching figure, the imploring gesture.

"Not another word. Go!" she said again.

Patricia turned her eyes on Dora. Dora was crying, with a slightly scared look on her flushed face;—sincerely sorry for poor Patricia; sorry, too, for Mrs. Hamley, who wounded herself as much as she hurt her niece; hating herself and Sydney and all that had led to this miserable complication—nevertheless keeping silence.

"Good-bye Dora," then said Patricia. "Make my aunt forgive me," she added, as with a stifled sob she left the room.

The innocent scapegoat on whom was laid the burden of many sins, if ever she needed faith of the best kind it was now!

That day Patricia was driven down to the Fletchers' with her boxes. Bignold had had orders to pack up everything belonging to Miss Kemball, and the coachman took her, wondering, to the Hollies. It was very like a dismissal, he thought; more especially when he saw by the maid's astonishment that the young lady was not expected.

"A rumpus, I make it out," he said to Mary Anne confidentially; and Mary Anne thought he was about right.

"My child!" cried Catherine Fletcher as Patricia came into the room, the shadow of her former self; thin to as much gauntness as a young girl can have; depressed, strange, subdued; all her brightness dulled; her former abounding vitality gone; the whole being and manner of the brave and cheerful Barsands nymph changed as if she had been transformed—changed as a green wood is changed when a fire or a storm has swept through it. "Good heavens what has happened?" she cried in real alarm.

"Oh! Miss Fletcher, do not think me mad, but do take me for awhile! Let this be my home; I have none other!" cried Patricia flinging herself into her arms. "You are my only friends. Keep me just a little while till I can keep myself."

"Child—my dear, dear girl! what is all this about?" cried Dr. Fletcher? coming to her.

She held out her hands.

"Will you take me, Dr. Fletcher?" she cried prayerfully. "Just for a little while till I get strong and can see my way?"

His face changed.

"For life, if you will, Patricia," he answered, holding her hands in his. "Don't say, 'only for a little while.'"

"Oh, how kind you are," Patricia said, looking into his face ; "but don't be too kind to me just now—I don't want to cry."

"I should not like to see you do anything weak or silly," said Miss Fletcher gravely ; "so don't cry, but tell us what it all means."

"It means that I am in utter disgrace at Abbey Holme, and that my life is too intolerable there. I cannot go on as I am," said Patricia ; "so I asked aunt if I might come here. I felt sure you would take me for a few days ; and she was angry, and sent me with all my things, as if to live here. This was her punishment to me because I asked."

"She was quite right," said Catherine Fletcher kindly "She never did a better nor a wiser thing. She knew that she could not have made me a more delightful present if she had given me half her wealth."

"Quite right," repeated Dr. Fletcher. "I scarcely gave the old lady credit for such perspicacity. So now, missy, you are at home remember—at home for life if you will."

"But now you must hear my story before you take me," said Patricia with her eager candour. "I do not think you will disbelieve me, but it is just possible you may, and I should like you to know what has happened."

"Will it take long ? Shall I keep the carriage with the boxes at the door till you have made your confession ? or shall I walk by faith and have them carried into the blue bedroom ?" asked Miss Fletcher pleasantly.

"You had better keep them till you have heard," was the grave answer.

"As if my Patricia could do anything worthy of condemnation !" said Catherine Fletcher, putting her comfortable arm round the girl's neck and looking into her face lovingly.

Patricia caught her hand, and kept it there on her shoulder.

"You believe me then ? you will believe me, however much appearances are against me ?"

"If you say that you are innocent—yes," answered Catherine emphatically.

"And you too?" Patricia turned to Dr. Fletcher.

"I? I would not believe that you could do anything wrong if you tried," he said. "And if you were even to confess to a grave misdemeanor, I think I should have recourse to a blister on your head and a dose of blue pill. I would rather accept the theory of temporary monomania than that of intentional immorality."

She drew a long breath.

"That is comforting," she said. "It seems to heal me somehow."

Then with her hands clasped over her friend's, but every now and then turning her eyes to that friend's brother, she made her simple statement—how that she had been asked to change a cheque at the bank and to say nothing about it; how that she had done so, and had agreed to say nothing about it; how that cheque had turned out to be a forgery, for which she was held responsible because of her silence.

"But," she said with a kindling face, "as I promised faithfully not to tell, I must keep my word, whatever it costs me. I know nothing about it in any way. I simply did what I was asked to do, and I had not the faintest idea there was any wrong connected with it."

"And the person who asked you knows all that has happened since?" asked Dr. Fletcher.

"Yes," answered Patricia.

"And has made no sign?"

"No," she said; "but," nervously, "please do not ask me any questions. I want to say nothing, because I might say too much if I did. I must be true to my word."

"So you shall be, dear," said Miss Fletcher, kissing her. "We will never question you. We both believe in you implicitly, don't we, Henry? and can see how it all happened as clearly as if we had been there. So now go up-stairs and take off your things. At last I have a daughter of my own!"

"A friend to share our home, to make it bright for us and to make her own happiness in it," said Dr. Fletcher hurriedly.

"It is so strange to hear myself loved again. I scarcely know if it is pain or pleasure. It feels almost too strong for me," Patricia murmured rather than spoke, pushing up her hair dreamily.

Brother and sister exchanged looks.

"Come, dear," said Catherine Fletcher briskly, " we don't dream at the Hollies. We must have the boxes seen to, and your things put away, child ; and, now I remember, there are three or four gowns and things of mine hanging up in your wardrobe. What an intrusion ! Come, let us make haste and get all in order before dinner-time."

Her voice and manner roused the girl pleasantly. With a little laugh that had just the beginning of a natural joyousness in it, she left the room with her friend, and in less than an hour was unpacked and homed, with a delicious sentiment of rest and peace stealing like sleep over her.

When they were alone together, Catherine asked her brother ; " What do you think of all this, Henry ?"

"I think it is evident; Miss Drummond," he answered.

"So I think ; but what does it all mean ? There is a mystery beyond ; what can it be ?"

"That is just the difficulty," he said ; "but the person for whom Patricia acted was evidently ' dear Dora,' as Mrs. Hamley calls her."

"Yes ; evidently ; I always felt she was underhand."

"Tyranny. Tyrants make slaves, and all slaves are false," was his answer.

"But how cruelly they seem to have treated this poor child. How changed she is !"

Dr. Fletcher's quiet brown eyes glanced with an angry vivacity—rare in him.

"Cruelly ! They have tried to kill her, body and soul !" he cried. " As if cruelty is only physical! Why, this girl has been assassinated—murdered ! All that was best and most beautiful in her they have tried to crush out, because it did not square with their wretched, shallow lives ! Had she died under their hands it would have been substantially murder— if not legally so."

He spoke with a vehemence his sister never remembered to have noted in him before. She looked at him anxiously ; then rubbed her eyes with her forefingers, which was a trick of hers when she was puzzled. Just now Henry puzzled her immensely ; and the key to the riddle was wanting.

CHAPTER XXXVL

DISILLUSIONED.

NO other arrangement could have helped Patricia at this moment so well as this of making her home with the Fletchers. Not even the return of Gordon and the fulness of her love with him would have done her so much good—taking the phrase in its highest sense. Had he come back and married her off hand, as he would have done, she would have been intensely happy, of course ; and happiness with some natures is a fine soil for the growth of the lovelier virtues ; but she would not have learnt all she was learning now, and she would therefore have lost the spiritual richness given by the sympathy which comes of knowledge.

She was eminently purposeful in character, and she was leading now a purposeful life. And one different in kind from anything she had known before. As her uncle's housekeeper and companion at Barsands, she had had her work and her uses in a small sphere, but wholesome so far as it went ; but here and now her horizon was enlarged, and her mind gained in proportion. She was Doctor Fletcher's pupil indoors, and Catherine's companion abroad. By the one, her intellect was trained with more mastership than it had ever been trained before : and the other took her among her old friends, the poor, where she must perforce pity and was able to help. Her life was passed out of herself as it used to be at Barsands, but on a higher platform ; and the more it was dedicated to the service of others, the more her own sorrows and perplexities fell into the background and became of less magnitude and importance. She went among the poor and heard the sorrowful stories of their lives ; she saw their hard struggles with misery, disease, and debt ; and she watched their pathetic patience under their afflictions. Sometimes it was their brutish patience, the submission of "dumb driven cattle" too spiritless to wish for better things, too degraded to strive for them ; and sometimes,

it was the recklessness which grows on that sandy soil where
there is no hope—the scamped work, the filched time, the
husbands who left their wives to starve, and cared neither for
home nor duty so long as they could drink away their ill-earned
wages; the wives that were slatternly shrews who drank too,
and cast to the winds every womanly virtue and every lesson
of decent living; the mothers whose children were unwelcome
enemies, fetters and hindrances in the great battle of life, so
many extra mouths to feed out of the common stock, which
they wished the fever or the frosts would take away, and which
were taken away with at least the help of neglect if of nothing
more active; men and women whom poverty, ignorance, and
the terrible conflict in which they found themselves worsted on
all sides, oppressed by man, forgotten by God, had reduced to
the level of savages, and some to the level of beasts—all this
she saw with a burning heart; her inherent desire to be of use
breaking out with tenfold force as she came to a more accurate
knowledge of the work that had to be done. And she was of
use, and never weary. Like Catherine herself, she gave up
herself to the service of humanity and to the alleviation of
suffering. Her life was passed among the poor, with no superior
patronage demanding gratitude and submission, no fine lady
daintiness playing at benevolence for a country pastime that
went no deeper than croquet or a new costume; but as a sister,
a child, more richly endowed than themselves, and sharing her
treasures with those who had none. Reading to the sick and
to the old; taking girlish gifts of use, or prettiness, or pleasure
only, to the children; adding the grace and brightness of her
youth to the motherly prevision of Miss Fletcher; comforting
those in sorrow; helping those in need; speaking good words
of human fellowship to those who had hitherto so sorely failed
—digging down into these arid souls for the sweet waters of
conscience and self-respect, and seldom digging in vain—this
was her work now done hand in hand with her older friend.
And it made a beautiful life for her; a life full of blessing given
and received; a life wherein she grew into a loveliness of soul
and body surpassing all she had yet attained; a life which
gave back the nobleness it wrought and the happiness it dispensed, such as is ever found, no matter what the pattern of
their flag, by those who have thus consecrated themselves to
this service of humanity.

In the beautiful activities of the present she wondered more than ever at the purposeless existence of Abbey Holme ; its ladylike excuses for idleness in those eternal strips of needle-work and endless rolls of parti-coloured knitting which filled up the hours for her aunt and Dora with such a comfortable conviction of industry ; its want of depth at home or of interest abroad ; its absence of all object or intention save the mainte-nance of the proprieties and the smoothest manner of passing time. She wondered just as much now at their material ar-rangements too, as she did in the beginning ; and still more at herself, that she had lived through them for th~ ~ long weary months. How stifling it was! Those drea!ful flues which went through the house and made it all as hot as a greenhouse ; those thick velvet-pile carpets and heavy curtains and closed windows and huge fires ; those dull evenings when she was expected to interest herself in bézique which she could never understand, and was not allowed to read or employ her hands in such work only as she could do—and it was not fine work ; those dull days ; those languid, compressed, silent weeks and months ! She felt she could not have lived there at all had it not been for Dora ; and how kind Dora was in the beginning ! Kind, yes, always ; at the end quite as kind as in the beginning even when she had ruined her doing her best to make her pain less painful ! But how all that sweetness of manner had van-ished into a mere bubble of no meaning, as she found out the unworthiness underlying the real nature ! It seemed to her, looking back and reflecting, that Dora would have been less unworthy had she been less amiable ; for to Patricia, as well as to Mr. Hamley, stratified characters, part noble, part base, were distressing, and she thought that a bad person had better be bad all through than only in bits, souls that are like Dead Sea apples being apt to mislead the innocent to fatal issues.

Ah; it was a dreadful time and place to remember! like gazing back into a prison, where " an angel beautiful and bright" had come down and looked her in the face, like that angel who bewildered the poor knight of whom Dr. Fletcher read to her the sweet sad story the other night ; an angel who had made the gloom shine like sunlight while she stayed, but who had vanished one day, making the worst darkness of all ! Sometimes a horrible dread used to come over her that perhaps

z

her aunt would fall into a softer mood towards her and send for
her again, to tell her she was forgiven, and that she was to be a
better girl for the future, and copy Dora with more zealous exactness, and be sure not to tell any more stories, or have to do
with forgery or shameful secrets.   She used to wake at night
in terror, dreaming that this had happened, and that she was
being dragged back to the Abbey Holme drawing-room where
she could not find the door and where the windows were all
closed. It was a dream that always shook her nerves for days
after, and that made both Dr. Fletcher and Catherine intensely
anxious when it came, for it was a sign that had a bad meaning.
Patricia, however, could not get rid of the thought ; it haunted
her waking as well as sleeping.   She used to ask herself what
she should do if this chance came about ; and sometimes she
used to ask the Fletchers, with a clinging kind of mental terror
that distressed them even more than did her dream.   When she
did, Catherine, to cover her deeper feeling, would laugh and
promise to hide her somewhere among the rocks like an old-
world fugitive ; but the feeding would be difficult, she used to
say ; and once Dr. Fletcher, not looking up, said in a constrained
manner ; " It will be your own fault if you go ; you have a
home here for life, if you wish it."

There did not seem to be much chance, however, of this
recall. As things stood, Mrs. Hamley refused to see either the
Fletchers or Patricia. She held the one as a criminal and the
others as her aiders and abettors ; and, as she said in her note
to Patricia wherein she declined a visit her niece had proffered,
she had always made it a rule in life to give up the acquaintance of people who did wrong. She did not understand else
what difference those who honoured the Ten Commandments
could make between vice and virtue ; and as she considered
that Patricia had sinned heinously, she necessarily held that
Doctor and Miss Fletcher had made themselves parties to her
offence by taking her as they had done from under her protection, undoing all the good she had been at such pains to effect,
and defying her right of anger and punishment.

So the breach was very wide and very pronounced between
the Hollies and Abbey Holme, and Milltown had a comfortable
little dish of gossip to discuss, wherein not one of the guesses
was true and not an arrow hit the right mark. Enough was

known, however, for abundant speculation ; and the Milltown people did not neglect their opportunities.

Chief of the humble friends to whom Catherine and Patricia went with their kind acts and heartsome words, was poor Mrs. Garth doing her brave battle with misfortune single-handed, and bearing her husband's collapse as well as their joint sorrow with a steadfast courage that was as sublime in its own way as any of those deeds of heroism which have stirred the world's imagination for all time and changed the current of history. Ah, how many of these poor hard-handed, rough-speeched brothers and sisters of ours, whom now we despise as " the common people" just admitted into the outer courts of humanity will be shining angels in the days to come ; while we who wear soft clothing and walk delicately, will be turned down in the ranks and set to learn some elementary lessons of virtue far beneath their feet ! Between the Hamleys and the Garths of society lie more gulfs than one ; and the "wisdom which is conversant with God " does not always dwell with the former.

Yet how brave soever Mrs Garth was, her path was very rough ; and she felt it to be so. There was no lack of immediate means ; but the future—that terrible future troubled her greatly ; and not without reason— it was all so utterly dark ! Time seemed to work but little good for James. He was still as broken-spirited as ever ; though to be sure he had twice done a day's work for Dr. Fletcher, and it seemed to have heartened him and brought back a flash of his old cheery manhood while the impulse to be doing lasted. The worst of it was, it lasted for so short a time ; and then he sank back into the wandering idleness of his former state, haunting the lanes that looked on to Long Field Farm, and breaking his heart at every change being wrought in field or fence. If he had lost his land fairly, perhaps he would have been as brave in his sorrow as his wife ; but it was the sense of having been tricked, and tricked by Mr. Hamley above all men, that was the poison in the wound and hindered it from healing. It was madness, granted ; but it was pitiable all the same.

One day Patricia was out for a walk by herself. The Fletchers were calling at the Quest, and she was to be picked up on their way home. She had never told them why she did not care to go to the grand house, but they could imagine plenty of

reasons, if none of them the true one ; and she was therefore
left behind as a matter of course, without questions or explana-
tions. She went up by the farm on her way to meet them,
taking the lane where she and Dora had walked that botanizing day when they had met Lord Merrian, and Mrs. Garth, as the
farmyard Constance, had broken the conventional canon of fitness by railing in Doric against a rich man's injustice.

What a lifetime had passed between this and then ! She felt
as far removed from the perplexed and entangled self of that
day as she had felt removed then from the joyous Barsands Patricia who had never known a heartache and never a tear, till
that last sad hour when all had gone to wreck together. How
changed the whole aspect of life was now from what it had been
both then and in the old, old days of the dear home ! Little in-
trospective as she was, her heart was perforce turned back on
itself to-day and she could not choose but look within, asking herself how things were with her and noting where they differed from
the past. The answer was well. She was happier now than
she had been, in spite of that terrible shadow under which she
lived ; but how much graver, how much less joyous ! how the
scales of girlish blindness and unconscious romance had fallen
for ever from her eyes, and what terrible truths had been revealed to her !

Then she thought of Lord Merrian, and his strange love for
her. What was there in her, a simple country girl without
family or fortune, to attract a man in his position ? Why, nothing ! It was just a day-dream to him—no more ; his reason had
gone to sleep, and he had wandered in his dream. She remembered with a blush that one rapid thought which had come like
a vision of temptation, of the good she could do the world
through him, and the power she would have had. And then
she looked up, as if some one had been walking with her to
whom she was speaking aloud, as she thought; " But I have
found that I can do good as I am ; that we all can if we like ;
and that I need not be Lord Merrian's wife to make a few hearts
lighter and a few lives better."

The root of this thought was a miserable young couple fast
going to ruin, whom Catherine and she had visited much and
taken in hand to teach and improve, and whom they had both
taught and improved. The chief evil had been the young wife's

incapacity and the young husband's impatience; but a well-ordered home, the means whereof had been partly taught and partly given, had closed the ginshop door and made a worthy household out of a pauperized and vicious hovel. This was just one of the instances of remediable ignorance of which they so often spoke at the Hollies, where it was held as a cardinal article of faith that human lives can be redeemed if only there is energy and love enough to do it.

And while she was thinking thus she came upon the gate where James Garth usually took his mournful station; and found him standing there in the old attitude, his chin resting on his hands, staring down on the fields that had been his father's, but would never be his son's. He was so wrapped up in his own thoughts, that he neither saw nor heard her, though she said "Good-day, Mr. Garth," cheerily.

Had he still been the proprietor of Long Field Farm, she might have called him Garth, simply. As a ruined man she was careful to give the little note of respect.

As he did not hear he did not answer her; and then she drew down into the gateway and touched his arm. He started and muttered a savage oath; but when he saw who it was, he dropped his eyes, and touching his battered cap said, mildly enough:

"Beg pardon, miss, I did not know it was you."

"I thought you were coming to the Hollies again to finish that bit of garden you left half done," said Patricia, not as an opening by way of improving the occasion, but simply because she thought he had been coming; and she wanted to see the bit which the Fletchers had taken in from the field finished and made into the rose-garden they said should be called after her—"Patricia's portion."

"I have no heart for work!" said Garth more sadly than sullenly, turning away.

"Oh! don't say that!" she cried with a kind of grieved surprise in her voice; "what is life good for if we do not work!"

"Life is good for nothing now to me," he answered.

"I cannot bear to hear you say so; is that like a man?" she said very earnestly, leaning forward and looking into his face. "Why, Mr. Garth! I should have thought you would have had more courage than this!"

"It has taken the heart out of me," he said; and put his head down into his hands with the old despairing gesture.

"But surely the very good of trial is to prove our strength!" Patricia answered. "What would become of the world if we all gave way like cowards as soon as things went wrong! And we can be cowardly in mind as well as in body."

"I am no coward, miss!" said Garth, lifting up his angry face.

The word caught and stung him, not unwholesomely.

"No, I dare say you are not; I should not think you were," Patricia answered; "at least not in the usual way.. But whatever you may be in one way, you cannot say that this kind of thing is either brave or manly! It does no good. It will not give you back your farm—and even if it would, all this gloomy despair would not be a worthy kind of purchase money; as it is, it only makes you more miserable than you need be, and adds to your poor wife's troubles."

"It is well for a young lady like you to talk," said James Garth with some scorn. "A soft young lady as has never known a cross nor a strain, how can you judge for a man like myself with such a sorrow as I have on me?"

"Have I known no sorrows?" answered Patricia in a low voice. "I think I have; and very bitter ones too! I have lost all that you have, Mr. Garth—my old home where I was brought up, and where I was so happy; my uncle who was like my father and that I loved like my father; my only friend; and—more;" she added with a flushed face: "more than I can tell you. And I too, nearly broke down as you have done, but—" with the old Joan of Arc look in her bright young eyes lifted up so straight and earnest into the sullen face beside her, "I made a better fight of it than you have! I am only a girl and you are a man—a man with a wife and children depending on you—but I would have cut off my right hand before I would have wasted my time and strength and neglected every duty as you have done, just to give way to all this useless regret! It is unworthy of you; and however angry you may be to hear me say so, I feel as if I must!"

"You are a bold speaker, miss," said Garth with a dark look.

Once the sunny temper of him would have been no more ruffled by a woman's words than his flesh would have been hurt by a child's blow ; but he was easily made angry now—and for the moment looked, as he felt, like a murderer.

Patricia shrank back at his eyes ; then she seemed to nerve herself, and held out her hand.

"Forgive me if I have spoken too roughly," she said with a noble self-surrender, as if she had been speaking to a king. "But I am so sorry to see you so broken—I do so long to know that you have taken your griefs into your own hands, and conquered them as a brave man should, that perhaps I have said too much ! You are doing yourself so much harm too, in every way, and making us all so unhappy ! I want you to forgive me now if I have hurt you, but to try and be braver than you have been, all the same. You *must* come out of this trouble, Mr. Garth !—you must be a man and conquer it ! "

She spoke passionately, with a pleading look and manner that could not fail to touch any one, not a madman nor a savage, It is the power that truth and love possess ; the faith which at times removes more than the material mountain.

There was silence for some moments, he looking down, she looking at him.

"Perhaps you mean well, miss," he then said with a deep sigh, and turned away his head.

Whether he would or no he was touched ; but he did not want to yield to her. He had not taken her proffered hand when she held it out to him, now she put it into his, and clasped her fingers over the rough brown skin.

"I do mean it well." she said with a fervent ring in her voice. "Show me that you believe I do, and that you are not angry at my speaking so plainly—for after all you are so much older than I— by coming to-morrow to the Hollies. If you would only take up work again, Mr. Garth, you would conquer everything—live it all down ! "

"Wages for working on another man's property are not pleasant to a man who has been his own master, and held his own land all his life, and his father's before him." said Garth.

"But if you have not got your land any longer, wages are better than nothing, and work on any man's property is better than no work at all," said Patricia with a deeper wisdom than perhaps she knew. "Do come to the Hollies, Mr. Garth ! you know that Doctor and Miss Fletcher are as much interested in

you as if you were their brother. **I** cannot tell how you have
distressed them by the way in which you have borne your
trouble, so unlike what might have been expected from you ! "

She was still speaking with the same passion of earnestness;
pleading with the man's better self and judgment against his
lower state ; her hand in his, her fingers pressed close in her
zeal. She looked like some girl-saint preaching the truth to un-
converted ears, calling the darker soul into the higher life **As**
indeed she was ; and as James Garth felt her to be.

Her courage and enthusiasm touched the dying spark of manhood in him ; her woman's zeal woke up his pride ; her frank
friendliness lifted him back to his old state of self-respect, and
seemed to heal the wound in his sore soul ; the warm girlish
grasp did him good, as he told his wife ; and looking at her
with his hollow eyes kindly, a smile came over his gaunt face
and he said, shaking her hand :

" I'll come to-morrow, miss , I'd scarce be a man if **I** could
refuse a young lady like you who speaks so well ! "

And as they stood there, with the warmth of the moment on
them both—she to save and he to yield—the clatter of horses
came near, and Lord Merrian, riding with a fair pretty girl,
passed them at a slow pace and took in the whole scene.

They had never met since that last interview in the drawing-room at Abbey Holme ; and when they did meet now all
things were changed. Patricia was no longer the possible co-
heiress with Dora Drummond ; no longer Mrs. Hamley's beautiful niece who was worth even a young lord's looking after ;
but a discarded relative, evidently living in disgrace and as
evidently having done something to deserve it. And Lord
Merrian was no longer the enthusiastic Numa worshipping his
hidden Egeria, but the wise and far-seeing young statesman
who had just ideas on the value of matrimonial alliances, and
who had come to the rather tardy possession of his senses and
the knowledge that a Lady Maud, born in the purple and educated in the shibboleth of the aristocracy from the beginning,
would make a fitter wife for him than even a Joan of Arc who
was a heretic to the inner creed, and not quite up in the accidence of the outer observances.

Lady Maud was a good, well-behaved, placid young person,
untroubled by doubt social or religious, and who would have

condemned an original thought, either in herself or any other
woman, as dangerous and unladylike. She was one of those
who accept the present arrangements of society as final, and
who cannot understand what people find to perplex and discompose them. There are the Queen and royal family ; the
aristocracy ; the two sections of the middle classes, both the
moneyed who may be known and the professional and poor
who may not ; and then there are the common people who have
to work for all these grander creatures, and who are not of the
same human nature somehow, neither living nor suffering nor
yet feeling as the high people, and who are so horribly vulgar
and dirty ? And then there is the Christian religion, which is
the only religion in the world ; all the rest being shocking
idolatries destitute of the first principles of morality ; and the
English Church, which is the only true centre of Christianity,
every other embodiment being so absurd that the wonder is how
people can be found to believe them ; and what can folks find
in all this to make them unhappy or discontented ? Things are
as they were ordered from the beginning ; the England and
English society of this our nineteenth century being the very
perfection of God's counsels , and people are very wicked who
try to change the established order. To be sure a few Acts of
Parliament may be passed that just touch an unimportant law,
but nothing more. As for these dreadful doctrines of liberty
and all that, Lady Maud thought they ought to be put a stop
to and done something with. She believed they were all mur-
derers in heart who held them ; and could not understand any
woman, still less a lady, with such awful opinions. Nevertheless, Philistine as she was, she was a good little girl who would
make a faithful wife and a tolerably efficient mother ; who
would give recherché dinners to ambassadors and royal princes,
and would regulate her household with discretion. She had a
fair understanding, and was by no means dull to talk to if you
kept in the shallows ; but she was lost on all subjects wanting
thought, being utterly devoid of philosophic instincts, and never
seeing the cause or the outfall of any emotion whatsoever.
She was immensely popular in society, being pretty, accomplished, amiable, and with perfect manners ; and when she
caught Lord Merrian's heart at the rebound, and made it her
own, the world congratulated him on his good luck and told

him he had chosen the very girl made for him. So they were engaged with much rejoicing on all sides, and the young lord himself felt that he had chosen the better part.

As they rode along the lane, however, his head would run on Patricia to-day. She seemed very near to him, with a strange surge of memory that distressed him ; for he was honest-hearted, and did not want to have his allegiance to the lady of his choice disturbed even by a memory. He was quite content with his pretty fiancée, and had no wish to look up into heights impossible for her to reach. Still, his Egeria had been very dear to him ! She had been like his good angel— the voice which had called to him from above, and to which he had replied Excelsior— before he failed and fell.

He was a little silent as they rode between the leafy hedges. His imagination, always his strongest or his weakest point, had invested Patricia with even more than her rightful share of charm and beauty ; and just now she seemed to come before his eyes like some glorified creature, half angelic, half heroic, who would have compelled crowds to kneel to her had she appeared and spoken.

Then they passed the Long Field gate, and he saw a tall, rather badly-dressed girl, with her hat pushed unbecomingly off her face, standing holding a peasant's hand in hers and speaking to him as equals together ; speaking to him with the same love, the same passion, the same fervour as she used to show when speaking to him, Lord Merrian, a gentleman and the son of a peer.

He took off his hat as he passed and Patricia bowed too ; but the spell was broken. Henceforth Lady Maud had no need to fear the past. There would be no rival in his memory to dwarf her mental stature and pale her spiritual charms. He acknowledged his folly and the blindness of his fascination. That kind of thing would never have done ! It is all very well to talk of brotherhood and equality and helping on humanity and all that : it is a beautiful theory, and one that warms one's heart when speaking of it. But when you come to its practical confession, standing thus shaking hands with a dirty, unwashed, unshaven peasant—Lord Merrian's blue blood asserted itself then with an indignant throb ; and Patricia fell for ever from her pedestal. She was simply a handsome girl with rather low tastes and an inferior kind of manner ; and he wondered, like a child suddenly conscious that its coveted plaything was a snake and would have stung him, what they should all have done had she taken him at his word, and become Lady Merrian and his mother's daughter-in-law. What a mercy she did not ! And as he thought this he looked at Lady Maud with as much gratitude as love, and closed the Kemball episode for ever.

Soon after this the Fletchers drove up, and Patricia got into the carriage with them ; but not before she had made Garth promise again that he would come to-morrow to finish his work in the garden, and not before she had poured still a little more life and courage into the poor fellow's sunken heart.

" What an extraordinary thing, that girl to whom you bowed, shaking hands with that common man ! " said Lady Maud after a long pause.

Lord Merrian looked innocent.

" That is Miss Kemball," he said ; " niece of the people who live there," pointing with his whip to Abbey Holme. " She is an enthusiast, and goes in for communism and all that ! "

" And you know her ! " Lady Maud's face had just a shade of possible displeasure athwart its surprise. " She is not quite in your style I should think," with a nervous little laugh.

" No, she is not ; but of course I know her slightly," was his answer, made with a reassuring indifference and a wise suppression of the identity of Egeria.

" I cannot bear to see women go out of their sphere in this manner," said Lady Maud. " I think all these theories and extravagance perfectly awful. The idea of any one holding the position of a lady being so familiar as that with a common man ! I wonder how she could ! "

" Yes, it is odd to what lengths enthusiasm will carry people," said Lord Merrian simply ; and turned the conversation by a master-stroke

CHAPTER XXXVII.

HAMLEY, M.P.

THE whole country was in a fever of excitement. A fête was to be given at the Quest, surpassing in magnificence anything that had ever been done before even in that lordly domain ; and the world of Milltown stood still to watch the proceedings. All the visitable people of the locality were of course invited, and there was to be a large gathering of notabilities from London as well as of magnates from county places. A popular novelist who went into society for his raw material, and looked on a dinner as copy and a ball as a dozen pages written to his hand and only needing to be transcribed ; a handsome young poet of high renown who made love to married women and celebrated them afterwards in verse ; a sprinkling of able editors, modern Joves whose thunder-bolts tell, and whom the great ones of the earth are fain to court as the kings of the fourth estate ; and a couple of distinguished artists who lived like princes and with them—represented the aristocracy of talent beside whose glories, in the minds of some, stars grow dim and garters and ribbons are of no more value than so many yards of coloured tape. It indeed, all sorts and conditions of men were represented at this fête ; and even the industrial had his envoy in the person of a rich cotton-spinner who had bought for a hundred pounds his foreman's invention for the better winding of thread, and who, by saving fractions of farthings on the reels, had rolled up millions of pounds as the gross results.

But among all these favoured guests bidden to see the show and swell the court of the local royalties, one house was passed over ; and the Hamleys of Abbey Holme were not invited.

It was an impolitic omission ; and no one knew exactly how it came to pass. When things turned ill in consequence the Countess threw the blame on the house steward ; not ashamed, proud woman though she was, to make her subordinate suffer for her own deed. On his side the steward swore that her lady-ship had run her pen through the name when she went over the list; and that he was bound to obey a sign as much as a word.

" A signal's an order," he said ; and his hearers agreed with him that it was.

As no commission of inquiry was appointed, and the private visiting-list of the Quest was not submitted to official inspec-tion, the thing passed as an inadvertence, regrettable but by no means to be apologized for, even when the consequences be-came evident a week or so later, and the mistake in policy fructified so disastrously.

By whose fault however it might have been that it came to pass, my lady's or the steward's, the fact was undeniable ; the Hamleys were not invited to the fête, and the whole country knew of the slight. It was delightful to Colonel Lowe. It re-joiced his spirits like his morning cordial brewed of double strength, and stood for so much per centage off that terrible mortgage money which had to be paid else Cragfoot must pass from his hands like a dissolving view. It reconciled him for a moment to his hard fate in being obliged to do without the cakes he had already eaten, and to pay for the pipers to whom he had danced. It was a day worth living for, he said to his son, to see that old shoe-black slapped in the face as he de-served, and he hoped he should live to see him slapped on the other cheek before he had done with him.

"I should like to see him a beggar at my door," he said ; " and I would not give him a crust to keep him from starving."

To which Sydney answered in the manner of a rebuke : " There is no good in wishing impossibilities ; but cannot some one put a bullet through his head ? "

" Easily, my boy, if no hemp was handy," laughed the colonel unpleasantly.

" By Jove ! the old Italian society knew what it was about ; and a hired bravo is a useful kind of scavenger after all," said Sydney.

" He cleared off the vermin," answered his father, " when all other means had failed," significantly; and Sydney's thoughts went back from James Garth, whom in his heart he cursed for cowardice, to Julia Manley to whom that day at the fête he had

determined to propose. There was no help for it. It was bigamy sure enough, or would be, and bigamy was a felony; but
murder would have even more unpleasant consequences, and
between the two he took credit to himself for choosing the
minor crime. He had not chosen without long deliberation,
many qualms, and a few angry tears ; but he had chosen now,
and so must make the best of it and go through to the end.

This slight stung the Hamleys deeply. It was too evident to
be concealed, and no varnish could gloss it over. It hurt the
master of Abbey Holme in his most sensitive part—his recognised social position ; and even when he went about explaining
to every one that the reason of it was—his wife's niece had refused the offer of Lord Merrian's hand—he did himself no good
and mended matters not a whit. For the mischief of it was
no one believed him, and a few said the Quest people should
really take it up and prosecute him for libel. It was impossible that a girl in her senses, and without prospects to be called
prospects, should have refused the heir to an earldom ; and just
as impossible that she should have had the chance. Lord Merrian might have trifled with her ; they saw nothing to condemn
in that, for was not he a viscount and Patricia Kemball a comparative nobody ?—and her vanity might have taken as serious
attentions which he meant as just so much amusement ; but he
never made her an offer, they said with an incredulous intonation. It was not in the nature of things, and some one told
untruths. It was just one of that conceited fellow's brags,
said Colonel Lowe ; or the girl's own falsehood which had im-
posed on him.

Thus, though Mr. Hamley talked of it everywhere, Patricia's
lofty action gave them but a very barren kind of honour at the
best. To be able to boast of a brilliant offer of marriage refused by a wrong-headed young person—his wife's niece—who
had absurd ideas about loyalty, when half the world doubted
the statement, was a poor exchange for the actual recognition
of an invitation ; and so the master of Abbey Holme felt. He
was not a business man, accustomed to weigh the comparative
values of investments, for nothing ; and he understood as well
as most the worth of a fact over that of a word. The word
melted into air, but the fact stood like granite.

Mr. Hamley was scarcely a Christian of the kind to receive

an affront and forbear to pay it back. On the contrary, he
upheld the doctrine of an eye for an eye as the soundest ever
preached, and boasted that he had always given tit for tat in
his life; a method of proceeding quite in harmony with the
fluent good nature of the man when not ruffled nor thwarted.
He was in no wise minded now that "the Dovedales" should
escape their tit; they had to have it, he said, and he meant to
give it them, hot and strong. If he could not make them serviceable friends he would be their formidable foe; and as they
declined to give him a hand up the ladder, he would teach
them what it was to have a saw rasping their own rungs.
They wanted Lord Merrian to represent the borough, did they?
and my lady had canvassed him when she thought he would be
of use, had she? She seemed to have forgotten that now, but
he had not; and when the next election came, as it would, a
fortnight hence, they would find the course my young lord was
to walk over pretty hotly contested, and in all probability the
peer would lose what the parvenu would win. He had the
most money to jingle in the ears of the free and enlightened;
and, ballot or no ballot, local influence tells and votes are
marketable all the same as before.

So Mr. Hamley set to work at once on the plan of his campaign; and soon all Milltown was on fire again with the news
this time that Ledbury's successful office-boy was going to contest the borough with Lord Merrian; and every one said he
would win. He had large local influence, and he represented
the self-made. Though a swell now of appalling magnitude,
had he not known hunger in his day, and been ragged and
barefooted? The working classes held a kind of vested right
in him in their own minds, and regarded him as a flower from
their root, a crystal from their clay. And beside these there
were the people who disbelieve in youth and prefer maturity
without any reference to the intrinsic quality of either—people
who would rather trust the bag to a bearded Judas than to a
boy-saint with a woman's face, and to whom Mr. Hamley, as a
man having experience, was to be infinitely preferred to a raw
lad who had not even a wife to help him.

The game was by no means desperate. Indeed it looked
marvellously hopeful; and the Countess repented herself afresh
that she had listened to pique rather than prudence, and been
more instinctive than politic.

"Spite never pays," she thought ruefully; "it would have been better if I had asked them and kept that monster in good humour."

With all this encouragement the monster had fierce opponents as well; none fiercer than Colonel Lowe, who made the vote a personal matter, and resented it as an insult offered to himself if yellow was worn and not blue; and none more influential in his quiet way than Dr. Fletcher. Between an impressionable young soul full of fluid convictions, and a cast-iron mind welded through and through into wrong ones, he thought there was more chance of good from the former. Lord Merrian would probably drift into the wrong lobby on some divisions, but then he would go into the right one on others; but Mr. Hamley would be invariably wrong. If the one had everything to learn, and most of all a central idea round which his theories of life might crystallize, the chances were even between learning good and evil; but what was to be hoped from a man who had adopted finality, and perfected his views on every point, yet who had spelt all his lessons backward and learnt nothing of life but the religion of success? Wherefore, though the bustle and insincerity of an election time were not much in Henry Fletcher's way, he consented to be one of Lord Merrian's committee, not because he affected him warmly but because he wished to keep out the other. And this more than ever widened the breach between the Hollies and Abbey Holme, and gave increased tangibility to Mr. Hamley's wrath.

The campaign, though short, was sharp.

Mr. Hamley stood on the high Tory interest. He despised as trumpery palterings with great questions all the boneless liberal-conservatism of young England, he said when he addressed the free and enlightened on his nomination, and was required to give the text of his convictions. To blow hot and cold was not his motto, and whatever he was he was Thorough. The altar and the throne; our glorious institutions and our national flag; England the home of the free, and the knavish tricks of socialists and reds confounded by the high good sense of the people—that was his platform—let those find a better who could! The people's heart was good, their judgment was sound. They knew where their best interests were to be found —in the union of all classes, not in class division. They would vote then, for the man who understood them best, who had been one of them, and whose success was as much an honour to them as to himself. They would vote for him rather than for the young gentleman who had no definite policy to offer them, who knew nothing of the great questions he was setting himself forward to decide, and who would be simply so much material for clever whips and unscrupulous Ministers. To elect that young gentleman would be to confide their interests into the keeping of hands that could not hold them, to steer by a weathercock that veered with every breath. As for the third candidate, who had been sent down at the last moment as a feeler by the republicans, he, Mr. Hamley, being a law-abiding man did *not* recommend the horse-pond, but he supposed the men of Milltown would have more self-respect than to choose for their representative a friend of petroleum and the Communists; a wretch who would deluge the fair face of England with blood, and who would leave neither religion nor morality nor yet property standing.

His speeches and addresses which were written for him were effective; his showy presence also had its own value; his ready tongue, his definite views, all as positive and final as the multi-plication table, pleased many; his money did more; and his uncompromising toryism, which yet bade for the working man as integral to imperial greatness, did most of all. Milltown was conservative to the backbone; and though Lord Merrian carried many of the gentry and the more independent thinkers with him, his admixture of philosophic liberalism gave Mr. Hamley just the advantage which won the day. The radical candidate of course was nowhere. He had been sent down merely as a gauge, and his exit from the town was ignominious.

Thus the game was lost and won in spite of Colonel Lowe and Henry Fletcher; and Mr. Hamley's name came out at the head of the poll, beating my lord by some scores.

It was a proud day for him. Jabez Hamley, M.P. It was a glorious rubber in the game of bowls that had begun between him and the Quest since that memorable day of omission! Jabez Hamley, M.P., and my young lord with the influence of his name, his earldom in the distance, and the flag flying from the Quest like royalty itself at home, defeated. Who says that the working man has not the power of station and riches in his

AA

hand if he chooses! Good sense, energy, and will—and here
you see him, the richest landed proprietor of Milltown, and
M.P. for the borough!

The man's self-congratulations were inexhaustible and even
his closest adherents were weary of them. He was as if possessed by a peripatetic demon of pride and elation, and neither
street nor road was free from him. Wherever you went you
met Mr. Hamley, florid, condescending, self-satisfied ; with his
head held high and his shoulders set square ; his radiant
humour shining out all over him like a sun ; inexhaustible in
talk of the election, and what he did, and how he had beaten
my lord by pluck and energy and right views ; and how splen-
didly his fellows had fought for him, and how ill my lord had
managed everything—yes, even with my lady the countess, and
the young person he was to marry all over the shop with their
fair speeches and more tangible bribes. But pluck and energy
—" Oh ! that eternal pluck and energy ! " said Mr. Borrodaile
sarcastically, after he had listened with smiling politeness to a
full hour's declamation on the Hamley qualities as interpreted
by the Hamley intellect.

Hamley, M.P.

He wrote the name as many times as a love-sick school-girl
writes her lover's and her own. He spent all his quiet time in
devising a proper flourish, one that would replace the ordinary
scroll he had elaborated up to this time, and that should be like
an ornamental fence-work about the cherished initials. He
gave Dora a new bracelet on the occasion, with " From Hamley
M.P.," engraved in bossed and fanciful letters that looked like
flowers about his photograph, which formed the centre orna-
ment ; and he bought his wife a diamond ring, which he presented to her with a set speech that pleased the poor lady whom
long habit had rendered less critical than of old. It was a
speech in the worst possible taste, and would have set her teeth
on edge in former days ; but now she smiled in her frosty way,
and said " Thanks, Mr. Hamley, you are very kind, and I
like this token of your success." And she was, as she said,
really gratified by his gift.

Thus the Hamley sun shone bright and warm, and there was
not a shadow anywhere save one—Patricia Kemball, and the
breach existing between her and them.

As for the " cut with the Dovedales," as Mr. Hamley phrased
it, he regarded that now as a providential ordering—providence
being on his side. Had they asked him to the fête he would
have still been their humble servant, and would have worked
for Lord Merrian for the wages of their social patronage ; but
having cast him off they had made a free man of him, and an
M.P. to follow. No, there was not a shadow anywhere ; and
even Patricia Kemball was but as a mote in the sunbeam of
really no importance. When Mrs. Hamley dropped, her niece
would be wiped off the slate as though she had never been.
He had no kind of ill-feeling to her; quite the contrary ; but
she had been a mistake, and Mr. Hamley was too keen a man
of business to cherish mistakes. Things that begin with bother
end with loss, he always said, and Patricia Kemball was no exception to the rule. Wherefore he looked to her aunt's decease
as the sponge over the slate where her name stood : when he
would have no more to do with her. What else might remain
rested in his own mind only.

CHAPTER XXXVIIL

WHAT MILLTOWN SAID.

IF Mr. Hamley could afford to be philosophic and magnanimous about that " uncomfortable young person," as he called Patricia, society was less patient. After the excitement too of the fête and the election, and the odd rumours that were afloat concerning many things and people, Milltow.a wanted something special in which to interest itself, as a kind of aftermath of gossip. So it fastened on the extraordinary state of things existing between the Hollies and Abbey Holme, and made it a personal matter as to which was right and which was wrong ; the two sides quarrelling fiercely together. The fact was people could not make it out, and were angry in consequence. Why had she so suddenly left her aunt's house, they said, speaking of Patricia, and taken up her abode with an unmarried man of no nearer kinship than Adam ? Some said it was infamous in Mrs. Hamley to allow it, and others said it was shameless in the young lady to do it. To be sure, Henry Fletcher was an old fogey, and there was a sister to stand sponsor for the girl to Mrs. Grundy ; but it was a very odd position all the same. And when people talk about an odd position they mean something wrong in the background. If it is a woman who is athwart the lines, her false perspective is sure to be accounted to her as a sin ; and no one could persuade the Abbey Holmeites that Patricia was not a good-for-nothing young baggage who had done something abominable for which she had been justly turned out of doors. But what a wicked thing of those Fletchers to take her in and countenance her as they did ! It was just like them ! Look at the servants they had—that Mary Anne, quite an improper girl ; and Alice Garth, who had been dismissed from Abbey Holme at a moment's notice ; and now Miss Kemball ! It seemed as if a woman need only go wrong and be disgraceful to ensure their patronage and friendship, and it was really shameful.

So the Abbey Holmeites stormed, and the partisans of the Hollies, being few and feeble, were for the most part discomfited, having only vague charity to go upon for their defence. And this never does much good in a local slander.

Mr. Wells too had been a little incautious, and had hinted at some things and told others. He was as much in the dark as everybody else as to the truth of that forgery, and he did not believe that the young lady had done it herself. But he had no clue to her accomplice; and at all events it was too strange a secret to keep entirely to himself. People are for the most part generous with strange secrets and like to share their wealth with their neighbours, and Mr. Wells was no exception to the rule; though he was a good, inoffensive soul who picked up caterpillars and small frogs from the dusty roads and put them into the moist banks, when taking his evening rambles, and was otherwise meek and benevolent. Still, he told more than he should about that hundred-pound cheque, and he hinted more than he told. Whence it came to pass that Patricia's name got more and more into the public mouth, and that people were beginning to regard her as a scandal to the place. A society so eminently respectable as that of Milltown does not like its young ladies to be talked of. Ever on the look-out for causes of offence, and ever in the mood to imagine what it does not find, it punishes the victims it creates. As it had chosen Patricia for its present victim it assumed that she must have been guilty of something bad because she was being talked about. It is a circular kind of logic common to narrow communities; and the Milltown community was very narrow.

At last some one took heart and spoke to Miss Fletcher seriously, warning her against her guest affectionately, as is the way with people when they have put on their armour of unrighteousness and mean mischief. It was the rector's wife, Mrs. Borrodaile—chosen spokeswoman by the rest on account of her official position which gave a reflected sanctity to her warnings—who came one day to the Hollies and begged to see Miss Fletcher alone. She hoped she did not offend in her zeal, she said; but was she quite satisfied with her young friend?— quite sure that she was all she seemed to be, and as simple and good as she had once represented her? Strange reports were going about the town concerning **her. There was some dis**-graceful mystery connected with **the Bank and a cheque of** which she, Mrs. Borrodaile, had not **full particulars ; but it was** something very dreadful, and she knew quite enough **to make** her uneasy. She was a very odd young person too she had heard in opinion ; and was quite a freethinker and **all** that ; with queer notions about morality, **and the most** objectionable habits—a very unsatisfactory young **person indeed, and one to** beware of.

So the good lady sat and talked, **and stabbed a** young crea-ture's fair fame with the best intentions in **the** world ; think-ing she was performing the part of a Christian minister's wife as it should be performed, and feeling satisfied that her matronly purity and propriety were justly incensed **against** youthful iniquity.

Catherine Fletcher smiled while **Mrs.** Borrodaile spoke ; and **her** smile, though genial and pleasant, was not reassuring.

"Yes, I know all the story," she said ; which was a long shot measured **by** facts ; "and I know that Miss Kemball was used most shamefully in that transaction—used in a double sense," she added meaningly. "You can tell me nothing new about it, Mrs. Borrodaile."

"And you are satisfied you know the truth?" asked that lady emphatically. "I am very fond of young people, as you know, dear Miss Fletcher ; but I am bound to say that my ex-perience of girls is unfavourable. They are generally untruth-ful, and I would not trust one of them."

"I, on the contrary, would trust most of them greatly, and Patricia Kemball entirely," said Catherine.

"I call that simply offering a premium to deceit," Mrs. Bor-rodaile answered.

She was a woman who held fast to the doctrine of inherent depravity, and considered trust in one's fellow-creatures an heretical doctrine to be discouraged like Wesleyanism or Soci-nianism, or any other objectionable weed in the garden of ortho-doxy.

"I think if you knew Patricia you would not say this," was Miss Fletcher's answer. "I never knew so lovely a character, so beautiful a nature."

"It is very odd," said Mrs. Borrodaile crisping her lips. "If she is so charming as you represent, how was it that she could not get on with Mrs. Hamley? I am sure a more correct-minded woman never breathed than dear Mrs. Hamley; and we can judge for ourselves of her kindness by the way in which she has brought up Miss Drummond—a no nearer connection than her husband's cousin! If Miss Kemball was really so sweet, I wonder she did not manage to make things pleasanter for herself at Abbey Holme than by all accounts they were."

"If they were unpleasant, of which I have no doubt, that does not prove that the fault was Patricia's," said Miss Fletcher.

"Of course it proves nothing; but the supposition would be that it was. And at all events it is pleasanter to believe in one's old friends, people too of mature age, rather than in a young stranger of whom one knows nothing."

"I think it is pleasanter to believe in the truth," said Catherine simply, and Mrs. Borrodaile bridled.

"Well," she said rising, "it is of course no business of mine. I merely thought it my duty to warn you, and to let you know that the most unpleasant reports are going about the place in connection with Miss Kemball. This horrid Bank affair for one—her ungovernable temper, so that her poor aunt could not possibly put up with her for another—her loose opinions, so shocking in a young person!—and then this ridiculous assertion that Lord Merrian made her an offer of marriage, which she refused."

"I hear so little gossip I had not heard that before," said Catherine.

"Not that Lord Merrian proposed?" cried Mrs. Borrodaile shrilly.

"No; not a syllable of it."

"Why all Milltown is ringing with it."

"Who says so?"

"Every one."

"But who first set the report afloat, I mean? Patricia did not, I am sure,"

"Oh! I believe Mr. Hamley first mentioned it. I wonder you never heard it, Miss Fletcher! He told Mr. Borrodaile before the fête came off—so long ago as that; and said that this was the reason why Abbey Holme had been excluded from the list of invitations. So I suppose it is true. At least, Miss

Kemball must have made them believe it." This was said with
a little natural feminine spite ; for Mrs. Borrodaile had nailed
her colours to the mast now, and was determined to find Patricia faulty on one count if not on another.

" You may see how little she boasts by her not telling me,
her nearest friend, that she had had such a flattering offer,"
said Catherine.   " She never gave me the faintest hint of anything of the kind ; so she did not plume herself very much on
her conquest."

" You might say instead how insincere she is not to have con-
fided in you ; but I see that you are infatuated, Miss Fletcher,
and no good is to be done with you. However, I have performed
my duty," was Mrs. Borrodaile's rejoinder, as she shook hands
indigna. ly, more than ever annoyed with Patricia as the innocent cause of her rebuff.

Had Catherine Fletcher been more skilful—say as skilful as
Dora—she would have done Patricia more good. She would
have agreed with Mrs. Borrodaile up to a certain point, by
which she would have asserted her own sympathy and won her
informant's respect. This would have put the envoy of Milltown morality into good humour, because people like to be
successful in their work whatever it may be—private slander
or public benefaction. Then, by a cleverly-dropped word here
and a kindly suggestion there, she would have modified some of
the harsher tints, softened some of the broader lines. And Mrs.
Borrodaile would have adopted her suggestions, thinking them
her own original impulses of charitable judgment. Thus she
would have seemed to hold with the righteousness of matronly
indignation while sweetening its sour doctrine of youthful iniquity ; but this kind of thing was as little in Catherine's way
as Patricia's. By which she too failed in her possibilities in a society which cares mainly to be flattered and which dislikes to
be taught. This two-faced faculty which the world calls tact,
is that wherein the children of the generation are stronger than
the children of light, and wiser in the way of work-a-day policy.

Without a line of deception in her whole character, Patricia
was yet not a girl to talk of herself, or to tell the facts of her
life unasked. She had but few to tell, indeed. Her uncle's
death, her engagement with Gordon, and her refusal of Lord
Merrian, were the three most important items in her inventory ;

but as she had never been asked about the last she had not
spoken of it. It would have seemed to her dishonourable had
she done so. Of Gordon she had often talked ; but naturally ;
with none of the shyness, the blushing consciousness, which
betrays the girl's love-affair. Had he been her brother she could
not have spoken of him with more open affectionateness,
more confessed pride. It was this very openness which threw
her friends off the track ; so that it never occurred even to Catherine, who had the woman's keen scent in such matters, that
her child, as she called Patricia, was engaged in the formal
manner recognised by the world. And Henry Fletcher, who
had heard the name of Gordon Frere even less frequently than
his sister, suspected less in proportion.

The evening of Mrs. Borrodaile's visit the three were sitting
in the drawing-room after dinner, when Catherine, looking up
from her book, said somewhat suddenly : "Patricia, Mrs. Borrodaile has been telling me the oddest story about you to-day !
I wonder if it is true ?"

There were never any secrets at the Hollies ; so that Catherine's speaking out before her brother was neither a breach of
confidence nor an embarrassment.

" A story about me ? What can it be ?" said Patricia meeting the kind smile with one as frank.

" It is about Lord Merrian."

A sudden flush that made her face flame to the tips of her
ears was Patricia's first answer ; her second, in words, was the
natural inquiry : " What did she say ?"

"That Mr. Hamley has been telling every one the reason
why they were not invited at the Quest, when that fête was
given, was because Lord Merrian had made you an offer, and
you had refused him."

" I think Mr. Hamley ought to hold his tongue," said Patricia indignantly.

Dr. Fletcher looked at her narrowly. He was arranging a
microscopic slide, but he spoilt his object and had to begin
again.

" Then it is true ?"

"Yes," said Patricia. "But I think it very dishonourable of
Mr. Hamley to speak about it."

" You refused Lord Merrian ! It was a brave thing to do,

child!" cried Catherine warmly, her mind taking in at a
glance the whole situation, with the pressure that must have
been brought to bear on her.

"I could do nothing else," the girl answered; "I did not
love him; besides, how could I, with Gordon?"

Dr. Fletcher put down his hands.

"What has Gordon to do with it?" asked Catherine opening her soft brown eyes.

"Everything," Patricia answered with grave simplicity.
"Uncle gave me to him the night before he died."

There was a pause of a few moments.

"I did not know you were engaged," then said Catherine,
to whom the information had come rather as a shock.

"No? I thought you did. I have spoken of him so often I
thought you knew everything," Patricia answered.

"Not so much as I do now," said Catherine glancing at her
brother. "I had no idea that our country lassie had been a potential countess, or that we were some day to lose her."

"Oh, as for losing me, you will not do that for a long time!"
said Patricia innocently. "Gordon will not come home for
another year at the earliest—perhaps not for five. It all depends on the Admiralty; and no one ever knows what their
orders will be." She looked up wistfully. "The time seems
long when I think of it." she added. "I should so like to see
him again! But it does no good to grumble, and I would rather
he did his duty to the service if I did not see him for twenty
years, than shirk his work and come home to me."

"That's the right spirit, dear love," said Catharine. "Is it
not, Henry?"

"Surely," said Dr. Fletcher rather slowly.

He had taken no part in the conversation; but this was not
extraordinary. He was a silent man by nature, and it amused
him to hear his sister and her young friend talk, as they did,
every evening on all sorts of subjects, while he sat by, generally
occupied with his microscope and listening to what they said
in between his graver observations and the notes made thereon.
But though he was silent, he had become very pale during these
last sentences; a kind of greyness had stolen over his face that
startled his sister when she looked at him. It was only a
change of colour and expression. His manner was the same as

ever, quiet, tranquil, self-possessed. And when he called Patricia to come and see the little shell he had at last fixed for her conveniently, not the keenest watcher could have detected a shade of difference in his tone or bearing. Unless indeed, it had been that he was more tender to her than usual.

So the evening passed, and the conversation after a time drifted into other topics; but not before Patricia, the ice being now broken, gave as circumstantial an account of all matters as she could, which showed the springs of Mrs. Hamley's conduct in a clearer light, if not a fairer. To have been implicated in a crime of which she would not betray the real offender, and to have refused a viscount, were both together reasons sufficiently strong to account for any amount of reprobation from a woman of her nature ; and neither Catherine nor her brother wondered now at Mrs. Hamley's practical desertion of her niece—" a loss by which we have made our gain," said Demeter lovingly, when Patricia had gone to bed.

And Henry Fletcher assented and said, " yes, indeed," without looking up from his work. How that evening's conversation affected him, or if it affected him at all, no one ever knew; not even Catherine, his confidante and favourite friend. He was not of the kind to wear his heart on his sleeve for daw or dove ; nor yet of the kind to nourish impossible desires or unavailing regrets. Whether he had hoped that Patricia Kemball would have remained with them for ever as their daughter and delight, or whether he had hoped for a still nearer and dearer love, who can say ? And was it only a coincidence, the degradation of health which followed so soon on this conversation ? No one knew.

All that any one could say or see was that Dr. Fletcher was looking very ill, and had grown quite an old man lately. His hair was greyer, his leathery brown face more marked and puckered, his mild kind eyes more mournful than of old ; and these had always been his characteristics. But as he did not complain no one took much heed of him. They supposed he had been poisoning himself with some of his abominable chemicals, or chilling his poor thin blood by star-gazing when he ought to be in bed and asleep, like a rational Christian gentleman. And if he was ill he had brought it on himself, they concluded ; so shut up their hoard of compassion for some better occasion—

such as poor Colonel Lowe's embarrassments which **Mr. Hamley**
took care should now be public property, and the pity **it would**
be if Cragfoot was obliged to be sold.   For though Milltown
was content to have a self-made Colossus bestriding their town,
it did not quite **like** to see the huge splay **foot set** down **on one**
of their real gentry.   That huge splay **foot** might crush the
Garths of humanity, as many as it would, **but** society itself was
interested in the Nemesis overtaking a spendthrift born in the
local purple.   Society was just now full **of poor** Colonel Lowe
whose house was tumbling about **his ears ; so that** between him
and Patricia Kemball the Milltown hoppers **were full fed with**
grist, and tea-party tongues wagged **merrily.**

They wagged still more when it **became known** that young
Sydney was engaged to Miss Manley, who had a hundred thousand pounds at least for her fortune ; and they all said it was
the most barefaced thing of its kind they had ever known.   In
this perhaps, they were not so far out ; for the **fact of an un-**
personable young woman with a large fortune being demanded
in marriage by a man of somewhat mildewed name, when the
ruin of his house had just been made public, carries a doubtful
look with it somehow, and seems to justify unfriendly comment.

Not that either father or son cared for what was said of
them, so long as they touched the material advantages for which
they sold themselves.   When, years ago, Colonel Lowe had
married Lady Anne Grahame's daughter, and had married her
without settlements and against the wishes of her clearer-sighted
friends, the world had made pretty free with the gallant young
officer's assumed motives ; but the Colonel came in for the Cragfoot estate, and let the world play at ninepins with his motives
as it liked.   And now when his son was treading in his steps
the same kind of disfavour was repeated.   They only hoped
however, that Miss Manley would be advised by those who
knew, and have her fortune settled on herself.   She had warning enough in her poor mother-in-law that was to be, they said,
who had married in that irrational trust which possesses weak
and loving women.   The handsome young officer full of fervour
and very much in debt, with a halo of Crimean glory round his
curly head, was more to be believed, she thought, than her staid
old tiresome friends who drew gloomy pictures, and wanted to
have no end of legal straps and backstays.   She did not accept

their gloomy pictures as in any way applicable to her. Men had married for money and ill-treated their wives afterwards, she acknowledged ; of course they had ; and would again ; but Charles was an exception ; and it was absurd, she argued, to give herself to a man she could not trust with her property. In giving herself she entrusted him with something far more precious than Cragfoot ; so the two might well go together, and the estate follow her happiness. Wherefore the marriage was celebrated according to their joint wishes ; and Lady Anne Grahame's well-endowed daughter gave herself in haste and had repented for a lifetime at leisure.

And now the same thing was going to be repeated with Sydney and Julia Manley in that odd way in which events double themselves in certain families. Miss Manley was as much in love with the son as Miss Grahame had been with the father, and the ravens of ill-boding croaked their ugly prophecies in vain. She only desired to show her lover how much she believed in him and loved him ; and the resolve of a weak woman for love or spite is for the most part unalterable.

Milltown was all agog with the news ; but aghast too ; for poor Miss Manley was liked well enough in the place, and Sydney was, as we know, distrusted.

Mr. Hamley came home one evening full of the report. He waited until he had drunk his prescribed amount of claret before joining the ladies, and then he began.

" Well, Dora, that precious lover of yours has not been long before he has given you a successor," he said, planting himself on the hearthrug, and speaking with a kind of contemptuous jocularity, which was not his most becoming manner.

" What do you mean, Mr. Hamley ? " answered Dora innocently.

" That precious scamp, that young Lowe, has engaged himself to Miss Manley ; and the fool is going to marry him."

" Indeed ! " cried Dora, who just then dropped her book and had to stoop rather a long time before she could pick it up again.

" Yes, I think it is, indeed ! when such shamelessness takes place before one's eyes. He has taken her for her money, that's as plain as the nose on one's face ; and that's why he wanted you," was Mr. Hamley's answer.

"You are not very complimentary, Mr. Hamley," said his wife. "I had no more wish that Dora should be his wife than you had, but I would not say so rudely as you do that he wanted her only for her dower. Dora and Julia Manley are not very much alike, I think!"

"You dear!" purred Dora. "You are always so good to me! But Miss Manley is a great deal better than I am, and perhaps Sy—, Mr. Lowe, does really like her."

Let those explain the contradictions of human nature who can. Dora did not want to go away with Sydney, and she was sorry for his distresses; she did not want to share his poverty, nor indeed did she wish him to be poor at all; she repented her own marriage with him; she was even ashamed of it now that the first excitement had worn off and she had realized the difficulties and dangers of her position; yet with all this, when she heard that Sydney Lowe was really engaged to Julia Manley, she was almost choked, partly with rage and partly with tears, and could scarcely command herself to speak in her usual tone and manner. Nothing but the deadly fear of discovery, with Mr. Hamley's small keen eyes watching her so narrowly, could have nerved her for her part; but power comes when it is needed, as it came to her now in calmness and self-control.

"I grant all that, Lady," Mr. Hamley answered. "I am not fool enough to place such a cart-horse as that Manley woman and our little Arab here in the same harness; but it looks fishy all the same——"

"It looks what, Mr. Hamley?" interrupted the slow, severe voice of the wifely critic.

He laughed, and shifted his feet noisily.

"A lapse, Lady, a lapse," he said. "Well, then, it looks doubtful when a young man pretends to be broken-hearted for Dora one day and makes up to Miss Manley the next. It looks more like money-bags than love, I must say. For my part," with an assumption of patriarchal experience, "I cannot understand the young fellows of the present day. I am a man as doesn't change myself, either in my admiration for the ladies, or in my sentiments elsewheres. The lady as I have loved once I should for always, and I don't understand this game of skip-jack—one down and another up before you can say Jack Robinson. I think that's the way to do, isn't it, Lady?"

He spoke to his wife but he looked at Dora; and Mrs. Hamley smiled and said yes, she approved of his fidelity. It was one of the virtues she always had admired in him, and she hoped she should have reason to admire it to the end.

Not much more was said at the time of this projected marriage, and Dora escaped the detection of her secret with her usual cleverness; but when Patricia heard of it, she startled the Fletchers by a curious outburst of anguish and terror, which they had some difficulty in calming. She would not say why the news so powerfully affected her; not even to Catherine, from whom she had not a thought unshared. She only looked white and scared, and said, " No, no, it ought not to be," and " it must not be," weeping hot heavy tears, and falling back again into her old position of self-torture—not knowing whether to tell what we know and so prevent further evil, is the right thing to do, or to keep silence in the presence of sin, and by silence to consent with sinners, may not be at times the truest good. Catherine comforted her as well as she was able, but she could not console her entirely; for, to which side soever she turned, she found grief and perplexity and one form of moral evil. Do what she would she could not keep herself pure nor hold her action harmless.

While she was sitting there doing her best to face her difficulties bravely, the Hamley carriage dashed up to the door, and a note was brought in to her from Mr. Hamley desiring her instant presence at Abbey Holme. Mrs. Hamley was ill. Had it then come at last? Patricia thought, as with trembling hands she threw on her hat and jacket. Had her aunt discovered the whole thing, and was she to be assoiled and reinstated?—taken back to favour, and perhaps taken back to the house? she would be glad of the former; but the latter?

As she turned to go she threw her arms round Catherine with a feverish grasp.

" Whatever happens we are always friends together, as we are now?" she whispered. " You will not give me back to them?"

" No," said Catherine kissing her fondly; "you shall not go back to Abbey Holme, my love, save at your own desire."

"Then that will be never!" cried Patricia with a shudder, as she got into the carriage and was borne away—borne away to this house of falsehood and fair-seeming, where nothing was as it looked, and where evil was accepted for good and deception for truth.

CHAPTER XXXIX.

THE LAST LOOK.

MRS. HAMLEY'S health had long been declining. She was one of those lean and ascetic women who, with a *cordon bleu* in the kitchen and all sorts of cometic vintages in the cellar, eat dry toast for breakfast and drink plain water for dinner. She gave one the impression of being only half-nourished and always insufficiently clad ; a woman to whom the senses were things accursed, and who kept her luxurious table and wore her magnificent clothes as matters due to her position rather than as personal indulgences in which she took pleasure-obligations for the pride of life, not delights for the lust of the flesh.

This last year had tried her severely. Ever since Patricia's arrival she had been more or less disturbed in mind, and her frail body had suffered in consequence. The last three weeks had put the coping-stone to her troubles. That her niece should be implicated in a crime which she refused to confess, that she should have thrust aside the providential settlement offered to her, and lastly, that she should have preferred the Hollies to Abbey Holme, and Catherine and Henry Fletcher to herself and her husband—all this was too much for her. Add to this the excitement consequent on her husband's election ; the breakfasts she had to give, the luncheons, the dinners, at which she must preside ; the uproar and confusion introduced into her well-ordered household ; the bodily fatigue and mental excitement she had to undergo ; and it was small wonder if, lying awake all night and fretting all day, now resenting Patricia's absence from their unusual festivities, now resenting those festivities themselves, exhausted and feverish, her health went down as Mr. Hamley said "with a run." Her scanty bit of dry toast grew smaller at each breakfast, her temper more uncertain. She was evidently very ill and profoundly wretched : but she would not allow them to send for Dr. Wickham, nor would she recall Patricia. She would own to nothing but fatigue and the east wind; and had it not been for dear Dora, she used to say, she did not know how she should have survived either.

Dear Dora was everything to her. In truth, the girl was sorry to see her suffer, and desperately frightened lest she should die. Her death would indeed be shooting Niagara, with that terrible "and after?" to follow. She was perfectly aware of the contingency it included; indeed she had known it for years; and though she had encouraged it when it suited her purpose, the knowledge of what had to come when Mrs. Hamley's death should leave Mr. Hamley free, had perhaps had something to do with the ceremony in which Mr. Sydney Lowe had been the principal performer more than a year ago behind the New Road caryatides. But though Mrs. Hamley's death would always have been a terror and a trouble, it was doubly so now when Sydney's engagement with Miss Manley was made public, and she could not claim even such slight protection as a confession of her love for him might have given. Would she have had courage for that, had she been able? Look where she would the waters were closing rapidly round her, and she saw no way of escape to the right or to the left.

Dear Dora was intensely unhappy at this time; terrified and distracted; and her own secret sorrows gave her such a delightful appearance of sympathy—as much from an instinct of self-preservation as from her natural amiability she attended on Mrs. Hamley with such unremitting care, so deliciously unobtrusive yet so full of thought and charming management—that, with the propensity there is in human nature to round off characters harmoniously and to find velvet coats without seamy sides, no one who had seen her at this time would have believed that a girl, so sweet and full of thought for her dying friend, was able at the same time to be so false and base.

Day by day Mrs. Hamley had grown worse and drawn nearer and nearer to the Great Hour. She had no perceptible ailment that could be catalogued. Weakness, loss of appetite, loss of sleep, frequent faintings, a gradual decay—that long slow death of which the stages are so many before the last is reached, and passed—these were the symptoms and the root of her malady. There was nothing special to combat in all this. The machine was wearing out; that was all; and she knew it. She had a

BB

tough spirit and had always made a good fight of it.   In poverty
of circumstances as in distress of mind she never showed what
she suffered, save by increased acerbity of temper.   She was
peevish in affliction, but she was grim and determined.   Even
now she had not given up till forced to do so.   She had come
down punctually to breakfast, and read the prayers in her
quavering treble, though she was obliged to yield so far to her
weakness as to sit during the office.   She had poured out the
tea to the last with her frail and shaking hands that could
scarcely lift the massive silver pot, both together ; and she had
had her poor old face and head dressed with her usual care and
precision.   It was painful to see the unnecessary struggle that
she made.   If only she would have consented to her state, and
been a comfortable unpowdered and unsightly goody wrapped
up in flannel without beads or bugles, lace or ribbons about
her, how much better it would have been, dear Dora used to
think ; while she said sweetly, to please her : " What a pretty
cap that is, dear !   Bignold certainly knows how to make
caps."

At which Mrs. Hamley would smile complacently, and think
she was masking her batteries and fading cleverly.

And all this time she was fretting about Patricia.   Too
proud to yield to her inward wish for a reconciliation, or to
write telling her to come and see her, she was angry that the
girl whom she had repulsed so severely did not again beg for
grace, divining the moment when it would be granted.

"She must know that I am ill," she used to think, half between tears and anger.   "My own flesh and blood—my only
relation to whom I have been so kind, a very mother—to treat
me with such ingratitude, such heartlessness !   It is her evil
conscience.   She knows that she has sinned, and she is ashamed
and afraid to see me."

So she thought, lying awake during the long watches of the
night, tossed between her secret consciousness of Patricia's innocence and her determination to find her guilty for her own
self-justification ; growing weaker day by day ; more harassed
night by night ; till at last the moment came when her will
had to go down before disease, and when she must perforce
keep the bed from which she could not rise.

Then, and not till then, she desired that Patricia should be sent for ; she not having heard of her illness, and to whom Mr. Hamley's hurried note : " Miss Kemball, return with the carriage if you please ; Mrs. Hamley is ill and desires to see you," was scarcely sufficient preparation for the terrible change she found.

Propped up in bed, her hair restorers, pads and braids, laid aside with her smart dress-caps, and her scanty whitened locks pushed off from her pinched and sallow face ; her eyes sunk in her head ; her thin lips, black and dry, drawn back from her teeth ; her body wasted ; and her hands idly plucking at the sheet—Patricia, suddenly ushered into the presence of her aunt —into the presence of death—could not at first realize what she saw. It was like something unreal ; a picture, or a dream. She could scarcely believe that that formidable power of whom she had been so often afraid should be lying there, a poor weak helpless thing appealing only to human pity and dependent on compassion for every act of her life ; her arbitrary will set aside ; her autocratic power gone ; nothing left now but the bare bones of humanity. It was very terrible to her ; a sudden reversion of conditions—she so strong, and her aunt who had mastered her so weak—that made her feel almost cruel and undutiful.

She could not repress a grievous little cry as she came up to the bed, and took the wasted hand that moved feebly across the sheet towards her, saying as she carried it to her lips, " I did not know that you were ill, darling aunty ; no one told me till this moment."

" I thought you might have come to see me, Patricia," said Mrs. Hamley with feeble reproach.

" If I had only known that I might, I would not have waited to be sent for," she answered tenderly.

The dying woman looked up.

" In spite then, of your wickedness, you feel that you owe me some respect ? " she said.

Had she been in her ordinary state her severity of accent would have chilled and checked Patricia ; now her assumption of moral superiority was almost tragical from its impotence.

" I only wanted to love you with my whole heart. Oh, let me hear you say that you believe me ! " Patricia said earnestly, her honest eyes full of tears.

" I dare say you did," Mrs. Hamley answered after a pause ; " I did not see it, but I am willing to believe it—now."

" I never meant to offend you, aunty dear, at any time. I have been ignorant and clumsy, I know ; but I always wished to do what was right," said the girl kissing her hand.

" But you did what was wrong instead," Mrs. Hamley answered, looking up with that strange and awful death-bed scowl which seems more like demoniacal possession than human anger.

Patricia shivered as she met her look, and shut her eyes for an instant ; then, as if she put it from her, she said :

" Yet indeed I tried hard to satisfy you, dear, though I failed."

" Yes, you failed—you failed," repeated Mrs. Hamley, half closing her eyes.

" I know I did, to my bitter sorrow ; and I never understood how nor why," returned Patricia, bending over her with an earnest caressing gesture, as if she would have taken the poor sick head to her bosom, and given some of the fulness of her own life to the fast-ebbing stream pulsing each moment more faintly in those shrivelled veins.

" If you are sincere in saying that, tell me the truth about the cheque," cried Mrs. Hamley suddenly, with a quick flaming up of her old angry tenacity.

Patricia looked across the bed to where Dora stood, distressed truly, but self-possessed and fully alive to the danger of the moment. She had not braved all the perils which had surrounded her for so many months to yield now to an impulse of weak compassion or puerile conscience. She was sorry for both Mrs. Hamley and Patricia, but she would be more sorry for herself if things were different. Hard as it was on both that the one should die deceived, and the other be condemned while innocent, it would be harder she thought, on herself, if the mask which she had worn with such success should be taken off now at the last moment, and the labour of a life be undone.

" Dora, help me !" cried Patricia in an imploring tone.

Dora looked at her steadily.

" I cannot help you, Patricia," she answered. " I know nothing about it—you know that I do not," emphatically.

Patricia covered her face. It took all her strength and
loyalty to stand up against the agony of this moment, to bear
this terrible burden. That her aunt should die believing this
grievous falsehood true, believing Dora pure, and ignorant of
the awful chapter of further crime contemplated and announced,
was of itself sorrow enough for a sincere nature; but also, unselfish as she was, it did seem hard that she should be forced
to sacrifice the appearance of honour—the thing which was
dearest to her in life—for the reality, in maintaining the false
repute of another.

The dying woman plucked her feebly by the sleeve

"Tell me," she said. "Why do you trouble Dora about
it?"

Patricia lifted up her face, pale, quivering, but steadfast.

"I cannot tell you aunt," she said in low distinct tones "I
have promised faithfully that I never would, and I have not got
leave to break my word. Only believe that I was innocent in
the whole matter—oh believe that, dear, for it is true!"

Her aunt gave a pathetic little sigh. She was too weary, too
weak to combat longer. She must resign herself to defeat.
Undutiful and self-willed even at this supreme moment, she must
leave that stubborn spirit now to its own hard course. She had
done all she could; and life was fading too fast for struggle.

She turned her wan eyes to Dora. It was rest to her to look
at the soft-flower-face she knew so well and loved so dearly!—
the face that had been, to her fancy and belief, like an open
book of which she had read every page from end to end! It was
her haven, her comfort; and yet, with the natural sense of family, she regretted even in this her last hour that her own niece
had not been as dear and good as her husband's cousin, and had
not been able to at least share in the love she gave so freely to
this.

"God bless you, my child!" she said in the gasping, interrupted utterance of the dying. "You have been my comfort
ever since you entered the house. You have made me happy."

"I have loved you, dear," said Dora, laying her soft hand on
the fleshless fingers.

Mrs. Hamley smiled faintly. "Take care of her, Mr. Hamley," she said; for Mr. Hamley had just entered by a side door,
and now stood by Dora.

"I will, my dear—I will," he answered **fervently, and put** his arm round his young cousin's slight figure, **drawing her close** to his ample chest.

"She deserves your fatherly care," **said Mrs. Hamley.** "I leave her to you. God bless her! God bless you, **Dora!**"

Dora sobbed, and Mr. Hamley pressed her to him tenderly. Tears were in his eyes too. The woman who was dying there before him had been his true friend, if never his beloved. Though she was leaving the way open for the happiness he had waited for so patiently and defended so jealously, still she had been staunch and loyal in her day. And then his very tenderness for Dora made him pitiful for his wife, just as his natural emotion for her death made him yet more loving to Dora.

"Don't fret my darling, I will take care of you," he said in a low voice.

Mrs. Hamley looked pleased.

"Right," she whispered. "Be her father—take care of her."

"Have you no word for me, aunt?" cried Patricia with the passionate cry of the Esau unjustly defrauded. "Bless me too!"

There was a pause. Mrs. Hamley looked at her niece wearily, sternly, sadly.

"God forgive you, and turn your stubborn heart. I forgive you," was then her feeble response made with an effort, and again her eyes turned to Dora. "God bless you, my Dora!" she murmured.

No other word was spoken. The evening sun **streamed** into the room and showed the pallid face of the dying woman; Patricia's silent agony, yet clear of self-reproach; the grief, the fear, but the self-control that comes of the very need of terror, of Dora; the subdued and decent regret of Mr. Hamley divided as he was between pity and love, regret and relief. The silence was broken only by the harsh rattle of the labouring breath growing harder, slower, at every instant; by the stifled sobs of the onlookers gathered there to watch but unable to help; when suddenly Mrs. Hamley opened her eyes. It seemed as if she saw something beautiful in the air before her, for a smile, softer and more divine than ever had been on her face before, irradiated her whole countenance. She half raised herself from her pillow, turning towards Patricia. The last spark of life blazed up in her eyes with a sudden vividness that burnt more like

fire than human life. She could not speak, though her dry lips
moved ; but her look fastened itself on the girl with a yearning
and intense desire, a passionate longing that was as mournful as
a cry.

Patricia stooped over her and took the half-raised body in
her arms.

"What is it dear ?" she said. "Do you know me now ?"

The face that looked into hers was scarcely Aunt Hamley's
face at all : it was that of a creature divinely illumined, brightened with more than human knowledge, burning with more than
human love. It lasted only for a moment ; but that moment
seemed an eternity, during which her very soul had looked from
her eyes into Patricia's. Then her head sank back on the girl's
arm, her glazed eyes turned, her jaw dropped, her laboured
breathing ceased ; and she was dead. But she died in her niece's
arms and her last look had been hers.

Patricia laid her head reverently on the pillow, and with a
strange superstitious feeling kissed her mouth for the faint lingering breath that might be about her lips.

Mr. Hamley stretched out his large hand and closed her eye-
lids.

"Thus die the just," he said with pompous solemnity ; while
Dora drew a deep breath as one who has safely skirted by a
danger, though the next instant she slightly shivered, knowing
what was before her.

To Patricia the world felt wider and darker somehow now
than it had done this morning. Her last relative had gone, and
she remembered with a pang of self-reproach—how base it
seemed !—her terror lest her aunt should send for her to live at
Abbey Holme again, and once more plunge her into the old life
of misunderstanding and "consenting with sinners." If it
could have brought her back again how willingly she would
have returned to the stifling air and unwholesome morals of
Abbey Holme ! If her own sorrow could have ensured that
poor dead soul's peace, how gladly she would have paid the
price ! But the door was closed and the seal set for all time
now ; and as the past had been so must it remain for eternity.
She could only hope that what had been wrong here was made
right there ; but for this world all was over.

Yet it was cruel. Dora blessed and loved and thanked, and

Dora the cause of it all! Dora who had lived a life of deception from the first, who had simply offered a manner for a
reality, a facile temper for a heart, and falsehood for truth ; and
she who had failed—she scarcely knew why, but surely not for
want of trying to succeed by faithful endeavour—yet she was
simply forgiven and Dora was blessed! She wished her aunt
had blessed her too. She was glad of that strange loving look;
it seemed to soften the hardness of the last word, and lessen its
injustice ; but she wished that she had blessed her? She had
not forfeited this holy consecration of death ; she had been
loyal to her promise, but in her loyalty she had not injured her
aunt, and she had done nothing to make her unworthy of her
blessing. It had been a less sorrow to believe her, Patricia,
guilty of some mysterious misdemeanor than it would have been
to have known Dora's life of deception and falsehood. She saw
no different way of action for herself had she her time to come
over again ; unless indeed she had suspected Dora from the beginning, and refused to do the service asked of her. But still
her thoughts went back to the central point of her sorrow at
this moment; she wished that her aunt had blessed her—that
she had spoken just one comfortable word of love and trust before the time for speech had passed for ever!

Presently Mr. Hamley spoke.

"Your dear aunt has died forgiving you," he said to Patricia.
his arm still about Dora ; "so do I."

He held out his hand over the bed, and Patricia, waking up
from her dreamy thoughts, put hers into it. It was like a com-
pact across the dead.

"Thank you," she said simply.

She knew he meant well, and she accepted his meaning in
lieu of the right. They shook hands solemnly ; after which
Patricia stooped down and lovingly kissed the white still face
on the pillow. Dora and Mr. Hamley kissed it too, both with
a certain shudder ; and then they all went down into the drawing-room, when Patricia prepared to go.

"Must you leave now?" said Mr. Hamley, meaning to be
kind. "If you must you must ; but remember that Dora will
always be your friend."

He said this as if he had offered her a coronet.

Patricia did not answer. She looked at Dora hurriedly, not

wishing to draw suspicion on her, and indeed on her own account not caring to look at her longer or more narrowly than was absolutely necessary.

The fair downward-bended face had a look on it of such abject terror overmastering it for a moment, as humiliated Patricia to see. How would she act now? Dora thought. Her silence during Mrs. Hamley's lifetime had been always sure, but she did not feel so certain of it now. There was this marriage with Miss Manley publicly talked about: would she keep her counsel faithfully even through this? But what of the future? When she too had heard that word which had to come, what would she do? Would she lift up her voice and cry aloud, and, to prevent the commission of a sin, tell all she knew, and so dash her former friend headlong to destruction? or would she still keep loyal silence and consent with sin and sinners for the sake of truth? This was why she looked so terrified that it touched the braver heart with a sense of shame and shared humiliation to see it.

But Patricia was far from suspecting the truth of Mr. Hamley's feelings or Dora's cause for fear. She, like her aunt, had no other idea but that of a fatherly affection on his side and a filial love on hers; and as for Sydney Lowe, she supposed that now, Aunt Hamley being dead, Dora would come forward openly and prevent the illegal marriage of her husband by taking up her own publicly. She was sorry for her too, all things considered; and notwithstanding her own griefs against her would not have added a feather's weight to her troubles.

"I hope you understand that it will be a good thing for you to have Dora as your friend," Mr. Hamley went on to say. "Dora will have a large amount of power in her hands; she will be mistress of Abbey Holme, and you will want some one to stand by you. Dora will stand by you. I make bold to say so much. You make her your friend, and all will come out square."

"Thank you, but I shall not ask her for her help," said Patricia hastily.

Dora looked up, but over her head, not into her face. She avoided Patricia's eyes as she spoke.

"I will always be glad to help you, dear," she said sweetly. "You are *her* niece; and this kind, good friend," turning to

Mr. Hamley and looking at him with shy affection and covert and most delightful consciousness, "this dear friend has always wished you well and been good to you. I can do nothing better than carry out his wishes."

'I do not know what you mean exactly," said Patricia with a certain stately bearing, drawing herself away. "I want no help of any kind, and what I want more than I have I can work for. The greatest good that you could have done me, Dora, before she died, you refused ; I want nothing of you now !"

" You take high ground, Miss !" said Mr. Hamley with an annoyed air.

" I mean nothing offensive, but I can accept no favour at your hands, Mr. Hamley, nor at Dora's," said Patricia.

" You need not be afraid. Affairs will be properly conducted, and not the most particular-minded person, as I call it, will have a word to say," put in Mr. Hamley hastily.

He took it that she knew his heart and mind, and that she resented his intentions. And for a moment the thought flashed across him whether " that tale of Gordon Frere was all a bam, and had the girl taken a liking for himself? She had always been uncommon good to him, and more unlikely things had happened."

" I am sure you will do all that is right," answered Patricia, believing him to mean the funeral, or the disposition of his wife's property to Dora, or something else in the way of business, she did not know what ; "but Dora knows quite well why I would not accept a favour from her, and why now that poor aunty has gone I have no place here and never shall have again."

" My goodness ! Patricia, I know nothing of the kind ! I have not the least idea of what you mean !" cried Dora roused to unusual energy of voice and temper by the imminence of her peril.

" Dora ! how can you carry on this awful thing with what I know, and you know too, and with what we have just seen !" cried Patricia pressing her hands on her heart.

" What the dickens does the girl mean ?" cried Mr. Hamley looking at her in a curiously embarrassed way.

If it was what he thought, her sentiments, though flattering and predisposing him to generous treatment and kindly judgment, were decidedly in the way at the present moment, and he wished her to understand as much.

" I have not the remotest idea," said Dora sternly. Then
in a low voice she added, " Our poor dear thought her mad,
and I do really believe she is."

" It loo... .ike it." he answered in the same key.

He went up to Patricia, and took both her hands in his,
speaking to her in that peculiar way in which people speak to
maniacs—rather loud, in an artificial voice, every word staccato
and distinct.

" Yes, yes, Dora knows all about it," he said wagging his
head in a soothing manner. " Dora quite understands it all—
you hear ? she quite understands what you mean ; so go home
now like a good girl, and tell Miss Fletcher to put your feet in
hot water   It will draw the blood from your head. Bad
thing, blood in the head, my dear," pointing to his own forehead
with his forefinger ; " hot foot-bath will do you good."

" I don't understand you," said Patricia looking at him in
blank amazement. " What do you mean ?"

Mr. Hamley rang the bell.

" Jones," he said when the man entered the room, "is the
carriage waiting "

" Yes, sir," answered Jones.

" Now my dear Miss Kemball, let me send you to your
friends," said Mr. Hamley graciously. " Jones tell Bignold to
put on her bonnet and escort Miss Kemball to the Hollies.   I
do not like her to go alone, Mrs Hamley did not like her to go
alone," with a sudden sigh. " She might do herself a mischief,"
in a whisper to Dora.

And Dora answered, " Yes.   It is better to send Bignold."

How lucky it was that she thought of making Patricia mad !
Whatever she might say now Mr. Hamley would not believe
her, and if she said too much she could easily get her locked
up.   Only the ravings of a diseased brain taking the false impressions characteristic of disease and accusing those who are
the nearest and dearest of impossible crimes ?   It was a happy
thought, and she was infinitely relieved by it ; though indeed
she was not cruel or hard by nature, only driven into both
cruelty and hardness by fear and falsehood.   And when she
thought of getting Patricia locked up in a lunatic asylum if she
told too much, she felt something like a person who is being
fast surrounded by the tide, when he suddenly strikes on a path-

way up the cliffs which he had not known nor foreseen, and whom it would but little discompose if he had to fling down an unoffending sheep or lamb that stood in his way and made his escape else impossible.

Patricia at first refused both Bignold and the carriage ; but when Mr. Hamley insisted so strongly that her refusal became contentious, she yielded, and suffered him to take her out to the door on his arm, as he had brought her in just about a year ago. As she passed through the hall she gave one sudden sob as if her heart would break ; and Mr. Hamley patted her hand affectionately. The new idea that had taken possession of him was flattering, if inconvenient ; and he felt that he could afford to be compassionate to the poor soul. Then they shook hands together, and he was really quite tender to her ; so much so that she wondered at it, and the servants wondered too ; as he assisted her into the carriage, and so sent her back to the Hollies in state, and guarded. She little suspected however that the former maid was her present keeper, and that she was regarded by Mr. Hamley on the one hand as a lunatic, dangerous to leave alone, on the other as a poor dear unfortunate young woman who had contracted a not unnatural but wholly unreturnable affection for himself.

" And now," she said, after she had told her friends how her aunt had died—told them too with many tears of that strange earnest look, and how she seemed to feel in it that the poor darling had at the last moment recognised her innocence, and what a comfort it was that she had died actually in her arms—when all this was told, " and now," she said, " we must come to some understanding about myself. I did not mind staying here so long as poor aunt lived—somehow it did not seem like fastening myself on you because, I suppose you could have sent me back at any hour when you were tired of me. But now it is different. I cannot live on you for ever ; I must do something for myself."

" Nonsense !" said Henry Fletcher.

" Henry is right," said Catherine. " Besides my dear, to take up your own point, you cannot do anything that will keep you. No one who has not a specialised education can make a reasonable income ; and so few women have a specialised education ! You, my darling, certainly have not."

"But I can learn something," said Patricia a little vaguely.

" We must first of all arrange what you can learn, and what you can utilise when learnt," Catherine answered, as if arguing a possible point.

' You know how much I love you both," said Patricia tenderly, as she returned to the charge. " You know I came to you like your own child when I was in trouble ; but how can I go on living here, perhaps for years, till Gordon comes home and is able to marry me ? I am sure you must both feel it would be better and nobler to do something for myself."

"So it would, if we were not ourselves," Dr. Fletcher said. "If you were with any one else, I would counsel you to go out into the world and be industrious and independent ; but not from us. We love you too well," he added, looking at her quietly.

" Patricia," said Catherine glancing at her brother. " I am going to tell you something ; something about myself that you have never heard. Henry knows it all, so it is nothing that will shock or startle him. Long before you were born, long before your father married, he and I were friends—the dearest friends ! My darling, he was the only man I ever loved ; and at one time he loved me. But then," she added hastily, " he had not seen your mother. Still, we were friends and lovers in earlier days, and but for a mere chance we should have been married. And does not that give me a certain claim to be your pro-mother now ?"

Tears stood in her eyes, and the round, soft matronly cheek was pale while she spoke. A woman's heart never grows old, and the love which, by long years, has become a habit of remembrance and is no longer a present influence, has nevertheless always the same power to move her when spoken of. Catherine Fletcher's love had been very true and very deep. It had saddened her life for many a long day ; and, for all that it was a thing of the past now, and she was entirely happy in her life, for all that she was a childless old maid and her only love had married and died so many years ago—she could never speak of him without tears. The habit of remembrance was the habit of sorrow too ; and deep down in her heart was that everlasting spring of grief which, however closely it might be covered up, would never run dry. Ah ! the graves we all carry about with us ! the sorrows that time only scars over and never heals !

"Then uncle knew it !" cried Patricia, as she suddenly remembered her uncle's look when Gordon was speaking of Mr. Fletcher the solicitor, and how he had mentioned " bonny Kate" so kindly.

"Yes, I have no doubt he did ; what there was to know, which was not much," said Catherine. "He and your poor father were very fond of each other, and trusted each other entirely, though they were so different in character and your uncle so much the older of the two. But now I think the question is settled. You will look on me as a kind of step-mother, Patricia ? They are not all as bad as the fairy-books make out. I think I have known one or two who have been faithful, and who have deserved the love they gained."

"Yes, you are my mother !" cried Patricia, throwing her arms round Catherine's neck with a passionate burst of self-surrender ; "and I will be your daughter, now and for ever. This is home, it is not dependence !"

"Now you are a good girl and a wise one," said Henry quietly ; while Catherine, crying too, for the silly sympathy of tears to which even strong-hearted women yield, could only kiss the dear young face that was resting on her breast ; and call her " daughter " and "dear child," while feeling as if she was holding Reginald with her in her arms,—while feeling as if he was there and knew what she felt, and loved her for what she was doing.

So that little hitch was got over satisfactorily. Patricia was formally adopted into the Hollies as the daughter of the house, and Dr. Fletcher was careful to call her " my sister's child " when he spoke of her—which was not often.

But Milltown, having a suspicious mind, was not quite certain whether it approved of the arrangement or not ; and at all events it was quite sure that the Hollies was just the worst home that odd girl could have found, and that she, in her turn, was just the most undesirable kind of young person those foolish people could have adopted. And, good heavens ! why did they want to adopt any one ? These things always turn out badly, prophesied the malcontents ; and the best wisdom in life is to accept the fewest responsibilities, and to interfere least with other folks' concerns.

CHAPTER XL.

FREE TO PLEAD.

MR HAMLEY did the thing handsomely. If the Countess of Dovedale herself had died there could not have
been a more splendid show of grief ; perhaps there
would not have been one so splendid. The shops put up their
mourning shutters, and all the blinds of the private houses were
drawn as the magnificent cortége, the best Milltown, helped by
the county capital, could furnish—tramped slowly down the
High Street to the intense enjoyment of a hundred peeping
eyes. The two or three little fishing-boats lying in the harbour
had streamers hoisted half-mast high—they had been sent down
by order, and were scarlet and buff, the Hamley colours, with a
black bar for mourning across ; half the community were made
mourners by the undertaker, and had hat-bands and scarves as
symbols of their grief ; and on the Sunday following Mr. Borrodaile preached the funeral sermon, wherein he called the de-
funct Mrs. Hamley a mother in Israel, and said that at the last
day the poor, who were her children, would rise up and call her
blessed. Seeing that the practice of almsgiving was held in
abhorrence at Abbey Holme, and that charitable contributions
were condemned as bad political economy, this was taking rather
more than the ordinary ecclesiastical license, which as a rule
goes even beyond the poetic.

As for Mr. Hamley's private and personal emblems of woe
they were of the most expressive and expansive kind. The
crape on his hat did not leave a quarter of an inch of beaver to
be seen ; his jet studs and watch-chain were of the largest size
and broadest and most florid pattern made ; and his glossy black
clothes seemed as if an extra dip in the dyeing-vat had been
given to them. Dora's mourning was almost as deep as a
widow's ; save the characteristic cap indeed, it might have been
a widow's. She looked very fair and interesting in her sables
—" black always did become her," said Bignold, who had been

promoted—black, just touched round the face with a narrow
line of transparent white; and when she came into church,
leaning on Mr. Hamley's arm, she created quite a sensation by
the unusual prettiness of her person and the presumed desolate-
ness of her condition.

She was assumed to be so desolate, and Mr. Hamley's grief
was taken to be so sincere, that Garth was heard to say bitterly : " He's had it out of the Psalms now, and God has cursed
the unrighteous as He promised ! "

After this Sunday there was a great deal of talk throughout
Milltown about Dora.   What would become of her no one could
exactly determine. Of course she could not live at Abbey Holme
with Mr. Hamley alone ; and until he married again, which he
was pretty sure to do, her case seemed a hard one, brought up
as she had been and made so much fuss with, they said among
themselves.   A few wondered whether the great man would
marry Dora herself; but for the most part they believed he
would look higher than his cousin, and maybe plant his foot in
the peerage this time. Besides, men don't generally take for their
wives their own dependants whom they have seen grow up under their roofs from childhood. So it was settled by the majority
that Dora would have to leave Abbey Holme, and that Mr. Hamley would marry some grand lady of high degree and small possessions, and found the Hamley family at last.   •

Colonel Lowe, discussing the great event of the hour with
his son, supposed for his part that Mr. Hamley would marry
Dora. He could understand now the old shoeblack's policy, he
said.   He had loved the girl himself, and in all probability
everything had been understood and arranged between them
long ago ; which was the secret of his refusal to give her a dowry
when he, Sydney Lowe, had done her the honour to propose to
her.

" Any one can see it with half an eye. It was clear as daylight to me at the time, as you must remember I hinted broadly
enough to you," said the Colonel in his disdainful way. " These
low-bred people have always their mysteries and intrigues on
hand ; and Syd, my boy, you are well out of that *galère*. You
have made better terms for yourself by a long way, and chosen
as a gentleman should."

This he said joyously, with his hand laid kindly on his son's shoulder, who looked sulky and by no means responsive. He had not seen Dora since his engagement with Julia Manley, and he dreaded though he longed to see her. He did not know how he could face her with such news as he had to bring, but he thought she would understand the necessities of his position, and he did not want to lose her—in the future. He did warmly and honestly love her with such warmth and honesty as he possessed ; and though his love sprang from, and rested on, only the lowest stratum of a man's fancy and passion, still it was all he had to give ; and if gold cannot be got from brass, what qualities brass has in itself may at least be recognised.

Among the other qualities however, which this love of his possessed, jealousy was one of the strongest ; and when he heard his father speak of Dora's possibly belonging to Mr. Hamley, he felt as if he should go mad on the spot—mad enough to throw Julia and her thousands to the wind, confess everything, and take Dora away—into poverty if it must be—so long as it was into his own keeping before the world, safe from any other man's intrusion. But the habits of a lifetime, and the sordid aims of a selfish nature, were too strong for him. Poverty was Sydney Lowe's Apollyon whom he dared not fight and could not conquer ; and rather than meet this terrible demon, whom we of the nineteenth century dread more than all the others drawn up in line of battle together, he would consent to be perjured on his own account, and to give up the woman he loved—and had married. He was essentially the child of the age ; indifferent to everything but physical enjoyment and social well-being, and with no more belief in morals than he had in religion.

Provided a man is not found out, it does not much signify what he does, according to Sydney Lowe ; and rather than be found out in a folly that would carry consequences, he would commit a crime for concealment. Money and position were his two gods of equal height and power ; and to these everything in heaven and earth, in life and humanity, had to give way.

Not being able, however, to bear his father's cynicism, and being as profoundly miserable as he could be—and if shallow, he was passionate—he dashed from the room, determined to see Dora at any cost, and to come to some definite understanding with her—his wife ; his wife, married to another man ! That

he should destroy his own secret marriage was one thing, and
in the circumstances in which he found himself quite allowable,
if to be regretted ; but that Dora should give herself and her
smiles to Mr. Hamley—no ! he could not stand by and see that
done ! She might commit a crime as well as himself, so far as
the sin was concerned. It was not that which troubled him.
But she should not give him a rival ; and the liberty he took
for himself he would kill her before she should share.

While he was fuming at his unlucky position with all its
detestable surroundings, cursing Julia, his father, Dora, Mr.
Hamley, every one concerned but himself, Mr. Hamley at
Abbey Holme was talking seriously to Dora.

It was Monday evening, the day after the funeral sermon
which had closed the cycle of the burial solemnities. Everything was done now. Even the undertaker's bill was paid, as
well as the bills for servants' mourning and liveries, the carriage
trappings, and the like : by which Mr. Hamley got off a large
discount for ready money. At home, everything characteristic
of and belonging to Mrs. Hamley was put away. Her special
little work-table had been placed like a shrine in a corner ; her
special chair removed ; her pile of handsomely bound religious
books was laid up in the library ; and her whole personal property was made over unconditionally to Dora, with the exception of the few poor trinkets and ornaments she had possessed
before her marriage. These were sent down to Patricia labelled
"Family heirlooms," and accompanied by a note meant to be
kind but worded with unconscious offensiveness, wherein Mr.
Hamley conveyed these precious deposits to her keeping as the
last representative of the Kemball family ; at the same time
begging to enclose a sum of fifty pounds in token of respect for
the dear departed whose niece she was, and to meet expenses
incidental on the melancholy event. It was kindly thought if
clumsily and pompously done ; and Patricia had no idea she
should hurt him as she did when she returned his fifty-pound
note with thanks. But he was really hurt. The man's heart
just then was softened, and he was more sensitive than he had
ever been in his life before.

Well ! the Kemball page of his life was turned down now for
ever ; and as he said, with a not undeserved sense of satisfaction, judging by his lights, it was a page of which he was not

ashamed, and where he had done his duty like a man. But now he was free—the last word had been spelt out, the last line written. He had gone through his lesson triumphantly, and now his play-time had begun. He was free—free to plead, free to enjoy. The man had never looked so well, so near to a strain of nobleness as he did this evening when he came into the drawing-room after dinner, prepared to receive the crowning mercy of his life.

Dora was sitting in her accustomed place alone, dressed for dinner as usual; pretty, soft, amiable also as usual; but devoured by secret fear and anxiety, knowing exactly what was to come but not knowing how it would end.

When Mr. Hamley entered, and she met him with her pretty smile subdued to the proper melancholy tone of the moment, making a graceful, half-receptive movement of her head and hand as if welcoming him to her apartment—she saw her fate. She saw it in the man's white, moved face; in the subtle change from master to wooer, from friend to lover which was in every line and movement, as he drew a chair close to her and in his turn motioned her to sit down. It was a queer, theatrical manner of meeting; but it was the kind of thing that pleased him. All display did.

He came to plead. He came confident of the result, but timid too, as real love makes even strong men before they are assured. He came to pour out such wealth of affection as he possessed like hoarded treasures in her lap; and Dora looking up at him with her sweet, affectionate little face, and heart that seemed to stand still for dread, only wished that he might die —fall dead there at her feet—before he had got time to say what he had waited almost these ten years to say, and what she herself had made it a crime to hear.

He sat down beside her, and took her dainty hand in both his own.

"Dora," he said in a husky voice, so low and changed it scarcely sounded like his voice at all; "I have something to say to you."

"Yes," said Dora innocently.

Had she not had nerves of steel she would have shrieked aloud in her terror. As it was, she smiled tenderly, and looked with the sweetest friendliness, like a child or an angel by his side.

"It cannot be a matter of amazement to you what I have to say," began Mr. Hamley oratorically ; but his grand manner ill accorded with his trembling hands and unsteady voice. "You must have discovered it for yourself that I love you— love you very dearly, I may say."

"You have always been the kindest of the kind to me," said Dora, lifting her eyes with her special look of shy girl's gratitude.

"I have tried to be so," he answered. "It was not difficult, feeling what I did for you. From the first moment when you came into the house, a pretty little girl, just budding as one may say, up to this hour when I have your hands in mine over my desolate hearth, I have loved you."

Dora gave his hand a little press, but said nothing.

"Year by year as you grew prettier and more and more the lady, I grew more to love you," he went on to say, drawing a deep breath. "But I do not think I ever took advantage of my position, or treated you with anything but the respect which I should naturally show a lady. You have been always the lady with me, Dora. I loved you—no man more; but I think I may claim to say that I did not show it to you rudely, or make the sainted soul who has just left us anxious or uneasy."

"You have been always very good to me," said Dora softly. "No one could have treated anyone with more kindness or gen erosity than you have treated me."

"I have wished to do so, Dora ! I have wished to do so ! But it has been hard work at times to control myself ; and when other men came after you, it was a struggle then, I can tell you. Still, I did ; and I am proud of myself that I did. At one time I was afraid of that young dog—that young Lowe."

Dora raised her pretty shoulders with a movement of disdain. "Oh !" she said, with a satirical little laugh.

"But you assured me it was not so, and I was content. I said to myself, Dora does not know my heart. Dora does not see that I love her—as a man and a husband I must control myself, and not let Dora know my great designs for her when the sainted soul shall be taken from us. If I could show myself to Dora, and let her understand me and the future I design for her, I should have no fear ; but as I cannot, I must do my best to keep her safe, and to save her from mere tuft-hunters, greedy of money, like that mean fellow Lowe. So I put it to you, Dora, as you may remember; and I cannot tell you how you lightened my heart when you said you did not love him. Dora, you gave me new life that day!"

He said this with a burst of tenderness that nearly broke him down. It was pathetic in its own way to see the coarse, strong face of the man softened and quivering with emotion, to see his eyes turned with such tender longing on the fair drooping head beside him, his self-complacency absorbed in the intensity of his love for this girl who was fooling him. Whatever of pure and true and noble there was in Mr. Hamley's nature was all centred in his love for Dora—Dora, the wife of Sydney Lowe—the Rachel for whom he had waited so long, and who had deceived him as she had deceived everyone else.

"And you do not love him!" continued Mr. Hamley in the tone of a question. He was sure of his answer, but he longed to hear it again. There are some things which never tire in repetition, and the assurance to a jealous man that he has no cause for jealousy is one of them.

She lifted her eyes to his face with her sudden swift look, dropping the lids immediately.

"Love him!" she said with the most enchanting contempt. "No!"

"And, Dora, you do love me? Let me hear you say so, darling! You have often told me so with those pretty eyes of yours; tell me so now in words," he pleaded. "I must hear you say it—'I love you!'"

"I love you!" replied Dora in a low voice. It was her task, and she must get through it in the best way she could. "Poor Syd!" she thought a little ruefully; which did not prevent her saying her prescribed formula in the most bewitching manner possible.

He caught her to his heart. Strong, conceited, arrogant as he was, at this moment he was nothing but the humble and enraptured lover whom a pair of blue eyes and two red rosebud lips had transported into heaven.

"Now I have won all that I care for in life!" he said, smoothing her hair with a tremulous hand. "Dora as my wife puts the finishing touch to it all. Oh, Dora, you have made a happy man of me to-night! My darling, my pretty pet, my little queen, how happy I shall be! how happy I am!"

" You have made me happy too," said Dora from the breadth of his chest where her golden head was resting; " how shall I get out of this awful scrape!" being the unspoken commentary that ran side by side with her words.

He passed his large hand over her face. It was such a delicious luxury to him to feel that he had so far the right. He had, as he truly boasted, always treated her with self-restraint and respect, and the slackening of the curb was a joy so great he scarcely regretted the price of so many years' control he had paid for it.

" But we will keep it secret between ourselves, my dear," he said. " I should not like to do anything that would be offensive to that sainted soul's memory. She was a good wife to me, if a trifle crabbed and stiff, and I would not like people to say that I danced on her grave, or took my second wife before my first was cold. We will keep all this to our two selves; and when the year is out we will be married quietly, you know, and without much of a spread. Don't you think I am right, Dora?"

" Certainly," she said. " No one must know!"

She said this quite warmly. It was a reprieve to her so far, and who knows what that reprieve might not bring forth? Mr. Hamley might die—he did not look very like it though; or Sydney might die; or Julia Manley; or a thousand things might happen which would set her feet free from their present fetters. Wherefore she assented with alacrity, and so gave Mr. Hamley cause to congratulate himself again on the possession of a prospective wife so full of nice feeling and so entirely the lady as dear Dora.

Furthermore it was agreed between them that Dora should sometimes visit friends, and sometimes live at Abbey Holme, where there should always be some married woman to be her chaperon and bear her countenance, as Mr. Hamley said; and that everything should be conducted in such a manner as to give no cause of scandal to a world only too ready to find cause.

" I must have my Dora's name kept as clean as a new pin!" said Mr. Hamley with more poetry of feeling than of speech. " We both owe so much to the memory of the dear departed."

To which Dora, sighing with the most admirable imitation of melancholy, said, " Yes, we do," and was rewarded for her sweetness by a kiss.

So the evening passed, and there was not in all England a happier heart or a prouder man than Jabez Hamley, M.P., and the accepted lover of Dora. Not all the wealth of England could have won him from his present position. He had not a wish ungratified—not a care, not a cloud in his horizon any where. Accustomed to self-control and fond of display, it was no great trial to him to have that year of probation before he could call Dora really his own. He wanted the world to see how decorously he could mourn for the sainted soul who had just departed. He too, like Mrs. Hamley, knew that affection and harmony are the only things which render marriage respectable, and that one of open disunion is also one of open scandal. It would have been painful to him, and would have brushed the bloom from the flower of his happiness, had any one been able to suspect that he had, as he said, danced on his wife's grave, and taken a second before the first was cold. It was even an additional pleasure to him that he was obliged to conceal his joy. It seemed to make it more entirely his own ; and the secret which no one shared with him and Dora was so much the closer bond between them. Yes he was thoroughly, divinely happy. He stood on the pinnacle, and asked no more of man or gods.

The next day he went down to Mr. Simpson's office.

"Simpson," he said in a melancholy voice, " I wish to add a codicil to my will."

Obsequious Simpson bowed. "Certainly, Mr. Hamley ; certainly, sir," he said. " Your instructions ? "

" Only a few words," said Mr. Hamley. "Absolute and unconditional bequeathment of all of which I may die possessed, in whatever form the property may consist, to my cousin, Dora Drummond."

Mr. Simpson was too wise to show any feeling, but he was profoundly astonished all the same. He was even more so when Mr. Hamley declared he would not leave the office till this codicil had been written, signed, witnessed, and delivered. The man's whole nature seemed changed. With his widower's sorrowful air was a certain abounding sense of inner joy that did not escape a man so astute as the Milltown lawyer ; but he made no comment farther than that it was natural for Mr. Hamley to wish to ensure the well-being of his only relation :

and that, wishing no ill to Miss Drummond, he yet hoped she would not profit by his generous disposition in her favour for many a long day yet to come, if indeed she ever did.

To all of which Mr. Hamley answered judiciously, and rode away with a light heart ; feeling that should he meet with any accident, which however he did not expect, dear Dora would be fully provided for and would wear his memory in perpetual magnificence and sorrow. He wished though, that he had made a proviso against her marrying. In his lover-like haste to as-sure her good fortune, he had not thought of that ; but he felt it would be enough to make him turn in his grave, as people say, if Dora should marry on his money ; and he was deter-mined to repair the omission to-morrow. Taking time by the forelock was one of Mr. Hamley's principles as well as Colonel Lowe's ; and to-morrow he would act on it.

Meanwhile he went home to what it pleased him to call out of doors his desolate hearth, where he found a superb little din-ner, and a beautiful young woman in the most becoming dress possible to be constructed out of crape and bugles, waiting to receive him with a mixture of open friendliness and secret bash-fulness which seemed to him just the most fascinating mixture of manner any lady could evince.

This evening too passed like the former, save that the softer tremulousness of the as yet unassured suitor had gone, and a certain fever of delight—a certain bounding, irrepressible, and enthusiastic joy—had taken its place. He could not go to bed ; he could not sleep ; and when Dora stole down the stairs in her old noiseless way, and went out into the garden to meet her husband, from whom she had had a peremptory letter to-day (she could receive private letters now), Mr. Hamley was in his own room thinking of her, and of all she had said and done to him to-night. She was like a fairy or an angel, he thought with a smile ; and that fairy, that angel, loved him and was his!

" Where nothing is, but all things seem!" How much of life is real anywhere? Prosperity, happiness, truth, even love —what is actual, what only an appearance? More secrets lie behind the closed doors of hearts and homes than the world outside ever dreams of ; and more men worship shadows and are made happy by pretences than ever come to the knowledge that they have been tricked.

CHAPTER XLI.

THE SHADOW IN THE WOOD.

" SYD, it has come at last!" cried Dora as she ran into her husband's arms in the shrubbery.

What had come? thought Sydney. Her knowledge of his intended marriage with Julia Manley? or had Mr. Hamley discovered all? or could it be that his father was right, and that this vulgar ruffian had dared to lift his eyes to the prize he had won?

"What has come, Dora?" he asked quickly.

"Mr. Hamley," said Dora.

"What about Mr. Hamley?" repeated Sydney. "You speak in riddles to-night—do please be plain!"

Dora felt all the awkwardness of the confession she had to make; but as it must be done she had better get over the bad piece of road as quickly as possible. It was a curious position for a woman to have to tell her husband that she had pretended —only pretended, mind!—she was going to be married to another man, even when that husband had announced his intention of marrying another woman!

"Mr. Hamley has proposed to me," said Dora, clasping her hands in each other and resting them on his bended arm.

The moon was bright enough for her to see her husband's eyes, and she did not like the look in them. She felt there was mischief behind them; and angry as she was with him she instinctively met it with a caress.

Caresses do a great deal with some men, and in general they did a great deal with Sydney Lowe. But though, when she looked as she looked now, she had hitherto always made his will her own, to-night she failed. Between love and jealousy the latter was the stronger of the two.

"And what did you say, Dora?" he asked, griping her hands harshly.

"What could I say, dear?" she answered deprecatingly.

"I did not ask that. You could say a great many things. I asked, what did you say?" he repeated, still with his dead-white face and flaming eyes and dangerously calm manner.

"Dora looked at him innocently.

"I said, yes, of course. What else was there for me to do?" she answered, arching her eye-brows.

With a savage oath he flung away the hands which until now he had been grasping, and lifted his arm as if to strike her. Had she shrunk or cowered, he would; but she stood her ground so quietly, and looked at him so prettily, that in a manner she unnerved him. She was desperately frightened nevertheless; but it would never do to let Sydney see that she was afraid of him, she thought. She must hold her own now or never, and make him understand that by his own iniquity he had made himself responsible for all that had come, or was to come. But if he did beat her, and make her black and blue —he looked capable of it—and Mr. Hamley saw the bruises, and asked her about them to-morrow, what should she say to him? Her difficulties were really very great. How she wished one of these two men would die! At this present moment she was quite indifferent which of the two, so long as she was free of one.

All these things she thought in the moment during which she stood with her hands clasped in each other, her head a little bent and her blue eyes looking up with the tenderest sweetness into Sydney's angry face.

"What nonsense, Syd!" she said, creeping up to him and taking hold of his arms. "How absurd of you to go on like this, dear! If I had not said yes, and pretended that I would, what would have become of me? He would have turned me then and there out of doors, and where could I have gone? Your father is ruined, and you cannot give me a home; besides it is all over the place that you are on the point of marrying Miss Manley, and I should like to know what I am to do!"

"Starve, rather than do such a shameful thing as this!" cried Sydney violently.

"Willingly, if you will starve with me," said pretty Dora amiably. "But I tell you Syd, frankly, if you marry Julia Manley for money I will marry Mr. Hamley; so now you know."

"Dora, you are too detestable!" cried Sydney. "You seem to forget altogether that you are my wife."

"No I do not, dear," she answered. "I remember it too well; for it makes the whole thing so dreadfully complicated. If we had been only lovers all this time there would have been nothing to be afraid of; but it will be a horribly awkward position for us both when you walk out of the church with Miss Manley on your arm as your wife, and we go out to our bridal dinner-parties afterwards. We shall meet at some of them."

"Oh, Dora, do not say such awful things!" cried Sydney, fairly writhing under her words. "I always thought you had some kind of feeling, some kind of sympathy. You will send me wild if you go on like this!"

"Well, Syd, you are the most extraordinarily unreasonable person I have ever seen!" said Dora. "You first of all marry me under false pretences; then you discard me, and are going to marry somebody else; but you will neither hear it spoken of, nor let me secure myself from ruin. What do you propose? or have you anything to propose at all?"

"I have," cried Sydney.

"Well? what?"

He turned away. Sydney Lowe was not much troubled with conscientious scruples nor moral delicacy, but even he hesitated before he propounded the scheme he had devised, whereby he should take all the infamy on himself and make it unnecessary for Dora to imitate him.

"No, Syd," said Dora, when he had taken the bad courage to speak, "I will not do that. We are in an awful scrape, but I don't think that would make it much better. At least not for me. It would be pleasant enough for you; but for myself —no I don't see it, Syd!" quite gravely.

"And you prefer that low-lived ruffian, that big brute, to me?" cried Sydney, savagely.

"No, Syd, I don't. I loathe and hate Mr. Hamley, and you know that I do; and I love you, and you know that too. I have never loved any man but you, and never shall."

Her head went down on his breast, and his arms were round her dainty waist. His passion changed in an instant to despair, and his anger to a woman's grief.

"Oh, Dora, how can you leave me!" he sobbed. "It breaks my heart to think of it when it does not send me mad!"

"How can you leave me!" she retorted, also sobbing. "You

are going to be married now at once; I only said I would in a
year's time, to keep things quiet and see what could be done.
It is you, not I, who are the deserter."

"What else can I do, darling?" he pleaded. "We are
ruined, all of us, unless we can get money, and I know of no
other way than this."

This was the first time he had confessed to his intention;
and it brought the present frightful state of things very vividly
before Dora. She turned away and shook herself free from his
arms: but if the movement was petulant she softened its harshness by sobbing vehemently. At that moment she hated Mr.
Hamley and loved Sydney to distraction; so she thought; and
would brave everything rather than give him up to Julia Manley, and accept the bitter portion assigned to her on her own
side. Her tears unmanned him more than ever. He clasped
her to him again, frantically crying—

"Dora! my wife! my own little wife! I cannot give you up!
Whatever happens, poverty or no poverty, let us keep together
and make the best of things as we have them."

"I will if you will," said Dora between her sobs; and then
they kissed each other and cried afresh, and were both profoundly and intensely miserable. They knew well enough that
they not could face poverty, but none the more did they wish to
part. Selfishness, deceit, recklessness, treachery, crime—all these
lay heaped in burning flames on their young heads; but all the
same, utterly worthless as they were, they loved each other at
the moment and they suffered. It soothed them to cry: "Let
us go into ruin together, so long as we are together." It was a
deception born of love and despair. Each recognised the deception in that deeper reasonableness which passion never stirs
in some people; but it was a sweet if passing solace, and each
thought the other believed in it.

So they stood there in the shadow, clasped in each other's
arms; Dora crying on Sydney's shoulder, and he crying over
her golden head too, in between alternations of hope and misery,
impossible suggestions, untenable promises, and sometimes blank
confessions of necessities; feeling that the final moment had
come, and that the calm counsel of the morning would show
them the madness of the night, while both pretended that this
madness was to last and to be acted on. More than once, how-

ever, Sydney begged her to forgive him for the wrong he had done her so unintentionally in marrying her; assuring her—and here he spoke the truth—that he had no kind of knowledge of his father's affairs when he made her his wife, and that he thought the sole hitch was that father's possible refusal to accept her as a daughter-in-law; and Dora assured him—which was not the truth—that she had never until last night had the least idea that Mr. Hamley loved her or regarded her as other than a daughter. Then they spoke of their running away together, and even went to the length of comparing their joint possessions. They did not reckon ten pounds between them. Mr. Hamley paid bills to any amount without remark, but he made no allowances, and he disapproved of ladies possessing much pocket-money; and ten pounds was but a small sum on which to begin life for two young people who could not do a hand's turn for themselves. On which they kissed each other again; and Dora wept as she had never wept in her life before; and Sydney felt that he should go mad or do something hideous and desperate if this kind of thing went on much longer. He was in fact wrought up to that pitch of fierce excitement wherein a man is no longer master of himself, where consequences are not calculated, results are not foreseen, and where the impulse of the moment, whatever it may be—the passion that lies uppermost—must be obeyed; and is; because reason, conscience, all that renders humanity human, has gone to sleep and only the animal remains. His own tears maddened him, and Dora's distress but added to his madness. A voice seemed to sound in his ear, just two words repeated again and again, "Kill him! kill him!" it said; "kill him! kill him!"

No ways and means presented themselves to his fancy, nor when nor how; only the impulse, only the voice: "Kill him!"

As he held his wife strained in his arms as in a vice, she felt his heart throb against her bosom while he groaned with a kind of angry despair that was scarcely human.

"Sydney," she said, in terror, "are you ill, dear!"

He made no answer, and as the last breath of her words passed over his cheek they heard the door of the house unbolted and unbarred, and presently a man's footstep came heavily down the broad stone flight that led from the door, and on to the gravel of the drive, turning to the left where they were hidden.

Dora clung to her husband in terror. **There was no danger** of her sobbing now.

"Mr. Hamley!" she gasped.

They shrank back among the **trees, but they dared not go** very deep into the wood. The **night was still, when sound** travels far, and the crisp fallen leaves would have betrayed them. Sydney grasped the heavily-loaded life-preserver he always carried with him in these midnight **expeditions—an in-** strument much after his own pattern, slight **and inoffensive to** look at, but deadly if used in earnest—then **pressed his arm** closer round Dora and whispered to her hoarsely not to be afraid. But she was even the more afraid for his **very words** ; he looked so dark and deadly, like a human tiger somehow.

Her mind took it all in ; discovery ; the men struggling together and one of them badly hurt ; her disgrace ; the public scandal and the open shame ; and then the enforced poverty after all ! A minute ago she had been bewailing her hard fate in being forced to separate ; now she shuddered at the **harder** prospect of being forced to keep **together.**

The steps came nearer. They **were firm and** heavy, and **with** them they heard Mr. Hamley's voice, sometimes speaking to himself, sometimes breaking out into a **few** false notes of song, and sometimes laughing softly as a man whose heart is too full of joy for thorough self-containment or repose.

He crossed the broad carriage-drive and came along the walk that skirted the croquet-lawn, and so into the shrubbery path where his fiancée and her husband were hidden. They heard his breathing and the very fret of his watch-chain as he passed.

"Dora!" he said in a tone of such abounding love, such intensity of passion, that Sydney felt the blood leap like fire to his face, "My Dora! my wife! How she loves me! Little angel, how devoted she is to me! I always suspected it—I knew it—but to hear her say it, 'I love you!'"—in falsetto— "Gad! it nearly did for me for pleasure! Dora! beauty! little angel! how I love you!"

He went on a few paces, then he came **back** again, singing softly what **he** thought was one of Dora's favourite songs. And then he sat down on a garden chair placed so close to **where** the young couple stood that Dora thought he must surely hear their breathing and the beating of her guilty, frightened heart.

"What hands she has!" Mr. Hamley said to himself after a moment's silence. "What lips! That good-night kiss of hers—I thought I should have turned faint and lost my head! How delightful to feel her soft hair and her velvety cheeks— she is like a flower; and she is my own. Dora! her very name is the prettiest in the world. Dora Hamley! They'll say in London that the M.P. for Milltown has the loveliest little wife in England; and they'll say right. Not the Queen herself can show such another in all her court! And to think of that young beast Lowe, presuming so high! The wife of the Member for the borough of Milltown is rather a cut above a profligate blackleg and his son! My Dora; no other man's Dora; only mine! And she loves me so much, and says it so prettily! To think of her saving herself for me; refusing them all because she loved me! Jabez Hamley, you are a happy man to-night! There's not a happier on the whole face of the earth, let him be who he may!"

So he went on talking in broken interrupted sentences to himself; the man's heart too full for sleep, too rich in joy for rest. He felt as if he should have been suffocated in the house, had he stayed there. He had that strange yearning to carry his joy into the infinity of nature which we all have, even the most prosaic of us, the least sensitive and refined, when our cup is very full and the gates of heaven have rolled back and let us in. The passion of happiness that possessed him was almost more than he could bear, and he came out into the fresh night-air to throw its burden on to something stronger and holier than himself.

He had been happy before this in his life; indeed, his life had been singularly blessed, he said to himself. He had been prosperous in all ways, successful on all points of his ambition; but he had never felt as he felt now, so possessed with his joy, so overpowered with his bliss. He had to keep silence to all the world of his happiness in Dora. To the outside onlookers he must wear crape round his hat and a sorrowful countenance for the due observance of the decencies; he could tell his secret to none; but like the man who must whisper what he knew of the king to the reeds, he too must whisper what he felt to the night. It was very un-English, very boyish, but it was nature. His life hitherto had been arid of love. He had married early for ambition, and he had prudently resolved to make that marriage a success. To do this he had not suffered his fancy to stray to the right or the left; and his very love for Dora had been a growth, not a sudden passion, and never fully confessed even to himself in its intensity, if it had been in its hope, because he had never dared to indulge in it till now. And the first love of a man's life matured at nearly fifty, is a deeper and more absorbing passion than even the most fervid fancy of earlier youth.

He did not sit there long, though it seemed like an age to the two hidden behind the trees listening to his boastful gladness—the one in such chill of abject terror, the other in such fire of torturing rage. Restless, feverish, with his chest expanded and his head held high, he wandered down the avenue, and presently they heard the gate leading into the wood from the shrubbery creak as it swung back, and the last of his footsteps died away.

Then Sydney, putting Dora from him without a word, without a sign, turning only upon her a pair of flaming eyes burning like fire beneath his dark brows, motioned her silently to the house; while he, drawing a deep breath, shifted his loaded cane to a yet more convenient hold in the middle, and set off with a swift and stealthy pace down the avenue.

"Sydney!" whispered Dora.

But he was gone. Keeping in the shadow of the trees, and with that light walk of his which he had practised so often and which was scarcely more noisy than the tread of a panther, she could neither see nor hear him; and after lingering for a moment, she too turned and ran, and was soon safe in her own room, unseen and unsuspected. No one who had seen her fair pretty face half an hour after, nestled among the lace and linen of her luxurious pillow, sleeping as tranquilly as a child, her cheeks just touched with a pink flush like a monthly rose, her small hand half-hidden among her golden hair, would have imagined that she had just escaped from one danger to herself, while leaving in the thick of peril the two men who loved her. She was of the tribe felis femina, not cruel of nature if she was of need, and preferring her own ease before all other things above or below.

Still softly singing to himself, Mr. Hamley walked on through the little wood. which when he first bought Abbey Holme was the boundary of his possessions. He had a special love for this tangled thicket: it was pretty and picturesque, with a pleasant trout-stream running through, broadening into a fair expanse of water where he kept a couple of swans and some favourite fowl. He remembered how glad he was, years ago, when he walked through this very path and took possession of the wood as master and owner. He had often stolen over the fences and got nuts and blackberries there in his ragged days; he took care that no ragged urchins stole over the fences now for nuts or blackberries!—and he remembered his proud delight in finding himself the lawful master of his former filched Paradise. It was eighteen years ago. How time had passed and prospered with him since then! Year by year he had gathered more, and year by year he would gather more still. His wealth had got to that point when it increases by itself; for spend as much as he could—that is, as much as he cared to spend—he could not get through all his income. He had that Cragfoot estate to get in yet, he thought; and maybe more land might come into the market, which he would secure. There were outlying bits he was beginning to covet, and that he thought would fit in well with his fields; but for these he could afford to wait.

He was glad about Cragfoot though. He would make it a Dower-house for Dora. Had Patricia Kemball been a sensible girl and done as she ought to have done in her aunt's lifetime, he would have made over the whole concern to her as her portion; now he would give it to Dora, and call it "Dora's Dower," as a remembrance. He laughed right out when he thought of this. It would be a pleasant revenge on that young profligate who had dared to ask him for Dora's hand!

How beautiful the night was!' The scented autumn air hanging in a light vapour that shone like silver among the trees, veiling the direct brilliancy of the moon and softening it into a general atmosphere of mild radiance rather than a specialised light, seemed more delightful to him than he had ever known an October night to be, or indeed, any night of any year. It was quite summer-like he thought, as he took off his hat and flung back his coat, looking about him. He had got now to the Oval; a cleared space by the side of the lake, as the broadened reach of river was called; and stood there bareheaded in the

DD

moonlight, watching the white swans floating lazily on the water. His back was towards the house, the chimneys of which could be seen over the tops of the trees in daylight.

Watching the swans, something in their graceful gliding movement struck the imagination of the man whose very soul seemed transformed to-night. It was the whiteness of Dora, the grace of Dora, the caressing, subtle charm of Dora, the purity of Dora. He saw her everywhere ; earth and heaven and all forms of loveliness were filled with her, and everything was but a type—a repetition of her excellence and beauty.

"My Dora !" he said aloud. Then, with a sudden rush of feeling, the like of which he had never known before, he cried out as if in an ecstasy ; "Thank God for her love !"

A whistling noise as a stick cut sharply through the air, the crash of breaking bone, a stifled cry, a heavy fall, and Mr. Hamley's life was over ; his love, his joy, his prosperity, his vainglory, nothing more now than a handful of dust fanned by the midnight air—the thought of a man which had passed like a summer's cloud. Had his death been by any other method, had his heart burst in his great joy, had he died by the visitation of God or by a thunderbolt from Heaven, one would have said that he had died at the right moment. To-morrow the ecstasy which had lifted him to-night beyond himself would have withered down into the vulgar narrowness of his everyday life ; his soul, which had expanded into poetry, would have shrunk back into its old groove of ignoble ostentation, of insolent self-assertion ; and his very love for Dora would by time have become first the mere pride of possession, then indifference, and perhaps have ended in jealousy and estrangement. He would never have been so great again, so near to nobleness as he was to-night ; for thought the cause of his passionate emotion was a cheat, his feeling was true. The tragedy by which all was over for him in life was a foul and cruel crime, but it gave him a pathos he would never have had else, and crystallized for ever the dignity and sublimer passion of the hour.

As Mr. Hamley fell a slight young figure shot quickly by ; plunged again into the shadow of the wood ; leaped wall and fence and gate, going always by circuitous paths till it struck the high road, where running still, always keeping in the shadow, Sydney Lowe soon gained the shelter of his own home as entirely unsuspected and undiscovered as Dora had been. Creeping noiselessly up-stairs, he went into his private room; carefully examined his clothes whence he removed certain damning stains and spots; stirred up the dying embers of the fire, and burned in the flame a heavily-loaded life-preserver, running the lead through a bullet-mould, as he had often done when a boy. And then he went to bed, where he laid as if in an ague fit till the morning. He had obeyed that haunting voice, and committed the crime he had been half-unconsciously meditating for many weeks, and now stood face to face with the consequences. His chance of detection? It all depended on whether he had been seen or not, or if seen recognised. And if seen and recognised, what then was he to do?

He lay there calculating, inventing, his brain on fire, his thoughts incoherent in their activity, half resolving to leave the place and England to-morrow, then again feeling that his only policy was to remain and trust to his good stars and his own cleverness, should suspicion arise and his name get bruited abroad. And while he was torturing himself with the criminal's coward fears, James Garth was making his way too, from the wood, carrying a bagfull of game which he had just netted in the preserves. Not half an hour before Mr. Hamley came to the Oval, he had passed through the paths with his snares, and had lifted what his last night's setting had brought him.

For Garth had turned poacher of late days, more as an act of revenge than for any other reason. It pleased the man's savage feeling to rob Mr. Hamley, who he always said had robbed him. It was his crude version of the law which gives an eye for an eye and a tooth for a tooth; and he helped himself pretty freely. More than once the head-keeper had warned him. They had been old friends in the days when James held his father's land, and he did not want to be hard on him. Still, his duty was to watch the game, and let no man meddle with it; and so he said; and each time he had it to say he spoke more sternly than before. He had been about the preserves to-night as usual, and had seen a figure come out of the little wood and run across the open in the moonlight for a moment, then dart under cover again. It was a younger, slighter looking man than Garth, it seemed to him, and evidently carrying nothing weighty. But there was not much doubt in his own

mind that he had made a mistake, and that it was Garth whom
he had seen, when all the circumstances came to light ; for
who else was it possible to have been ?   When he and the un-
der-gamekeeper, making their rounds the next day, came upon
the stiff body of their murdered master lying in the Oval with
his skull battered in by one tremendous blow given from behind, and a piece of white spotted blue bandana hanging on one
of the bushes near, the man's heart stood still ; for he recognised the neckerchief as the one James Garth habitually wore,
and the whole crime became clear.

" Whosever throat this fits has done it," said the under-
gamekeeper pointing to the bush ; and the police, when they
were sent for, said so too.

And what excuse could Garth make ? There, under his
bed, was the bag of game ; round his neck the torn bandana,
with its missing piece found on the bushes close to where Mr.
Hamley was lying murdered.   There was no denial of the one
fact, and the inference was too strong to be gainsaid.   The
poacher was arrested on suspicion, committed on the capital
charge, and sent to jail to stand his trial at the coming assize,
Milltown having but one mind on the matter—that he was
guilty.   For again and again they asked who else could have
done it ? Mr. Hamley was not the beloved of all men, but he
had no enemies save this gloomy, discontented peasant whose
land he had bought, and whom he had thus made his foe for
life—and death.

CHAPTER XLIL

TRUTH AND SEEMING.

THERE is nothing of which a poacher is not capable. Given a pair of hands bold enough to set snares for the squire's game, and you have a heart black enough to compass the squire's murder. This is a logical sequence in the minds of the landed gentry, and they act on it when they have the chance with singular uniformity of feeling. A poacher is the common enemy of all men with game preserves ; and they think they do the community good service by getting rid of him on any pretext that will serve.

Whether it is he who is intrinsically bad, or the law which makes him so, does not trouble them. Men in possession are not given to abstract reasoning, the first principles have nothing to do with Acts of Parliament. To break the law has an ugly sound with it to those whose gain is to keep it, and practical protest against inequitable decrees is a crime where readjustment would pare off some of the golden fringes from the rich man's garments to give decent clothing to the poor. So it is that a poacher has but hard measure meted out to him at the hands of magisterial game preservers ; and class enmity, always bitter, is never more so than when it has to deal with a man who has snared a pheasant or netted a salmon by the right of nature, and against the game law.

Thus, when it became known that James Garth had taken to poaching, his arrest on a charge of murder was quite in the order of things. Discontent and springs together make an amalgam that renders the worst crime of all easy ; and the poor fellow was condemned long before he was tried. When that conclusive bit of white-spotted blue bandana was compared with the yeoman's neckerchief and found to correspond with the torn end, there was then not the shadow of doubt left, nor the chance of escape. The whole thing fitted in piece by piece with as much accuracy as those two ends of torn silk; and the hypothesis was as clear as demonstrated fact.

Garth had been poaching; Mr. Hamley, suspecting something, or perhaps only restless from grief at the loss of his wife, had gone out into the wood and had caught him in the fact. There had been an altercation; and Garth, being ordered off, had gone sullenly away, when he had turned, and creeping noiselessly behind his detector had struck him on the back of the head with some round, heavy instrument, and so had killed him treacherously on the spot. Nothing could be clearer. The game was found under his bed, and the gamekeeper, his own friend, had seen him running across the open. He had not known him at first; at least not for certain in the shimmery moonlight; the man he had seen looked younger and of lighter build, he said, and he had not taken him to be his old friend and mate; but enlightened by after events he reconsidered and corrected his first impression, and was prepared now to maintain, sadly enough, that it was James Garth, and none other, whom he had seen escaping from the place of murder. For you see, said the man, as all Milltown said in concert, who else could it be?

All the bitter words Garth had said, all his discontent and angry despair. Mrs. Garth's loud-voiced passion at the dismissal of her daughter, every small and until now half-forgotten incident, and specially that scene where he had had that kind of fit, and had cried "Murder!" at the Long Field Gate came back to the memories of those who had heard and seen. And then that torn fragment of bandana! It was a small thing on which to hang a man; but it hanged him nevertheless. All saw in it the finger of Providence, which forces a man who commits a crime to leave some betraying sign by which the old saying that murder will out may be justified; and the finger of Providence was accepted as a guide pointing in the right direction in this instance.

A proved poacher; confessedly out in the preserves on the night of the murder; seen escaping from near the very spot by his friend the gamekeeper, a reluctant if honest witness; and with a fragment of his neckerchief found fluttering in the bushes close to the spot—what could save him? Not the absence of the instrument with which the deed was done; though the woods were searched far and near for something that would fit into that awful wound ; not his own protestation of innocence made once and never repeated, for he became sullen on the trial and stood as if he did not care which way the verdict went; not his previous good character, seeing that even good men may lapse and that no saint is sure; not even the current rumour that his brain was touched, for the jail surgeon certified his perfect sanity ; nothing that could be urged had any weight in face of the overwhelming force of the circumstantial evidence brought against him, backed by the hypothesis born of his notorious enmity and discontent.

He was tried ; well defended ; but found guilty all the same ; and sentenced to be hanged by the judge in an impressive speech which lost its point so far as the prisoner was concerned, from the simple fact that he had not done that thing for which he was exhorted to repent and condemned to die. But it moved the judge who delivered it and the audience who heard it, and indeed was a fine bit of eloquence full of good, honest human feeling.

After sentence was passed, a petition headed by Dr. Fletcher, but sparsely signed by the rest of the community, was forwarded to the Home Secretary praying for commutation of the capital sentence. The petitioners were either those few who did not believe, in spite of appearances and no one else possible, that James had done this murder—those half superstitious and wholly unreasonable people who have more faith in character than in circumstantial evidence ; or those kindly apologists who believed that he had done it sure enough, but who thought him mad and therefore not responsible. But the Home Secretary was a strong man, and returned the memorial with the answer that he saw no reason to interfere with the regular course of justice. The prisoner had had a fair trial, and the laws must be obeyed.

There was no help for it then. In heaven there might be a re-arrangement of the sentence, but on earth it was final ; and James Garth was hanged within the precincts of the county jail ; his last words, while Calcraft was arranging the drop, being " Gentlemen, I am innocent ! " as he lifted his wan face to the light and looked as a brave man does when he meets an ignoble doom nobly. But all the thinking and educated people of Mill-

town said he richly deserved his fate. All save Henry Fletcher; whose defence however had done the poor fellow no kind of
good, and himself that amount of harm which comes from the
open expression of unpopular opinions. The gentry took grave
exception at this continual advocacy of the poor characteristic
of him. They said, bitterly, that it did not signify what a common man did, if it would only injure and annoy the rich that
mad fellow was on his side. They might all have their throats
cut, and he would move heaven and earth to get the interesting criminal off, without a thought for the victim. It was infamous, disgusting, and he ought to be drummed out of society
for it.

No one was so indignant as Colonel Lowe; though to make
amends no one was so silent as his son. The Colonel liked
Henry Fletcher well enough, he said, as they all knew; and he
had always disliked that poor Hamley fellow, as also they all
knew; and he had never concealed his contempt for him nor
kowtowed to him as the rest had done; but when it came to
taking sides with his murderer—good heavens! that was another matter. A gentleman may keep aloof from a vulgar up-
start and yet not hold with the ruffian who has assassinated
him in his own grounds. A petition for a reprieve? No! If
Garth could be hanged twice over the punishment would not be
more than he deserved; and he, Colonel Lowe, would vote for
the second drop. What would become of the country if such
crimes as these were winked at? No.; none of these sentimen-
talities suited the Colonel. Gag such mischievous demagogues
as Henry Fletcher; let Garth swing; and above all things defend the majesty of the law and keep up the due subordination
of classes.

So Garth did swing, and no living soul knew the real truth
but one—he who had burnt a slight cane in the fire one October night, and run a lump of lead through a bullet mould. And
no living soul suspected the truth but one—she who had seen
her husband steal, with his panther-like tread, on the traces of
her lover in the shadow of the wood, and who knew what was
in his heart.

After this a subscription was got up for Garth's widow and
orphans, and they were shipped off to Australia, as creatures
too tainted for the purity of Milltown. They were the victims

of circumstances, as so many of us are; martyrs crushed under the wheels of that tremendous car where sits the Justice of the World; the helpless struck down by the blind; sinless Cains bearing the brand unrighteously, but none the less shunned of men because of that unrighteousness. It had been a frightful page in Milltown history; there had never been such a one before; and the citizens felt the best thing to do was to obliterate the last traces as quickly as possible, and wipe out the name of Garth from the annals of the place.

When Mr. Hamley died and was buried, his will was read; and Dora Drummond was proved his heiress. He had made it hastily—a mere codicil of a few words—the very day before he was murdered, poor man! as if he had had a prevision of his fate, they said, with pale cheeks. Nothing touched the public imagination more than this. There was a pathos, almost a poetry in the action that counted much in the general indictment against Garth; and the popular feeling ran high in favour of the murdered member for a disposition of his effects which betokened such a generous and fatherly interest in his young relative.

Thus Dora came into absolute possession of everything untrammelled by a single condition. No guardian, no trustee had been appointed; nothing but her own sovereign will to administer and distribute all this immense fortune. She was the mistress of Abbey Holme and of the whole estate; the richest woman for miles round; before whose wealth poor Julia Manley's hundred thousand pounds shrank into insignificance, and to whom rumour gave even more than she had.

It was marvellous to see how beautiful and beloved she became all at once to Milltown; how much every one suddenly found out she had been always admired and liked; and how each person claimed to have specially discerned her worth, and valued it, in the bygone years. Not a house failed in its sympathetic respect for the young heiress, and the Countess of Dovedale was among the earliest condolers. Perhaps she gave a half rueful thought to Lady Maud who accompanied her; at any rate, that young noblewoman imagined, as Patricia had so often done in her past world, that her future mother-in-law had a headache, and had best be left to herself during the drive. When they had deposited their cards and driven away, my lady spoke of Miss Drummond quite warmly. She was so perfectly well-bred, she said ; and such a lovely creature ! She must be fabulously rich—too rich indeed for a woman ; and she, the Countess, hoped she would marry soon, and marry well. It was too heavy a responsibility for such a young and lovely creature as she was ; she ought to marry into a good family where there was a sensible mother—a woman of the world who could guide and direct her—and where her money would do good and be the means of exalting herself ; one of the aristocracy, in short. To which Lady Maud answered tranquilly ; yes, she ought, and perhaps under the Countess's wing and her own, when she should be Lady Merrian, she would.

All these kindly speculations however, were soon set at rest ; and in a very short time it became known that Dora Drummond was going to marry young Sydney Lowe. People of course found fault with her choice and ridiculed her taste, and cried what a pity ! to each other when they met in the market-place ; but a few of the robuster kind—those whose wealth-worship nothing could chill nor shock—affected to have known of this attachment from the beginning, and to find it an exquisite instance of human constancy. To be sure, there were a few awkward whispers about Julia Manley ; for the Colonel, to clinch the decision he had good reason to consider wavering, had told every one exultingly of his son's engagement to this young lady, whose excellences he had vaunted in almost poetic terms. Now, within twelve hours of the reading of Mr. Hamley's will, an occasion was found for a rupture between the lovers ; and though Julia humbled herself, poor soul, to that point where submission ends and degradation begins, she could not soften her angry idol. He definitively and somewhat coarsely broke with her for ever ; and the heart-broken creature fled away with her thousands and her sorrows into Cornwall, where she established herself in a mining town, embraced Wesleyanism, and became a thorn in the side of the Broad Church clergymen.

Dora and Sydney married quite soon after all these stirring events. The world said she was right. She was too young to live alone, and though Mr. Hamley had made her his heiress, and she owed all imaginable respect to his memory he had not been a near relative ; and, considering all the circumstances she need not wait long. Indeed in view of these circumstances she need not have waited long had he been her father. A quiet marriage giving her a companion and protector was far the best thing for her; and they applauded her decision. A month after that melancholy murder then, she was united to Sydney Lowe, very quietly and without parade. Colonel and Mrs. Lowe were the only people at the wedding, Patricia Kemball refusing to be bridesmaid. But the bride was dressed in white, with a long lace veil, all the same as if the wedding had been one according to conventional rule, having no other meaning attached to it.

For one thing she was greatly blamed by all sensible people, her gross imprudence in having no settlements. It was a curious bit of irony that Mr. Hamley's wealth should pass unconditionally into the hands of Sydney Lowe, but the world is full of such. Mr. Simpson urged her to secure at least something; and even the Colonel, not planning villany, thought she would do well to have her own dower properly assured; but Sydney said he would marry no woman on earth with settlements; and after a private conversation with Dora, she gave in, and his will triumphed as the man's should, he said. No one suspected the root of this imprudent arrangement; and Sydney got great credit for generosity in making a post-nuptial settlement which assured Dora a fair share of her own wealth. For the rest, he made no bad use of her money. Indeed he became rather close-fisted than otherwise, responsibility seeming to have worked a radical change in him somehow, and to have even gone beyond the point of steadying him. He released Cragfoot, paid off his father's debts, and set him on his legs again; but he told him sternly that this was the only thing he would do for him, and that if he fell into the mire again he might pick himself out the best way he could. He was as little like the old Syd, now that he had money, as was the law-respecting king like the law-breaking prince. He was gloomy, stern, morosely pious, would keep no society, and of frightfully irritable nerves. His health broke suddenly, and he was soon startled, soon made angry and uneasy. He had a listening look about his eyes that struck people as odd, and he hated to hear the names of Hamley or Garth. People said he drank in private; some that he ate opium; others that he gambled. A thousand reasons were whispered from one to the other to account for this extraordinary change in him; and none hit the truth. For so far from any such vice as secret drinking or drugging, he seemed afraid to trust his senses into the keeping of any one or anything but himself, and always slept with locked doors, and a loaded pistol lying handy.

He and Dora got on together pretty well, judging by appearances; which were fallacious. She was too well trained in the way of concealment to show him what she suspected or the world what she felt; nevertheless she often cried in secret, and wished she had never known Sydney Lowe, and that she was once more under the Hamley rule. She had but exchanged masters; and of the two her husband's hand was the heavier.

She got a small amount of feminine consolation however, in the quiet impertinence with which she treated the Colonel and Mrs. Lowe. Once she had courted them by all her pretty arts in vain; now they were obsequious to her, while she snubbed them with merciless good-breeding, and made them regret that they had not had enough prophetic insight to have secured her when they might, and before she had become publicly a prize. This was their judgment of affairs: and it was as false as all the rest.

On the whole then, the Abbey Holme household, though a failure and a wreck if judged of by truth and principle, was sufficiently well ordered for outward purposes. True, Dora lost her beauty, and became old and haggard suddenly, with a scared look in her eyes that seemed the reflection of her husband's abiding expression of listening and watching; but she was always graceful and conciliating to her world on those rare occasions when she appeared in society, and if Sydney was not popular he had abundant obeisance done to him. No one cried out against him that he had committed theft, forgery, and murder, when he stood up in the Abbey Holme pew on Sundays, and enriched the choir with his clear tenor that sounded above all the rest. Nor when he sat on the bench and leaned ever to the side of rigour and righteousness, did his brother magistrates denounce him as a greater criminal than the poor half-witted clods whom he judged so severely. What was done, was done; and no one knew or ever would know; and for the rest he passed through life in the odour of respectability, beloved by none, known by none, bearing ever with him the con-sciousness of crime and the belief in his own eternal damnation, but bowed down to by all. Was he not the master of Abbey Holme, and the wealthiest man for miles round? Does the world ask more, or seek to know more than this?

Patricia spent her days tranquilly enough at the Hollies in the midst of love and duty. There were no brilliant meteors in her sky, but no clouds and no storms; it was sunlight of the best kind—the sunlight of affection, contentment, and a pure conscience. Her happy girlhood had passed for ever, but it had left a womanhood greater and nobler than itself had been; a womanhood of deeper thought and higher aims—yes, and of a more exalted love than would have come to her had she re-mained untaught of sorrow.

Yet she was always under a cloud at Milltown, and she never lived down the vague disrepute that hung about her fair fame. Every one said that she had done something very wrong once, though no one knew exactly what it was; and the Fletchers were too "queer" themselves to reinstate her by their respect. Her very severance too from Dora told against her; and, as the world argued, if she could have estranged one so sweet and amiable and forgiving as Mrs. Sydney Lowe, what must she not have done, what must she not have been! She was con-scious of this public disfavour, which she neither braved nor feared. She knew that she had not deserved it, so bore with equanimity the high estate and public honour of those who had done the wrong, and the general condemnation of herself who had only suffered by it. Between truth and seeming she had chosen the better part, and she never regretted her elec-tion.

Years passed before Gordon returned, but years that did good work in both. When the drift-time was over, and they stood once more together hand in hand on the seashore as in the old days, she was no longer a girl living only in the joy of her own youth and love and innocence, but a woman who had learnt the deeper meaning of life through the high teaching of suffering and trial; a woman self-consecrated to live, like the Fletchers, by principle rather than expediency; for truth, not seeming; for the inner law of nobleness, not the outer gain of pleasure. And he too was no longer the mere boy who had the boy's hope and the boy's courage, but a man who had learnt like herself something of the deeper meaning of the Great Riddle, and had set himself to live according to his knowledge.

She and Gordon were poor enough when they married ; and Dora, now that she was no longer afraid of Patricia, knowing by experience how entirely she might trust her silence and loyalty, pitied them profoundly from the luxurious depths of her gorgeous, loveless, miserable home. She would have helped them generously, if they would have taken help at her hand. But Patricia, though she had long ago forgiven her freely and fully—long ago resolved to bear that burden of shame for her to her life's end, patiently and faithfully—would never enter into terms of friendship with her again. Besides, though poor in the world's goods she was infinitely richer in heart and spirit than the faded, frightened, melancholy mistress of Abbey Holme ; the wife of the man who slept with locked doors and a loaded revolver by his side, and who had bad dreams and believed in his own eternal destruction.

She never felt so keenly how far better truth is than seeming, and love than riches, as when, one summer evening, she and the Fletchers and Gordon were standing on the high cliff road, looking at the golden sunset just now flooding earth and sky with that glory which no words, no pigments, can possibly describe. They were watching the gradual passing of the gold to crimson, and then to deeper purple, in that quiet, half-entranced way which makes silence so eloquent when a carriage drove slowly past. It was the Abbey Holme carriage, containing Dora and her husband. Dress, appointment, equipage—all were of the costliest kind, the most absolute perfection. The land they drove over was their own ; the men they passed did homage to them, their masters ; they had conquered fortune and distanced justice ; they were above even the accidents of life ; and they had means to gratify every conceivable desire. But the inner misery of the faces that looked out from those superb surroundings sufficiently confessed their worthlessness.

"Well ! for all their money I would not exchange places with those people," said Gordon, as they passed. "It is not what we have, but what we are, that tells ; and of the two we are the more to be envied—what do you say, Pat ?"

She looked up into her husband's handsome, manly face, bending down to hers with such frank and trustful love.

"I think so," she said earnestly.

"And I know it," said Henry Fletcher taking her hand on his arm. "Between Dora and Patricia the world would make no doubt which was the more to be envied; but I fancy the judgment of God will not go with the verdict of the world; and that truth and seeming were never at greater odds than they are and have been all through the history of these two girls!"

"Thank God the truth has come to my share!" said Gordon fervently. "I should have done ill with a whited sepulchre. Don't you remember, Pat, how I always counted on your true-heartedness?"

She laughed a little shyly, and blushed vividly.

"Yes," she said, looking at him tenderly. "I remember how good you always were to me! And so long as you and these dear ones are satisfied with me I am quite happy. And I don't think people want much more than love, and that their own consciences should not condemn them to make life only sweet!"

"Dear child," said Catherine caressingly. "How sweet life must be to you then!"

"To us all!" she answered.

"Yes," answered Gordon; "to us all!

THE END.